THE STRATEGY OF WORLD ORDER

Volume I

TOWARD A THEORY
OF
WAR PREVENTION

Edited by

RICHARD A. FALK
SAUL H. MENDLOVITZ

WORLD LAW FUND

1966   *New York*

Library of Congress Catalog Card No. 66-14524
Copyright © 1966 by the World Law Fund
Manufactured in the United States of America
First edition, 1966

Foreword

As we move through the closing years of the twentieth century the most enlightened and humane among our contemporaries are in a state at once apprehensive and exhilarated. The sources of apprehension are spread on the face of the modern world. These are the brute facts of a globe divided against itself and armed with excess capability for annihilation. Exhilaration comes in part from defiance of danger. It is, also, grounded in knowledge of the abounding opportunities in reach of our techno-scientific civilization. This universalizing culture flies precariously between utopia and cremation.

The idea that serious intellectual effort can play an important role in achieving a positive resolution of the dilemmas of the age is a declaration of confidence in the human mind. The four volumes in the present sequence, remarkably enough, show no regression to the intellectual postures and methods of a simpler time. The volumes are no perfumed garden of ruminative essays sweetly resigned to the end of civilization or of life itself at the hands of the barbarian. Nor is the series a rhetorical exercise attuned to more varied moods. Only at the edges are the chapters ironic, sardonic, or laced with recrimination. The tone is sternly professional. It is responsible, scholarly, scientific, predictive, inventive, and critical.

Professors Falk and Mendlovitz have planned and executed a program designed to shape an academic discipline oriented toward the principal policy question of the epoch. It is entirely appropriate that such a program should spread among professional and graduate schools, and ultimately permeate college and precollege years. The task of building public order on a world scale is no ephemeral topic that has been escalated to transitory effulgence by isolated incidents that have been inflated with the helium of Madison Avenue. Why, one may ask, is there no inclusive system of at least minimum public order? Before replying, it is necessary to have a firm grip on the web that ties world disunion to world society. Problems of this scope and depth have all the seriousness that is traditionally regarded as the essential hallmark of a question that is properly academic.

Modern intellectual innovations are reflected in the composition of the team of authors whose publications are included. Most numerous are lawyers, political scientists and economists; and they are supplemented by an occasional public leader, journalist, or physical scientist. It is the presence of such a natural scientist as Herman Kahn that demonstrates the distinctive structure of the policy sciences of the twentieth century. Clearly, if available information is to be rationally processed into action, public policy must draw upon every field of knowledge. Hence self-chosen professionals diversify their competence by reaching across the gap that separates experimentalists, field researchers or theorists from community decision-makers.

The scope of the policy sciences is twofold. In addition to obtaining information relevant to particular policy issues, policy scientists are responsible for improving theoretical and practical knowledge of the decision process itself. By tradition this has been the responsibility of political science (including students of international politics) and jurisprudence. The problems of "transnational" or "international" arenas are set apart from other power relations by the persisting significance of the expectation of violence as a chronic sign and source of division.

The proposed disciplinary concentration on world order is congenial to the future-oriented outlook of modern man. The tempo of change in population and in all sectors of civilization is accelerating with such speed that the necessity of looking forward is now conceded, even in relatively conservative circles. It is feasible for Bertrand de Juvenel, for example, to induce a team of colleagues in Western Europe to anticipate the pattern of coming things.[1] Or a prominent figure in Dutch planning, Frederick L. Polak, is led to publish two volumes designed to outline a systematic method for thinking about future events.[2] In the recent past even adventurous-minded professors have felt out of their metier when confronted by theoretical models of significant past-future relationships. Today we think about world order because of the obvious importance of seizing all occasions to navigate every ship of state toward safe harbor.

Implied in the foregoing is another dimension of the mind of modern man, which is the candid acceptance of value goals for public policy. These four volumes do not pretend that human cultures are of one mind about the dignity of the individual; or about the relative importance of sacrificing freedom or security. But every thoughtful person can be of one opinion in support of the obligation to *consider* these questions and to act accordingly. The general editors have no intention of initiating or conducting the world forum on terms that preclude participation by men and women of many preferential maps. Only those who love war and dominion as ends in themselves and who despise inquiry will find no hospitality between the limits of the present undertaking.

Linked with futurity and with overriding conceptions of goal is another perspective that comes easily to the contemporary mind. The approach is inventive. It searches the literature for creative proposals of two kinds: potential structures of public order; possible strategies for passing through the configuration of today toward a preferred structure tomorrow. Hence the frequency of allusion to the panorama outlined by Clark and Sohn and the attention given to plans of arms reduction and control. Hence, too, the hope of seizing on doctrinal formulas such as "peaceful coexistence" in order to gain purchase on realizing the ancient obligations and opportunities of cooperation.

The material assembled here is drawn for the most part from the work of American scholars. To some extent this is a concession to the institutions most willing and able to further the educational objective of the enterprise. But this is not entirely so. The intellectual community of Western Europe has not yet recovered from the disastrous impact of two major wars, several waves of revolutionary activity, and many minor upheavals. The United States of America has gone through these destructive decades uninvaded, unconquered, and relatively unstrained. And the USA, having learned of the global arena the hard way, is mobilizing its talent to come to grips with the formidable insecurities that cannot be charmed or wished away.

It is not too much to say that the distinctive mix of philosophy, history, science, prediction and ingenuity that has helped to shape the modern study of international relations, and which is now focused on world order, has been importantly shaped by the American academic community. Given the physical, legal and other assets at the disposal of the American scholar, it would be an unforgivable slackness of mind and character if this were not the case. Given the obstacles that have blocked the path of universities in many if not most other nations of the globe, one can do no less than express gratitude for whatever has been accomplished anywhere in the domain of free scholarship.

As in other controversial matters, the present undertaking finds a home for conceptions of jurisprudence that sometimes jar with one another. Whatever these differences may be, they will not blind an analytic reader from perceiving that a book of this timeliness, scope and vitality gives expression to a view of the place of law in world society that sweeps past traditional formalism. For the law that is the subject of this series is more than words divorced from deeds, more than norms unphased with facts, more than memories unhinged from expectations, or goals unjoined with concrete specifications. The changing subjectivities that define authority are themselves understood to be open to change even in the act of study.

Whatever the differences that must be taken into account throughout the length and breadth of the world arena, the volumes of this series are an opportunity for any motivated and qualified person to busy himself directly with his own business, which is a common interest in the life or death of man.

HAROLD D. LASSWELL
Yale University

---

1. *Futuribles; Studies in Conjecture,* Geneva, Switzerland, Droz, 1963.
2. Frederik L. Polak, *The Image of the Future; Enlightening The Past, Orienting the Present, Forecasting the Future,* New York, Oceana Publications, 1961. 2v.

Preface

AT THIS STAGE in the development of international society there is a need for the systematic study of world order. Systematic in the sense of bringing all relevant intellectual skills to bear and of using all the accumulated knowledge on the subject. In particular, advantage is sought to be taken of the disciplined inquiry associated with work in the fields of international law, international organization, arms control and disarmament, and economic development. This set of materials is offered as a step toward the creation of an autonomous academic discipline of world order.

Within the subject of world order primary attention is given to the avoidance of war through the creation of a war prevention system in international society. War is studied from a special point of view—its prevention—but in the spirit of social science rather than in the manner of a moralist or millenarian. As a potential academic discipline it is synthetic, cutting across such established educational divisions as law, political science, sociology, economics, history.

These materials adopt as a guiding method or organization and conception the orientation provided by what has come to be called "international systems theory." We propose study of the existing international system, of a postulated alternative system designed to achieve the objectives of war prevention, and the means available to transform the one into the other, which process we refer to as "the transition." It is the emphasis on achieving transition that gives a problem-emphasis to these readings. The postulated alternative system selected to illustrate the attributes of war prevention is the world projected by Grenville Clark and Louis B. Sohn in *World Peace through World Law*. It is not selected as an expression of the ideological preference of the editors so much as to provide a model, specified in some detail, of what an alternative international system might be like. Such a model of one future for the international political system facilitates our understanding of international society as it exists and operates at present and informs us more clearly about the kind of changes that must be made to fulfill the objectives of war prevention. (A fuller account of this endeavor is to be found in the selection by Mendlovitz at the end of Chapter 4.)

To conceive of world order as the strategy by which one system is transformed into another more in accord with a posited set of human values (e.g., survival, peace, welfare, human dignity) is the essence of this undertaking, and accounts for the choice of title.

RAF
SHM

May 31, 1965
Noordwyk aan Zee
The Netherlands

NOTE: *Where references are made in the text to other volumes of* The Strategy of World Order, *the volume is designated by roman numeral, the chapter by arabic numeral, and (where applicable) the section heading by letter. Thus,* **II-4B** *refers to Volume II, Chapter 4, Section B. Reference to materials contained in the same volume are designated by Chapter number. Thus, "see Chapter 4."*

THE STRATEGY OF WORLD ORDER has been made possible through the generosity of the D. S. and R. H. Gottesman Foundation and the Miriam and Ira D. Wallach Foundation.

Acknowledgments

The sheer mass of an enterprise of this sort makes its principal organizers very dependent upon the aid and comfort of many others, a dependence that far exceeds the gesture of acknowledgment. We mention here only those who made contributions beyond the normal line of duty.

First of all, we wish to thank the Rutgers Law School Secretarial Pool, especially Mary Connolly, Eleanore Yurkutat and Florence Wotherspoon for their patient and expert labors.

In The Netherlands the editors were especially lucky to have the benefit of the prodigious and proficient secretarial service of Miss Norah W.. Allen who made a habit of twenty-hour working days.

We thank Willard Heckel, Dean of the Rutgers Law School, for making available the funds for research assistance, and Blair Crawford, Barbara Kulzer, and Miriam Nusbaum, for giving us much needed assistance with the research and related matters. Thanks are also due to the Harvard Law School and especially the staff of the International Legal Studies Center for providing Mendlovitz with office and library facilities, and to Klaus Knorr, Director of the Center of International Studies at Princeton, for providing similar facilities in the final stages of the study, thus speeding the collaborative process considerably.

We are most indebted to Professor Ellen Frey-Wouters for many kindnesses, including especially the delicate handling of permissions with several of the more refractory of the foreign publishers.

William Cowan deserves especial mention because he did such an excellent job as technical editor with such short notice. Susan Newman's proofreading under similar circumstances is also greatly appreciated.

We are, of course, very grateful to the staff of the World Law Fund for handling the whole undertaking, and to Miss Florence Goldstein for her superb managerial services in masterminding the entire complex process of translating an assemblage of materials into a series of books.

And in the spirit of dedication, Saul Mendlovitz seeks also to mention Roberta Mendlovitz and their family—Jessica, Michael, Jamie, John, and Martha.

Contents

*WPTWL is the abbreviation used to designate *World Peace through World Law* by Grenville Clark and Louis B. Sohn.

2. The Causes of War and of Peace

3. The Nature of International Society

A. *Differing Views of the World*

B. *Differing Methods of Viewing the World*

4. The Shimoda Case: Challenge and Response

Volume II INTERNATIONAL LAW

Volume III THE UNITED NATIONS

Volume IV DISARMAMENT AND ECONOMIC DEVELOPMENT

THE STRATEGY OF WORLD ORDER

Volume I

TOWARD A THEORY
OF
WAR PREVENTION

The Problem, the Plan, and Some Preliminary Considerations

As the Preface suggests, these volumes attempt to draw upon the accumulated knowledge and developed techniques of several academic disciplines and to build toward an integrated approach to the study of world order. The readings are intended to present a synthesis of relevant perspectives organized around the central idea of system change. In this opening chapter the objective is to translate this conceptual task into as vivid substantive terms as possible.

The central problem of world order is assumed to be the avoidance of thermonuclear warfare. All other issues of world order stem from the effort to grapple with this overriding problem of our times. This focus of concern does not suggest by any means that other issues are really subsidiary in any significant sense. It would indeed be an egocentric approach to world order if Westerners subordinated the terrible afflictions of poverty, disease, overpopulation, and sheer chaos that so much of the rest of mankind now endures. However, the danger of nuclear war imperils the overall achievement of the prosperous and fully developed countries in such a singular fashion that it must inevitably dominate their political imagination.

It is a premise of these readings that all major sectors of mankind must find benefit in the international system if a stable peace is to be achieved through reforms in the existing system. The interests of all must be made consonant with the administered renunciation of political violence. Not only does stability require this minimum degree of affirmation, but the cooperative effort needed to transform the existing system presupposes that the major actors in international society will find that the new system will give them net advantages, otherwise they will refuse to take the steps to bring it about.

To pose these issues and to assess the prospects for a new international system capable of war prevention, attention will be given throughout these materials to *World Peace through World Law* by Grenville Clark and Louis B. Sohn (Harvard University Press, 1964). The Clark-Sohn work presents a model of a drastically revised international system that is designed to eliminate warfare from international life. It is a model that depicts in detail the character of the new system and outlines a set of procedures for dealing with conflict in such an altered international society, altered especially by the elimination of national military establishments as a result of total disarmament. Clark and Sohn present their model in the form of a proposed provision-by-provision revision of the present United Nations Charter. Properly used, such a setting facilitates a comparison of the two systems by highlighting the differences between the existing structure of world order and the proposed structure. The Clark-Sohn plan, in addition to being the most celebrated and competent set of proposals for the radical change of international society, is also a sophisticated effort to make the new world appeal to various kinds of states by trying to create expectations that their interests, other than the common interest in peace, will be advanced by its adoption. For example, the populous states are promised weighted voting according to population, the poor states are promised capital assistance, and the rich states are assured that their obligations, fiscal and otherwise, will not be onerous. At this stage it might be helpful to read an outline of the Clark-Sohn plan in *World Peace through World Law*, pp. XV-LIV, and, because the point of origin is war prevention, to examine their elaborate scheme for disarmament by reading their introduction to it on pp. 206–213.

A. Preventing Thermonuclear War

The article "The Prevention of World War III" by Kenneth E. Boulding from *The Virginia Quarterly Review*, vol. 38, no. 1. (Winter, 1962) pp. 1-12, faces squarely the problem of preventing a general thermonuclear war. The starting point of his analysis is to conceive of international society as a system. As the term is used here by Professor Boulding, "system" implies that the conduct of significant international actors form recurrent and relatively stable patterns of behavior which can be discerned and understood. In this view, the network of patterns, taken as a whole, is assumed to possess a strong tendency to persist through a considerable period of time, although not indefinitely. Boulding states that the present international system faces the probability of "irretrievable disaster" because its most influential actors have failed to realize that modern weapons render anachronistic the idea of a security community based on the national state. In light of this conclusion and of his portrayal of the high level of existing international tension, Boulding develops a dynamic model for world order. It consists of five stages of gradually increasing international social and political integration. The first stage is *tacit contract* and the last is *world government*.

It may help to orient your thinking in terms of comparative international systems to compare Boulding's five stages with the set of operative principles offered by Clark and Sohn. Are they fully compatible? If not, in what·respects do they differ? Can they be reconciled? If not, which is the more correct?——the more useful?——in what respects? Do both models make a similar analysis of the nature and role of conflict in international society? Does either propose the elimination of conflict, or merely the effective regulation of the means used to wage conflict?

THE PREVENTION OF WORLD WAR III

By KENNETH E. BOULDING

WHEN we talk about preventing something we imply two things. We imply, first, that there is a dynamic system which is now proceeding that, if allowed to proceed unchanged, will result in an event which is regarded as undesirable and which, therefore, we want to prevent. We imply also that it is possible to change the dynamic system in question and replace it by another dynamic system in which the unwanted event does not occur. Thus, suppose we find ourselves driving towards a railroad crossing and suddenly we see the red lights flashing and a train approaching. Our dynamic system at the moment consists simply of velocity and direction. We are proceeding, say at 50 miles per hour, towards the crossing. The distant early warning system of our eyes informs us the crossing is dangerous. The knowledge which we have of our existing dynamic system informs us that if it continues we will arrive at the crossing at the precise moment when the train is there. The combination of a distant information system coupled with the simple dynamics of automobiles enables us, however, to prevent the disaster. We do this by putting on the brakes long before we get to the crossing. This in effect changes the dynamic system under which we have been operating. It introduces a new variable into it, indeed a new dimension, deceleration. Because of this, we are able to prevent the disaster, as we are able to avoid simultaneous occupancy of the crossing by ourselves and the train.

We must be careful, of course, in applying the analogy of a simple psycho-mechanical system like a man driving a car to the enormous complexities and uncertainties of the international system. However, the international system is still a system, even though it has important random elements in it. Because it is not entirely random, it has elements of predictability. One of the greatest difficulties lies precisely in the stochastic nature of the system. We are driving a car, as it were, that may or may not respond to brakes according to whether dice held by the driver indicate "respond" or "fail." The situation is made all the more difficult by the fact that we face here a stochastic system with a very small universe, that is, a very small number of cases. Stochastic systems with a large number of cases can be treated by the theory of probability. We have a pretty fair idea, for instance, how many people are going to die in automobile accidents next year, although we do not know exactly who they are.

The problem of reducing the total number of automobile accidents is a very different kind of problem from the one that faces the driver of the preceding paragraph. Nevertheless, even with our present knowledge it would not be difficult to design an automobile and a road system which would kill, let us say, 20,000 people a year instead of 40,000. What we would be doing here would be to reduce the probability of disaster on the part of a single individual. It is by no means impossible to think of the international system in a rather similar way, and to talk about the things we can do to reduce the probability of disaster. What we mean by this is that if we had a very large number of planets roughly identical with our own we could postulate changes in the system which would reduce the number of cases in which disaster occurred. This would be the analogue of treating road deaths as a public health problem and seeking to reduce their probability. As far as we know, however, we do not have a large number of planets like ours and for our purposes at least there is only one. Hence, reducing the probability of disaster does us very little good if the disaster actually occurs. The problem of stochastic systems with a small number of cases has received insufficient attention in the theoretical literature. It is precisely this kind of system, however, with which we have to deal in international affairs.

I believe the present international system to be one which has a significant probability built into it of irretrievable disaster for the human race. The longer the number of years we contemplate such a system operating, the larger this probability becomes. I do not know whether in any one year it is one per cent, ten per cent, or even fifty per cent. I feel pretty sure, however, that it is of this order of magnitude, not, shall we say, of the order of magnitude of .01 per cent. The problem of system change, therefore, is urgent and desperate, and we are all in terrible danger. This is largely because of a quantitative change in the parameters of the international system under which we now live. This is still essentially the system of unilateral national defense in spite of the development of the United Nations and certain international organizations. Unilateral national defense is workable only if each nation can be stronger than its potential enemies in its home territory. This is possible under two circumstances. The first is that the nations must be far enough away from each other, and the extent to which their power declines as they operate further away from their own home bases must be sufficiently great. Then each nation can be stronger than the other *at home* with on-the-spot forces because of the fact that in a nation's home territory the enemy operates at a certain disadvantage. There is a second condition, however, which is that each nation must be able to dominate an area around its home base equal in depth to the range of the deadly missile. Because of quantitative changes in these conditions even in the last few years the system of unilateral national defense has become infeasible on a world scale. No nation is now far enough away from potential enemies to be sure that it can dominate even its own territory. Furthermore, the range of the deadly missile is rapidly reaching 12,500 miles, which means that the second condition cannot possibly be fulfilled. The condition which unilateral national defense attempts to establish, therefore, which I call *unconditional viability,* is now no longer possible.

The urgent and desperate nature of the present situation is created by the universality of the disaster with which we are threatened. The system of unilateral national defense has never given permanent security. The rise and fall of nations and empires is a testament to this fact. Indeed, looking with a large historical eye, one may say that unconditional viability has never existed except perhaps for brief periods and the best that unilateral national defense could do for any society was to postpone disaster. The situation of the individual society, that is, is rather analogous to that of the individual, whose life, on this earth at any rate, must also end in irretrievable disaster, that is, in death. Where we have a large number of individuals, however, death for the individual is not death for the race. In fact death for the individual is necessary if the race is to survive. Where the number of individuals becomes smaller and smaller, however, there comes to be a critical point where death for the individual is also death for the race and the irretrievable disaster which the individual suf-

fers is likewise irretrievable disaster for the species. The unilaterally defended national state now seems to me to have got
to this state in its development. It is no longer appropriate
as a form of organization for the kind of technical society in
which we live. Its death throes, however, may destroy the
whole human race. The age of civilization out of which we
are passing was characterized by a large number of nation-
states or independent political organizations practicing unilateral national defense. Because of the large number of these
organizations there were always some being born and always
some ready to rise into the places of those which suffered disaster. With the number of effectively independent nation-
states now reduced to two or perhaps at most three, the possibilities of irretrievable disaster become much greater.

The problem which we face, therefore, is how to effect a
system change in the international order, or perhaps we
should say the world political order, sufficient to lower the
probability of disaster to a tolerable level. The critical
problem here might be described as that of "system perception." To revert again to the analogy of the car and the
railroad crossing, if the driver of the car does not see that he
is approaching the crossing, if the warning lights are not
working, and if he cannot see the train approaching, he will
naturally not take any steps to avert the disaster. The world
problem here is perhaps psychological rather than mechanical. There is a fairly widespread sense abroad of impending
doom. The doom, however, is so large that we do not really believe it and we go about our daily actions as if it did not exist. This is the mechanism, as Jerome Frank has pointed out,
known to the psychologists as "denial." Up to a point this is
actually healthy. We all know that we are going to die some-
time and we may die tomorrow; but we act pretty much as
if we are going to live forever. We do not spend much time in
taking tearful farewells and in writing our last wills and tes-
taments. We plan ahead for months and even for years, in
spite of the fact that these plans may never come to fruition.
This perfectly legitimate response to uncertainty becomes
pathological when it prevents us from taking steps which
would postpone disaster or make it less likely. The man who

is afraid that he has a cancer but who will not go to a doctor because he might find out that he has one is a good example. Where the prospect of disaster, therefore, is so vague or so uncertain that it merely results in pathological denial, it is necessary to bring the actor to a more realistic appraisal of the system within which he is acting.

If the problem of "denial" is to be overcome, it is necessary to do more than merely scare people with horrendous pictures of the possible future. Indeed, the more horrendous the picture which is drawn, the more it is likely to result in denial and pathological inactivity. The future which faced our driver at the railroad crossing was also horrendous, but instead of denying this and continuing on his way he presumably applied the brakes, that is, initiated a system change. The problem in the international system is that we seem to have no brakes. That is, it is hard for people to visualize the nature of the system change which is necessary for survival. This, then, is one of the major tasks today of the political scientist, the philosopher, the journalist, and the prophet: to give the people an image of changes in the international system which seems small enough to be feasible yet large enough to be successful. It is not useful to picture Utopias which seem utterly unattainable—this perhaps is the main difficulty with the World Federationists—even though the function of Utopias in providing a constant driving force in social dynamics should not be underestimated. The present situation, however, calls not for Utopia, but for political solutions. Indeed, one of our great difficulties today is that we have too many Utopias. We need to think, therefore, in terms of a world social contract: that is, a minimum bargain between the contending parties which will give the world a sufficient system change to relieve it from the intolerable burden which it now bears. This social contract does not even have to be explicit or contractual. It can begin by being tacit; indeed, one can argue that a world social contract already exists in a tacit embryo form. We can visualize perhaps the following five stages of development.

I. The stage of tacit contract. In systems which have an inherent instability, such as duopoly in the relations of firms, or a bipolar system of mutual deterrence in the relations of states, it is often possible to maintain a quasi-stable position for a long time through tacit contract: that is, through mutually consistent unilateral behavior on the part of each party. A quasi-stable position is like that of an egg on a golf-tee—it is stable for small disturbances but not for large. For considerable periods of time, however, the disturbances may be small enough so that Humpty-Dumpty does not fall. Comes a slightly larger disturbance, however, and all the King's horses and men cannot put him together again. The international system under the Eisenhower administration exhibited this kind of quasi-stability. An important element in that stability was a tacit agreement between the United States and the Soviet Union to do nothing effective about civil defense. We agreed, in effect, that our civilian populations should be mutually exchanged as hostages, for we each had the power to destroy large numbers—at least half—of each other's civilians. This meant that the chance of deliberate nuclear war was very small, though the chance of accidental war was appreciable; indeed, the missiles almost went off on at least two occasions. A natural accident, such as a large meteor, or an electronic breakdown, or a social accident, such as a mad pilot, or a political accident, such as an unwise commitment to an irresponsible third party, could under these circumstances easily set off a mutual exchange of nuclear weapons, so that the system could not be regarded as more than a temporary expedient.

Another example of tacit contract was the mutual suspension of nuclear tests, recently broken by the Soviet Union. Here the fear, perhaps, of world opinion, and the fear also of the technical consequences of an uncontrolled race for technical development of weapons, created a temporary tacit agreement. We have had similar tacit agreements in regard to spheres of influence and intervention in third-party quarrels. The United States did not interfere in Hungary, nor the Soviet Union in Egypt during the Suez crisis. The Russians allowed themselves to be thrown out of the Congo, and are not threatening to be more than a nuisance in Cuba. The conflicts in Korea and Viet Nam were temporarily settled by latitudinal partitions. The Arab-Israeli conflict does not become an arena of the cold war. All these represent systems of mutuality of conduct which might be classified as tacit agreement.

II. The fate of the tacit agreement on nuclear testing, and what looks like the impending fate of the tacit agreement on civil defense, is a testimony to the inherent instability of the tacit agreement in the long run. It is something like the gentleman's agreement in economic competition, which suffers from the defect that not all people are gentlemen. The danger is that in the absence of organization between contending parties their only means of communication is by a "threat system." A threat system, which is characteristic of unilateral national defense, is based on the proposition, "If you do something bad to me I will do something bad to you," by contrast with an exchange system, which is based on "If you do something good to me I will do something good to you." Both systems tend to lead to consummation, but whereas the consummation of exchange is an increase of goods, the consummation of threats is an increase of "bads." War is mainly the result of the depreciation in the credibility of threats in the absence of their consummation; and hence a threat system has a basic instability built into it, which tacit contract may postpone but cannot ultimately avoid. The great problem, therefore, is how to get rid of threat systems. This, I suspect, happens historically mainly by their being overlaid with other systems of relationship—trade, communication, organization—until they fall so much to the bottom of the pile that they are no longer significant.

The essential instability of threat systems and the weakness of tacit agreements, therefore, make it highly desirable to pass into the second stage of formalized agreement, and the building of what might be called "peace-defending" organizational structures. The first of these obviously is an arms control organization designed at first perhaps only to limit the present arms race but capable of the ultimate hope of policing genuine disarmament. We could begin, perhaps, with an organization for the prevention of accidental war. This will be a joint organization of the major armed forces of the world. Once this has been accomplished, a major system change is under way. It is the organizational disunity of the armed forces of the world which constitutes the real threat to humanity. If they were united they might threaten us with a great many disagreeable consequences but they would not threaten us with extinction. An arms control organization, therefore, would be the beginning of a very powerful social change. It would constitute the formal recognition of the fact that unilateral national defense is no longer possible. Once this initial break is made, system change may be expected to take place quite rapidly. It may be that we shall have to look forward to a substantial separation of the armed forces organization from the states which they are supposed to defend, and which they can no longer defend. Just as we solved the problem of religious wars by the separation of church and state, so we may be able to solve the problem of nuclear war by the separation of the armed forces from the state. The plain fact is that today the threat which the armed forces of the world present to their own civilian populations is much greater than any conflict among the nations. Arms control will be the beginning of the recognition of this social fact.

III. Arms control must move fairly rapidly into disarmament; otherwise it will be unstable. The organization of the world armed forces will be a loose and unstable one at first, and it will always threaten to break up. It may be, of course, that the major pressure towards disarmament will come from the economic side. Once the threat of war is removed by arms control and by organizational unity of the world armed forces, the economic burden of maintaining these monstrous establishments will seem intolerable, especially in view of the fact that it is the arms burden (equal to the total income of the poorest half of the human race!) which perhaps prevents the world from really tackling the problem of economic development and which condemns hundreds of millions of people and their descendants to live in misery. One looks forward, therefore, to the third stage of rapid and total disarmament, under the arms control organization. There are many difficult problems involved in this which have not been worked out and on which research desperately needs to be done. One research program is on the way at the moment on the broad problems of the economics of disarmament, conducted by Professor Emile Benoit of Columbia University. The United Nations is about to inaugurate a similar study. However, the organizational and social-psychological problems involved are very great and quite unprecedented. Growth is always much easier than decline and the problems of adjustment involved in a rapid decline in the world's armed forces still have to be faced. These problems, however, are difficult rather than insoluble.

IV. Even universal total disarmament, however, is not enough, for this too is likely to be unstable even though disarmament itself will reduce many of the sources of conflict, especially those which arise out of strategic considerations. It will not eliminate all conflicts by any means. In a world as divided as this, ideologically and economically, we may expect serious conflicts continually to arise. These conflicts will constantly present the temptation to the losing side to resort to violence and to redevelop organized armed forces. If disarmament is to be stable, therefore, there must be a system of conflict control. Conflict control is one of the essential functions of government. It is not, however, the only function. In thinking of world government, this is probably where we ought to begin. In the early stages it is more important to establish conflict control than to establish justice or to solve all social problems. Conflict control as a function of government has been inadequately studied and identified. This is perhaps because the study of conflict systems themselves is still in its infancy. However, this is a rapidly developing body of social science and one hopes that it may be possible in the not-too-distant future to develop a substantial body of knowledge on the identification and control of conflict systems. The problem, of course, is the identification of conflict processes in early stages before they become pathological. There are very difficult problems here in the definition of the pathology of conflict, as this, of course, goes very deep into our value systems. Conflict which is regarded as pathological by one person may not be so regarded by another. If, however, we regard violence as generally a sign of pathological conflict, we may be able to identify the processes of social dynamics which lead towards it, and we may therefore be able to interpose counterweights which will correct these processes. We may revert once more to the analogy of the car at the crossing. We need to develop both perception of dangers ahead and also organizations which can act as brakes. These processes have been fairly well worked out in industrial relations, where a whole profession of mediators and conciliators and personnel experts has come to being. There is no reason why these principles should not be applied in other fields of social life and especially to the conflict of states.

V. The last stage, of course, is true world government, capable not only of controlling conflict but of expressing and developing the common concerns and aims of mankind. At the moment this seems to be a long way off. Fortunately, the prevention of war does not depend, I think, on the establishment of full world government. If the stages of development which I have outlined can be pursued rapidly enough, war may be postponed for longer and longer periods until the postponement becomes indefinite by the establishment of a true world government. We must therefore find half-way houses and quarter-way houses which are moderately habitable. We must not allow Utopian longings to deprive us of political bargains. The actual negotiation of the world social contract is going to be a long and arduous business. We need to put many more resources into this than we are now doing. Nevertheless, there is something here which can be done. There is a road which leads somewhere. If we are to break out of the apathy, irrationality, and despair which beset us, we must gain a vision of that road of escape and make at least one step along it. This is the great significance of the growing movement for peace research. Just as we no longer accept depressions as "acts of God," wholly unpredictable and uncontrollable, so we need no longer accept mass violence as unpredictable and uncontrollable. The fact that we cannot yet predict or control it should stir us to a great intellectual effort in this direction, for this way lies hope. The only unforgivable sin in the present crisis of mankind is despair.

NOTES AND QUESTIONS

1. Is there any evidence available to oppose or to support Boulding's startling conclusion that "the present international system. . . has a significant probability built into it of irretrievable disaster for the human race"? If unable to refute this assessment how would you propose taking it into account? Do you believe that your government is sufficiently aware of the seriousness of the situation? Assuming its awareness, how much freedom does your government have to adapt national policies and postures to take account of these new risks of catastrophe? See *The Anglo-American Tradition in Foreign Affairs* edited by Arnold Wolfers and Laurence W. Martin (Yale University Press, 1956); Stanley Hoffmann, "Restraints and Choices in American Foreign Policy," *Daedalus* (American Academy of Arts and Sciences, Cambridge, Mass., Fall, 1962) p. 668. Do answers to these questions vary with the character of the domestic political system? For instance, is it easier or more difficult for a centralized and authoritarian bureaucratic state such as the Soviet Union to adapt its policies to changing circumstances? Does Soviet ideology place constraints on the foreign policy-making process? Is a revolutionary ideology more sympathetic to proposals for radical change in the social order than an evolutionary ideology? May a government be revolutionary in international affairs and evolutionary or even conservative in domestic affairs, and vice versa?

2. John Herz writes persuasively about the inability of the nation-state to uphold national security interests as a consequence of nuclear weapons. See his "Rise and Demise of the Territorial State," *World Politics,* vol. 9 (Princeton University Press, 1957) p. 473; see also Herz' book *International Politics in an Atomic Age* (Columbia University Press, 1959) pp. 97–106.

3. Boulding argued against the utopianism of "world federationists" on the ground that their program is unattainable. However, he contends that the first four stages of the system-change must be accomplished within a relatively short time and since his proposal involves a radical increase in world organization structures, is it any less utopian than world federation? — than the Clark-Sohn plan? — in what respects? Satisfactory answers cannot be given until more reading has been done, but the relevance of the matters raised by these questions is important to appreciate now. What characteristics of Clark and Sohn or Boulding seem utopian? What does it mean to characterize something as "utopian"?

4. It should be noted at this point that Kenneth Boulding is a distinguished economist who has made the control of conflict a major concern in his recent professional research. Founder of the Center for Conflict Resolution at the University of Michigan, he has been among those responsible for the quarterly publication of *The Journal of Conflict Resolution* (University of Michigan) and for many of the research activities in the field. Boulding's approach extends beyond making the study of war prevention merely a course within any one academic department. His attempt is to create an entire new discipline that deals integratively with all forms of conflict. For an assessment of this endeavor, see Thomas C. Schelling, "Experimental Games and Bargaining Theory," *World Politics,* vol. 14 (Princeton University Press, October, 1961) p. 47, and Schelling's own book, *The Strategy of Conflict* (Harvard University Press, 1960); see also Anatol Rapoport, *Fights, Games and Debates* (University of Michigan Press, 1960).

5. Although the use of system analysis is well established in engineering and in the physical sciences, its introduction as a tool of analysis for the social and behavioral

sciences is relatively recent. In fact, the assertion that international soceity can be treated as "a system" remains controversial. There is already a rather large body of literature on the subject. The following books are recommended because they use systems analysis to appraise the control of violence in international society; Morton A. Kaplan, *System and Process in International Politics* (Wiley, New York, 1957); George Liska, *International Equilibrium* (Harvard University Press, 1957); Richard N. Rosencrance, *Action and Reaction in World Politics* (Little, Brown, Boston, 1963); *The International System: Theoretical Essays*, edited by Klaus E. Knorr and Sidney Verba (Princeton University Press, 1961).

6. The concept of "denial" mentioned by Boulding suggests that many of the problems involved in establishing a war prevention system concern psychological, psychopathic, and anthropological aspects of human nature. We shall consider these perspectives, but only marginally. For a good collection of readings with these emphases, see *War: Studies from Psychology, Sociology, Anthropology*, edited by Leon Bramson and George W. Goethals (Basic Books, New York, 1964); Arthur & Lila Weinberg, *Instead of Violence* (Beacon Press, Boston, 1963); Malcolm P. Sharp, "Aggression: A Study in Ethics and Law," *Ethics* (University of Chicago Press, July, 1947) pp. 1–39. Any conception of law and formal organization embodies assumptions about the character of human nature as well as about the relationship between certain psychological variables and the social environment. The extent to which these variables may be isolated and shown to be causally connected to the problem of preventing war remains a major unsolved methodological problem; given our present level of knowledge about human nature and social organization, it seems likely that we will have to deal with a system of thought in which the "variables" of the social and behavioral sciences are known to interpenetrate one another but in a manner that has not yet been clearly or operationally specified. Talcott Parsons has made a notable attempt to integrate these various levels of analysis in the following three books published by the Free Press of Glencoe, New York: *The Structure of Social Action* (2nd ed., 1958); *The Social System* (1951) and *Social Structure and Personality* (1964). Recent interesting attempts in the area of law and organization include Kenneth S. Carlston, *Law and Organization in World Society* (University of Illinois Press, 1962) and Ernst B. Haas, *Beyond the Nation-State* (Stanford University Press, 1964).

B. The Arms Race

The following essay by Herman Kahn from his book *On Thermonuclear War* (Princeton University Press, 1960) has been widely read. His formal analysis of the manner in which a war might begin has influenced the entire style of discourse in which these matters are discussed. His analysis derives from certain assumptions about military strategy and about the rate of technological innovation in the arms race. Kahn's discussion demonstrates the complexity of military security when it is based upon a strategic nuclear deterrent. These issues are reconsidered in the chapters in Volume IV devoted to arms control and disarmament.

Kahn is quite optimistic about the possibility of avoiding a major nuclear war during the next two decades without general and complete disarmament. Nevertheless, he agrees with Boulding and the Clark-Sohn plan that curtailing and, perhaps, eliminating armaments, is crucial for a war prevention system. Kahn writes that the technology of weapons development in the nuclear age produces revolutionary changes in armaments every four or five years and thereby makes obsolete, in part at least, the prevailing strategic doctrines upon which national security is supposed to rest. This strategic lag has been responsible for a deficient foreign policy. For influential conservative criticism to this effect, see Henry A. Kissinger, *Nuclear Weapons and Foreign Policy* (Harper, New York, 1957) and Kissinger, *The Necessity for Choice* (Harper, New York, 1961).

An important implication of Kahn's comments on the rate of technological innovation is that in some sense the arms race or the competition for military superiority is itself an independent contributing factor to the probability of a major thermonuclear war. For influential studies that explore, with the aid of mathematical techniques, the hypothesis that wars are caused by arms races, see Lewis F. Richardson, *The Statistics of Deadly Quarrels*, edited by Q. Wright and C. Lienau (The Boxwood Press, Pittsburgh, Pa., 1960) and Lewis F. Richardson, *Arms and Insecurity*, edited by N. Rashevsky and E. Trucco (The Boxwood Press, Pittsburgh, Pa., 1960); for a more standard account that reaches the same conclusion, see Philip Noel-Baker, *The Arms Race* (Oceana Publications, Dobbs Ferry, N.Y., 1958).

Kahn's discussion of the Doomsday Machine, Doomsday-in-a-Hurry, and mutual homicide pacts are intended not merely to terrify—as indeed they do—but also to demonstrate that the arms race threatens to undermine the supposed stability of the deterrent system, the stability that arises from the capacity of either superpower to inflict unacceptable damage on its opponent, even if it is the victim of a surprise attack. Such a prospect of retaliation is said to deter the attacker.

Finally, by way of introduction, it should be obvious that Kahn is sensitive to the political, as well as to the strategic and military problems involved in curtailing the arms race. Given the dynamic complexity of our world in the past six years, it is remarkable that Kahn's analysis retains its original vitality.

The Arms Race and Some of Its Hazards

HERMAN KAHN

PREFACE

IT IS EASY TO WRITE GRAPHICALLY AND PERSUASIVELY OF THE DANGERS of the arms race, nuclear and otherwise. Such documents are often well received: the author's heart seems to be in the right place; he is for people and against the abominations science and technology have produced. Yet, this question remains unanswered: Why do nations in general, our own in particular, continue to play such a dangerous and pointless game?

Here we hit on the nub of the matter: the game is indeed dangerous, but not pointless, since not to play it (even to reduce forces or submit to arms control) can also be dangerous: a Pearl Harbor or a Munich is all too possible. If we examine the whole range of possibilities, beginning with unilateral disarmament, surrender, appeasement, or accommodation, and ending with an accelerated arms race, preventive war, Mutual Homicide Pacts, and Doomsday Machines, we discover that there are no pleasant, safe, or even unambiguously moral positions for the individual, for a nation, or for civilization. Unfortunately, the discussions that concentrate on one facet of our dangerous future tend to create a psychological atmosphere conducive to the neglect of the remaining problems of security. This is no reason for not discussing the dangers of the arms race (or any other dangers), but only for emphasizing the ultimate need for a balanced comparison of all the dangers.

I have written elsewhere * on why adequate arms control may be essential if we are to reach 1975 and later years without a major thermonuclear war, while emphasizing that we may also need military establishments of a much higher quality than is usually conceded, even by people who think of themselves as "militarists," and the many difficulties and dangers of arms control. I will not summarize the arguments here. I would only be doing myself a disservice if I did so. This is a difficult, unpleasant, and emotional

---

* This chapter is based in part on my book, *On Thermonuclear War* (Princeton, N.J.: Princeton University Press, December 1960).

subject; the points raised are often irritating or dismaying, and many readers transfer their irritation and dismay to the author. For example, if one presents a balanced account of the risks an attacker might face from a retaliatory blow, it is easy to show that, subject to some chilling uncertainties, there are many circumstances in which the risks the attacker faces are considerably less than is generally believed. As a result, there are plausible situations in which a perfectly sane (but calculating, decisive, or ruthless) attacker might decide that "it is less risky to go to war than to live with the current situation or crisis." At this point, many readers conclude that the analyst is advocating preventive war; in other words, instead of examining the arithmetic, they conclude that anyone who calculates this way wants to act this way.

While the most important problems of the 1960's and 1970's may result from the arms race itself, rather than from the political and military dangers against which the arms race is supposed to protect us, those dangers exist. Today they are manageable only because the arms protect us from them; *ill-advised* measures to control the arms race can still reduce our security.* We are trying to negotiate some very rough and dangerous terrain. While it is by no means clear that there are any "reasonable" routes to wherever we want to go, it is clear that there are precipitous and unscalable heights in all directions. Let us now examine some of this terrain.

VARIOUS WAYS IN WHICH WAR CAN START

The major danger of the arms race lies precisely in the fact that the arms may be used; thermonuclear war may be unthinkable, but it is not impossible. Arms control can reduce the risks that ensue from the ever-present possibility of war by reducing:

1. The number of events, both international (tensions and crises) and technical (false alarms and misunderstandings), that could give rise to war.

2. The probability that an event of the kind that could cause war will actually result in war.

3. The damage of an actual war, not only by abolishing the use of certain weapons and controlling the use of others, but also by facilitating ahead of time the machinery by which wars are ended before they become overwhelmingly destructive.

There is no space here to expand on these possibilities; they are all discussed elsewhere in this book. However, it may be well now to discuss systematically how a war could arise and indicate some of the problems to be considered. I will begin by listing a number of possibilities, in a semi-technical jargon intended to categorize and describe them.

1. *Unpremeditated war* (human or mechanical error, false alarm, self-fulfilling prophecy, unauthorized behavior).

* The possibility implied by the author's use of the word *still* in this sentence is to be noted.—ED.

2. *Miscalculation* (game of "Chicken," rationality of irrationality strategies, escalation, overconfidence).

3. *Calculation* (Type II Deterrence situation; preventive war; pre-emptive war; world domination; solution to a desperate crisis).

4. *Catalytic war* (ambitious third nation; desperate third nation).

The items in these four categories are neither exhaustive nor distinct from one another. They are not exhaustive because our weapon systems are so new, and their impact, both on one another and on international relations, is so little known that it would not be surprising if a war started in some manner not heretofore thought of. However, I have made the list as exhaustive as possible; in doing so it has been convenient to list categories that occasionally overlap. This is probably better than to strain too much to prevent duplication or leave out some important possibility.

Unpremeditated War. The four categories are ordered by the writer's personal estimate of their likelihood of actually being a cause of war in the next decade or two. I have put unpremeditated war at the top of the list, the fearful possibility that a war may occur almost unintentionally. There is a widespread fear that this could occur; that a button may be pressed accidentally, an electrical circuit short, a relay stick, a telephone call or other message be misunderstood, an aurora borealis or meteor or flock of geese be mistaken for an attack, a switch fail, some ICBM's launched through some mechanical or human error, some stockpile weapons accidentally exploded, and so on. Such things have happened in the past and may happen again. However, unless one side or the other is careless enough to install a quick-reacting, nonrecallable strategic system, it is most unlikely that any single one of the above events would trigger off a retaliatory attack. It is just because radars do indeed occasionally give false alarms and accidents do happen that it is essential for both sides to install weapon systems that either have so-called "fail safe" or "positive control" features built into them, or that are large enough and well enough protected that they do not need to be "trigger happy" to survive. If a system can accept the enemy's attack and still strike back effectively, the decision maker has time to evaluate and decide—time to be careful. Such systems may use an ambiguous warning so as to take some temporizing measure that will reduce vulnerability to enemy attack or provide a better posture from which to retaliate. But the commander can then wait for further confirmation before making any irrevocable commitments.

There is a danger that the temporizing measures that are instituted on an ambiguous warning will remove some of the psychological, legal, and physical safeties that normally govern the strategic force, so that there is a greater load thrown on the remaining safeguards. For this reason several accidents in a row or even a simple accident during a period of considerable tension could be dangerous. Actually, the greatest danger is the possibility that a chain of "self-fulfilling prophecies" is set into motion. It is perfectly conceivable for one side's temporizing action to be observed by the other side and to be misinterpreted as being aggressive rather than defensive, thus causing the other side also to make some temporizing defensive move. This second defensive move can in turn be misread by the side originally alerted as confirming his suspicions, so he may make some further moves. It is then possible for reactions and signals to be set into motion which trigger off further reactions and signals by both sides until a point of no return is reached. This is one reason that it is necessary for each side not only to be cautious and responsible, but also to make sure that the other side also understands what is happening. In so far as any temporizing measures depend on doing things which raise apprehensions on the other side, it is important to be prepared to allay those apprehensions. This is possibly a very fruitful area for arms control.

The Soviets are completely aware of the problem. For example, in a Security Council debate of April 21, 1958, Arkady S. Sobolev made the following statement:

American generals refer to the fact that up to the present time the American planes have taken off on their flights and returned to their bases as soon as it became clear that it was a case of false alarm. But what would happen if American military personnel observing their radar screens are not able in time to determine that a flying meteor is not a guided missile and that a flight of geese is not a flight of bombers? Then the American planes will continue their flight and will approach the borders of the Soviet Union.

But in such a case the need to insure the security of the Soviet people would require the USSR to make immediate retaliatory measures to eliminate the oncoming threat. The Soviet Government would like to hope that matters will not go so far.

In order to get a clearer idea of the extremely dangerous character of acts of the United States [that are] dangerous to peace, it is enough to ask the question what would happen if the military Air Force of the Soviet Union began to act in the same way as the American Air Force is now acting? After all, Soviet radar screens also show from time to time blips which are caused by the flight of meteors or electronic interference. If in such cases Soviet aircraft also flew out carrying atom and hydrogen bombs in the direction of the United States and its bases in other states, what situation would arise?

The air fleets of both sides, having observed each other, having discerned each other somewhere over the Arctic wastes or in some other place, apparently would draw the conclusion natural under those circumstances, that a real enemy attack was taking place. Then the world would inevitably be plunged into the hurricane of atomic war.[1]

In spite of their awareness of the problem, the Soviets have tended to emphasize disarmament almost, but not quite, to the exclusion of other aspects of arms control. For example, at the 1958 Surprise Attack Conference, they stressed larger issues and refused to discuss narrow technical issues although our own position may have been excessively narrow. To this writer it seems dangerous to wait for a settlement of the political issues before considering this problem, but in this kind of a problem it takes two to make an agreement. However, even informal implicit agreements or, on some aspects, unilateral concessions can be helpful.

It is also conceivable that some pathological or irresponsible person will deliberately try to start a war or crisis. The Soviets have made much of the possibility that a deranged or irresponsible American pilot on airborne alert would take it into his head to attack Russia alone. Not only are there many safeguards against this, but it is most unlikely that a single-plane attack would touch off a war. A much more ominous possibility is given in the book *Red Alert*,[2] in which a determined SAC general, who, unknown to his superiors, is sick with an incurable ailment (and whose judgment and sense of discipline are thus affected), decides personally to end the Soviet problem once and for all. The most interesting part is the clever way he gets around the rather elaborate system set up to prevent exactly this kind of behavior.

I should make clear that I believe that, currently at least, the probability of unpremeditated war is low. The reason I put it on the top of the list is because I believe (assuming, perhaps optimistically, that both sides are careful, competent, and responsible) the other ways in which a war could occur should have an even lower probability. It is also clear that many of the methods recommended to reduce the probability of war by accident might very well result in increasing the likelihood of war from one of the other causes. After both these points are made, it must also be mentioned that nobody can estimate realistically what the probability of accidental war is. (There seems to be some tendency to underestimate the probability of war. For example, Wheeler-Bennett reports in his book, *Munich: Prologue to Tragedy,* that on January 1, 1939, Lloyds was giving 32 to 1 odds against war in 1939. This was three months after Munich and eight months before the war actually started. While it would be hard to convince me that it is as high as, say, 1 in 10 a year, still, if it were this high, the situation would be entirely unsatisfactory. Even if it were 1 in 100 a year, it would still be unsatisfactory, because the current state of affairs could not be allowed to continue indefinitely. One must eventually introduce a major change in the situation, or expect to get into a war anyway.

The really dangerous intensification in the probability of unpremeditated war is likely to come in the future, partly as a result of increased alertness or dispersal of weapons carriers in the missile age, partly as a result of the increase in the number of buttons that can be pressed accidentally, but mostly as a result of the proliferation of independent nuclear capabilities to other countries, each with its own standards of training, reliability of personnel, and safety practices.

War by Miscalculation. Nearly as worrisome as the possibility of unpremeditated war is the war which is more or less premeditated (perhaps as in the *usually uncalculated* "calculated risk")—but the decision maker doing the premeditating has miscalculated or misunderstood the risks or consequences of his actions. Many believe that the most likely way for this to occur is as a result of the use of a committal strategy. For example, one side may make it clear that it is going to stand firm in some crisis in the belief that "since neither side wants war," the other side will back down. If the other side does not back down, then war can result. A graphic if somewhat oversimplified example of such a situation is given by Bertrand Russell:

This sport is called "Chicken!" It is played by choosing a long straight road with a white line down the middle and starting two very fast cars towards each other from opposite ends. Each car is expected to keep the wheels of one side on the white line. As they approach each other mutual destruction becomes more and more imminent. If one of them swerves from the white line before the other, the other, as he passes, shouts "Chicken!" and the one who has swerved becomes an object of contempt.[3]

It is clear that if one side really wishes to win this game its best (rational) strategy is to commit itself irrevocably to going ahead. If one can convince the other side that one has done this, then the other side must back down. However, if the other side still refuses to back down after the irrevocable commitment has been made, it would be irrational to carry out the rationally made commitment. Since both sides will be attempting to use this strategy, it is also quite clear that the game may end in a disaster.

According to Bertrand Russell, the game is played by degenerates in America, and by nations everywhere. It is a caricature, because Russell ignores the fact that it is a major purpose of diplomacy to prevent a crisis from arising which can only be settled by the total and humiliating defeat of one side or the other. Most bargaining situations involve gains for both sides, and the major question is on the division of these gains and not the humiliation of the other side. However, the game of Chicken may occur. Barring enforceable adjudication, the less one is willing to play the game, the more likely it may be that one may end up having to play it. Life, liberty, and security may depend on being willing to play this dangerous game. As Russell states:

Practical politicians may admit all this, but they argue that there is no alternative. If one side is unwilling to risk global war, while the other side is willing to risk it, the side which is willing to run the risk will be victorious in all negotiations and will ultimately reduce the other side to complete impotence. "Perhaps"—so the practical politician will argue—"it might be ideally wise for the sane party to yield to the insane party in view of the dreadful nature of the alternative, but, whether wise or not, no proud nation will long acquiesce in such an ignominious role. We are, therefore, faced, quite inevitably, with the choice between brinkmanship and surrender."

The game of Chicken is an extreme example of the use of "rationality of irrationality" strategies. Because these are so important it may be worthwhile to dwell on them briefly. In any bargaining situation, even the most innocuous, it can make sense to commit oneself irrevocably to do something in a certain eventuality, and at the same time it may not make sense to carry out the commitment if the eventuality occurs; if one could, one would revoke the "irrevocable" commitment. The analogy with the game of Chicken should be clear. It should also be clear that if both sides commit themselves to incompatible positions, there will be no bargain. But if the bargaining is carried on with skill, and if both sides are cautious, then the bargaining will take on the aspects of a normal commercial transaction in which both sides gain, the exact division of the gains depending on their relative skill, but in which neither is driven to the wall.

Unfortunately, in any long period of peace, there is some tendency for governments to become more and more intransigent. The thought of war may become unreal. Even more important, every government is likely to build up a background of experiences in which it did very well by standing firm and very badly when it displayed a flexible, reasonable, or conciliatory attitude. It is only when peace fails that the governments are likely to learn that standing firm on incompatible positions is not a feasible symmetrical strategy. One can almost confidently predict that unless arrangements are made for adjudication or arbitration, somebody is going to play the international analogue of Chicken once too often.

The rationality-of-irrationality war should be distinguished from one caused by the two sides having incompatible objectives which they are determined to achieve, no matter what the risks: in this case war must result. The rationality-of-irrationality war corresponds to a situation in which neither side really believes the issue is big enough to go to war over, but both sides are willing to use some partial or total strategy of commitment to force the other side to back down. As a result, they may end up in a war they would not have gone into, if either side had realized ahead of time that the other side would not back down, even under pressure.

A typical circumstance in which such a situation could arise results from the use of Type II Deterrence.* Imagine, for example, that the Soviets had done some very provocative thing, such as invading Western Europe with conventional armies, on such a large scale that we felt that we could not stop the invasion by any limited actions, and that we would not be able to rescue Europe at a later date. We might still not be willing to strike the Soviets with our SAC, in view of the terrible price we would have to pay to their retaliatory blow, even if we struck them first. However, we could evacuate our cities and place our forces on a super-alert status, and thus

* As in my book, I would like to distinguish three kinds of deterrence. Type I is the deterrence of an "all-out" direct attack. Type II is the deterrence of extremely provocative acts, other than an all-out attack on the nation using the deterrence. Type III might be called a graduated or controlled deterrence: it is the deterrence of provocations by making the potential aggressor afraid that the defender or others will then take limited actions, military or nonmilitary, which will make the aggression unprofitable.

put ourselves in a much better position to strike first and accept the retaliatory blow. We might then present the Soviets with an ultimatum. We
would in effect be presenting the Russians with the following three alternatives: to initiate some kind of strike; to prolong the crisis, even though
it would then be very credible that we would strike if they continued to
provoke us; or to back down or compromise the crisis satisfactorily. We
would hope that the Soviets would prefer the third alternative, because our
Type I Deterrence would make the first choice sufficiently unattractive, and
our Type II Deterrence would do the same for the second; but we might
be wrong, and they might take the first alternative. Or they might take the
second alternative in the assumption that we would back down, and we
might not.

Another method of getting into a war by miscalculation would be as a
result of a limited move that appeared safe, but which set into motion a
disastrous sequence that ended in all-out warfare. This increase is called
escalation. One can imagine some sort of crisis which gradually increased
in violence or scope until it triggered one of the reactions already discussed. This could occur either because the limits of a limited war are not
being observed, or because more parties are being drawn into it, or because
the isues themselves become fraught with significances that did not initially exist, or because of some unauthorized or accidental behavior by
subordinates. It is difficult to supply a plausible reason for escalation (except, of course, as a move in the game of Chicken), when it is to everybody's interest to control things, yet almost everyone considers that it can
and perhaps will happen.

Escalation is possible particularly if one of the two contending sides does
not think through the consequences of its actions. To return to the Type II
Deterrence situation discussed above: it is perfectly conceivable that the
Russians, looking at the 60 million hostages we have in our fifty largest
cities, might decide that it was safe to attack Europe, and that we would not
attack them in retaliation. They might also vaguely realize that if they attacked Europe, we would probably evacuate the 60 million hostages; but
they might not understand the full consequences of that evacuation, in
terms of the psychological stiffening of the backbone and the enormous
decrease in the risks this country would be running if it went to war.

The possibility of escalation may actually play a useful role in deterring
certain kinds of crises or limited wars. For example, it is quite clear that
the nuclear-weapon systems we and the British have in Europe are on the
whole fairly vulnerable to Soviet attack, so that they have little second-
strike capability. Yet the Soviets might be afraid to destroy them in a
limited European attack, for fear that the level of by-product destruction
would automatically cause escalation into an all-out World War III. On the
other hand, if the Soviets did not destroy them, the Europeans might use
them, and this in turn would not only be damaging to the Soviets, but
might also cause escalation into World War III. This means that lower than

all-out attacks may be deterred for fear they will escalate. The same mechanism holds, for example, if we decide to open a route to Berlin by force if the Soviets or East Germans try to close it. As of 1961, the Soviets have the capacity to apply all the counterforce they need to stop any such action. The purpose of the action is not to overwhelm Soviet countermeasures, but to make it clear to them that the stakes are large. It is clear that we might be willing to take a small but appreciable risk of an all-out war, even if we were not willing to go immediately into an all-out war. The action might be effective precisely because it was so dangerous. To the extent that various types of arms-control measures reduce the possibility of escalation, then to that extent the deterring effect of escalation on limited actions is decreased. The author finds this no reason for not carrying through such control measures, but he knows many Europeans who are antagonistic to any reliable limits on the use of violence, for the very reason that such limitations may increase the probability of a provocation at that limited level.

Another possibility of a war by miscalculation occurs when one side goes to war in the mistaken belief that it has a sufficient preponderance of force or a clever enough war plan to be able to win satisfactorily. The mistake can occur through some uncertainty being underestimated, some imponderable ignored, or sheer ignorance or recklessness. Given current beliefs in the West, it is almost impossible to imagine this happening to a Western government unless the decision makers have their judgment clouded by desperation or madness. The situation is less certain in the Communist bloc. The Chinese clearly underestimate the effects of nuclear war. Hopefully, it will be some time before they have the power to use nuclear weapons, and time may bring them greater wisdom. The Soviet estimates, as gleaned from their public statements, seem plausible, though whether this comes as a result of more or less sophistication than is prevalent in the West is hard to tell. They talk of the possibility of great destruction and suffering together with the likelihood of the "victor" surviving and recovering. The Soviets do not seem to be trigger-happy or reckless, one judges at this writing, so that it does not seem to be necessary to put much effort into attempts to educate them on the danger of being overconfident about the use of modern weapons. The Soviets may underestimate the need for collaboration in controlling the technological development and dissemination of new weapons and thus be unwilling to make the necessary compromises entailed in getting feasible arms-control programs accepted by both sides. If they go to war, however, it is as likely to be as a result of calculation as of miscalculation. This thought brings us to our next topic.

War by Calculation. War could result from calculation. After due study, a nation might decide that going to war would be the least undesirable of its choices. Common belief, of course, holds just the opposite: that war could arise only as a result of miscalculation—but this is based on the unsophisticated view that all wars result in automatic mutual annihilation.

This could happen, but in all likelihood it would not. One type of war by calculation could occur in the Type II Deterrence situation referred to above. If at that point we attacked the Soviet Union, the damage we received in return would be considerably reduced. We might well decide that our nation was better off to accept this retaliatory blow rather than let Europe be occupied, and also to accept the costs of living in the hostile and dangerous world that would result.

Or, to give another example, the Soviets suffered from 20 to 30 million casualties in World War II, and in addition they lost about one-third of their wealth. It is sometimes pointed out that this did not happen from calculation but was inflicted on a day-by-day basis: no alternatives were ever really put up to them. However, given the nature of the Nazis and their program, I would believe that even the average Soviet citizen (not to mention the government) would have been willing to accept the cost of World War II in order to achieve the position they have since won, as an alternative to Nazi domination.

Another war by calculation would be the so-called preventive war. This does not necessarily mean that one side believes the other is planning eventually to attack the first, which is therefore merely getting in the first blow. One side has only to feel that a war is inevitable—or so likely that it might as well get the disaster over with as soon as it gets a sufficient lead, so that it is safer to seize the opportunity than to wait. Such an edge is most likely to result from a technological change to which the other side has not reacted. The so-called missile gap illustrates how this problem could arise.

The United States SAC (Strategic Air Command) is supposed to be based upon about fifty home bases. If the Soviets happened to acquire, unknown to us, about three hundred missiles, then they could assign about six missiles to the destruction of each base. If the Soviet missiles had, let us say, one chance in two of completing their countdown and otherwise performing reliably, then there would only be 1 chance in 64 that any particular SAC base would survive a Soviet attack. There would be better than an even chance that all the bases would be destroyed, about one chance in three that one base would survive, and a small chance that two or more bases would survive.

A missile gap of the sort described is especially dangerous because missile attacks are so much more calculable than any other kind of attack. They are so calculable that many people feel that even a cautious Soviet planner might be willing to rely on the correctness of his estimates; that Soviet decision makers might find it the path of caution to attack while the opportunity was still available.

Actually the results of missile attacks are not mathematically predictable. There are imponderables and uncertainties with regard to such things as reliability of basic data, field degradation, intelligence leaks, and firing discipline so that the probability of something going wrong cannot be predicted. But so many laymen and professionals persist in regarding the reliable prediction of the results of missile attacks as simple problems in engineering and physics that it would be irresponsible to rely on Soviet caution and sophistication alone as a protection. And if such an attack were successfully carried out, it would truly be a war by calculation.

The need for a quick reaction to even "hypothetical" changes in the enemy's posture is likely to persist indefinitely, in spite of the popular theory that once we get over our current difficulties we will have a so-called minimum nuclear deterrent force that will solve the Type I Deterrence problem. (Some even maintain that it will solve all strategic problems.)

It should be noted that if a serious deterrent gap ever occurred, then, even if the Soviets were not willing, either out of caution or morality, to use their superiority, the situation would still be dangerous. They might well be tempted to a strong (even reckless) foreign policy, if they believed that their military technology entitled them to some gains, or that if they got into trouble they could use their missiles to rescue themselves. This kind of situation could be especially dangerous if the Soviets considered that they could not disclose their superiority, since if they did so, we could take remedial action (e.g., an airborne alert). Still, they might be willing to hint at their superiority, in the belief that this would be just enough to make us weak or uncertain in our response in a crisis, but not move us prior to a crisis to institute the airborne alert in time.

Another possibility for preventive war could occur if an arms-control agreement broke down and one side had a considerable lead, either because of its previous success in evading detection, or its greater ability to rearm. This side might well feel that, rather than see the world subjected again to all the dangers of an arms race, it would be doing a public service to stop the race, once and for all. And this could best be done by stopping the cause of the race—its opponent. It might be especially willing to start the war soon after the arms-control agreement terminated, because the risks, even if things went awry, would not be so great at the existing low level of arms than before the arms-control agreement had lowered the absolute level of the balance of terror. The rather high probability of war breaking out after the arms race had begun again (but before both states were fully armed) is often ignored. Most writers focus attention on the situation existing at the time of the breakdown, when the posture is still determined by the agreement and on the feasible violations of the agreement, rather than on the situation some months or a year or two later.

Then there is the idea of "pre-emption," or as Einstein called it, "anticipatory retaliation." Almost all authorities agree that at present the advantages of striking first are so great that if there seems a high probability that the other side is actually attacking, it may be better to take the certain risk of a relatively small retaliatory strike rather than the high probability of a much more destructive first strike. This calculated pressure for pre-emption is especially likely in one situation very similar to that of "self-fulfillment," previously discussed. Even if only one side suspects that the other may attack, each can easily become convinced that it should attack— not because it wants to, or even because it believes the other side wants to, but only because it believes the other side may attack simply to pre-empt a supposed attack by the first (which is itself being launched as a pre-emptive attack). Schelling has labeled this situation, "the reciprocal fear of surprise attack."[4] As described, it is not a case of miscalculation, but a case of calculating correctly. This is clearly a situation in which each side has nothing to fear but fear, yet the knowledge that the other side is afraid fully justifies that fear.

Many things could touch off a "reciprocal fear of surprise attack" situation. The only reason I have put this possibility low on the list of possible causes of war is because of the belief that as long as decision makers are consciously in control of events, they are very much more likely to draw back from pressing buttons and accept any resulting risks, than to do something which would make war inevitable—particularly, if this war were to occur at a time and under circumstances not of their choosing. However, complicated and dangerous situations can occur. For example, suppose that one of our own Polaris submarines accidentally launched some missiles at our own country. Even if the submarine commander succeeded in informing us of what happened before the missiles landed, the accident could still cause a war. The Soviets might observe these missiles exploding and if they did know where the missiles came from, they might decide that it would be too dangerous to wait. Even if the Soviets knew that the missiles had not accidentally come from a Soviet submarine, they might not believe that we would wait to find out.

We might ourselves be under pressure to attack even if we thought the Soviets knew nothing about the incident because we could not be sure they did not know. It might appear safer to pre-empt than to let precious minutes slip away while we tried to persuade the Soviets that we knew they were innocent. The possibilities for trouble are almost infinite, and it would be wise to reinforce the natural caution of decision makers with explicit measures, both unilateral and multilateral, to facilitate communication and persuasion and to make waiting safe.

The line between preventive and pre-emptive war is sometimes very fine, and it is on this line that some of the most plausible war-making situations can occur. For example, let us imagine the Type II Deterrence situation discussed earlier, in which the Soviets were hypothesized as invading Europe, and we as evacuating our cities as a preliminary to delivering an ultimatum or otherwise exerting pressure. If the Soviets struck us at that time, it would not be a pre-emptive war, because very likely we would not have made up our own minds as to whether we would strike or not; in particular, we would intend to give them the option of backing down or compromising. However, we are so close to making up our minds that this cannot be labeled as a preventive war, either—a war to head off some generalized future threat. Similarly, if after evacuating our cities, we gave the Soviets an ultimatum, and the Soviets chose the alternatives of prolonging the crisis, we might decide to strike, even though we thought there was a big chance that they were going to back down eventually. We would not be sure, and if we had already evacuated our cities, the risks of going to war would have been sharply diminished.

There is also a possibility of going to war simply to achieve world domination. Most people (the author included) believe the risks involved in going to war are so great today that no matter how promising an attack might look on paper, the "imponderables" and other "uncertainties" are large enough so that not even a moderately irresponsible decision maker would go to war for positive gains—though one like Hitler might. However, if we ever disarm, either unilaterally or bilaterally, to the point where the available weapon systems do not present the awful potentialities present today, then, of course, this possibility reappears.

Even if decision makers are unwilling to go to war for positive gains, they may still be willing to go to war, if, in their opinion, "going to war" is less risky than not doing so. There are many situations in which this could occur. One could imagine an internal or external crisis getting out of hand, and one which was being aggravated by the opponent, perhaps merely by his very existence. One may then be tempted to go to war, not because it looks so tempting, but because it looks like the least undesirable alternative.

Catalytic War.[5] The last possibility is the catalytic war. This is the notion that some third party (or country) may deliberately start a war between the two major powers for reasons of its own. As it is usually discussed, the concept holds that some power which is third, fourth, or fifth in the international hierarchy wishes to improve its position by arranging for the top two nations to destroy each other, thus moving itself up two notches. This is one of the major reasons why some people fear the dissemination of nuclear weapons to "ambitious" powers. However, there are several reasons why this particular concept is not considered plausible: (1) risks are so great for the triggering power that it is difficult to believe that one power could make and carry out such a decision, (2) more important, the United States and the Soviets will probably put into effect slow-reacting systems with a lot of stops in them before the decision for all-out war is reached. This means that it will be much harder for a third party to start a war than is often imagined, though if it tries hard enough and has a large enough capability, it is not impossible.

There is another type of catalytic war which I think much more likely and important: a desperate third nation thinks it has a problem that can be solved only by war. Let us imagine a war between India and China which the Indians were losing. The Indians might feel that if they induced the United States to strike at China and Russia, this would solve their problem, and any method they used to achieve this end was as good as any other. Conversely, let us imagine a situation in which the Chinese felt hard pressed (possibly over Formosa) and told the Russians, "We are going to strike the United States tomorrow, and you might as well come along with us, for they will undoubtedly strike you, even if you do not do so."

As stated, the situation may seem somewhat implausible, but one can devise hypothetical situations which make it seem more plausible than I have done here. One may wish to broaden the definition of catalytic war. Any method by which a nation uses military or diplomatic power to embroil larger nations or increase the scope of the conflict could be called catalytic. By this definition, World War I was a catalytic war, set off by Serbia and Austria, which also had some overtones of "reciprocal fear of surprise attack" and "self-fulfilling prophecy," because the side which mobilized first was likely to win. It meant that even a defensive mobilization (by the Russians) touched off a defensive-offensive mobilization (by the Germans), in much the same way some believe that a badly designed, quick-reacting force can be touched off by defensive moves by the other side.

SOME HYPOTHETICAL ULTIMATES

Stability Is Not Enough. Many experts and laymen believe that the best method of preventing any of the four potential causes of war from actually causing a war is to procure what are called "stable deterrent systems." This term implies a military posture which will deter a surprise attack and also not be accident prone or "trigger happy." Even this limited goal is not enough for those strategists who also want stability against provocation (i.e., they also wish to have adequate Type II and Type III Deterrence). However, many strategists, and even some arms controllers, overlook the important requirement that a failure of stability should result in limited and "acceptable" consequences.

In order to illustrate this remark, I would like to discuss the strategic theory of three conceptualized devices, which I shall call respectively the Doomsday Machine, the Doomsday-in-a-Hurry Machine, and the Homicide Pact Machine. To discuss these hypothetical (almost allegorical) devices will not only focus attention on the most spectacular and ominous possibilities of the arms race, but it will also clarify a good deal of our current strategic thinking. In particular the discussion should make clear that:

1. The sole objective of maximizing deterrence is an unacceptable criterion for a weapon system;

2. There is a very difficult fundamental problem in deciding the permissible stakes at risk in the event of failure of deterrence;

3. Although current weapon systems are already quite disturbing, their potentialities could be dwarfed by some of the devices that may be practical in the near future.

The Doomsday Machine. A Doomsday weapon system might hypothetically be described as follows: let us assume that for 10 billion dollars one could build a device whose function is to destroy the world.[6] This device is protected from enemy action (perhaps by being situated thousands of feet underground) and then connected to a computer, in turn connected to thousands of sensory devices all over the United States. The computer would be programmed so that if, say, five nuclear bombs exploded over the United States, the device would be triggered and the world destroyed. Barring such problems as coding errors (an important technical consideration), this machine would seem to be the "ideal" Type I Deterrent. If Khrushchev ordered an attack, both Khrushchev *and* the Soviet population would be automatically and efficiently annihilated. (The emphasis is deliberate: most deterrents are more likely to destroy populations than decision makers.)

Even if this is the ultimate in Type I Deterrence, the Doomsday Machine is an unsatisfactory basis for a weapon system. It is most improbable that either the Soviet Union or the United States would ever authorize procuring such a machine. The project is expensive enough so that it would be subjected to a searching budgetary and operational scrutiny, one which would raise questions the project could never survive.

The Doomsday-in-a-Hurry Machine. Before considering these questions, let us consider how one might adapt the Doomsday Machine to purposes of Type II and Type III Deterrence. For reasons that will become clear, let us call this model the Doomsday-in-a-Hurry Machine. The computer would be given all the facilities it needed to be "well informed" about world affairs. We could then publish a "Soviet Criminal Code." This would list in great detail all the acts which the Soviets were not allowed to commit. The Soviets would then be informed that if the computer detects them in any violations it will blow up the world. The logicians (and some so-called practical men) might then believe that we had solved all our deterrence problems. After all, we would then have drawn a line the Soviets would not dare to cross. We could relax forever our interest in defense and turn our attention to other matters.

Unfortunately, the world is not that simple. First, the Soviets would rush to build their own machine. There would be a race to publish first. This race to publish first involves more than prestige. There is almost a certainty of an incompatibility between the two sets of rules, since Paragraph I of each probably states that the opponent shall not build a Doomsday Machine! To many people, to build a Doomsday Machine would be the greatest provocation short of an attack that the opponent could commit. In fact, because it may destroy so many people, some find it more provocative than an attack. Even if we succeed in publishing first, and even if the Soviets believe our machine will work as advertised, and are deterred from publishing, trouble is still almost certain. It will simply prove impossible to draw a useful, unambiguous line that covers most Type III Deterrence situations—it may even be difficult to cover unambiguously all possible Type I and Type II situations. The first time there is a difference in interpretation the world would be blown up.

The Unacceptability of Doomsday Machines. Let us examine the use of both the Doomsday and Doomsday-in-a-Hurry Machines as deterrents. It is desirable that a deterrent should be: frightening; inexorable; persuasive; cheap; and nonaccident-prone.

As measured by these characteristics, both Doomsday Machines are likely to be better than any current or proposed competitor for deterrence. They are as *frightening* as anything that can be devised. They are more *inexorable,* since they can be made almost invulnerable to direct physical destruction (electromagnetic waves which would set them off go faster than shock waves which might destroy the device); the operation is in principle so simple and reliable that one can really believe it would work (as opposed to a complex weapon system which requires the split-second coordination and almost perfect operation of many complex parts in a strange post-attack environment); and the automatic operation eliminates the human element—including any possible loss of resolve as a result of either humanitarian consideration or threats by the enemy.

The machines are certainly *persuasive.* Even the most simple minded should be able to understand their capabilities. Most likely such machines would be *cheap,* compared to present weapons expenditures.

Finally, they are relatively *foolproof,* in the sense that the probability of an accidental or unauthorized triggering should be low. This means, while the possibility of an unauthorized or accidental use of the machine, in spite of all precautions, would be too high to be acceptable, it would still be lower than the probability of such an action in complicated and dispersed systems such as Polaris, Minuteman, and airborne alert. Not only is the number of buttons very low, but the Doomsday weapon system is so simple that one should be able to see clearly the places where trouble could occur, and then take all possible precautions.

The difficulties lie in the fact that the Doomsday Machine is not sufficiently *controllable.* Even though it maximizes the probability that deterrence will work (including minimizing the probability of accidents or miscalculations), it is totally unsatisfactory, for one must still examine the consequences of a failure. A failure will kill too many people, and kill them too automatically. There is no chance of human intervention, control, and final decision. Even if we give up the computer and make the Doomsday Machine reliably controllable by the decision makers, it is still not controllable enough. Neither NATO nor the United States, possibly not even the Soviet Union, would be willing to spend billions of dollars to give a few individuals this particular kind of life-and-death power over the entire world.

If one were presenting a military briefing advocating some special weapon system as a deterrent and examined only the five qualities on the list, the Doomsday Machine might seem better than any alternative system; nevertheless, it is unacceptable. We thus see that our list of properties should have included a sixth: It is desirable that a deterrent should be *controllable*. The fact that most public discussion ignores this last requirement could imply that either some of the weapon systems currently being proposed are unacceptable, or that the way we talk about these weapon systems is wrong—very likely both.[7] Most decision makers seem to feel very strongly about the unacceptability of Doomsday Machines. If forced to choose among accommodation to the point of surrender, a large risk of surprise attack, or buying a Doomsday Machine, they would choose one of the first two as against the last one.

This last statement may surprise many who feel that irresponsible governments on both sides have already bought the equivalent of Doomsday Machines, almost without a second thought. I used to be wary myself of discussing the concept for fear that some overenthusiastic colonel would issue a General Operating Requirement or Development Planning Objective for the device. For whatever it is worth, my experience in two years of briefings has been exactly the opposite. Except for some intellectuals, especially certain scientists and engineers who have overemphasized the single objective of maximizing the effectiveness of deterrence, the device is universally rejected. Doomsday Machines do not look professional to senior military officers (in a way it threatens them with a fourth service), and they look even worse to senior civilians. The fact that more than a few scientists and engineers do seem attracted to such devices is disquieting, but as long as the development project is expensive, even these dedicated experts are unlikely to get one under way.

A Fundamental Problem. The concept of the Doomsday Machine raises certain awkward questions which must be considered by both policy maker and technician. If it is not acceptable to risk the lives of the *three billion* inhabitants of the earth in order to protect ourselves from surprise attack, *then how many people would we be willing to risk?* It is clear that both the United States and NATO would reluctantly envisage the possibility of one or two hundred million fatalities (i.e., about five times more than those in World War II) from the immediate effects, even if one does not include long-term effects due to radiation, if an all-out thermonuclear war results from a failure of Type I Deterrence. Under somewhat more controversy, similar numbers would apply to Type II Deterrence.* We are willing to live with the possibility partly because we think of it only as a remote possibility. We do not expect either kind of deterrence to fail, and we do not expect the results to be that cataclysmic if deterrence does fail. However, even those who expect deterrence to work might hesitate at introducing a new weapon system that increased the reliability of deterrence, but at the

---

* For example, Brennan would concede the statement for his B Deterrence, but not his C Deterrence. [Primarily because I believe we have the capacity to deal with failures of Type C Deterrence by drastically less expensive methods.—ED.]

cost of increasing the possible casualties by a factor of ten, so that there would then be one or two billion hostages at risk if their expectations fail.

Neither the 180 million Americans nor the half billion people in the NATO alliance would be willing to procure a security system in which a malfunction could cause the death of one or two billion people. If the choice were made explicit, then the United States or NATO would seriously consider "lower quality" systems, i.e., systems which were less deterring, but whose consequences would be less catastrophic if deterrence failed. They would even consider such possibilities as a dangerous degree of unilateral disarmament, if there were no other acceptable postures. The West might be willing to procure a military system which could cause such damage if used in a totally irrational and unrealistic way, but only if all of the plausible ways of operating the system would not inflict anything like the hypothesized damage. Nor would we knowingly build a strategic system which forced the Soviets to build a Doomsday Machine in self-defense. On the other hand, we would probably be willing ourselves to go to desperate measures rather than give in to a cynical attempt by the Soviets to blackmail us by building or threatening to build a Doomsday Machine.

Possible Future Problems. Aside from moral and political reasons, and aside from the repugnance policy makers and practical men feel for a device that is poised to strike at their own population, the main reason the Soviet Union and the United States would not build a Doomsday Machine is that they are both *status quo* powers; the United States is one because it has so much, and the Soviet Union is one partly because it also has much and partly because it expects to get so much more without running any excessive risks. However, even if we believe that neither the Soviets, nor the Americans, nor other technically competent and wealthy but "satisfied" powers (such as England) would at present deliberately build a Doomsday weapon system, at least three important problems arise. Would a nation build one inadvertently? If not now, will it change its mind in the future? Would a determined non-*status quo* nation build one?

I do not believe that any nation will build a Doomsday Machine inadvertently, partly because it is so hard to build one, but mostly because current discussion is focusing attention on this problem, and decision makers are becoming conscious of its implications. As for a technically advanced *status quo* country's changing its mind, I could easily imagine a crisis in which a nation might desperately wish it had procured such a machine. Fortunately, it seems less likely that a nation would procure a standby capability that could be connected up at the last moment than that it would procure a continuous capability in being. The lead time for designing and constructing such a machine would be so long that the crisis would be settled before the project could get under way. In the long run (one to three decades), the third question, "Would a determined non-*status quo* nation build one?" may turn out to be the most important.

Many scientists believe that Doomsday Machines will inevitably become both clearly feasible and much cheaper than I have suggested, so that the developmental gamble will be much less risky than it is today. In addition, a number of powers which, unlike the United States and the Soviet Union, may not be cautious in outlook, will be getting both richer and more competent technically, yet may retain their non-*status quo* outlook. For example, there may be a nation (like the Germany of 1933) which is wealthy enough and technically competent enough to have an advanced military technology, yet desperate or ambitious enough to gamble all.[8] Or some of the underdeveloped nations may become rich in terms of gross national product, but have such a low per capita income or other social anomaly that they retain attitudes more appropriate to a desperate claimant on the world's resources than a responsible "bourgeois" member of international society.

China presents the outstanding possibility of this last type in the next decade or two. Such a third nation might well decide that an investment in a very high-quality Type I Deterrent would pay dividends. It is unlikely (though not impossible) that the leaders of that nation would plan on threatening the world with annihilation or extreme damage unless given their way. If they can do the damage gradually, they can make the threat clear and demonstrate their resolve, without actually committing suicide. As an example, suppose that the blackmailing nation started a process which it could reverse, but which could not be reversed or negated by others, in which the temperature of the earth was artificially dropped five degrees a year. If they also had a Doomsday Machine to protect themselves from attack (one which might depend on the same mechanism), one could easily imagine that they could demonstrate enough resolve to bring most of the other major nations to terms. A much more likely possibility for the possessor of a Doomsday Machine would be to exploit the sanctuary afforded by his "excellent" Type I Deterrent to be as aggressive as he pleased against his neighbors and to threaten any who interfered with all kinds of punishment—for example, some form of controlled nuclear retaliation, in which he destroyed two or three of the major cities of his interfering opponent. Even if it were feasible to retaliate in kind without setting off the Doomsday Machine, the social and political impact of accepting such losses would raise much more serious internal and external problems in the United States than in China. It seems most likely, for example, that having to accept and explain the rationale of an exchange of two or three major United States cities for an equal number of Chinese cities would result in political suicide for the party in power in the United States, as well as in some instabilities in our alliances, but only in some serious inconvenience to the Chinese government. It should therefore be a major objective of arms control to prevent such hypothetical, but not unimaginable, problems from occurring. (Here is one clear case of joint Soviet–United States interest.)

The Homicide Pact Machine. There is another hypothetical deterrent which, while not a Doomsday Machine, is still an "ultimate" of a sort. This could be called the Homicide Pact Machine, an attempt to make the failure of Type I Deterrence mean automatic *mutual* homicide. The adherents to this somewhat more practical device hope to divide the work of deterrence in a natural way—we poised to destroy the enemy and the enemy poised to destroy us, and neither of us buying any effective active or passive defenses for our respective societies.[9] The Homicide Pact Machine is clearly more satisfactory to both humanitarians and neutrals than the Doomsday Machine, and both should note the distinction. As far as patriots and nationalists are concerned, I believe that the Homicide Pact systems have many of the same drawbacks as the Doomsday Machine, though not in so extreme a form. The major advantage of the Homicide Pact is that one is not in the bizarre situation of being killed with one's own equipment; while intellectuals may not so distinguish, the policy makers and practical men prefer being killed by the other side rather than their own.

It is just because this view no longer strikes some people as bizarre that it is so dangerous. The Homicide Pact used to be, albeit only half-intentionally so, NATO policy and recently has come extremely close to being consciously adopted as official United States policy. It is not known to what extent the Soviets are planning to live up to "their part of the bargain" and move in the same direction. While Khrushchev's speech of January 14, 1960, indicated that Soviet decision makers have begun to accept some of the concepts of deterrence which have so persuasively swept the West since the mid-fifties, there is no indication that this acceptance will lead to a relaxation of current Soviet attempts to attain a capability of fighting and surviving wars as well as of deterring them. The opposite may be true. The main point of the speech was not that the Soviets were disarming, but rather that, by cutting back on conventional capabilities, they would gain in their capability to fight a modern thermonuclear war. Whether this is the somewhat misleading "more bang for the buck" program we once followed or a serious attempt to be prepared for any eventuality, only time or Khrushchev can tell.

THE ARMS RACE ITSELF

In discussing the Doomsday Machine as a weapons system, including computer and sensors, I have ben dealing with a somewhat romanticized and (one hopes) very remote possibility. I have spent so much time on it partly to highlight and satirize some current strategic notions (e.g., some extreme forms of Finite Deterrence). For this reason, much of the section on "hypothetical ultimates" has been cast in a "reassuring" tone; but the mere fact that one feels it necessary to discuss soberly the use and construction of Doomsday Machines indicates in the most dramatic manner that the current arms race has changed in character from previous arms races. The issues are bigger and may eventually come to the stage of Doomsday Machines or close approximations of these devices. While this possibility now seems rather remote, if the event should ever transpire, it would of course constitute *the problem* of the twentieth century. However, one does not have to allude to the Doomsday Machine to be concerned about the arms race and current capabilities. Our normal military forces are frightening enough, and they are improving rapidly (though in some ways the newer systems—Polaris and Minuteman—are less destructive than the old ones).* The most spectacular thing about the arms race is that it *is* a race, and one that is being run with some celerity.

This is also a new thing. There has been some tendency in the past for the military to exploit the products of civilian research and development, but this attempt has been remarkably lackadaisical. There has been even less research and development done specifically for war. (The common belief that the search for improved weapons has been a major source of technological progress seems to be grossly exaggerated, at least for periods of peace, though long wars such as the American Civil War and World Wars I and II did see technological advances spurred on by the requirements of the war.) Previously, really big wars have tended to occur twenty and thirty or more years apart, and there has been a tendency for each war to start where the last one left off or even with more ancient techniques.

Even so, each war has brought startling and unexpected surprises. (For example, the development of the most characteristic feature of World War I, the long line of trenches stretching from the Alps to the English Channel, seems to have been considered by only one writer, Jean de Bloch, and though widely read, he had no impact on military planning.) Now, for the first time in history, we are having a complete technological revolution in the art of war approximately every five years. As a result, we are now three technological revolutions away from World War II. Any attempts to apply the concepts and rules of common sense derived from that experience run the grave risk of being as outmoded as some American Civil War concepts would have been in World War II. In so far as we are trying to plan for the late 'sixties and early 'seventies, we are projecting into an environment which is two or three revolutions ahead of where we are today. An examination of the development of military doctrine in the postwar years, in both the official agencies and the *avant garde,* indicates that the possibility of great success in such planning is not high. While doctrine has evolved with meteoric speed as contrasted with the rates before World War II, it has been hopelessly behind events rather than successful in anticipating the future. I will not try to describe this process in any detail, though I would like to describe the technological revolutions, so as to emphasize the difficulties both we and the Soviets have in understanding and coping with just the military environment in our search for security.

* This is because of weight restrictions on the warheads for these missiles, not because of humanitarian considerations.—ED.

The Technology of 1951. Let us start with the situation in 1951, a convenient date to mark the first peacetime revolution. What follows is a very partial list of the new possibilities (with particular reference to the United States and air warfare) that the military planner (or arms controller) of 1945 would have had to anticipate by 1951: third- or fourth-generation fission bombs; the B-50 and B-36, forming the backbone of the United States SAC; the initial production of the B-47; the first flight of the XB-52; a manual air defense system started; air defense having F-80, F-84, F-86, F-94; production order for Nike A; experimental aerial refueling; a nuclear-powered airplane under development; many organizations, in and out of government, formed to institutionalize innovations in air warfare and to rationalize research, development, procurement, and operation; the Russians possessing TU-4 and MIG-15, and having tested three nuclear weapons.

I will discuss only a few items on the above list and on other lists to be given later, but the whole list will remind us of the complexity and speed of the arms race.

The most pressing questions involve the impact of fission bombs. These devices had had a very vigorous development program, and in 1951 we had third- or fourth-generation models available. Would their use have been decisive or not? The Soviets did not think so: they talked smugly of the "permanently operating factors" and the impracticability of blitz-krieg tactics. Many Americans, particularly the advocates of air power, tended to think that nuclear weapons would be decisive, but we had not bothered to get as many bombs as we could or (from the strictly military point of view) should have. Of course, the Soviets had gone into a vigorous development and procurement program for nuclear weapons. But they did not seem to have made any preparations specifically designed to meet the threats that nuclear weapons pose, though they had done a great deal to meet conventional threats typical of World War II.

In 1951 there was still much talk of the scarcity of uranium, a view which was reinforced by most of the technical people. Few people in or out of government thought of the atom bomb as soon being plentiful; nobody realized that practical and convenient thermonuclear bombs would be available before long. But a few people with high security clearances knew that some work on a rather impractical thermonuclear device was going forward. Though there was some discussion in 1951 about "baby atom bombs" with about the same power as the Hiroshima and Nagasaki bombs but much smaller in both weight and size, not even the experts had any idea of the flexibility, efficiency, and economy soon to be available in the atomic weapons arsenal.

Almost all 1951 discussions of defense against nuclear weapons assumed that the bombs were too precious to be used on anything but important cities or the most valuable production targets, such as Oak Ridge and Hanford. Similarly, NATO planned on the assumption that nuclear weapons would not be generally available for the European theatre except for very special and very high priority targets. However, a few economists were already pointing out that since there was a large disparity between the value of uranium and the marginal cost of production, there was every reason to imagine that much more uranium could and would be produced. There was even some reason to suppose that this large increase in production would be roughly at current prices. Most of the military, the scientists, and the engineers did not think that way.

This overvaluation of bombs as being too precious to use on military targets affected defense planning in our Zone of the Interior. Because of the threat of Soviet attacks, the Air Defense Command and the associated Army Anti-Aircraft Command was set up in Colorado Springs in 1951, but they thought of their highest priority job as the defense of large cities and nuclear facilities; the initial deployment of their facilities (radars and fighters) almost ignored warning and defense for SAC in the event of a surprise attack directed at SAC and not at the cities.

In spite of the emphasis on short wars it was not until 1948 that we seriously started to mold SAC into an ever-ready instrument of war. (The accession of General Curtis LeMay to the command of SAC and the Berlin Blockade apparently played the main roles.) We had not quite finished the process by 1951. Neither had we accepted the implications of the Soviets' testing of an atom bomb. For example, the official point of view (to be reflected soon in the investment of some 11 billion dollars in war reserve tools and raw materials), as opposed to that of the air-power enthusiasts, held that an all-out war of the mid-1950's would be long—from three to five years—even though initiated with atomic weapons.

While it is easy to show that most of these planners had not thought about the problem and were just reacting in a World War II fashion, given the official asumptions as to the scarcity of bombs, they may well have been right about the length of the war. Nobody could show just by physics and engineering that a small number of fission bombs dropped on Russia would in fact have caused them to sue for peace. In fact, one could almost have shown the opposite: that the Russians accepted much more damage in World War II and continued to fight, so that unless such imponderables as the psychological and disorganizing impact of using even a small number of bombs were great, a long war would have been possible.

One thing was almost always completely overlooked in 1951: the possibility that war could have broken out under such circumstances that the United States might not have succeeded in using very many bombs. We had only a small number of SAC bases (18 in 1950,[10] including some strategic fighter bases that did not pose a serious threat to the Soviets) and no organized warning system worthy of the name. (There was not even a Ground Observer Corps, for this organization dates only from July 14, 1952.) Furthermore, under normal conditions, SAC operated unalerted and would have taken some hours before it could get its planes into the air just to evacuate—even longer before the airplanes could have been prepared to go on a mission. Under these circumstances, just a handful of Russian planes carrying a very small number of atom bombs might well have been able to wipe out a large segment, possibly approaching 100 percent, of our strategic military power in a few hours. (I use the term "few hours" deliberately. The Russians needed no superb coordination or piloting to do this task. They simply had to be able to fly from one point to another point, more or less on a Great Circle route.)

In some ways the lack of concern in 1951 for the ground vulnerability of bombers was surprising. Many people had written or lectured about the importance of our having a secure and invulnerable SAC. Furthermore, it was part of both Douhet * and Air Force doctrine that war in the air is decided by the destruction of the enemy air force on the ground. Last, less than a decade had passed since the "bolt out of the blue" at Pearl Harbor. Nevertheless, there was a real doctrinal lag, which by the mid-fifties was just being made up. It is rather interesting that it was the advent of the ICBM, rather than the fact that the Soviets had acquired a strategic bombing force, that persuaded most people to think the vulnerability problem through and learn to distinguish between First Strike (attack) and Second Strike (retaliatory) forces. As long as the problem had any subtlety at all, most people managed to ignore it. One wonders what subtle doctrinal lags exist today.

It was quite true in 1951 that even though the Russians had the basic equipment they needed—the bomb, and a plane which when refueled could reach its target—they probably had neither the tactical knowledge, the operational capability, nor the strategic doctrine which would have enabled them to launch such an attack out of the blue. In fact, given their strange lack of emphasis on aerial refueling (an absolute must for any Soviet war planner devising an attack on the United States), one could have argued that the Soviets were basically planning to refight World War II, and, for example, had built hundreds of submarines to stop convoys of the type of World War II.

In addition, Stalin and his military advisers seem to have been reasonably, if not excessively, cautious. They were willing to fill power vacuums and press relentlessly, but not too aggressively. They were willing to take small but not large risks. There is even evidence that they tried to restrain the Yugoslav, Greek, Indochinese, and Chinese Communists from being too provocative.

However, it also seems likely that Stalin's caution did not stem from fear of the atomic bomb as a decisive weapon. What alarmed him about the United States was Detroit—not SAC. He appears to have been convinced that no sensible government should tangle with a nation that had a gross national product of 350 billion dollars a year. We had both assets, the

---

* Douhet was an Italian strategist who developed in the 1920's much of the air-power strategy later used in World War II. See Bernard Brodie, *Strategy in the Missile Age,* Princeton University Press, 1959.—ED.

bomb and the GNP, so that any difference between the point of view of the United States and the Soviet Union was not crucial.

It should be quite clear, even from the superficial discussion above, that any arms-control system set up in 1951 might easily have been based on some serious misunderstandings of the implications of-the technology then current, and on even more serious misunderstandings of the future. In particular, some kinds of inspection schemes might have resulted in making our vulnerabilities both crystal clear and very tempting to Stalin or some of his military advisers. Even to force the Soviets to go through the intellectual exercise of thinking these problems through might have been dangerous. Before we could have safely started discussion of "the control of surprise attack," we would have had to fill in the gaps in our defense posture—that is, engage in a limited rearmament program.

The Technology of 1956. Let us now look at the technology of 1956. It included such factors as: third-generation thermonuclear bombs; three nuclear powers; the last B-47E produced; B-52 and KC-135 being phased into SAC; B-36 being phased out (the last B-36J was produced in August 1954); B-52D in production; B-58, Snark, and XP6M-1 (Martin Seamaster) flying; Regulus I, Nike-Hercules, and Falcon missiles in service; Atlas, Titan, and Thor in crash programs; many other missile programs in progress; Century Series of fighters (F-100 to F-104) being phased into the Air Defense Command; the DEW line being built; MB-1 (nuclear warhead for air-to-air rockets) being tested; production order for Missile Master and SAGE; classified intelligence projects such as the U-2, Turkish Radar, etc.; an atomic-powered plane and rocket under development; an atomic-powered submarine launched; research and development becoming the major business of the aircraft industry, and procurement becoming secondary; the Russians having the Badgers, Bears, Bisons, IRBM's, and their own models of H-bombs.

The most startling change was the development and perfection of thermonuclear bombs. Probably this introduced a more radical change into the technology of war than the introduction of the atom bomb did. The difference between megaton and kiloton is very large, in some ways relatively larger than the difference between kiloton and ton.

The effect of the innovation shows up in the nature of the questions one tends to ask. For kiloton bombs, one asks how much is destroyed—but, barring an extreme course of military events, no one doubts the the nation will continue in some form. With multimegaton weapons, the question of the continuation of the nation (to some, of civilization) is raised even in the shortest of wars. Megaton weapons are comparable to gross forces of nature such as earthquakes, hurricanes, etc. The prospective effects of the use of such weapons are not only extremely widespread, they are also occasionally very subtle and hard to predict. As a result, for the first time in the history of war we have what might be called *the problem of the post-attack environment.* Partly because of one of these environmental effects (fall-out), and partly because we had not thought about or prepared for nonmilitary defense including recuperation, it is most unlikely that the United States really possessed in 1956 and later years much objective Type II Deterrence. But nobody knew it, so we did not suffer any disastrous losses in 1956. However, the instability of such psychological capabilities began to show up even before the next technological revolution in 1961.

Let us look at this notion of post-attack environment in more detail. Multimegaton bombs are so powerful that even if they do not destroy a system, they may damage it by some subtle effects or so change the environment that the system will be temporarily inoperable. The various effects of nuclear weapons include blast, thermal and electromagnetic radiation, ground shock, debris, dust, and ionization—any of which may affect people, equipment, the propagation of electromagnetic signals, etc.

It is quite possible that some of our current systems may have important hidden defects that will only be disclosed by an attack. In the last few years I have worked on several weapon systems in which new weapon effects or new interpretations of old weapon effects were found that had not been thoroughly allowed for and which could have been disastrous. I therefore find it hard to believe that we have uncovered all of the problems from which our systems may suffer. An extreme dependence on such theoretical investigations as a substitute for (unobtainable) experience can be dangerous. For example, imagine that our total posture has ten serious weaknesses in it, but by dint of hard work and much investigation we discover nine out of ten of the weaknesses and correct them. Imagine also that the enemy is trying to find these same weaknesses and succeeds in finding nine of them. Unless the overlap is complete and we have found exactly the same weaknesses, then the enemy has discovered a weakness which he can exploit. If the processes involved were purely random, there would be a 90 percent probability that the enemy had found the one weakness we failed to correct. In practice, the situation should not be that bad: the weakness that was hard for us to find is probably just as hard for the enemy to find. But even if the enemy does not find some weakness that he deliberately exploits, it is not at all clear that we will be able to predict the post-attack environment in enough detail to be able to take into account adequately all of the phenomena that will occur.

Technological Advances by 1961. Let us now glance at some of the technology we shall be facing in 1961: arms control (techniques and capabilities); satellites, such as Tiros, Transit, Notus, Discoverer, Pioneer, Mercury; soft Atlas and soft IRBM's deployed; 25-psi Atlas, 100-psi Titan, and Polaris being phased in; several guidance "breakthroughs"; a crash program on Minuteman and other second-generation missiles; B-47E, B-52H, B-58 forming the bulk of SAC; BMEWS being phased in; Goose, Navajo, Regulus II, Seamaster, etc., canceled; SAC operating alert and dispersed; inexpensive, efficient, and versatile bombs; four nuclear countries; SAGE and Missile Master partially deployed; Bomarc A and Hawk being phased in; Nike-Hercules, F-100, 101, 102, and 104 in service; limited Civil Defense (?); X-15 test vehicle; a nuclear-powered plane and rocket still under development; experimental nuclear explosives; the Russians having . . . ?

The year 1961 will find arms control having some influence on our military posture. On October 31, 1958, the United States suspended the testing of nuclear weapons, and 1961 is likely to be the third year of no weapon-development testing on the part of the United States. Thus, 1961 should be the third year of an uninspected moratorium, and, in addition to all the other uncertainties of a United States military planner, there will be such questions as, "Are the Soviets cheating? If so, to what extent? And what is the military significance?" Even if a treaty were to be signed by the time this book is published it will take a period of from two to five years to install and proof-test whatever inspection network is agreed upon.

The test-suspension negotiations at Geneva illustrate the importance of doing our homework. In July and August of 1958, the Western and Eastern experts at Geneva agreed, after a short hectic conference (at which most of the technical facts were worked out in late evening sessions) that about 180 stations around the world (about 21 in the Soviet Union) would suffice to pick up illegal explosions greater than 5 kilotons in yield. Within months, on the basis of new data and experiments, the Western experts decided they had been off by at least a factor of four. A few months later, several ingenious schemes (testing in big holes or outer space) were worked out to evade the proposed inspection system almost completely, as far as tests of the kiloton type were concerned.

From the viewpoint of arms control, one of the most dangerous innovations of 1961 is the possibility of the experimental use of nuclear explosives in one or more peacetime applications. In May 1959 the Atomic Energy Commission sponsored the Second Plowshare Symposium on the Industrial and Scientific Uses of Nuclear Explosions. At an earlier symposium there had been much interest in the subject, but nobody expected anything to happen very soon. By the second one, many of the ideas had had time to mature. There were about fifty papers presented at the symposium on various aspects of nuclear explosives. The suggestions for peaceful uses of nuclear explosives included: artificial harbors, sea-level ship canals, underground oil storage, power, isotope production, geothermal steam plants, salt water distillation, improvement of underground water supplies, mining, shale oil production, meteorological experiments, and other scientific experiments.

The length of the above list should not surprise the reader. Nuclear explosives are a uniquely concentrated but very simple and relatively cheap source of power, heat, and pressure, as well as of neutrons and other radiation. Once they become even slightly available, many people will look for and find applications for these new devices, which in turn will make them even more available. In fact, the terms on which they are available at this writing were spelled out by the AEC at the Second Plow-share Symposium as follows: roughly a half million dollars will buy explosives in the low kiloton region, and perhaps a million dollars will buy them in the low megaton region. The AEC is careful to note that the above charges are for small quantities.

Very few people at the 1959 symposium would have accepted even odds that a number of the ideas discussed would not be in programs by 1961. In particular, a project to dig an artificial harbor in Alaska is definitely programed at this writing. Since some of the individual projects promised to use hundreds or even thousands of bombs, it is not impossible that even a private international market of buyers and sellers of nuclear explosives could eventually spring up. This last is particularly likely if there is technological progress in the design of very simple bombs made of readily available materials. Once there develops a legitimate market for nuclear explosives, then in the absence of controls many nations will manufacture them for sale or peaceful use, if not by 1970, then by 1980. However, unless one of these nations is very irresponsible, there should be a fair degree of voluntary control over the distribution of these devices.

I will discuss later some of the problems that might arise as a result of the possible dissemination of nuclear weapons. I should point out that at the present writing, however, it is rather unlikely that nuclear explosives will be as successful as I have indicated they might be. As Lewis Bohn has pointed out to me, the above discussion mirrors almost exactly the early (incorrect) postwar expectations on the speed of development of nuclear reactors and the consequent strategic and control problems. Much of the Baruch Plan for the control of nuclear weapons was preoccupied with this much overestimated problem.

I believe that a much better economic and technical case can be made for the use of nuclear explosives than could be made for the early postwar reactors. In addition, there is a much smaller distance between a nuclear explosive and a bomb than between a reactor and a bomb. In the first case, the distinction is often a semantic one; in the second case, one may need a major chemical industry. I therefore believe that if nuclear explosives do not present a problem, it is likely to be because of legal, social, and political obstacles to this development rather than technical and economic ones. This is one place where the pursuit of a higher standard of living for all may result in a drastic reduction.

The Mid-1960's. We have just been looking somewhat superficially at the early 'sixties. I would like to give only a bare listing of the possibilities of the mid-sixties, labeled 1965 for the sake of definiteness. (The reason there are only four years between this technological revolution and the last—I had been using five years between these revolutions—is that technological innovation seems to be even faster today. We are spending more money on research and development, and getting more skillful in its management.) By 1965, then, we would expect to have some of the following:

independent nuclear deterrents; Minuteman B and Polaris C; second-generation Atlas and Titan; Dynasoar; BMEWS-B, Midas, and SAMOS; protected B-52G and H, B-47E, B-58A and B; the limits of bomb technology (if testing is continued); commercial nuclear explosives; an airborne ballistic missile; super-guidance; SAGE B, Bomarc B and C, Nike-Zeus A and B, Hawk B, F-108, B-70 technologically possible, but perhaps canceled; antiradiation drugs; protected command and control; exotic fuels and propellants; an inexpensive reliable research missile; inexpensive satellites; a nuclear-powered airplane(?) or rocket (?); experimental climate control; bacteriological and chemical warfare; and astronauts.

The 1970's. Rather than comment on any of the above, I would like to deal with some of the possibilities for the late 'sixties and early 'seventies, which I will label 1969. We now have to take into account more than just the extrapolation of current technology. We have to consider the possibility of "breakthroughs" and other surprises. Although it is not possible to limit or describe in advance what breakthroughs might occur, it is possible to discuss some projects currently being studied which might be called breakthroughs, if successful. This method of trying to estimate the total impact of technological progress is likely to involve some large underestimates of the total change, since one can almost guarantee that many startling and unexpected developments will occur. I will try to make up for this by some judicious exaggeration in the areas to be discussed, for such an exaggeration will give a better "feel" for the over-all possibilities for the late 'sixties or early 'seventies than a more sober discussion of the few items I will consider: cheap, simple bombs; cheap, simple missiles; cheap satellites; controlled thermonuclear reaction; other sources of cheap neutrons; other sources of nuclear fuels; californium bullets; ground-effect machines; reliable sensors; super-calculators; cheap calories; medical progress; advanced materials; cheap, fast transportation (for limited wars); reliable command and control; Doomsday Machines; and disguised warfare.

When we enter the 1970's, the most advanced nations at least will know in theory how to make simple bombs and missiles, and in the absence of explicit or implicit controls will be making them in practice. For this reason, I have put cheap simple bombs and cheap simple missiles at the top of the list because, even with arms control, and certainly without it, these are likely to be the most characteristic features of the late 1960 or the early 1970 period. They may or may not present the most important (and dramatic) problem. This will depend on which nations actually have weapons in their stockpiles, on the explicit and implicit controls, and on the state of international relations.

Under the current programs, 1969 may be a little early for the diffusion of these devices to other than "advanced" nations. It is very difficult to predict the rate at which the technology, materials, and information will be disseminated. Even without explicit controls, it might be the mid-1970's or even a later period before they become cheap and simple for the majority of "developed" nations. But there are many things that could accelerate this dissemination process: the use of nuclear weapons in a limited war; successful programs for the peaceful uses of nuclear explosives in the mid-1960's might at least make nuclear "devices" widely available; the deliberate diffusion of nuclear technology, by either the United States or the Soviet Union, to enough allies so that there will be no more secrets; a breakthrough in technology or materials, etc.

As an example of this last possibility, consider the fusion reactor. It is improbable that this device will be practical by 1969; most experts in this field are somewhat doubtful about any real success before the year 2000. Let us, however, go ahead and outrage the experts by assuming not a qualified, but an outstanding success—such a success that even relatively primitive nations will find it possible either to build or buy a fusion reactor and thereby to acquire a virtually unlimited source of cheap power. This spectacular gift of technology has a significant side effect: it gives off neutrons very copiously, so copiously that it may not be exaggerating to state that the neutrons are for all practical purposes free.

Free neutrons would mean that many kinds of nuclear fuels would be very cheap. With these nuclear fuels and with the kind of technology that is likely to be available in 1969, it may literally turn out that a trained and technically minded person, even one who is a member of a relatively primitive society, would be able to make or obtain bombs. This would raise forcefully the question of the illegal or uncontrolled dissemination of bombs. (One can today buy machine guns, artillery, tanks, and fighter aircraft on the gray market.) Thus the 1969 equivalent of the Malayan guerrillas or the Algerian rebels or the Puerto Rican nationalists, or even less official groups such as gangsters and wealthy dilettantes, might be able to obtain such bombs.

Even if the controlled thermonuclear reaction does not prove to be a success by 1969, there are other possibilities for the cheap production of neutrons. For example, many of the commercial uses of nuclear devices would release neutrons as a by-product. This might lead to either the clandestine or open production of weapon-grade nuclear fuels. There are also possibilities that simple and inexpensive methods for producing weapon-grade nuclear fuels will be developed. It is also possible that we and others will learn how to make bombs using only or mostly materials already widely available, such as deuterium and lithium. (The widely discussed small "clean" bomb would probably use such materials.) In a word, 1969 (though more likely 1979) may see the introduction of the era of the conventional nuclear bomb in which (in the absence of adequate controls) any "legitimate" nation can get some models, and some illegitimate groups or governments may also get access to nuclear weapons, but presumably under more onerous conditions than those to which legitimate purchasers are subject.

Consequences of the Spread of Weapons. We may be too frightened of the possible consequences of the widespread diffusion of weapons. It is quite clear that if one gave the Egyptians and Israelis atomic weapons, one is likely to find both nations acting much more cautiously than they do today, simply because the consequences of "irresponsibility" would be much more disastrous. On the other hand, even a greatly increased sense of responsibility may only mean that, instead of falling upon each other the week after they come into possession of these weapons, the attack may be deferred for a year or two.

In fact, almost any sober analysis indicates that it is somewhat harder for "Nth" countries to cause a cataclysm than is often believed.[11] It is difficult to imagine that China or France, for example, could in the next decade obtain a large enough strategic force to strain United States Type I Deterrence seriously, although the situation in the 1970's and 1980's could become much more difficult. It is even difficult to imagine one of these nations being able to start an accidental war, if the Soviets and the United States have made sensible plans to prevent this eventuality, and it is a little difficult to understand why they would want to start one, unless they were in some kind of a crisis which would be helped by such an action. In this last case, the Soviets and the United States would be likely to be on their guard.

All of the above may be true. Even though it is going to be difficult to get nations to make the necessary concessions until the dangers are both more apparent and more pressing than they are today, nevertheless, I believe that we should still try to make international arrangements *before* the weapons have been distributed, rather than *afterward*. While it is quite possible that many laymen overestimate the immediate impact that the widespread dispersion of weapons will have, I strongly suspect that the "sober" analysts underestimate both the immediate and long-term problems. I will list ten such problems here. It would not be difficult to list many more.

In a nuclear world, the "small" powers, vis-à-vis one another, would have: greater opportunities for blackmail and mischief-making; greater likelihood of an accidental triggering of weapons; an increased possibility of a "local" Munich, a Pearl Harbor, and blitzkriegs; pressures to preemption because of the preceding three items; a tendency to neglect conventional capabilities because of an overreliance on nuclear capabilities; internal (civil war, a *coup d'état,* irresponsibility, etc.) and external (the arms race, fear of fear, etc.) political problems.

Nuclear diffusion to small powers would also: create a situation in which the diffusion of nuclear weapons to irresponsible or criminal organizations and individuals is facilitated; complicate future problems of control by making such control involve the small powers' having to accept an obvious reduction in their sovereignty (that is, they would give up something, rather than abstain); give the Soviet Union or another large power many opportunities to act as agent-provocateur; and create the capability, and therefore the pressure, for many nations to make a crisis serious or to exploit an ongoing crisis (such as by catalytic war or escalation).

In short, the diffusion of nuclear weapons may or may not increase the number of crises, but it will almost undoubtedly tend to increase the seriousness and the grim potentialities of any crisis or even the misunderstandings that do occur, besides increasing enormously the importance of having responsible and competent governments everywhere.

The widespread possession of nuclear weapons and delivery systems strikes many observers as similar to situations in physics that may be described as semi-stable equilibrium. For example, imagine a ball balanced on top of a small cup so that small movements of the ball can be tolerated, but not large ones. If this ball on the cup is isolated, it might sit there on top of its cup forever, but if it is submitted to the vagaries and chances of a sufficiently uncontrolled environment, one can guarantee that sooner or later it will fall. This may be true even though every "reasonable" analysis of the situation that looks at probable or plausible disturbances showed that the forces were in close enough balance so the ball should stay where it is. It takes an improbable or implausible force to topple the ball. But some improbable and implausible events will occur and, barring a major change in the situation, almost certainly the ball will eventually fall. While the analogy may simultaneously be apt and yet misleading, many who have thought about this problem have come to the conclusion that reliable stability can only come through an international agency with an effective monopoly of force.

For many reasons, I do not believe that the twentieth century will see a disarmed world, but it may see a world government or the equivalent.[12] Until that day arrives, it will be of great value to try to keep, indeed *make,* the problem of national security intellectually and diplomatically simple, and the diffusion of nuclear weapons would seem to go exactly the wrong way. The "two-power" case seems both intellectually and practically more controllable than the "N-power" case. The diffusion of nuclear weapons not only complicates the over-all "analytic" problem, but the stakes at risk if events go badly would seem to be less in the "two-power" than in the "N-power" case.

CONCLUSION

In this chapter I have scarcely been able to touch upon the complexities of the technological arms race and the stability of the United States–Soviet balance of terror. I have tried to point out that technological progress is so rapid that there are almost bound to be doctrinal lags. These doctrinal lags will in themselves be dangerous, leading to important gaps in our preparations, the waste of badly needed resources on obsolete concepts, the neglect of possible strengths, the excessive use of especially glamorous tools, and, possibly most important of all, heightened possibilities of serious miscalculations or accidents because we have not had time to understand and make provisions for the requirements of the newly installed systems. To the extent that arms-control measures are supposed to alleviate dangers or costs by allowing the current "balance of power" status and military competition to be conducted, by agreement, at cheaper or safer levels, or to the extent that one hopes to increase each state's objective capability of preventing surprise attack or other disaster, this inability to understand "the military problems" introduces almost intolerable complications. (The reason for the adverb "almost" is that we have these complications, whether or not we have arms control.) I have almost ignored the even more complex problem of the conduct of international relations in a world in which force is becoming both increasingly more available and increasingly less usable, a problem that is complicated by the spectacular increase in the number of sovereign nations, by increased nationalism, militarism, and "ambitions" in these new nations and governments, and by the revolution of rising expectations.

Any attempts to control the arms race must be able to live with all the stresses and strains that the above problems will create. It is most unlikely that all of these problems will be solved in an atmosphere of good will and common fellowship, or by the use of *ad hoc* committees and intuitive judgments derived from experience in almost irrelevant situations. And we may not have much time in which to work.

References

1. The *New York Times,* April 22, 1958.
2. Peter Bryant, *Red Alert* (New York: Ace Books, 1958).
3. Bertrand Russell, *Common Sense and Nuclear Warfare* (New York: Simon and Schuster, 1959).
4. T. C. Schelling, *The Strategy of Conflict* (Cambridge: Harvard University Press, 1960).
5. The term seems to be due to Amrom Katz.
6. While I would not care to guess the exact form an efficient Doomsday Machine would take, I would be willing to conjecture that if the project were started today and were sufficiently supported, one could have such a machine (or close approximation to such a device) by 1970. I would also guess that the cost would be between ten and a hundred billion dollars. Even then it might not be possible to destroy groups of especially well-prepared people. The mechanism one would use would most likely involve, not the breaking up of the earth, but the creation of really large amounts of radioactivity, or the causing of major climatic changes.
7. I should make the point, though, that contrary to many common statements, current (1961) weapon systems are not Doomsday Machines or even close to being such devices.

8. This is actually an extreme view of the German situation. During most of the period 1933–1944 Hitler was restrained by "responsible" elements, and many of his gambles were actually hedged. On many occasions on which he seemed too reckless, military groups prepared a *coup d'état* should he go too far.

9. It is more feasible to survive and recuperate from a war than is generally thought. RAND Report R-322-RC, *Report on a Study of Non-Military Defense,* June 1958, has a description of the possibilities.

10. Testimony of General LeMay before the 1956 Subcommittee on the Air Force, Senate Armed Services Committee, p. 135.

11. See Fred C. Iklé, *Nth Countries and Disarmament* (RAND Corporation Report P-1956), April 1960, for further discussion of this important problem.

12. An international agency with a near-monopoly for force might come from any of the following possibilities, listed in order of apparent probability rather than desirability: (1) a Soviet- or United States-dominated world arising most likely out of war; (2) some other results of a war; (3) a Soviet Union–United States combination which is in effect a world government, though it may not be openly called so; (4) some of the NATO nations and China added to the above combination as influential, if not equal partners; (5) the haves against the have-nots, probably without exploitation, and, perhaps, with aid to underdeveloped nations, but with stringent arms control in which authority and responsibility are roughly proportioned to military and economic development; (6) a sort of world federal state in which power is proportioned to sovereignty and population, as in the United States Congress.

While many of the above possibilities may strike most readers as unpleasant or undesirable, it is quite possible that even a "bad" world government is preferable to an accelerated and uncontrolled arms race. It is to be hoped this last will not be the only choice available.

NOTES AND QUESTIONS

1. How can you verify Kahn's contention that revolutionary changes have taken place in weapons technology every four or five years since World War II? What revolutionary changes in weapons technology have taken place since the end of World War II? What changes might take place in the next twenty years? Does strategic thinking increase or decrease the dangers of nuclear war? For representative studies in strategic doctrine, see Herman Kahn, *On Thermonuclear War* (Princeton University Press, 1961); Glenn H. Snyder, *Deterrence and Defense* (Princeton University Press, 1959); *NATO and American Security,* edited by Klaus E. Knorr (Princeton University Press, 1959); Raymond Aron, *The Great Debate—Theories of Nuclear Strategy* (Doubleday, New York, 1962).

2. For a more elaborate and detailed analysis of the escalation process, see Kahn in *National Security: Political, Military, and Economic Strategies in the Decade Ahead,* edited by David M. Abshire and Richard V. Allen (Praeger, New York, 1963), especially pages 475–481; and Herman Kahn, *Thinking About the Unthinkable* (Horizon Press, New York, 1962).

3. For Kahn's view of what the world might look like in the year 2000, see his chapter "The Arms Race and World Order" in *The Revolution in World Politics*, edited by Morton A. Kaplan (Wiley, New York, 1962). The spread of nuclear weapons and the possible steps to retard or avoid this spread is taken up in a later chapter, **IV-2**. Kahn's comments concerning the possibility of the outbreak of thermonuclear war are pertinent to our discussion here. His estimate is that "a nuclear war is likely to be avoided only for a few decades," unless the spread of nuclear weapons is halted and some significant changes are made in the present system of international relations. For a somewhat similar appraisal, see Oskar Morgenstern, *The Question of National Defense* (Random House, New York, 1959). At the same time, Kahn lists some reasons why it might take as long as thirty or forty years before the current system would break down. See p. 341, *supra*. Kahn has commented upon *World Peace through World Law*. He had an exchange with Richard Hudson, editor of *War-Peace Report*, on the value and merits of the Clark-Sohn approach. This is to be found in *War-Peace Report* (War-Peace Report, Inc., New York, March, 1963) p. 3. Kahn's position seems to be, first, that world government would not necessarily produce a pleasant world. And secondly, that if world government does come about, it is likely to occur as an aftermath of a major crisis or following the use of nuclear weapons.

This aspect of Kahn's thinking is disclosed by the following extract from an essay "The Arms Race and World Order" from *The Revolution in World Politics*, pp. 350–351 (see above):

In any case, the search for a solution less makeshift than the current one must go on. The time available probably is to be measured in one or two decades, rather than one or two centuries. This seems to indicate that our old concepts of national sovereignty are either obsolete or soon will be. To many this last remark implies that we should be unwilling to risk or fight a war solely to preserve the nation state as an independent sovereign entity. That seems reasonable. But it does not mean that we should not be willing to risk or fight a war to influence or to vote on the system which replaces national sovereignty and independence. However, it is difficult to decide what one should be willing to risk unless the alternatives are spelled out.

It would, therefore, be useful to touch on the most important possibility of all, the comprehensive agreement. Included in this are many of the suggestions for international police forces, world governments, and near world governments.

Probably the most detailed and comprehensive proposal has been worked out by Grenville Clark and Louis B. Sohn. It is difficult for practical politicans, hardheaded statesmen, or professional planners to take such proposals seriously–except as manifestations or symptoms of the impracticality of the "do-gooders." As a result, such studies are rarely read by critics except from the viewpoint of content analysis; their substantive audience tends to be restricted to "friends and relatives." As a result, the Clark-Sohn proposals have not had the benefit of as much hostile informed criticism as they deserve. This is singularly unfortunate because their book is not only an extraordinarily worthwhile basis for continued work but it also may succeed in influencing history, even in its current, relatively unfinished state.

Consider, for example, the following hypothetical scenario of what could happen. The United States and the Soviet Union are today each supposed to have a handful of missiles. Imagine some of these missiles being shot off accidentally. Imagine also that this accident touches off a reprisal by the other side and, possibly, further exchanges on both sides until most or all of the ready and reliable missiles are launched. Imagine further that the accidental nature of the strike is soon discovered (since there is no immediate follow-up bomber attack and since the pattern and timing of the missile launchings do not conform to a reasonable surprise attack, this should become clear to both sides quite rapidly). Imagine finally that communications between the two countries are established soon enough so that both sides (today miraculously) succeed in calling off or preventing massive bomber strikes.

With current missile forces, it is most likely that at this point in history possibly five or ten or even more cities on one side or the other, or both, might have been destroyed. But both countries would survive this blow. One could confidently predict that the morning after this event there would be a deeply felt conviction among all the nations, particularly the two antagonists, that deterrence and anarchy were not a good way to run affairs, that we simply could not go back to the old precarious balance of terror and assume the same risks over again. Under these circumstances, it would not be at all surprising to find the United States and the Soviet Union ready to sign something resembling the Clark-Sohn proposals within a few days. It would be realized that unless an agreement were made within days, that is, before the dead were buried, one side or the other would quite likely try to exploit the common danger for unilateral advantage. In this case the negotiations would probably degenerate into the usual unproductive Cold War jockeying.

The proposals of Professors Clark and Sohn are enormously valuable. They constitute an alternative preferable to the current arms race. However, their proposals do seem to have serious defects. Therefore, in the absence of an immediate war or crisis, they have given us only a foundation on which to work. Much better proposals can be devised. But the improvement will come about only if hard-headed and realistic people take such proposals seriously and either work on them, or criticize the labor of others. Although much is being done now, more can be done. This is one place where the lone scholar, working without either an inter-disciplinary team or access to classified information, can hope to make a major contribution. However, the big inter-disciplinary studies will also play an important role. Let us, therefore, make a conscious attempt to encourage the design and analysis of "Utopias" or other alternatives that might be brought about through the agency of a war or crisis. Bleak as this prospect is, a war or crisis is the most likely route by which we shall achieve a more stable international order.

4. Is a major nuclear war likely in the next two or three decades? This concern has been made familiar through mass media and ordinary social discussion. Many people either have an opinion on the matter or find that they can formulate an opinion relatively quickly. On the other hand, the absence of relevant information produces a sense of bewilderment for some. A prediction of this sort, or your inability to make one, might also make you curious about what, in general, guides our anticipations about the course of social life. Are these guide lines persuasive? Can your judgment benefit from any additional evidence? Is there some systematic way in which you can make your predictions more accurate? What sorts of evidence are needed? To forecast the prospects of nuclear war would it be helpful to study the outbreak of war during pre-nuclear periods of international history? The attempt to explain your answer, or to account for your inability to answer, may give you insight into why some seek to change the world in a manner that expresses their preferences, whereas others are passive. Is social action based more upon psychological predispositions than upon rational evidence?

Certainly one reason why some people work so hard to avoid war is because they are impressed with the likelihood that it may come about. It is relevant, perhaps, to observe that if enough people, especially among policy-makers in leading governments, share a worry about the likelihood of nuclear war, there is an increased probability that steps will be taken to make its occurrence less likely. That is, whether the prediction is right or wrong, a sense of danger tends to reduce the danger as it induces precautions.

Another reason why some people are more willing than others to seek ways to avoid war is their image of what such a war would be like if it were to take place and their varying sense of just how negative it is to experience, or run the risk of experiencing such a war as compared to running other risks.

We pose questions concerning the risk of nuclear war because without some explicit sense of the risk, it will be more difficult to assess how much should be done to avoid it, and such an assessment influences attitudes toward different schemes of world order. To ask the following series of questions may seem absurd, in view of the absence of evidence available for their answer, but consider the deeper absurdity of refraining to ask them:

(a) What is the likelihood of a major nuclear war by 1980–1985? How "big" must a nuclear war be to qualify as "major"? Relevant indices include casualties, megatonnage, recovery time, duration of violence, property damage, and political consequences.

   If you think there is only a remote possibility of such a war, what are the facts on which you base this judgment? Assuming that there will be no major war by 1980–1985, what do you think the world political structure will look like then? The articles by Ducci, Waltz, and Yalem in Chapter 3 will respond to this question.

   If you feel that the likelihood of war is great, in what way is this war likely to begin? Who will be the participants, what will be its magnitude, and what will be its effects?

(b) What is the likelihood that there will be significant implementation of a major disarmament proposal by 1980–1985? On what information do you base your judgment?

   Do you agree with Herman Kahn that war can probably be avoided until the year 2000 without general and complete disarmament? If not, why not? If so, why? On thinking about the future, see Lasswell, Chapter 3.

(c) What steps can be taken to reduce the risk of thermonuclear war? Do these steps differ in any marked degree from the principles of world order accepted by Clark and Sohn? In what way? Is it necessary to implement all the Clark-Sohn principles? Which ones are crucial and why? Have they omitted any important principles? Does one need also to consider what steps must be taken to make principles of world order that are as far-reaching as those incorporated in Clark and Sohn politically acceptable to both the leaders and their publics in the world's major nations?

(d) Some have argued that the danger of nuclear war has been responsible for maintaining international peace and that if nuclear weapons had not existed, then the cold war would probably have been a hot war of World War II proportions. How does one take steps to avoid nuclear war without increasing the risks of conventional war?

5. Further reading on war, in addition to the readings cited, includes: Quincy Wright, *A Study of War* (unabridged ed., University of Chicago Press, 1965); Myres S. McDougal and Florentino P. Feliciano, *Law and Minimum World Public Order* (Yale University Press, 1961); Julius Stone, *Legal Controls of International Conflict* (rev. ed., Stevens, London, 1959); *International Aspects of Civil Strife*, James N. Rosenau (Princeton, University Press, 1964); Kenneth E. Boulding, *Conflict and Defense* (Harper, New York, 1962); Raymond Aron, *Paix et Guerre entre les Nations* (Cale-

mann-Lévy, Paris, 1962); John W. Burton, *Peace Theory* (Knopf, New York, 1962); Raymond Aron, *The Century of Total War* (Beacon Press, Boston, 1955); Alfred Vagts, *A History of Militarism* (rev. ed., Meridian Books, New York, 1959); John U. Nef, *War and Human Progress* (Harvard University Press, 1950); Theodore Ropp, *War in the Modern World* (rev. ed., Collier Books, New York, 1962).

6. The essays that we have read contend that the arms race is a factor aggravating the possibility of the outbreak of war. But it should be clear that aside from an accidental war caused either by a mechanical failure, by unauthorized conduct, or by a misinterpretation of an adversary's behavior, political leaders in control of a social organization must come to the decision to initiate the war. See Sidney Verba, "Assumptions of Rationality and Non-Rationality in Models of the International System" in *The International System: Theoretical Essays*, edited by Klaus E. Knorr and Sidney Verba (Princeton University Press, 1961). To assess this decision-making link it is essential to examine carefully the contemporary political system as it operates both within the nuclear powers and in international society as a whole. Under what conditions, and to what purpose, would it be appropriate for the leaders of the United States to use nuclear weapons?——on the basis of what level of provocation?——against what targets?——against battlefield targets?——against enemy cities? Would you grant the same authorization to leaders of other nuclear powers?

C. Some Considerations Concerning Disarmament

In the course of studying the means available to achieve a disarmed world under law, it is essential to appraise the present prospects for disarmament. The following extract from Richard J. Barnet's *Who Wants Disarmament?* (Beacon Press, Boston, 1960) pp. 128-134, raises important questions that pertain to the disarmament process itself and to its culmination in a totally disarmed world. Barnet makes two main points. He suggests first that we have given insufficient attention to the problems that might arise in a disarmed world, and that this failure is by itself a formidable obstacle to the present conduct of serious disarmament negotiations. For even aside from mistrust, until we have examined the possible image of a disarming world, it is unlikely that a political system will take drastic disarmament proposals seriously. The stubborn bargaining of participants and the intractability of the issues so visible in the negotiating process might, in part at least, be a consequence of this failure to exercise our intellectual powers of anticipation.

Barnet's second point, obviously related to the first, is that neither the American government nor the American public has been prepared, or is preparing itself, to give serious attention to the various problems connected with disarmament such as economic adjustment, the maintainence of political stability and national security, the management of world conflict, and the administration and technique of disarmament itself.

PREPARATIONS FOR PROGRESS

by
RICHARD J. BARNET

Disarmament has seemed so fundamentally at odds with the hard facts of a divided world that it is widely regarded as a utopian solution. The question is, however, whether disarmament is any more utopian a means of preserving peace than the mechanism of deterrence on which we have put such great reliance. The success of each appears to require a basic change in existing patterns of behavior. Peace through disarmament would demand a willingness to look for security through means other than military power; peace through deterrence, a willingness to accept permanently a threatening status quo. Historical support for each alternative is pessimistic, although perhaps less conclusive in regard to disarmament since so little has been tried. Deterrence by threat of violence—our historical legacy—has never prevented war. Unilateral disarmament and the few cautious steps towards mutual disarmament that have been taken have never prevented war either.

To be "for" or "against" disarmament in our world, therefore, seems a singularly unrealistic approach. Neither the military planner who sees no end to the arms spiral nor the pacifist who calls upon the world to make itself over by a sheer act of will offers any practical basis for progress towards peace. To tell the world to go on making and testing nuclear weapons is like telling a drunk to go on drinking. To say "there has *got* to be progress on disarmament" is as fruitful as telling the drunk to pull himself together.

It is difficult to envisage much progress on disarmament until we stop treating it as a theoretical problem and recognize that it is an approach to salvation that is peculiarly appropriate to our own world. This does not mean that disarmament will necessarily work, but it does mean that it is worth the kind of research we are quite willing to devote to marketing techniques, satellite construction, or refinements of the atomic bomb. Valuable research has already been completed on aspects of inspection, but the mechanics of the disarmament treaty represent only one phase of the problem and by no means the most important or difficult one.

There is, for example, a series of questions waiting to be faced concerning the achievement of security in a disarmed but still divided world. Where can we put our trust in a world where we have abandoned our trust in arms? If an international authority with police power over the major nations is impractical, what alternative stabilizing mechanisms would be available? How much (or, more realistically, how little) would Russia have to change its approach to international relations before the United States should take the risks of substantial disarmament? And what would be the effect of disarmament on our national goals? In a disarmed world would we retain the capacity to guarantee the security of our allies against Communist infiltration? Against spontaneous revolution? Would it be crucial for us to be able to guarantee their security in either such case? Would retention of our system of alliances be desirable? Are we irrevocably committed to the prevention of Communist expansion merely by military means, or must we for our security resist all Communist encroachments by whatever means effected? Would we dare to contend with Russia in a world without arms for the friendship and loyalty of the emerging underdeveloped peoples, or would any competition bound to become so threatening to one side or the other that the use of force would be resumed? In a world disarmed would a revolutionary power be more likely to moderate its ambitions, or would it exploit the physical defenselessness of its neighbors to work their destruction through the treacherous use of force? Would we be willing to see the balance of power shift decisively to the other side as a result

of peaceful competition without lifting a hand in anger to stop this course? Would the Soviet Union? What kind of assurance would we want from Russia that it would not try to destroy us whenever it acquired sufficient relative power to justify the attempt? What kind could it give and what would the assurance be worth? What kind of guarantees could we in turn give the Soviet Union?

Then there are questions concerning the conditions under which disarmament might prove acceptable. It has become quite clear by now that neither the Soviet Union nor the United States is willing to make gratuitous contributions to an "atmosphere of mutual trust." Each concession for the relaxation of tensions, quite properly, has a price tag. Arriving at the

right price while the arms race continues is particularly difficult because the subjects of possible concessions are themselves intimately involved in the military competition. For
example, the reunification of Germany is as much a military as
it is a political problem. In a disarmed but still divided world
Germany would continue to be the subject of competition, but
its overriding importance would be diminished because it
would not represent a military threat to either side. Today,
however, any solution of the German problem would vitally
affect the military balance of power in Europe. In the context
of an arms race each side, therefore, has been reluctant to
offer real concessions for fear of appearing weak and encouraging the other to make further demands. Concessions
have been in such short supply that prices have remained
inflationary.

One of the most difficult problems of a disarmament
agreement is caused by the natural desire of the signatories to
hedge against disaster in case the system should fail. Keeping
bombs in reserve for such an eventuality is unsatisfactory because their very existence poses a threat. Is there any other
way of providing each signatory an escape in the event of the
treachery of its rival without thereby wrecking the treaty? Is
there a mechanism for restoring the innocent power to a relative position equivalent to, or at least not much worse than, the
relative position he was in with respect to his rival before each
of them agreed to disarm? Or must we in order to give disarmament any chance of success burn our bridges behind us?

A related problem involves the integration of arms reduction and arms control. The French delegate to the U.N. Disarmament Commission described the goal in this area in these
words: "Neither control without disarmament; neither disarmament without control; but progressively all the disarmament
that can be controlled." [1] Implementing this program has
proved extraordinarily difficult because the equation in any
particular situation is uncertain. To put the question from the
Russian viewpoint, how much of a weakening of American
military power should be required to offset the disadvantage
incurred in exposing such Soviet military secrets as the location
of missile launching sites? Or, to put the same question from
the American point of view, how much of a guarantee of
Soviet compliance should we require before we reduce our
strength? Technical studies of the mechanics of control indi-

cate that the more comprehensive the system of inspection the greater the guarantee of compliance.[2] Since comprehensive inspection will only be acceptable in the present world if accompanied by comprehensive disarmament, which involves serious risks in the event of noncompliance, we are in a paradoxical situation in which the disarmament treaty offering the greatest security against evasion also presents the greatest risks if in fact it is evaded. Is there a point at which we would assume those risks short of a millennial change in the Communist world? If so, what is the point and how do we arrive at it?

What about the impact of disarmament on the domestic economy? The Russians are undoubtedly convinced that American business leaders, fulfilling the prophecies of Lenin, are conspiring to keep America armed. Lenin believed that the "crisis of capitalism" could be postponed only by massive military expenditures. Communist propaganda repeats this theme today. And it is undeniable that military expenditures play an important role in our economy. Each year some $25 billion is spent for weapons and military facilities.[3] Conceivably, there might be more general interest in disarmament if the demands of defense production resulted in a shortage of the consumer luxuries to which we are all accustomed. But, unlike the economy of the Soviet Union, where production of consumer goods has been sacrificed in favor of military requirements, the American civilian economy may have benefited from the stimulus of military expenditure.

We have boldly answered the Communists that the American economy can take substantial disarmament in its stride and still produce prosperity. But we have yet to start the necessary planning to make good on our claim. Whatever the ultimate effect of disarmament on the American economy, such a step will require a number of important decisions which must be made well in advance of actual reconversion. Indeed, they ought to be made before serious negotiation begins. We must face such questions as these: How much of the capital presently devoted to weapons production and research should go to support disarmament machinery? What program should be adopted to soften the effects of the unemployment that will result during the transition of the economy from military to nonmilitary production? How should America spend its surplus when disarmament does begin to release resources for other purposes? What kind of additional foreign aid programs would we feel a need to promote for our security in a disarmed world? What domestic projects would deserve our attention?

Answers to these questions are as vital to an approach to disarmament as they are to life in a disarmed world. Yet we do little to answer them.

The investigations of the Senate Subcommittee on Disarmament reveal that as of September 1957, after eleven years of disarmament negotiations, "no agency of the executive branch has made efforts to ascertain the economic consequences of a reduction in armaments." [4] And over a year later, in October 1958, in its Final Report the same Senate subcommittee made this observation:

> There are only some 6 or 7 persons who work full time on disarmament in the State Department. The subcommittee is struck by the disparity in the effort the world is putting into thought and action for controlling and reducing armaments and the effort going into the development, fabrication and build up of armaments. [5]

And outside of the State Department in the other executive agencies there is little sustained and intensive attention to disarmament. From time to time, the Administration has called upon distinguished private citizens to review our policy, make recommendations, and even negotiate agreements with the Russians. The contributions of these individuals have been important, but it is unquestionably true that no one can acquire the background essential to deal with these stubborn problems in a few months of service. There is no more reason to put the responsibility for formulating disarmament policy and negotiating disarmament agreements in the hands of conscientious, but inexperienced, amateurs than there is to put the Pentagon under the control of *ad hoc* committees or part-time generals.

Moreover, the only agencies in the government that do have a continuing interest in disarmament are those which have a primary responsibility for and hence a commitment to military defense. Since bureaucracies are notoriously inefficient at seeking their own dissolution, it is too much to ask those to whom our defense effort and atomic energy program are entrusted to prepare for disarmament as well. This fact has been recognized by a number of prominent political figures, including Senator Kennedy, Governor Rockefeller, and former Governor Stevenson. Clearly what is needed is a permanent agency with responsibility for conducting research in disarmament and advising the President in the formulation of disarmament policy. *

But this is not enough.

Not only the government but the American public must prepare ourselves if there is to be any hope of achieving the breakthrough to peace we are all seeking. While many aspects of disarmament are highly technical and are perhaps completely comprehensible only to experts, the ultimate decisions, whether to take one kind of risk or another, are appropriate to the democratic decision-making process. Indeed, no statesman —of whatever stature—could make the kind of commitment which disarmament requires unless he had the public with him. In the final analysis, the public must sit as a jury to weigh the opinions and recommendations with which we are confronted, as best we can, and then decide. And the decision cannot be delayed. The longer the arms race continues, the more difficult a solution becomes and the greater the risks of war. It is, therefore, more urgent than ever to face the challenge of disarmament and decide whether we *want* disarmament, for upon our decision may well depend the future of civilization on this planet.

Notes

1. U.N. Document DC/SC.1/PV.-69, as quoted in *Final Report, supra*, p. 179.
2. See *Inspection for Disarmament, supra*, p. 8.
3. *Final Report, supra*, p. 66.
4. *Id.*, p. 67.
5. *Id.*, p. 16.

NOTES AND QUESTIONS

1. In September, 1961 Congress authorized the establishment of the United States Arms Control and Disarmament Agency. The Agency is an independent executive agency, having a special affiliation with the State Department; its Director reports directly to the President of the United States as well as to the Secretary of State. According to the original legislation the purposes of the Agency were:

An ultimate goal of the United States is a world which is free from the scourge of war and the dangers and burdens of armaments; in which the use of force has been subordinated to the rule of law; and in which international adjustments to a changing world are achieved peacefully. It is the purpose of this chapter to provide impetus toward this goal by creating a new agency of peace to deal with the problem of reduction and control of armaments looking toward ultimate world disarmament.

Arms control and disarmament must be consistent with national security policy as a whole. The formulation and implementation of United States arms control and disarmament policy in a manner which will promote the national security can best be insured by a central organization charged by statute with primary responsibility for this field. . . .[22 USC 2551.]

The Agency has been in operation for several years now. It would seem appropriate to assess its accomplishments to date. How many of the questions, for example, which Barnet (who was, incidentally, the Deputy Director of Research in International Affairs in the Agency for two years) places before us in the following excerpts have lost their relevance as a result of the Agency's existence? Our knowledge of ACDA's work is restricted by the fact that many of its labors are undisclosed or are based upon classified materials. Althought the ACDA has stimulated inside and outside of government an unprecedented amount of research which has dealt with problems of arms control and disarmament, it seems accurate to report that a very small percentage of ACDA's work deals with proposals for drastic disarmament. Its staff is preoccupied with limited and isolated measures of arms control in those areas where the prospects for negotiating an agreement soon seem most favorable.

Congress has also seen fit to prohibit ACDA explicitly from engaging in any kind of work designed to promote public support for disarmament, and the Agency's activities are scrutinized very carefully each year. A reading of the Congressional Hearings indicates that the hostile critics of ACDA, who are the most extreme opponents of arms control and disarmament in Congress, have not diminished their criticism as the years have passed.

The next selection by Walter Millis appeared in the *Saturday Review* (September 15, 1962) pp. 18-21 and p. 31. Millis considers the problem of maintaining order in a warless world, that is, in a world in which states have agreed to abolish the capability to wage major warfare. In this respect a warless world is equivalent to a disarmed world; Millis and others use the phrase "warless world" to evoke an image of a radically transformed international system. For some representative discussion, see additional articles in *A Warless World*, edited by Arthur Larson (McGraw-Hill, New York, 1962); Millis' fuller account can be found in his book with James Real, *The Abolition of War* (Macmillan, New York, 1963).

A world may be "warless" even if wars occur. That is, wars on some scale will always be possible so long as mankind is organized into political groups in competition with one another. In addition, even under conditions of total disarmament it would remain possible for states to be in violent conflict and even to threaten or carry out a program of partial or total rearmament. In fact, such a danger would be a probable ingredient in the political life of a disarmed world, especially in its early phase, and rearmament threats might be made by those dissatisfied with their status. See Schelling, **III-9C**.

Millis assumes a world in which general and complete disarmament has been agreed upon in a form that includes enough centralized enforcement machinery to discourage rearmament. Even when states are totally disarmed they will retain police and paramilitary force to maintain internal order. This will leave a military capability that might be mobilized for external purposes, as well.

The central focus of Millis' analysis is upon the relationship between law and order in domestic society, and law and order in international society. In view of the present ideological conflict, the nation-state structure, and the lack of a strong, positive identification with a world community, Millis argues that it would be impossible and unwise for a world legal order to attempt to police all violent behavior throughout the world. He argues that for this reason it would be necessary, even in a warless world, to rely heavily upon domestic legal structures to contain violence. Millis' analysis leaves unanswered the very difficult questions that today torment international relations: what characteristics of internal or civil wars make them appropriate matters for supranational concern, action, intervention? Note that many of the crises and confrontations in the nuclear age have taken place in circumstances of domestic violence arising out of attempts to influence the outcome of civil strife.

What is perhaps most striking in Millis' analysis is his conclusion that, with the exception of the elimination of "the corroding fear of catastrophe which today complicates and distorts every real problem of international politics, a warless world would be much the same as the world is today, and social, political, and economic competition and struggle would certainly continue and might even increase." Millis does not then envision a drastic change either in the nature of man or in the way in which inter-group conflict will be carried on. This is rather startling, when one considers it. In the past men have looked forward to a peaceful world. For example, in the Christian or Communist concepts of peace, the dominant element was the idea of a community of brothers, or a family of man, and it was expected to usher into being a new ethic and politics based on harmony and altruism.

An important aspect of this analysis concerns the process of transition to the warless world: To the extent that political movements exist in the world that wish to spread their values and political system to other societies, the idea of a warless world projected by Millis need not be unacceptable to them. That is, the acceptance of a warless world and the continuing propagation of a missionary ideology become, in this view, quite compatible. In fact, it might be maintained that if the risks of major war were seriously cut or eliminated, then there would be more incentive to wage political and ideological struggles. The risks of catastrophe would disappear, or at least diminish greatly.

Finally, Millis is aware that war and violence have been responsible for bringing about legislative changes in both international and domestic society. He makes clear, then, that if violence as a source of change is eliminated, new methods must emerge. Perhaps here Millis implies some form of world government in his version of the warless world more far-reaching than the war prevention system projected by Clark and Sohn.

WALTER MILLIS

Order and Change
in a Warless World

TO IMAGINE a warless world is to imagine a special kind of world order—a system of "law and order" which must nevertheless allow for the disorder, conflict, and change essential to the development of human institutions. An idea must be formed of how such change, which throughout history has been so often and so deeply associated with war, can come about with a minimum of physical violence.

That change through conflict will continue to come about, regardless, is scarcely arguable. The complicated struggles among individuals, groups, classes, communities, or nations for wealth, position, and power is inherent in human nature. No system of world law and order can eliminate these power struggles; it would be primarily a means of regulating or structuring them.

The relative "justice" of such regulation is highly important from the standpoint of support for the system, but it seems essentially secondary—a by-product, as it were—to the "order" which the system would impose. There have, of course, been highly unjust orders which have survived over long periods and others comparatively just which have suffered early collapse. The essential of any order, just or unjust, is that it force the competitive struggles among those subject to it into other than lethal or violent channels.

In any system of law and order one finds three elements, which are the mechanisms through which it achieves its purpose: (1) a sovereign "monopoly" of legal force to forbid resort to violence; (2) a system of general rules (law) defining in generalized terms the rights, duties, and, therefore, the power positions of all involved; (3) a judicial system to apply the general rules in specific conflicts and to provide in its decisions a generally accepted alternative to trial by combat or violence.

No system of this kind, of course, is ever perfectly successful. An irreducible minimum of violent crime, usually a certain amount of rioting and group violence, remains under the most developed systems of law and order. Nor has any such system ever completely inhibited change; even the most static and somnolent of social orders has never been "frozen" into a coma. It is true that a developed system of law and order has the effect, at any given time, of defining—crystallizing—the power relations of the individuals, groups, and classes subject to it, and that this crystallized legal structure of power may survive after the actual power relationships in the community have changed. But when the actual power structure tends to get out of line with the legal definition, it is, sooner or later, the legal definition which is altered, not the newly emerging structure of power.

WHEN the discrepancy between the fact and the form grows too great, such changes may be violent, reflected in great wars on the international stage or bloody revolutions within. But war and violent revolution are by no means the only or the necessary means of adjusting the system of law and order to changes in the underlying power structure. The modern world has recorded immense adjustments of this kind largely, if not wholly, effected by nonviolent means.

Nor is it true that these can occur only in those systems which, as in the Western democracies, include formal provision for popular participation in institutional change. Toynbee, in the opening article in this series, cites the abdication of the Tokugawa Shogunate in Japan—at the time anything but a democratic society—and the accompanying political and social revolution, all accomplished with very little violence. Since the death of Stalin, if not before, considerable shifts have plainly been occurring in the power structure both of the Soviet Union itself and among the constituent states of the Communist empire. But the Communist system of law and order (which is no less a system of law and order because it seems to us an unjust one) has accommodated itself to these changes in general without war or revolution. The one violent revolution of importance—that in Hungary—was suppressed by the Soviet police power, thus leaving Communist law and order outwardly intact. But the ruthlessness with which "order" was reimposed in Hungary does not mean that the system is perpetually unchangeable. The Hungarian revolt will still make its contribution toward those changes—hopefully nonviolent, but changes in any event —which shifts in the underlying Communist power structure are certain to bring about.

Even the existing international order, "anarchic" as it is commonly assumed to be, has since 1945 adjusted itself to very great changes in the basic power relations of peoples, states, classes, and groups with, on the whole, a rather surprising minimum of war or other violence. Discussions of a new world order usually overlook the fact that we already possess a more highly developed system of international law and order than ever before in history. It is a system not yet reduced to statutory form or fully embodied in treaty undertakings; and its institutional expressions, such as the U.N., are still quite rudimentary. It is a system, nev-ertheless. It is incapable, certainly, of "freezing" the political and social institutions of mankind into any perpetual mold; yet it is currently proving itself adequate to insure that for most peoples, most of the time, the infinitely complex struggle for power is carried on by essentially nonviolent means.

Perhaps two-thirds of the population of the globe live today under no more than four or five great, stabilized, and mutually more or less invulnerable centers of power, of law and of order: the United States, the Western European democracies, the Soviet Union, China, and perhaps India. They appear rather effectively to have excluded violence and bloodshed from their domestic affairs as instruments of practical politics. Each has effectively developed the essentials of rule by law: a police force quite capable of forbidding anything more than merely casual resort to violence; a system of general rules to govern the internal power struggles, and at least some kind of adjudicatory and regulatory system to apply the rules and to offer an alternative to trial by violence which, however imperfect or unjust, can be accepted as preferable.

These great systems of law and order differ widely in their efficiency, their subtlety, and their sophistication as social organizations. It is difficult, for instance, to find much parallel between the deliberations of the Supreme Court of the United States and the intrigues within the Soviet power elite in the Kremlin, except that both serve the same broad purpose. Each offers an acceptable (or at any rate accepted) alternative to armed violence and rebellion in the settlement of basic power issues. Different as they are, each of these great systems appears to have established its ability to keep order, with yet enough flexibility to permit necessary change to take place without extremes of violence.

THIS at any rate, appears to be the common opinion. No one, for example, can seriously suppose that the United States will remain fixed in the particular mold of political, social, and economic relationships which it has attained in 1962. We all look for great changes of one kind or another in the American power structure; but it takes a John Birchite mentality to imagine that violent revolution either will or can accompany them. Much the same is true of the great Communist states. The shifting and uncertain power relations between Moscow and Peking are well advertised in the Western press; but no serious student has been rash enough to predict that they will end in a Sino-Soviet war. It is not the likelihood of armed rebellion in China or the USSR that impresses most, but its apparent impossibility in the foreseeable future.

Thus two-thirds of the population of the globe already live under reasonably stable systems of law and order, so stable that no one predicts violent revolution or collapse for any of them (unless as a result of another world war), yet not so rigid as to be incapable of necessary change and development. By whatever paths of blood and misery the world has attained this result, it has attained it; one must recognize its novelty—for it is a phenomenon almost as unprecedented in history as are the nuclear arsenals themselves—as well as its obvious importance to the general problem of world law and order.

Unfortunately, much of the remaining third of the global population is less well organized. Southern Asia, Africa, and much of Latin America are being swept by the "revolution of expectations," inordinately complicated by nationalism, by racial and class conflict, by differences between the small educated elite groups, with their urban followers, and the peasant masses, as well as by the tendency of the great, stable power centers to exploit these difficulties for the advancement of their own power and influence. Speaking very generally, over much of this area the basic power structures (both domestic and international) are in a fluid state; it is the problem of the new leaderships not so much to "seize power" as to discover the new bases on which a viable power structure may be erected. What rules (law) are available, whether derived from decisions in the U.N., from the principles of international law, or from domestic constitutional and institutional arrangements, are clearly out of line with the highly complicated actual power relationships.

Over much of this area no general rule of law and order, even a repressive one like that which the Soviet Union has successfully established over its many different peoples and different conflicts of interest, seems possible. And it would appear that a good deal of violence—whether in the savage form that occurred in the Congo or in Algeria, or simply the military coup d'états that have, with relatively little bloodshed, interrupted the processes of "democracy" in so many parts of the world—is inevitable. No system of law and order can hope to avert all violence, or dispense justice with a hand so even that men, groups, and communities will never seek to "take the law in their own hands." But it is still surprising that so little, not so much, violence and bloodshed has attended the enormous shifts in group, class, and national power relationships which have taken place since 1945.

Such is the situation in which we find ourselves today. We have developed a system of world law and order unprecedented in human experience. It contains no global monopoly of legal force adequate to forbid violent solutions to the problems of nations, classes, communities, and groups, although for the time being the great weapons-systems seem to be providing an effective substitute. Change is certainly proceeding as rapidly as most could wish; yet within an order sufficient to permit the vast majority of the world's peoples to live currently at peace and keep such violence as does continue to occur within tolerable bounds. It is an order efficient to permit even more—to permit the growth of what Robert C. Angell has felicitously called the "interstitial tissue" of global organization: "Actually, an elaborate web of relationships is being woven among the peoples of the world. . . . There is live and growing tissue around us, interstitial tissue, if you will, which is spreading and becoming stronger every year." What would be the effect on this general situation of the assumed excision from it of the organized war system?

This is really the central question. All that we have been asked to assume in this series is an initial abolition of organized war, with the introduction of whatever (only vaguely specified) institutional arrangements may be necessary to maintain the abolition. How, so far as securing necessary social and political change is concerned, would the resultant warless system differ from the existing one? The easy answer is to say that it would differ very little; but there is an obstacle to the easy answer. This lies in the still obscure but clearly intimate relationship which has existed through most of history between domestic violence and revolution and international violence and war. The two have probably been intermingled in most of the major changes in human systems of law, order, and power-organization. Great wars have led to great revolutions; great revolutions have led to great wars. Perhaps the causal relationship was not in fact so simple as this would suggest; but the observation at least inspires an inquiry as to whether, if there are no more great wars, there can be any more great revolutions; or, conversely, if there are to be further great revolutions, will not great wars inevitably be revived?

Our presently existing world order seems to be both sufficiently flexible and sufficiently stable to meet the necessities of change without intolerable concomitants of violence. But so did the Atlantic world appear to its inhabitants on the eve of the French Revolution; so did the Western and the Russian imperial world appear on the eve of World War I. Both the Soviet Union and China today appear to represent stable systems of law and order. But the appearance may prove to be illusory. As power relationships continue to shift within the rigid frameworks of these great societies, it may be that nothing short of violent and bloody rebellion will suffice to break up the old power structures and institute the new.

Revolutionary violence in France after 1789 not only reorganized the domestic power structure; it fractured the international power structure of the time and led to the first total wars of modern history. Given an initially warless world, a similar violent breakdown of the Russian or Chinese power structures might have similar effects. No presently imaginable system of policed disarmament could deal finally or completely with such a situation. It is hard to picture an international police force endowed with either the physical force or, more importantly, the authority to intervene in a chaotic Russia in order to "restore order." It is easy to imagine the pressures upon the contiguous national police forces to intervene in one way or another in order to preserve their national interests; and to see that these pressures could lead to "escalation," rearmament, and war by processes which the international police would find difficult to control. All that one can say to this is that perfection is unattainable in this world; no system of politics will infallibly meet all the problems that may arise before it. But a politics which starts from a universal and policed disarmament, has a far better chance of meeting this sort of situation than has one which starts with the system of organized war.

There is the opposite case, often illustrated by the Russian Revolution of 1918, in which it is held that great international wars are necessary to break up encrusted and anachronistic power structures inhibiting human development. That wars have had this effect can hardly be doubted, but that major war is a necessary element in political and social advance is much more dubious. In the usual view, the Russian Revolution actually began with Alexander II's emancipation of the serfs in 1861, a voluntary recognition by the autocracy (not unlike the abdication of the Tokugawa Shogunate) that times were changing and that the legally established power structure in Russia would have to be modified accordingly. The process thereafter continued, haltingly, not without a good deal of violence on the part of government and revolutionaries alike, but rather steadily.

Even imperial Russia had within it the potentialities of necessary change; and many believe that the autocracy would have undergone a relatively peaceable "constitutionalization" of the new power relationships—rather as happened in Britain and was happening in Germany—*except* for World War I. The Russo-Japanese War of 1904-05 no doubt pushed the autocracy along the avenues to modernization; but World I simply paralyzed and finally destroyed it, leaving it as helpless to promote as it was to resist the change which was overdue. Power passed by default into other and more ruthless hands, who built and imposed a new power structure, one which was at least somewhat more responsive to the realities than the Czarist system had been, though hardly an ideal case of political and social evolution. World War I, in this view, was not necessary to political and social change in Russia; all that it did was to distort this change into extreme, and generally inefficient, forms.

ORGANIZED war and violent domestic revolution have thus been closely associated, historically, with the processes of political and social change. But the exact nature of the association is not too clear; and it is not easy to be dogmatic about the probable effect of the removal of one, organized war, from the global order. One may hazard some guesses. In the absence of international war, certain processes of violent internal change could not go on as they have done. Revolutionaries, for example, would have less chance of acquiring small arms and financial and propaganda support from rival outside powers than they have today. At the same time, they would have less to fear from outside intervention. To revert to the eighteenth-century examples, another American Revolution could not count on the assistance rendered by France as a strategic move in her war

with Britain; another French Revolution would not have to face the coalition of powers joined in defense of the *ancien régime*.

It is not easy to strike a plausible balance between such possibilities; but so far as the present great organized power centers are concerned, it seems reasonable to predict that the abolition of organized war among them would not seriously affect the problem of necessary change. After all, at the end of World War I, the Western Allies attempted to intervene with armed force in the Russian revolutionary situation, in a way they could not do in a world disarmed by assumption. Their lack of success at least suggests that the presence or absence of national armaments would not greatly affect such basic reorganizations of the power structure as were then taking place.

Perhaps the real question lies not with the great and relatively stabilized power systems, but with the less-organized areas. How far will a warless world order try to limit the more sporadic disorder and violence that one must expect here? In a generally disarmed world one may expect the simple absence of the hypertrophied weapon systems to supply an adequate equivalent for a global "monopoly of legal force." The want of the necessary weapons systems will generally forbid resort to violence by any of the great power centers. (The argument, it must be remembered, is based on the assumption that the weapons systems have been *voluntarily* laid aside and destroyed.)

But with the survival everywhere of national police forces, there will be no lack of at least light weapons in the world, accessible to bold or desperate men and to their followers. Riots and mob violence, the more organized use of such weapons as plastic bombs, the even more highly organized forms of guerrilla war, will still be possible. The military coup d'état will still be possible through the manipulation of the national police. (Indeed, most of the "military" forces which have participated in such affairs have amounted to little more than what one would expect the national police in a warless world to be.)

How far will a warless order, through its international police force, attempt to control all these forms of residual violence? It seems improbable that the attempt will go very far. The assumed elimination of major organized war must, after all, eliminate the one great danger in current minor wars and violence—the danger of escalation into a great-power conflict. It seems evident that the warless order must have not merely an international but a supranational (that is, veto-free) police force to control disarmament and to ensure that rearmament does not take place. But a supranational, veto-free police force can take on reality only as its empowerment (authority) as well as the physical force at its disposal is strictly limited to that requisite for its police functions. It is difficult to envisage an international or supranational police force as a great army, capable of coercing the states which must support it and overawing the national police forces which they will retain. One sees this force rather as comparable to the American Federal Bureau of Investigation, which wields very great power within the American system, but does so precisely because its weapons are of negligible importance and its empowerment strictly limited. The FBI obviously could not wage a successful armed battle with any state or municipal police force. It has other means of ensuring its power in state and municipal police circles; and it seems obvious that the real power of the supranational police force vis-à-vis the remaining national police forces with which it must

work will rest on similar bases.

THE concept of an "international police power" has a long, though generally unfortunate history. Experience seems to demonstrate that while some power of the kind is necessary to avert extremes of savagery, violence, and irresponsibility, it can succeed in this much only if it refrains from itself trying to settle or decide the power struggles out of which the violence arises. One may compare the U.N. "police action" in Korea with that which it was driven by circumstance to take in Palestine and the Congo. The attempt in the first case was to intervene in a major power struggle, and it ended, as probably it could only have ended, in a fairly major international war. In Palestine and the Congo the attempt has been to limit the savagery as far as possible, without authority to decide the power struggles involved. It seems probable that the patterns along which a supranational police force in a warless world order would tend to develop are to be found in the Congo, not in Korea. For its problems would, in a real sense, be police and not military problems.

Perhaps what was first advanced as the easy answer is the right answer as well. Assuming the removal of the organized war system, the political and social institutions reflecting the underlying power organization of the world, of its peoples, states, classes, communities, and groups, would continue to grow and change much as they are now doing in fact, but without the corroding fear of catastrophe which today complicates and distorts every real problem of international politics.

NOTES AND QUESTIONS

1. The causal connection, if any, between international violence and domestic violence, especially as it relates to social and political change, has been perplexing throughout history. It has been argued that the development of nuclear weapons has made it imperative for the organized international community to concern itself with wars within states, as well as wars between states. This concern is essential

because of the phenomenon of escalation, that is, the tendency of political violence to expand in scale from small to large encounters as the side losing at any level resorts to new tactics. Some authors have recently pointed out that the prevalent pattern of contemporary international violence is to grant military support to contending factions in situations of civil strife, and furthermore, that a tacit agreement exists among the major powers to the effect that violent conflict will be restricted to violence carried on within the boundaries of the states where these struggles are situated. Some examples of domestic wars that have solicited international participation are Korea, South Vietnam, Laos, Greece, and Burma. For a general treatment, see Morton H. Halpern, *Limited War in the Nuclear Age* (Wiley, New York, 1963).

Other analyses with similar orientations also often point to additional patterns of mutual self-restraint as possessing the character of an international "code" restricting violence. For a preliminary outline of this approach, see Chapter IV in Richard A. Falk, *Law, Morality and War in the Contemporary World* (Praeger, New York, 1963). The main "provision" in this code is the toleration of the use of violence by a superpower to maintain hegemony over a state defecting from its bloc or sphere of influence; the rival superpower confines its response to protests and denunciations, but refrains from direct or indirect military support for the faction it favors. Hungary (1956) and Cuba (1960–1962) illustrate the operations of this agreement. Samuel P. Huntington develops this kind of argument in the title essay of the volume, *Changing Patterns of Military Politics* (Free Press of Glencoe, New York, 1962). See also Georg Schwarzenberger, "Hegemonial Intervention," *1959 Yearbook of World Affairs* (Praeger, New York) p. 236.

2. The positive roles of violence in social affairs will be examined again in Chapter 2, especially in connection with Harold Nieburg's article. The need for procedures for social change in a disarmed world is discussed in Falk, Chapter XVI in *Security in Disarmament*, edited by Barnet and Falk (Princeton University Press, 1965). Consider also William James's famous arguments about the contributions of war to human character and the consequent need to find "moral equivalents" if war is to be eliminated as a social institution. See William James, "The Moral Equivalent of War," in *Memories and Studies* (Longmans, Green, New York, 1911) p. 265. See also, *War as a Social Institution*, edited by Jesse D. Clarkson and Thomas C. Cochran (Columbia University Press, New York, 1941) and Robert E. Park and Margaret Mead in *War: Studies from Psychology, Sociology, Anthropology*, edited by George W. Goethals and Leon Bramson (Basic Books, New York, 1964).

India's use of force to annex the Portuguese enclave of Goa is considered to have been an aspect, however unfortunate, of the decolonization process that has taken place in the period following World War II. See Quincy Wright, "The Goa Incident," *American Journal of International Law*, vol. 56 (The American Society of International Law, Washington, D.C., 1962) p. 617. It is difficult to assess the motivations of the use of armed force by the People's Republic of China against India. See Surya Sharma, "The India-China Border Dispute," *American Journal of International Law*, vol. 59 (The American Society of International Law, Washington, D.C., 1965) p. 16; and the July–October issues of *International Studies*, entitled "Chinese Aggression and India" vol. 5, nos. 1, 2 (Asia Publishing House, New York, 1963). The Chinese objectives seemed to include political intimidation, as well as the desire for a more favorable bargaining position from which to negotiate the settlement of an ordinary border dispute. China, whatever else she may have attempted, did not attempt to conquer India.

3. Do you think that Millis' view of a warless world is realistic? Or do you think that if national armaments were abolished there would be such a profound impact on social organization and human behavior that the world would necessarily be much more transformed than he anticipates? On the basis of your limited study of the Clark-Sohn proposals for the establishment and maintenance of a peaceful world, would you say that their scheme presupposes a world with more good fellowship than the kind of rough and tumble world postulated by Millis? Do Clark and Sohn make any assumptions about the need to transform human nature, or to moderate conflict among states in proposing their scheme? Is it more likely that states will disarm if the world remains organized as it is today, or if it is reorganized into some form of world government as Clark and Sohn propose? See Klaus Knorr, **IV-4**.

4. Millis suggests that given the present structure of international society, it would be impossible to·develop an international police force equivalent to the armies now found in the present nation-states. Compare Schelling, **III-9C**. Instead, Millis feels that the international police should resemble the United States Federal Bureau of Investigation. Is the alleged effectiveness of the F.B.I. dependent upon the fact that it is backed up by the might of the United States Armed Forces? How effective is the F.B.I.? Why has it been unable to eliminate organized crime? What changes in a domestic social system would be needed to permit an international F.B.I. to become fully effective within its various spheres of endeavor? Would this effectiveness pose threats to the maintenance of democracy?

5. We shall have occasion in **III-9** to discuss more thoroughly the development of peace-keeping machinery for the international community. Millis' view of the extent of international military forces needed to preserve the peace seems different from that set forth by Clark and Sohn (who propose a United Nations Police Force of 200,000–600,000 backed by a large military reserve). Which of the two conceptions do you prefer and why? Which is more attainable? Are there further alternatives?

6. To what extent does one's attitude toward the character and size of an international police force combine attitudes of *necessity* and *feasibility*? What kind of system is likely to be more politically acceptable to the Great Powers? Is the sovereign state, as the dominant mode of political organization, more or less endangered by the growth of a large world police force? Does one's response reflect the alternate fears of vulnerability to disarmament cheating by nations on hand, and a potentially hostile and despotic external center of military authority on the other? See the papers published under the title *Quis Custodiet?* edited by Arthur I. Waskow (Peace Research Institute, Washington, D.C., 1963); and see Fisher, **IV-5B**.

D. World Law, World Community, and World Order

One of the most formidable obstacles to the establishment of a war prevention system is the belief held by influential people throughout the world that war is virtually inevitable; this belief is buttressed not only by historical experience of war through centuries, but by the tendency to associate national security automatically with military power. The readings thus far suggest that weapons of mass destruction cause people to wonder whether international society cannot be changed to make large scale wars far less likely in the future.

When considering proposals to reduce the risk of war by the creation of world legal structure of the sort suggested by *World Peace through World Law*, one frequently encounters another formidable obstacle. This is the belief that the world is not yet ready for such an elaborate political structure and that recommendations for its attainment are premature. Even among those who contend that war can be avoided there are many who argue that such factors as lack of common values, ideological diversity and struggle, militant nationalism and economic inequality curtail efforts to strengthen supranational institutions.

A common rationale usually given to support this position is that some form of genuine community must precede the establishment of an organized and effective system of law and government. Those who argue in this way usually admit the theoretical possiblity that some form of world government could be established by force and maintained for the advantage of one or both of the superpowers. See e.g., John Strachey, *On the Prevention of War* (St. Martin's Press, New York, 1963). Even in the event that an imperium or condominium could establish centralized political authority, its stability, some would say, would require widespread support in community sentiments. However, given the present ideological dogmas and military postures of the superpowers, it is unlikely; too much cooperation is assumed for this form of world government to emerge in the near future. It seems as plausible to suppose that some form of limited world government will be established by the voluntary agreement of the principal states of the world. However, such an agreement assumes some consensus on how to organize such a world, including, especially, the procedures that would be used to settle conflicts arising within it.

The problem of the relationship of a legal order to community values and to a sense of community is, of course, complex. There is controversy about whether law is a dependent or independent variable within a social structure and if so, to what extent—that is, there is no clear agreement whether law can create order in any social context, or whether the context must first exhibit the cohesiveness needed to support a regime based upon law. In this latter regard, it is necessary to determine which values must be internalized, which interests must be

harmonized, and what kind of legitimized institutional processes create the social support requisite for stable government
on a global scale.

Although it is not possible here to discuss these matters very
fully, it is important to appreciate their general relevance to an
appraisal of such schemes as the Clark-Sohn plan that call for
the establishment of a revised United Nations with a structure
and authority tantamount to a limited world government. There
are several issues to keep separate. First, to what extent and
in what respects must international community exist before it
is feasible to adopt the Clark-Sohn plan? Second, to what
extent can one rely upon the Clark-Sohn plan, by the act of its
adoption, to foster the growth of a genuine international community? Third, to what extent and in what respect does an
international community presently exist?

The first selection relevant to these questions is an address
given in 1949 by Robert Maynard Hutchins, "Constitutional
Foundations for World Order," edited by The Social Science
Foundation (Denver University Press, 1949) pp. 97–114.
Hutchins raises explicitly the question of the relationship
between community and government and reminds us that the
experience in the United States after the Revolutionary War
suggests that a workable government might emerge in an
environment in which there appears to be little agreement on
values. For a study of many of these issues by a prominent
political sociologist, see Seymour Martin Lipset, *The First New
Nation* (Basic Books, New York, 1963). Hutchins argues that, in
fact, law and government in the United States have helped to
mold the consensual base that has resulted in bringing stability
and continuity to the society for an unusually long period of
time. In many modern states the role of law and government is
to mediate among conflicting ethical and social principles and
practices present within the society, rather than to eliminate
rather than to eliminate conflict.

Another major point touched upon by Hutchins is the extent
to which any government, to be effective, must satisfy various
kinds of demands on issues of social justice. To what extent
must the supranational authority in the world community satisfy demands for justice asserted by its members? Is it possible to achieve a war prevention system that deals exclusively
with the problems of controlling violence or wars? Or must
such a supranational authority also have the capacity and
ability to render social and economic justice? As we shall see,
if one concludes that order rests upon a sense of the justice of

the system, then the task of achieving limited world government or supranational authority is vastly more complicated. For then an agreement to take steps to avoid nuclear war must also reconcile to some extent the differing national conceptions of what constitutes social and economic justice so that they can, at least, coexist in a single world governmental authority. And it is more than a matter of differing outlooks. It also requires the adjustment of relations among states of greatly different wealth and at very different stages of economic development. On this, see Barbara Ward, *The Rich Nations and the Poor Nations* (Norton, New York, 1962); Gunnar Myrdal, *Beyond the Welfare State* (Yale University Press, 1960); William Paddock and Paul Paddock, *Hungry Nations* (Little, Brown, Boston, 1964); Gustavo Lagos, *International Stratification and Underdeveloped Countries* (University of North Carolina Press, 1963); B. V. A. Röling, *International Law in an Expanded World* (Djambatan, Amsterdam, 1960). Cf. **IV-6A**.

Authoritarian and totalitarian states have demonstrated the capacity of a government to maintain a stable society in the absence of community support. See Merle Fainsod, *How Russia is Ruled* (rev. ed., Harvard University Press, 1963); Samuel N. Eisenstadt, *The Political Systems of Empires* (Free Press of Glencoe, New York, 1963). Does this experience cast any light upon the social prerequisites of limited world government? Can we expect coercion to assure stability if world government comes about by the voluntary action of sovereign states?——if it comes about as a consequence of world domination by one or more centers of political power? Some of these issues are discussed in Francis H. Hinsley, *Power and the Pursuit of Peace* (University Press, Cambridge, England, 1963). See also Adda B. Bozeman, *Politics and Culture in International History* (Princeton University Press, 1960).

Does the relationship between law and community depend crucially upon the *kind of limited world government* that we envisage? Would it be worthwhile to tolerate an increase in governmental coercion or a reduction of economic prosperity in exchange for a greater prospect of avoiding nuclear war? How does one relate war prevention to the achievement of other social and political goals? What is worth sacrificing to decrease the likelihood of war? Or, to put the question differently, what risks shall we take to diminish the risk of nuclear war? Would you support a limited world government that gave high expectations of war prevention on condition that standards of living were equalized the world over? This might result in reducing the standards of living in rich countries anywhere from 40 to 70 percent. Is it

possible to answer these questions? If it is not, how then is it
possible to form rational attitudes toward the problems of world
order?

ROBERT MAYNARD HUTCHINS

Constitutional Foundations For World Order

The *New York Times*, in its editorial on the second anniversary of the
bomb, said that the ultimate protection against it can only be the abolition
of war itself. The Times suggested that the final success of efforts to abolish
war could be realized only in an ultimate world government.

I do not understand the use of the word "ultimate" in this connection. We
have now arrived at the ultimate stage in history. We cannot do something
intermediate now and ultimately do something ultimate. What is ultimately
required of us is required of us now. If what is ultimately required of us is
the abolition of war through a world government, then we had better set
about trying to get war abolished through world government now. . . .

It will be said, of course, that if nations will not collaborate in an alliance
or debating society or propaganda forum like the United Nations, they cannot be expected to come together or to stay together in a world state. The
American states could not or would not collaborate under the Articles of
Confederation before 1787, but they did come together, and, with the exception of one period they stayed together under the Constitution.

It may be admitted that there were ties which united them which do not
unite nations today. Moreover, they were remote from the rest of the world.
Both their enemies and their friends were too preoccupied to bother them.
They had the safety valve of a new country and western lands. On the other
hand, we should not forget that many differences deeply divided the American states, so much so that, three months before the Constitutional Convention, Madison wrote that he "trembled for the issue."

Mr. Hooker has lately shown in the magazine *Common Cause* how serious the divisions among the states in the confederation were. Virginia had
twelve times as many people as Delaware. Georgia claimed a hundred times
as many square miles as Rhode Island. There were so many Germans in
Pennsylvania that Franklin feared they might make German the language of
the state. It was impossible to get along in some sections of New York without knowing Dutch. The trip from Boston to New York, which now takes
less than an hour, took four days to a week along the finest road, or longer
than it takes now to go around the world.

Gouverneur Morris thought that a federal tax was impossible because of the extent of the country; and one member of the Convention asked, "How can it be supposed that this vast country, including the western territory, will, one hundred and fifty years hence, remain one nation?"

When Washington took charge of the armies surrounding Boston, he wrote that the New Englanders were an exceedingly dirty and nasty people. On the other hand, Ephraim Paine of Vermont complained that the southern members of Congress regarded themselves as a superior order of animals. Tariffs were levied by New York, Pennsylvania, and Maryland on the goods of other states; and New Jersey taxed the New York lighthouse on Sandy Hook. New York, New Hampshire, and Massachusetts quarreled about Vermont, and Pennsylvanians battled Virginians on the Upper Ohio. It is no wonder that when the Constitution was completed by the Convention, the principal attack upon it was that it was utopian, a visionary project, an indigestible panacea.

And it barely was accepted. In the conventions in the critical states it just squeaked through. In Massachusetts it carried by twenty-nine votes, in Virginia by ten; and in New York by only three.

What we are talking about is the relation between world community and world law. Reinhold Niebuhr, whom I greatly admire, takes the view that we cannot discuss world government because we have no world community to support it. The discussion of world government, he thinks, may even retard the development of world community and hence retard world government. . . .

But I am afraid that Mr. Niebuhr exaggerates the state of perfection which world community must achieve before world government can be considered. . . .

Those who oppose discussion of world government on the ground that a world community must precede a world government seem to me to overlook the interaction between the two. This is what the Greeks had in mind when they said that law was an educational force and that the city educates the man. The Constitution of the United States has educated the people of this country to believe in and support the Constitution of the United States. We are so used to thinking of law as repressive and constitutions as the embodiment of pre-existing agreement that we neglect the tremendous force which any constitution and any system of law exerts in behalf of is own acceptance and perpetuation. Anybody who has studied the relation between the political institutions of a state and its educational system, for example, must agree with Aristotle that politics is the architectonic science. One of the reasons Aristotle gives for this conclusion is that politics determines what is studied in the state.

The way to promote world community is to have world government. But since we, as private citizens, cannot establish a world government, the next best thing we can do to promote world community is to talk about world government. World discussion of world government, far from disrupting the world, may have some chance of uniting it; for the consideration of what is necessary to unite the world, the discussion of a common problem of overwhelming importance, should lead to a growing sense of community among all peoples.

An important reason for talking about world government is that nobody knows what it is. Should a world government aim at limited measures designed to maintain what is called security, or is security itself dependent on the pursuit of broader purposes? Should a world state be federal or unitary, or should it, perhaps, contain the best features of each? What should be the relation of the world government to the citizens of extant states? What taxing powers shall the world state have, and what order of military forces, if any? This list of questions can be prolonged indefinitely, and there are countless possible answers to each of them. Yet people go around saying world government is wonderful or world government is impossible. It may be that many forms of world government would be something less than wonderful; and it may be that some form of world government is possible. The only way to find out whether any form of world government is possible and practicable in our time is to work at it and talk about it. . . .

Tinkering with the United Nations will not help us, if we agree with the *New York Times* that our only hope is in the ultimate abolition of war through an ultimate world government. An entirely different constitutional foundation is required. A new set of commitments must be made. Commitments to an alliance can be transformed into allegiance to a government only by a change of heart which is embodied in a fundamental constitutional reform. . . .

If peace through intimidation and peace through purchase are failing and in the nature of things are bound to fail, we might try peace through justice. Justice means giving every man his due; it means not doing to others what you are unwilling to have them do to you. Justice is suggested to us by a well-known American document which states that all men are created equal. Justice is the cement which holds a political organization together.

If we will grant that what we want is peace, and that justice is the only way to peace, then we may begin dimly to perceive both the outlines of a policy for the present and the constitutional foundations of a future world order. We are required to abandon a policy of power and purchase and pursue a policy of justice at home and abroad.

In order to pursue this policy we have to make certain moral and intellectual commitments, commitments that threaten to take us, in fact, into the realm of metaphysics. We have to admit that men are different from the other animals and that their moral, rational, and spiritual qualities are the qualities that make them men. These characteristics prevent us from dealing with men as we are free to deal with other animals. Human dignity forbids us to apply force to men, except by law. It forbids us to regard other men as means to our ends, for every man is an end in himself. The prospects of a human community result from our common humanity.

To give every man his due, therefore, is to treat every man as a man, black or white, British or Russian, rich or poor, ignorant or educated. And we may remember, as John Stuart Mill pointed out long ago, that we cannot expect the slave to show the virtues of the free man unless we first make him free. To say that certain men cannot be treated as men means simply that they have never had a chance to be men, and they must be given that chance.

To give every man his due is to give him the Rights of Man. This means that he must be free from want as long as he is willing to work. It means that he must be free from the fear of tyranny, oppression, and exploitation. It means that his claims to life, liberty, and the dignity of the human person are inalienable. It means that the necessities of life must be common property of the human race, and that the management of the necessities of life by individual owners is a trusteeship which such owners hold subject always to the common good. It means that a world government must be a democracy, because only democracy gives every man his due.

It will be said that a world government which is founded on justice goes further than world government has to go and that we should limit ourselves to those objects as to which there can be no debate, the principal one of which is security. It will be said that nobody wants war and that all that a world government should do is to try to prevent war. This it can do by securing a monopoly of arms. Why talk about justice, the rights of man, and the law of nature when all we want is peace?

The answer is that men will fight until they get their rights. The minimum structural requirements of world government are plain enough. A world government, so as to preserve the cultural values that now exist in the states and regions of the world, must be a government which acts directly on the individual, wherever he may be; for otherwise it is merely a league of sovereign, and hence ultimately warlike, states. But these are minimum structural requirements. There are minimum moral and spiritual requirements, too; and these may be summed up in the single word justice. The advancement of man in spiritual excellence and physical welfare is the common goal of mankind. Universal peace is the prerequisite for the pursuit of that goal. Justice in turn is the prerequisite of peace. Peace and justice stand or fall together. Men will fight until they get their rights. . . .

NOTES AND QUESTIONS

1. As the essay by Hutchins indicates, the relationship between government and community has been subjected to investigation by political philosophers and scholars throughout the Western history. The Hebrews, the Greeks, and the Romans concerned themselves with this relationship. Discussions in a modern setting commenced in the 16th century with Jean Bodin's elaborate account of sovereignty as a rationale for the nation-state. Rousseau, Adam Smith, and David Hume are

a few of the most prominent thinkers who have explored the grounds for a stable and just order in society. For a synoptic classic on the subject, see Montesquieu, *The Spirit of the Laws,* translated by Thomas Nugent (Hafner, New York, 1949).

Thinkers as different as William Graham Summer and Karl Marx agree that law and government are superstructural reflections of more basic and underlying social and political processes. Given this pervasive similarity in social analysis, there is a tendency to discount law and government as independent factors in the process of creating or transforming a political system. Marx, for instance, considers the ownership of the means of production as the critical factor. Yet even Marxists give attention to the form and process of government in their study of how power is to be seized and maintained. Their strategy is a revolutionary one, disdainful of reform that merely ingrains more deeply the wrongful characteristics of the existing system. Accordingly, there is for the Marxist no gradual evolution which leads from one system to another; at some point there is only the violent overthrow of one system by another.

In recent years several leading behavioral scientists have studied the problem of achieving an integrated international community. An impressive attempt to isolate variables and make measurable the elements that constitute the processes of political integration can be found in two books by Ernst B. Haas, *The Uniting of Europe* (Stanford University Press, 1958) and *Beyond the Nation-State* (Stanford University Press, 1964). The writing of Karl W. Deutsch has perhaps exercised the greatest influence in recent years. See Deutsch, *Political Community at the International Level* (Princeton University Press, 1953); *The Integration of Political Communities* edited by J. V. Toscano and P. E. Jacob (Lippincott, Philadelphia, 1964); and Bruce M. Russett, *Community and Contention* (M.I.T. Press, 1963).

For a comparative and empirical study of the elements of cohesion in a domestic society, see Gabriel A. Almond and Sidney Verba, *The Civic Culture* (Princeton University Press, 1963). For a very perceptive account of the requisites of stability in a domestic society, see Harry Eckstein, *A Theory of Stable Democracy,* Research Monograph no. 10 (Center of International Studies, Princeton University, 1961.

At the level of international community a useful work is *The World Community* edited by Quincy Wright and published by the University of Chicago Press in 1948. A sociological view of the relationship of community to government is developed in the chapter by Louis With entitled, "World Community, World Society, and World Government."

For a general study of these problems in a national and international setting, see Carl J. Friedrich, *Man and His Government* (McGraw-Hill, New York, 1963). For an analysis of the varying impacts of nuclear weapons upon social moral, and political life at the national and international levels, see Karl Jaspers, *The Future of mankind,* translated by E. B. Ashton (University of Chicago Press, 1961).

For a recent attempt to analyze these problems from the viewpoint of the behavioral scientist, see Richard W. Van Wagenen, "The Concept of Community and Future of the United Nations," *International Organization,* vol. 19, no. 3 (World Peace Foundation, Boston, Summer, 1965) pp. 812–827.

Books approaching the problem from the viewpoint of law that might be helpful include Percy E. Corbett, *Law and Society in the Relations of States* (Harcourt, Brace, New York, 1951); Kenneth S. Carlston, *Law and Structures of Social Action* (Stevens, London, 1956); Walter Schiffer, *The Legal Community of Mankind* (Columbia University Press, 1954); C. Wilfred Jenks, *The Common Law of Mankind* (Praeger, New York, 1958); Dietrich Schindler, "Contribution à l'Etude des Facteurs Sociologiques et Psychologiques du Droit International," *Recueil des Cours*, vol. 46 (The Hague Academy of International Law, 1933); Myres S. McDougal and Associates, *Studies in World Public Order* (Yale University Press, 1960).

2. Ranyard West in *Conscience and Society* (Emerson Books, New York, 1945) has explored the relationship of government to community by inverting conventional belief. West asks whether we can ever expect a sense of community to precede the existence of governmental structure. As a psychiatrist he constructs his argument on the premise that the aggressiveness of man will predominate in the absence of the repressive apparatus of law and government. West is conversant with the philosophy of Hobbes, Locke, and Rousseau as well as with the literature of international law. He adds to his psychiatric perspective a sophisticated sense of the relationship of law, philosophy, and politics in international life. The result is a stimulating account of the preconditions for world order.

3. The case against supranational or limited world government is most effectively presented by Inis L. Claude in *Swords Into Plowshares* (rev. ed., Random House, New York, 1962) Chapter 18; and by Reinhold Niebuhr in "Illusions of World Government" in *World in Crisis: Readings in International Relations* edited by Frederick H. Hartmann (Macmillan, New York, 1962). Professor Hans J. Morgenthau, whose writings have been most influential in developing the national interest approach to the study of international relations (see especially his influential text, *Politics Among Nations* (3rd ed., Knopf, New York, 1962), writes trenchantly on this subject. According to Morgenthau a limited world government capable of providing security and eliminating war is quite improbable in the near future. At the same time Morgenthau maintains that unless such a reorganization of international relations occurs a disastrous nuclear war may take place.

4. Lincoln Bloomfield in "Arms Control and World Government," *World Politics*, vol. 14 (Princeton University Press, 1962) p. 633, an article dealing with the possibility of world government over the next fifty years, argues that unless there is a radical change in the behavior of the Chinese elite, which he doubts, it is almost impossible to believe that world government will emerge. Is it Chinese behavior or ideology, or both, that are presently most incompatible with the acceptance of some form of limited world government? A persistent argument against the creation of a limited world government arises from the observation that nation-states are unwilling to give up their sovereignty or their discretion to make unilateral decisions with regard to foreign relations. Without this willingness the whole venture is in vain. For a recent study of the attachment of men to nations, see Leonard W. Doob, *Patriotism and Nationalism* (Yale University Press, 1964).

One is reminded of Cardinal Fleury's reaction to the venerable Abbé de Saint Pierre's plan for perpetual peace: "Admirable, save for one omission: I find no provision for sending missionaries to convert the hearts of princes." Well how do we convert the hearts of princes and do they need converting?——all of them?—— which ones?——why? Or should we be concerned with the sentiments prevailing among their populations? Is this an educational task or must there be a bio-psychic growth of altruism in the human spirit? An optimistic account of the course of spiritual evolution may be found the Theilhard de Chardin, *The Phenomeon of Man* (Harper & Row, New York, 1959).

The skeptical viewpoint is sometimes stated as an ethical imperative—namely, that the nation-state should not give up its sovereignty. This view regards the nation-state as the best form of society possible within the present context of international relations. Reinhold Niebuhr's political writing often seems to support this view. There is a considerable literature glorifying the achievements and destiny of the nation-state. Perhaps none is so sublime in this regard as Hegel's *The Philosophy of Right*, translated by T. M. Knox (The Clarendon Press, Oxford, 1953). In general, see Hans Kohn, *Nationalism* (Van Nostrand, Princeton, N.J., 1955).

There has, however been literature expressing the opposite view. For example, the magazine, *Common Cause* (University of Chicago Press, 1947–1951), edited by a group of faculty members at the University of Chicago, produced a draft constitution for world government and printed a series of articles related to the subject. This constitution advanced what might be called a "maximalist" position on world government since it provided for a legislature with the ability to deal with matters of economic and social justice. Most of the articles were written in the form of short notes or essays. They do not have the usual documentation found in scholarly writing. However, some of the problems we have been discussing with regard to Hutchins' article are taken up in the magazine, especially in articles by Charles Merriam, Erich Kahler, G. A. Borgese, and Richard P. McKeon. A recent critique of national sovereignty can be found in an article by Kathleen Gough, "The Crisis of the Nation-State," edited by Roger Fisher, in *International Conflict and Behavioral Science* (Basic Books, New York, 1964).

5. Western democratic thought since the time of the American and French revolutions has stressed the notion of the consent of the governed, generally to be expressed through the mechanism of representative government and the popular vote, and resulting in some sort of consensus that permits a mediation of clashing interests so as to avoid recourse to violence by disappointed groups of citizens. Nevertheless, it is also clear that the proper instruments of coercion can be used by an elite to maintain power without the consent of the governed. Given what we know about the nature of totalitarian societies, authoritative structures, bureaucratic organization and the role of government, it is superficial to focus exclusively on the degree of consensus with regard to values. It is evident that an effective government may exist without much popular support. To understand what is needed for an effective government we need to study a series of factors: values, interests, social structure, social process, and institutional forms for the exercise and control of violence. Such a frame of reference suggests that the extent to which ultimate values must be held in common by members of a community depends on a whole set of variables. Such a conclusion shifts our attention from specifying some minimum consensus to the more complicated question of asking what mix of values and interests, under what conditions and guided by what strategies, might give rise to the kind of society within which we want to live. It is this style of thinking about the Clark-Sohn plan or about alternative schemes for limited or comprehensive world government that we recommend.

6. It should also be noted that the demand that values be shared as a precondition to work on the tasks of war prevention may very well increase both tension and hostility. In fact, it might be argued that there is both a conscious as well as an unconscious reason for avoiding accommodation and cooperation with other ideological groups and other nation-states so long as an agreement on values is deemed

essential. For any kind of cohesion so mechanically achieved is unlikely to with-
stand pressure and may have the unfortunate effect of raising false hopes or
creating sentimental deceptions. See Wolfgang Friedmann, *The Changing Sturcture
of International Law* (Columbia University Press, 1964).

7. We have not given much attention yet to the relevance of economic justice to the
achievement of world government. Hutchins, it will be recalled, indicated that
there could be no stable world community authority unless that authority was able
to provide justice for people throughout the world. Implicit in this assertion is the
conclusion that unless disadvantaged people are given a share of the world's wealth
and income they are likely to remain alienated from established political structures,
whether national or global. Clark and Sohn have made the establishment of a
world development authority a cornerstone in their war prevention system. See
IV-6. The Clark-Sohn proposal calls for spending up to about 50 billion dollars
a year for economic development. This huge sum is to be allocated for the benefit of
the non-industrialized and newly developing states with low standards of living.
The main source of this money is expected to come from the savings associated
with disarmament. At present the Soviet Union and the United States alone spend
between 95 and 100 billion dollars a year on armaments. Whether the officials and
peoples of these states would be willing to transfer the resources now used for
national defense to a fund for international development is a matter of conjecture.

The next selection by Quincy Wright, an excerpt from an
article entitled "Toward A Universal Law of Mankind," which
first appeared in the *Columbia Law Review*, vol. 63 (1963) pp. 440–
446, continues the discussion of the social preconditions for an
effective law government in world affairs. Wright seeks to get
away from any notion of mechanical preconditions by emphasizing that the extent to which legal government is attainable
varies with the international context and is always a matter of
degree. Even belligerents fighting one another usually recognize the laws of war governing each other's prisoners. All social
interaction exhibits some susceptibility to order, but not to the
same degree.

Wright emphasizes the role of public opinion in strengthening the basis for an expanding system of world order, and calls
attention to the improvement of transnational communication
facilities as a factor favorable to the recognition of common
interests and values by peoples everywhere.

The excerpt from Wright contains a valuable summary of five
forms of world order that are simultaneously present in contemporary international society. It is useful to go beyond the
simplistic image of world order made up exclusively of the
legal relations persisting among sovereign states, and Wright's
mode of analysis gives us an intellectual tool for doing so.

(Excerpt from)

TOWARD A UNIVERSAL LAW FOR MANKIND

QUINCY WRIGHT

III. Emerging Conditions for Universal Law

Let us assume that a universal society having some degree of integration is a condition for universal law having some degree of effectiveness, and ask: what are the conditions favorable to the emergence of a universal society, and what are the prospects for its more adequate development in our stage of history? We may look to history and sociology for answers to these questions.

Human history discloses processes of integration and disintegration. Empires, federations, and international organizations have developed and collapsed. Arnold Toynbee presents a picture of the rise, followed by the disintegration, of a score of civilizations. Some periods and peoples have been dominated by internationalism, cosmopolitanism, and pacificism, and other periods have been dominated by nationalism, imperialism, and militarism. H. G. Wells,[11] James T. Shotwell,[12] and the writers of the UNESCO history of the world[13] present a picture in which the forces of integration have the upper hand. Man, they suggest, has been evolving toward a conception and an awareness of mankind and of universal principles of peace, justice, freedom, and progress implicit in that conception. The people of the civilizations of antiquity and the Middle Ages, they point out, were more aware of mankind than the thousands of tribal peoples who preceded them. And even more aware of mankind have been the peoples of modern civilization who emerged after the discoveries of Columbus and his successors had established permanent contacts among all of the older civilizations. Mankind has never before achieved such a degree of law and organization as it has in the institutions that have developed since World War I.

Statistics of the financial contributions states have made to international organizations since the formation of the Universal Postal Union in the 1870's indicate that these contributions have been increasing by geometric progression tenfold every twenty-five years, and that these contributions, although still very small in proportion to the total budgets of states, have been increasing more rapidly than those total budgets.[14] Can we deduce from these historical facts a trend toward a society of mankind of ever increasing effectiveness, in spite of the recurrence of periods of war and disintegration, and the prevalence of extreme nationalism opposing attitudes of internationalism?

The sociologists distinguish the processes of communication, acculturation, co-operation, and organization. In proportion as men in different groups *communicate* with each other regularly and abundantly they tend to form a public opinion. This in the long run synthesizes the values and technologies of the communicating groups into a *common culture* and value system, even though the first effect of such communication may be defense reactions hardening each of the cultures and maintaining antagonism among them.[15] The participants in a common culture tend to become aware of that culture —especially if they come in contact occasionally with a different culture— to formulate in legal rules the standards, interests, and goals that culture

11. WELLS, THE OUTLINE OF HISTORY (1921).
12. SHOTWELL, THE LONG WAY TO FREEDOM (1960).
13. UNESCO, A HISTORY OF THE SCIENTIFIC AND CULTURAL DEVELOPMENT OF MANKIND (in progress), discussed in COMM. FOR THE STUDY OF MANKIND, REPORT OF CONFERENCE ON HISTORY AND MANKIND (1962) (discussion by Professor Gottschalk).
14. Wright, *The Mode of Financing Unions of States as a Measure of Their Degree of Integration,* 11 INTERNATIONAL ORGANIZATION 30, 35 (1957).
15. Pitirim Sorokin has presented detailed evidence of the convergence of the American and Soviet cultures in spite of their antagonism. 1 INTERNATIONAL J. OF COMPARATIVE SOCIOLOGY 143 (1960). See also LASSWELL, WORLD POLITICS AND PERSONAL INSECURITY 203 (1935); 1 WRIGHT, A STUDY OF WAR 174-76 (1942).

implies, and to *co-operate* for the realization of these rules. Such co-operation stimulates the acceptance of common policies and an *organization* to enforce the law and to achieve the policies.[16]

Society building may proceed by autocratic, rather than by democratic, methods. A conqueror may declare law and create organizations to enforce it over conquered peoples who gradually develop common values and a common culture as communication among them increases. Thus England emerged after the Norman conquest, and the universal Roman Empire after Caesar. This process may not succeed. "Self-determination movements" have often disrupted empires, as has happened in most of the modern empires since the American Declaration of Independence.

The processes of communication, acculturation, co-operation, and organization influence each other. Any one of them may, at a particular point in history, have the lead, but all are related to the progress of science and technology. This progress has been continuous from the caveman who invented fire and stone implements to the recent release of nuclear energy and solar satellites, ever widening the areas of cultural contact and of potential law, co-operation, and organization.

Can the speed and magnitude of these processes be measured by statistics? Can the relation of changes in one process to changes in the others be formulated in mathematical equations? These are questions with which the social scientists are wrestling.[17]

Perhaps the analysis of public opinion will prove the most fruitful approach to answers. Public opinion (which implies some awareness and some concept of the group), society, and law are closely related. All are states of mind as well as states of affairs. We must reject a purely mechanistic view of human affairs. A law of mankind implies that, in some degree, mankind is a society, and this implies that mankind is a public, the members of which, on some matters, have a relatively homogeneous opinion. In short, it implies a world public opinion. We live in a world whose people have many nationalities, ideologies, and religions expressing human values in different terms. We cannot develop a world public opinion through the avenue of any of these nationalities, ideologies, or religions. Each is so wedded to its own tradition and the conviction of its own superiority that others will resist incorporation.

Universal law, whether public international law or universal private law, can formulate values acceptable to all mankind only if it is derived from sources accepted by universal public opinion. From a short run point of view, authority with power to enforce may create rules of law that courts

---

16. See 2 *id.* at 970-82; WRIGHT, CONTEMPORARY INTERNATIONAL LAW: A BALANCE SHEET 8-9, 54-55 (1955) ; THE WORLD COMMUNITY (Wright ed. 1948).

17. See, *e.g.*, TECHNOLOGY AND INTERNATIONAL RELATIONS (Ogburn ed. 1949).

may generalize into principles of justice gradually accepted by public opinion. But in communities in which discussion is free and, in the long run, in all communities, public opinion rises from sources independent of government, creating intuitions of justice that become crystallized by courts and legislatures into rules of law, eventually generating a government having means of enforcement. Here again we have a "hen and egg" situation with regard to the priority of public opinion and enforcing power. In the long run, however, opinion—not physical power—is the mother of law, although in a large community it may remain vague and ineffective until formulated in law.[18]

Thus it is through the development of a world public opinion, manifesting general understanding and recognition of emerging principles of universal law, that mankind can become aware of itself, of its value, and of its intuitions of justice, and can become a functioning society capable of assuring observances of that law and of realizing the purposes declared by "We the peoples of the United Nations" in the preamble and first article of the United Nations Charter.

Law can be stated in a code, social organization can be prescribed in a written constitution, values can be formulated in a creed, culture can be described by social scientists, but all become realities only as they are supported by the public opinion of the group, manifesting and influencing the individual opinions of its members. Public opinion is continually changing, and may be measured: by the degree in which it is for or against a rule, symbol, or person; by the degree in which it is homogeneous or heterogeneous; and by the rate and direction in which it is changing in time. As every politician knows, in the understanding and influencing of opinion in all these dimensions resides the possibility of enforcing and changing law, of building organizations, of realizing values, and of modifying cultures—in short, of governing. A homogeneous and stable world public opinion on many subjects would tend to develop under conditions of declining international tensions and increasing transnational communications.[19]

Thus, both history and social analysis suggest that unless mankind blows itself up with modern weapons, the human society will increase in intensity and effectiveness. The analysis of public opinion may suggest the best approach to conscious control of this process and to creation of conditions for a more adequate law of mankind.

---

18. President Lincoln once said: "He who moulds public sentiment goes deeper than he who enacts statutes or pronounces decisions. He makes statutes and decisions possible or impossible to be executed." Quoted in Dafoe, *Public Opinion as a Factor in Government*, in PUBLIC OPINION AND WORLD POLITICS 3 (Wright ed. 1933) ; see Wright, *The Strengthening of International Law*, 98 HAGUE RECUEIL DES COURS 5, 30-35 (1959).
    19. See 2 WRIGHT, A STUDY OF WAR 1087-89, 1472-81 (1942).

IV. The Form of Universal Law

Universal law will not be viable unless supported by universal public opinion, but a national opinion will not support law seeking to maintain a universal order of society that it opposes. American opinion will not today support a world communist order, nor will Soviet opinion today support a world capitalist order. What form of world order can attract the general support of world opinion?

Should human society be conceived as: "international," as was customary in the nineteenth century; "cosmopolitan," as among the Stoics of antiquity, the medieval philosophers, and the world citizens of the eighteenth century Age of Enlightenment; "interideological" or "interregional," as conceived by contemporary cold war politicians and advocates of regional or ideological alliances or federations; "imperial," as by Dante and the empire builders of world history; or as a synthesis of all these conceptions. The latter seems to be implied by the United Nations Charter. Although formally based on an *international* conception, "the sovereign equality of all its members," the Charter demands universal respect for human rights and fundamental freedoms of all irrespective of race, sex, language, or religion, a *cosmopolitan* conception. It also permits regional arrangements and agencies thereby tending toward an *interregional* or *interideological* system, and, by giving a dominant position and a veto to five great powers on decisions binding all the members, it suggests an *empire* governed by what was called by some of its founders the five "policemen" of the United Nations. Should the basic units of human society be the state, the individual, the region, or the world? Or should there be a balance among all? Because the world social order must be reflected in the world legal order, this issue may be stated: should the law of mankind be conceived as a law among all nations, a law among all individuals, a law among the great regions, ideologies, or blocs, a law establishing the competence and authority of universal institutions, or a "transnational" law synthesizing all these points of view?[20]

That these issues are highly controversial is indicated by the ambiguity of the United Nations Charter; they involve not only the necessity of accepting the demands of groups based on power, prestige, and tradition, but also the utility of accepting the most efficient geographical and cultural scope of different rules of law and the morality of giving legal protection to values supported by world public opinion.[21]

A distinguished political philosopher wrote: "I must reserve the right to be a monist when I can and a pluralist when I must."[22] He thus re-

---

20. See Jessup, Transnational Law (1956); Wright, Problems of Stability and Progress in International Relations 74-75 (1954).
21. See Wright, *Fundamental Problems of International Organization*, in Comm. to Study the Organization of Peace, International Conciliation 454 (1941).
22. Sabine, *Pluralism: A Point of View*, 17 Am. Pol. Sci. Rev. 34, 50 (1923).

flected the effort of the rational mind to generalize, coupled with the sense of reality of the good observer. Balance between the two has brought triumphs in both natural and social science. Overemphasis on the first in human affairs has led to dogmatism, tyrannies, and conflicts. A jural law which seeks control rather than prediction should, to avoid these dangers, be based on the opposite principle. It should be local when it can, universal when it must, thus manifesting respect for the freedom of the individual and the local group, insofar as that freedom is compatible with the freedom and security of all. Rules for the use of a swimming pool in a town should be mainly local. It is not necessary to consider what people might like on this subject in other areas, although concepts of human rights may impose some restrictions. When, however, there is an impact of external usages, law must extend to a broader area. Saudi Arabia would like to regulate the oil concessions that it gives to foreign companies by its national law, but because it needs foreign capital and technicians it must recognize law broader than national in interpreting these concessions. Many relations between the American countries can be regulated regionally, but as to questions involving the interests of Europeans, universal international law may have to control.

In a shrinking world, in which all peoples are vulnerable to attack by missiles, propaganda, embargoes, and bacteria from the most distant parts, and in which universal communication continues to develop recognition of an increasing number of universal values, the criterion of efficiency, as well as the criterion of the dignity of man, demands that, notwithstanding the presumption that local law is preferable, an increasing proportion of legal rules be universal. The criterion of necessity provided by existing distributions of power may often require respect for rules in the interest of local traditions and sentiments inconsistent with the general interest or opinion.

If, however, due consideration is given to the general opinion of mankind, to the existing distribution of power, to the values, goals, and interests of states, individuals, and regions, and to the demands of other groups for self-determination—political, cultural, religious, or economic—, it is clear that the scope of rules of law must be greatly varied and the interrelation of rules of different scope very complicated. Neither individualism, socialism, nationalism, nor cosmopolitanism can be accepted as a universal guide. The present possession of primary physical power by sovereign states, the present dominance of the sentiment of nationalism among peoples, and the universal interest in preventing international war may justify the United Nations and customary international law in giving first consideration to the territorial integrity and political independence of the nation-states. So long as states monopolize power, peace requires that they accept the universal law, and most of them will accept it only on those terms. The claims of mankind represented by the United Nations, the claims of regions, of lesser groups, and of individuals for appropriate self-determinations have, therefore, been given recognition in the United Nations Charter secondary to that of sovereign states. Justice requires that the power of the states be curbed so far as practicable in consideration of these other interests. In a distant future, these interests, especially the interests of the individual for whose welfare other institutions exist in both democratic and socialist theory, may achieve a better balance in universal law with the national interest of sovereign states.

NOTES AND QUESTIONS

1. How does public opinion influence national policy with respect to war-peace issues?——with respect to foreign policy? Does "public opinion" exist in an authoritarian (or otherwise undemocratic) nation? Does Wright exaggerate the importance of public opinion to the growth of the social preconditions of a universal law of mankind?

2. Assess the relative significance for world order of the five forms mentioned by Wright. What was their relative significance in 1900?——in 1925?——in 1965? What will it be in 2000? From the viewpoint of war prevention, what is the optimal mix among the five forms? What information or reasoning is available to convince someone who arrives at different conclusions?

3. There is another passage in Wright's article (pp. 456–457) that is pertinent to this preliminary stage of analysis:

> The more primitive a system of law, the less effective are the decisions and policies of central authority and the more important it is that the basic rules of order be clear and precise. A system of "strict law" prevails. International law is a primitive system of law, the basic principles of which seek to establish respect for territorial integrity and political independence of equally sovereign states. It is an *international system* and differs from an *imperial* system organizing law and power over subject peoples from a single center, from a *military balance of power* in which relations are based on strategic calculations with little influence of law, and from a *cosmopolitan* system in which a wide consensus on values permits a unitary or federal organization to function with consent of the governed. In an international system, it is especially important that the fundamental rules of order be clearly defined.

Are the basic rules in international society clearly defined to uphold the integrity of the state system? See **II-1, II-3**. For instance, is it clear what constitutes "intervention" in violation of the territorial integrity and political independence of a sovereign state?

E. Big World and Small World

It has been suggested in connection with Hutchins' article that a good deal of writing has been done on the improbability and undesirability of creating supranational world authority or a limited world government. Most of this literature has dealt with the interrelationships of community and law, and is relevant to the discussion. The next selection by Albert Wohlstetter, Technology, Prediction and Disorder," from *The Dispersion of Nuclear Weapons*, edited by R. N. Rosencrance (Columbia University Press, 1964) pp. 274–289, does not directly concern the central problem of community and government. It is important, however, because it adds a new dimension to the discussion by its appraisal of the scientific and technical revolution going on throughout the world. Wohlstetter accepts the task of predicting the development of technology and the implications of this development for the quality of order in the world community.

Wohlstetter's concern is the relationship among three elements of the modern world: scientific and technological change, the probability of the outbreak of thermonuclear war, and the possibility of the development of an integrated world community. To explore this relationship Wohlstetter provides us with two felicitous constructs: the small world view and the big world view. Both of these constructs originate in speculations about the impact of technology upon the prospects for both world order and world community. The small world view, to state it very crudely, believes that instantaneous worldwide communication and the ability to transport men and equipment rapidly about the world have, in fact, created "one world," a world vulnerable to catastrophe as a result of nuclear weapons. Most people who adopt this small world view feel that the presence of these weapons of mass destruction in this tightly connected world makes it essential to achieve world government soon. Many of these people, according to Wohlstetter, are also likely to assume that world government will come about in a relatively short time as a result of the sense of community and as a result of fear arising from close contact and vulnerability to destruction, both of which are a result of the new technology.

The big world view, on the other hand, regards the nation-state as the effective political unit of international relations for some time to come and emphasizes a technological limit to military power that prevents any single state from acquiring the authority needed to achieve world domination. Wohlstetter believes that each of these views contains a partial truth concerning the probable character of world order during the next two decades and that each also incorporates a significant distortion.

The big world view, according to Wohlstetter, is inaccurate as a result of its assumption that technology is what prevents the formation of one world. Wohlstetter argues that from a military viewpoint and from the perspective of communication and transportation a world integrated as a whole is indeed feasible, but he believes that the problems of administering existing nation-states are so formidable and constricting that national elites will be unable to devote themselves to the pursuit of world domination. The small world view, in turn, is inaccurate because it fails to understand that technological progress in destructive capability does not necessarily lead to war, or make it more likely, or imply an end to social progress; at the same time, a technology that abolishes distance does not necessarily mean that world community will be strengthened. The intractibility of our present system of international relations militates against this. As a result of this analysis, Wohlsetter conjectures that "the actual rule of law. . .will not break out all of a sudden. Instead it is more likely to be built opportunistically, piecemeal like the common law." This kind of gradualism assumes that the process of international political integration will require a long period of time, if it is to happen at all. It contrasts with the Clark-Sohn proposal that calls for the immediate and abrupt establishment of a limited world government and for national disarmament phased over a period of twelve years.

Technology, Prediction, and Disorder

ALBERT WOHLSTETTER

The topic assigned to me joins in a familiar way science and technology. Not long ago this would have been irritating to pure scientists, and in particular to someone studying abstract mathematics. The connection is appropriate, however, because science is not very pure. Even mathematical logic turns out, to the surprise of most of those practicing it twenty years ago, to be very useful in electronic brains. Science and technology have always been linked—and inseparably. As both Leonardo and Francis Bacon at the dawn of the age of science knew very well, knowledge is not only understanding and therefore good in itself; knowledge is also power, the mastery of nature. Predicting is at least one condition for controlling, for changing things, shaping them to human ends. And since many of the purposes of men conflict, knowledge also inevitably involves the power to destroy. The duality of peaceful and warlike uses of knowledge is intrinsic.

Just listing some new and accelerating technologies today, in the standard way for all talks on the future of technology, will suggest both the duality of impending change and the enormous scale of that change: nuclear energy, synthetic new materials, the techniques of bio- and chemo-therapy, space technology, computers or information machines and the closely related technology of communication, and the possibilities of controlling weather both in the small and in the large. Let me run rapidy through this sample list.

In the development of nuclear energy, the two-fold application for peace or war is most obvious. Here the use for peacetime power has been slower than originally expected, though its long-term potential to replace fossil fuels still is very great. The tremendous scale of the change is directly visible in the use of nuclear energy in military explosives and in the transformation this has worked on military strategy and the power relations among states.

But the major change brought by the systematic exploration of nuclear reactions is likely to be in the massive transmutation of elements, a nuclear alchemy more fundamental than the chemistry of new materials and capable of almost unimaginable effects on our technology. In any case it is apparent that synthetic new materials will continue to benefit—and to disrupt—the world division of labor and the life of all of us, including especially life in the raw-materials-producing, less developed countries.

The widespread application of antibiotics and other modern medical and public health techniques will work wonders, as it has already, in the life span of people—and the possibilities of biological warfare illustrate the basic duality. But some of the *peacetime* uses sometimes seem as problematic as they are beneficial, as in the unexpected changes in the local balance of nature that have alarmed readers of Miss Rachel Carson, or in the critical case of the enormous and violent increase in the numbers of humans living—and needing work, food, and living space.

Space travel and space technology offer no promising solution for the population crowding problem. But the peacetime application in communication satellites is already patent, as is the use of satellites for detection and warning in time of war, and for the transmission of wartime commands, and possibly for bombardment.

One of the central and fastest developments, of course, has been in computers or information machines, the so-called electronic brains. These have been essential in guided missiles and other aspects of military defense. They are playing a major role in almost all the other developments I have mentioned. They are in essence, as the name "information machine" suggests, an improvement in communications within a mechanism or an organization. Capabilities of communication, both in the sense of transmitting messages as well as in the broader sense that includes transporting men and materials are accelerating enormously and are one of the plainest evidences of the increasingly tight—sometimes uncomfortably tight—connection of every part of the world to every other.

The last potential for changing nature that I shall mention, the ability to control weather, is still little understood; it is only in its dim beginnings in the small-scale, local attempts at rain-making. Even here, as public discussion has suggested, one locality might benefit at the expense of another, as in the diversion of water from a river. But the drastic changes in climate and in the atmosphere which might be effected by men—and are the subject of speculation today—include changes in the level of the seas, possible flooding of continental shelves and coastal cities, the long-term warming of vast regions and cooling of others. Quite apart from their deliberate use in warfare, the possibilities of diverging interests here dwarf anything we have seen in the Arab-Israeli disputes over the River Jordan, or even the water disputes between California and Arizona.

A mere roll-call then of the possible changes coming in our power to change things can be inspiring. Or terrifying. And usually both. Sometimes, in fact, the possibilities are presented in pairs. We are told we will have either the cataclysm or paradise, a world of light. But even paradise can be pretty terrifying, as is reflected in the fantasies of Aldous Huxley or in the current actual fears of automation. As a result, talks on the future of science and technology tend to be a competition in ominousness.

Prophets of technological change—or even a man writing a paper on impending changes in our enormous power to change things—may, I find, take on the awesome attributes of their subject matter. Some of all that massive power seems to rub off on the fellow who merely announces it, as if he could evoke the enormous benefits or the destruction he foretells, like a soothsayer or caster of spells. This has its advantages and temptations. Like the soothsayers, and unlike the messenger who brought bad news to the king in the past, messengers of technological bad news today have an assured welcome in the community. It is almost an occupation.

However, as I have said, control involves as a necessary condition successful prediction. And the prophecy business in technology is very shaky.

Its aura of power is sustained in good part because we do not keep tabs on how pronouncements on the future of science and technology turn out. Such scorecards would almost always prove chastening. Even some of the successful examples of extraordinary prescience, I have found when I recently had occasion to look at them closely, were rather more like the prophecies of Nostradamus than predictions deduced from a finished scientific theory. There are, of course, many notorious examples of unsuccessful prophecies —plain bum guesses—by famous and excellent scientists. There was Simon Newcomb's demonstration, published a few years after the Wright Brothers flew at Kittyhawk, that "no possible combination of known substances, known forms of machine, and known forms of force can be united in a practicable machine by which men shall fly long distances through the air."[1] For Newcomb, an American scientist of the first rank, "this demonstration" seemed "as complete as is possible for the demonstration of any physical fact to be." Then there was the great Rutherford's judgment, less than a decade before the first sustained nuclear chain reaction, that we were never likely to be able to control atomic energy to a useful extent. Forecasts by distinguished scientists of the growth and spread of nuclear weapons and rockets, in spite of a good deal of folklore to the contrary, far from being highly accurate, have hit not only the bull's eye, but on all sides of the target date; and sometimes these scattered shots in the dark were fired by the same marksman. This is nothing new. One of the best and most ambitious attempts to foresee the next ten to twenty-five years of our technical future was put out in 1937, and among other things missed totally: nuclear energy, antibiotics, radar, and jet propulsion.

Large changes are clearly impending, but the inability to foresee how fast they will come or even what they will be should not surprise us. Part of the difficulty is in the very nature of research. Finished science or at least tentatively completed theory enables us to predict. But trying to prophesy the *future* of science is something else again. It is predicting what we will discover, guessing what the dark will reveal when lit up. If we knew we would not need the research. It is in the nature of research, as Robert Oppenheimer has put it, that "you pay your 'two bits' first—that you go in—and you don't know what you're going to see."[2]

---

[1] Simon Newcomb, "The Outlook for the Flying Machine," chap. XXI of *Side-Lights on Astronomy* (New York and London, 1906), p. 345.

[2] J. Robert Oppenheimer, *The Open Mind* (New York, 1955), p. 7.

When we think we know what we'll see or won't see, we sometimes don't do the research even though we need it. The brilliant English geneticist, C. D. Darlington, has written very eloquently on the obstacles to further discovery that, in this way, can be erected within the ranks of science itself. "It is no accident," he thinks, "that bacteria were first seen under the microscope by a draper, that stratigraphy was first understood by a canal engineer, that oxygen was first isolated by a Unitarian minister, that the theory of infection was first established by a chemist, the theory of heredity by a monastic school teacher, and the theory of evolution by a man who was unfitted to be a university instructor in either botany or zoology." [3]

This resistance to the new within science itself troubles some of the proposals for departments or ministries of science and technology which come up from time to time, here and in England. Professor Darlington feels that great organs of authority, even in science —the scientific journals and the schools, the royal societies—tend so quickly to get stuck in the mud that what we need instead of a Ministry of Science is a Ministry of Disturbance, "a regulated source of annoyance; a destroyer of routine, an underminer of complacency, an *enfant terrible.*"

"Pure" (or fairly pure) science stimulated by the obscurity of its future, is moved to resolve uncertainty. But it is also troubled by false presumptions as to what that future might be, and the situation is rather worse for applied science or technology. One of the main reasons for this is that the progress of technology is not purely a matter of invention. It has to do with such grubby matters as costs, and uses, and competing purposes; in short, with politics, sociology, economics and military strategy. When even a great physicist talks of the future of technology, he isn't talking physics, but of matters which, if less profound, are enormously more complicated. Experience and all the academic disciplines devoted to illuminating these matters shed only a very dispersed, flickering, and fitful light. But they are all we have.

The implications of present and future technology for our future

[3] C. D. Darlington, *The Conflict of Science and Society* (London, 1948), pp. 5, 50.

course of action are much agitated in the current discussion. I am going to refer to two sorts of analyses to illustrate the limits of our understanding and the implications of these limits. Let me call the one the SMALL WORLD and the other the BIG WORLD analysis.

First the SMALL WORLD. All of the fast-growing technologies I have described earlier have in common that they enable us from any one point on earth to affect any other point and to do this with increasing speed and effectiveness. This will be true eventually of weather control, with massive possible effect. It is already nearly true of the possibilities of transportation and quite true of weapons delivery. It is nearly true of communications, but also of thought control. There is no longer space on earth simply to extend the area of operation of a technology. In this sense, we have run up against the finite limits of the earth. Not only can the range of delivery of weapons cover the earth completely from any point, but the area of destruction against unprotected targets is very large in relation to the accuracy of this delivery. There is very little time and room to absorb a blow and devise a response. The Atlantic and Pacific oceans and the distance from the Russian border to Moscow no longer suffice to shelter the United States and Russia. Moreover, the spread of nuclear weapons to more powers is likely to increase the instability, making both more complicated the problem of deterring surprise attack and more difficult the task of reducing the chance of war through "accidents" or misunderstanding, or the like. The great mathematician, John Von Neumann, suggested that a war between existing nations of the current size and closeness, with weapons of impending range and destructiveness, would be as unstable as a war with the weapons of 1900 confined to Manhattan Island. For this reason he felt that the world had become "undersized and underorganized."

One sort of inference typically drawn by scientists and technologists from this line of thinking (though *not* in his later years by Von Neumann), is the immediate necessity for world-wide agreement in controlling the technology of destruction—a control that amounts to organizing the separate sovereignties into one world—simply because the destructive implications of technology are so awful. To use the stark alternatives that were stated at the very start of the nuclear age, it is One World or None. One world, these technologists say, is a political necessity.

While scientists and technologists at the end of the war stressed with great urgency the necessity of one world, events, it seemed, were moving in another direction—towards the multiplication of sovereignties. Membership in the United Nations doubled and is on its way to tripling. It may be that the United Nations itself, with its one-nation one-vote and the large forum that it provides small powers, may encourage this multiplication. It offers some incentives to the leaders of small subdivisions of former colonies to achieve separate sovereignty status and to play a role on the world scene. In any case it is clear that we have not been going *steadily* towards one world.

This actual and growing diversity of the world receives some notice in the second view of the world and technology. That view I have for the sake of contrast identified as the *Big World*. It is represented by several distinguished diplomats, historians, and writers on foreign affairs.

Let me read a central passage from the recent work of one who is all three: diplomat, fine historian, and thoughtful critic of foreign policy.

Many Americans seem unable to recognize the technical difficulties involved in the operation of far-flung lines of power—the difficulty of trying to exert power from any given national center over areas greatly remote from that center. There are, believe me, limits to the effective radius of political power from any center in the world. It is vitally important to remember this, particularly in the face of the fears one hears constantly expressed today that the Russians want universal power and will be likely to take over the world if we fail to do this or that.

There is no magic by which great nations are brought to obey for any length of time the will of people very far away who understand their problems poorly and with whom they feel no intimacy of origin or understanding. This has to be done by bayonets, or it is not done at all. This is the reason why, despite all that is said about Soviet expansion, the power of the Kremlin extends precisely to those areas which it is able to dominate with its own armed forces, without involving impossible lines of communication, and no farther. There are geographic limits to the possibilities of military occupation; and such colonial regimes as can occasionally be successfully established at points remote from the ostensible center soon develop, as has been demonstrated time and time again since the days of the Byzantine Empire, a will and identity of their own and become increasingly ineffective as instruments. In this way, the exercise of centralized power is gradually reduced, once more, to something like its natural limits.

What I am asserting is that universal world dominion is a technical impossibility, and that the effectiveness of the power radiated from any one national center decreases in proportion to the distance involved.[4]

This view of the world then stresses that power is finite, that it diminishes in proportion to distance from its center, and concludes that—at least for any length of time—world dominion by Russia or any other single power is a technological impossibility. The theory frequently goes with a stress on the apparent growth of many centers of power, and in particular the growth in the importance of small powers. On the whole this multipolarity is taken as making the world more stable. But as for One World, on this view it is *technically infeasible.* It is something of a paradox, contemplating these two views of the world, that the technologists insist that One World is a political necessity and the diplomats and political historians assure us that it is technically infeasible.

The diplomats and historians who view the world as large, compared to the limits of technology, show an attractive and persuasive awareness of the diversity of competing national goals, the problems in the exercise of power, and the factual limits both to power and to national ambitions. These are matters that technologists tend to brush over all too lightly. Nonetheless, this view of the world has problems. For one thing, though military power comes in several varieties, none that I have examined in terms of the technology of nuclear or conventional warfare today falls off so neatly in a straight line from the power center. Even for conventional combat sometimes the costs of getting to a theater of war are very small and the capabilities very large, compared to the costs and capabilities of moving about *inside* the theater. And since the comparative advantage inside the theater may depend on many highly local phenomena—terrain and local transportation and communication—it sometimes turns out that a distant foe actually has an advantage

[4] George Kennan, *Russia and the West Under Lenin and Stalin* (New York, 1962), pp. 260–61.

over one nearby, whose access through local roads, ports, and airfields may be very poor. In the case of nuclear war the cushioning effects of space are much more radically transformed. And how important distance is will depend on what your objectives are. An aggressor may be considerably helped by proximity. But a so-called "second-strike capability" is likely to be aided by distance.

In any case the old geopolitical considerations on the balance of power which typify the Big World view, whatever their worth for past history, are too schematic and dubious to be very reassuring about the stability of the present world today.

Nor is the theory very reassuring about Soviet ambitions, though it seems the emphasis on the impossibility of world domination by any one power is meant to be. For one thing, all we are assured is that great nations will not obey a distant will "for any length of time." But even a short time—like the duration of the Byzantine Empire—could be unpleasant. Moreover, even if we assumed that total world dominion by a single power was infeasible, this is not completely comforting. A world divided between several nuclear-armed, contending communist powers, for example, might, if possible, be even worse. And finally we must ask how the finite limit to the effective radius of power which is stressed by these writers compares with that other finite limit stressed by the holders of the Small World view. How does the technical limit of power compare with the size of the globe? To be specific, is it less than twelve thousand nautical miles? That's halfway round. Two paths of that length starting from the same center could meet at the opposite side of the globe.

And the old empires, when you come right down to it, were rather impressive in extent. I have made some very rough estimates and some extremely unreliable calculations. I found that a direct path from Byzantium to the farthest extent of Justinian's domain on the Iberian Peninsula comes within a factor of three or four of making it halfway round the world. Justinian did pretty well. Genghis and Kublai Khan did even better than that—and did it, my friend John Williams has pointed out, with ponies. Communications and transportation have improved by very much larger factors than three or four. It used to take from a month to two months to go from

Byzantium to Rome. Now jets can make it in hours, rockets in minutes. And, while no one who has put a telephone call through from Istanbul (today's Byzantium) to Rome would ever think that arranging the connection is done with nearly the speed of light, still, the improvement over Justinian is tremendous. On the technical limits the Small World theory and the technicians are more plausible.

Our adversaries are restrained, but not by what is technically feasible. Long before technical limits are reached, they are restrained by the diversity of their goals, and by the costs of doing us in; and therefore by us. But the diversity of goals is essential. The diplomats and political historians are on firm ground when, in contrast to most of the technologists writing on strategy, they stress the complexity and multiplicity of political objectives. The Communists are preoccupied with a good many other problems than doing us in by force of arms. There are all the indirect methods and there are the problems of their own internal development, and the quarrels with their friends as to which one will do us in and how, and a good many other domestic and foreign concerns. No country in the communist or non-communist world has ever pursued the arms race with the single-minded ferocity assumed in the simple models constructed by writers on strategy and military technology. The world is getting small in relation to what is technically feasible, but it is not getting simple.

There are more severe limitations in the simplicity of the strategic and political views of the technologists. Technologists tend to treat these political and military problems as if they were pure technology. But as I have already suggested, in practice within any given nation a decision to speed the development and production of nuclear weapons or bombers or rockets will be affected by the costs of such a program, the many competing national purposes for which the same resources might be used, and the apparent rewards. The rewards themselves depend upon the behavior of other nations beyond national control and the expected payoffs may in some cases be rather easily frustrated. So, in spite of the great scientific competence of the English, their costly rocket program—the Blue Streak—turned out to be of very dubious value and was cancelled, not because of any technical failure in realizing the original plans, but because of the much greater capabilities the more powerful Russians have for getting countermeasures. Not nature, but the Russians, spoiled the original plans. Feasible Russian countermeasures would have found the Blue Streak vulnerable on reentry from space, but even more vulnerable on the ground before it was ever launched.

Some scientists and technologists talk of the imminent appearance of rocket programs so cheap that they will be available not merely to poor countries, but to rather wealthy individuals, a new sort of nuclear dilettante. In fact, military programs for nuclear weapons and delivery systems with other than ornamental utility or totally irresponsible use are an enormous enterprise. They have been rather consistently underestimated. Until very recently studies of the diffusion problem considered only what it would take for new entrants to the nuclear club just to make bombs, as if the bombs would deliver themselves and be unopposed. And it is still extremely rare in such studies to consider the delivery problem in a serious way, with full account taken of the problems of operating and controlling nuclear forces in the face of possible enemy counters.

The spread of nuclear weapons is a genuine problem and an important one. But the time scale for this diffusion and its characteristics have been woefully misrepresented by men who have taken the problem as one of improving technology to cut the cost of a standardized and universally desired product. When considered realistically, however, it becomes apparent that the product is highly complex and the standards it has to meet are continuously changing. Nuclear retaliatory systems have not been going down in price, but up. The first 100 B-58's, Atlas, or submarine-launched Polaris cost three to five times more than the first 100 B-47's. Wealthy dilettantes don't appear to be a very promising immediate market. In fact diffusion has gone very much more slowly than was predicted at the end of the war. And prophecy continues to be quickly outmoded by events. Only three years ago, Sir Charles Snow forecast at least a dozen new entrants to the nuclear club by 1966. Nothing of the kind is likely to happen.

Technologists who hold the Small World view tend to assume not only that any country will acquire all means of destruction within its technical capacity, but also that once acquired these weapons are sure to be used ("sooner or later") so we have had predictions that nuclear war is statistically certain before the end of the decade.

The danger of nuclear war is a very real one. But this sort of prophecy has no empirical foundation whatsoever. Sometimes the certainty of nuclear war is presented as a mathematical matter. Given a fixed probability of war, no matter how small it is, so long as it is greater than zero, "sooner or later" the nuclear holocaust will come. In this form, however, the prediction is mathematically impeccable but trivial. It has no empirical content, offers no index for action. It tells us essentially nothing. An equally impeccable bit of algebra would show that the outbreak of the rule of law and eternal peace is statistically certain—"sooner or later." This argument would run: In any given year there is some probability that the total rule of law among nations and the peaceful settlement of disputes will come into being. This probability may be very tiny right now, but it is greater than zero. And not decreasing. Well then, "sooner or later" . . . and so on. The parallel argument about the statistical certainty of nuclear war should be no more terrifying than this argument for the statistical certainty of eternal peace is reassuring.

Such impeccable but empty statistical arguments are very common—even among Nobel Laureates in physics. Still more common is the assertion that the probability of war in any given year increases year by year. For a variety of reasons, I believe this one simply to be wrong as a matter of fact. On the evidence of the greatly decreased vulnerability of our strategic force and the greatly increased centralization of command over nuclear weapons, the probability both of deliberate attack on U.S. forces and of their unauthorized or "accidental" or miscalculated use has declined in the last decade.

Most frequently what we get are bare predictions that the probability of war is very high in some next period of years. However,

I have recently run through the history of these predictions and can report something that is, at least partially, reassuring. They show a trend.

For example, one physicist of the first rank in 1945 was most pessimistic about the postwar years. He said, "If we manage to get through the next fifteen years alive, we shall probably emerge immune to atomic bombs." The next prediction I came across by this same physicist fell, as it happens, in the year 1960, that is, fifteen years later. He did not then feel that we were immune to atom bombs. But he now talked of the probability of war in the following *forty* years. Another physicist, a friend of mine and former colleague, was saying not very long ago that unless we had comprehensive arms control by 1970 the probability of war was extremely high. A little later, he moved the date to 1975; and I was somewhat relieved to find him writing recently that—with average luck—we just might last out the century.

I do not intend to minimize the dangers of nuclear war. They are, as I have said, very real. I believe that the most important goal of both our national defense and our foreign policy must continue to be to reduce the probability of war, year by year, and step by step. However, there is no basis for the statements that are made almost every day which fix the length of our lease on life. I feel moreover that all the urgent statements indicating that the lease is nearly up have some very large defects. Most important, they pretend to a knowledge of the future which we do not have, a knowledge not only of the technology but also of the evolving political and economic scene. Second, they lead not to science or politics, but to eschatology: they point to the establishment on this finite earth in the near future of an improbably final arrangement for settling the deep antagonisms between the East and the West and in fact among all nations. In doing this they express our wishes, but not our sober estimates of the durability of the antagonisms themselves. They focus on time intervals that are very little understood and ignore some time constants on which we have a good deal of empirical evidence.

We are in the dark about the future of science and technology,

still more about the long-term future of military and political developments in the world arena. We should be extremely skeptical,
therefore, if sweeping predictions on any subject come tied to a
prescription, an exhortation for urgent and sweeping action. We
have all heard the apocalyptic pairs of alternatives: "Destroy the
Russians or they'll destroy us"; or "Disarm or face world annihilation." These are counsels of desperation, fear of the dark. They
abandon not only patience, but intelligence.

However, if uncertainty is hard to tolerate, it is nonetheless a
very pervasive and hard fact of life. It demands, today, flexibility,
preparedness to change direction with new knowledge and the use
of every shred of knowledge that we have. This last includes our
knowledge of the glacial slowness of the Cold War's receding. We
have interests in common with our opponents, but we deceive ourselves when we talk of these as overriding all others. The utopian
proposals urged today by so many scientists and technologists ignore the durability of our political problems by calling for a final
and immediate solution.

As if the problem of peace were not enough to settle all at once,
such prescriptions for its solution are frequently coupled with reci-
pes for solving the extraordinarily resistant troubles of the less-
developed countries. It is frequently suggested that we can stabilize
the peace and launch the less-developed countries into self-sustaining growth at one stroke—simply by devoting all or most of the
money spent on national defenses throughout the world to provide
capital for these areas. Such formulae hardly take seriously either
problem: keeping the peace or economic development. Economic
and political self-development for the less-developed areas are not
at all likely to be accomplished quickly or by any simple formula—
not, for example, simply by large infusions of capital.

Utopian hopes also flourish in the less developed countries. The
stereotyped phrase, "the revolution of rising expectations," sometimes
denotes the awareness by the poor of the great gap between the poor
and the rich countries. But any suggestion that this gap is likely to
be closed in a matter of years, or even decades, encourages false
hopes. The stereotype would be better phrased "The revolution of

excessive expectations." These problems of technological backwardness—like the problems set by the extreme advance in military technology—are not simply technological. They are embedded in traditional ways of life that offer small incentive to innovation.

Innovation in any case will be no cure-all. The facile assumption that headlong economic development has some automatic connection with the development of democratic forms is little evidenced. The fragmentary evidence available, for example, in the studies of Seymour Martin Lipset, suggests that in the periods of social dislocation characteristic of rapid industrial advance, totalitarian forms may flourish. Advance, once achieved, can furnish a firm and partial basis for political democracy. But the process of innovation and swift technological advance can be painful. The ecstatic and violent millennial movements of medieval and reformation Europe exploded precisely at the times and places where change had uprooted peasants and journeymen, torn them from the support as well as the constraints of kinship, and thrown them into towns.

Millennial prescriptions of scientists and technologists in the advanced countries for the economic development of backward areas, with their simple stress on technology alone and the supply of industrial capital—sometimes even just electric power—form an unfortunately perfect match for some of the millennial characteristics of the leadership in newly independent countries.

John Von Neumann, who of all the scientists wrote most perceptively of our burgeoning technology and small finite world, did not draw the utopian conclusions of many who cite him. On the contrary, he wrote, "It is unreasonable to expect a novel cure-all."

For progress there is no cure. Any attempt to find automatically safe channels for the present explosive variety of progress must lead to frustration. The only safety permissible is relative, and it lies in an intelligent exercise of day-to-day judgment.

The one solid fact is that the difficulties are due to an evolution that, while useful and constructive, is also dangerous. Can we produce the required adjustments with the necessary speed? The most hopeful answer is that the human species has been subjected to similar tests before and seems to have a congenital ability to come through, after varying amounts of trouble. To ask in advance for a complete recipe would be unreasonable. We can specify only the human qualities required: patience, flexibility, intelligence.[5]

The sense of my own comments is much the same. There are without doubt large changes in technology impending. But how fast they will come and just what they will be is not really predictable. Still less are the widespread political and economic consequences of these changes. The future of technology is dark. Not black. But obscure. It is better, then, to direct our steps by the small and fitful illumination that we have and will obtain, to move with intelligence, rather than simply to make one grand leap in the dark.

The actual rule of law is not likely to come all at once, like the mythical social contract of the eighteenth-century philosophers. It will not break out all of a sudden. Instead it is more likely to be built opportunistically and piecemeal like the common law.

The changes coming are neither intrinsically benign nor malign. In any case they are best not viewed in terms of the apocalypse or the millennium. The apocalypse might come. But it need not. And the millennium is not about to.

[5] John Von Neumann, "Can We Survive Technology?" *Fortune* (June, 1955), p. 152.

NOTES AND QUESTIONS

1. Compare Wohlstetter's views on the probability of war with those of Boulding, Kahn, and Clark and Sohn. With which of these authors does he disagree and what is the character of the disagreement?

2. The argument is sometimes made that since there is some finite possibility of nuclear war each year, then over a period of years it is probable that war will occur. Wohlstetter suggests that such statistical reasoning is foolish and that it might make more sense to say that the absence of war over a period of years supports the inference of an "outbreak of peace" rather than one about the probability, or even the eventual inevitability of a major war. What do you think about this kind of reasoning? Does it help you to assess how great, in fact, is the danger of nuclear war?

3. Wohlstetter argues that the rule of law in world affairs will develop in much the same way as the common law developed in England and the United States. This does not mean that he thinks the pattern of development will be identical, or that the role of courts and executive will be similar in the international system to what has existed in various domestic systems. He merely intends to suggest that the process of integration will be comparatively slow. Does Wohlstetter underestimate the fact that rapid technological change in worldwide communications and transportation is developing a world culture at a much more rapid rate than English or American culture developed? It is plausible to maintain that the peculiar mix of

common culture, efficient organization, and technological ability needed for effective government was quite unfavorable during the period when the common law developed, but that today the facts are reversed and that institution building will proceed very rapidly on the international level. See, for example, "World Culture" by Margaret Mead in the book *The World Community* (University of Chicago Press, 1948), edited by Quincy Wright. For a somewhat conflicting view, see Julius Stone in his introduction to *Legal Controls of International Conflict* (rev. ed. Stevens, London, 1959). See also Quincy Wright, "The Strengthening of International Law" in *Recueil des Cours,* vol. 98, no. III (The Hague Academy of International Law, 1959) pp. 5–289, and the chapter entitled "Maintaining Peaceful Co-existence" in *Preventing World War III*, edited by Q. Wright, William M. Evan and Morton Deutsch (Simon and Schuster, New York, 1962) pp. 410–441.

F. Some Documents on Supranational Authority

The dividing line between dispassionate analysis and programmatic documents is probably not as clear as is frequently supposed. Certainly many pamphlets and books espousing programs of reform or even revolution are based on an analysis of existing conditions and on some sense of the possible given an image of nature and social organization. By the same token, writings presented as scholarly research possess values orientations and often cast light on what are the effective limits of programs offered by people with political action-goals in mind. The next two selections are documents with an avowed intention to establish a direction for political action. At the same time, the authors arrived at their program on the basis of an informed study of the issues that have been dealt with throughout this chapter, and might be expected to contend that their recommendations for action arise from findings they consider objective.

The encyclical letter of Pope John XXIII, *Pacem in Terris/ Peace on Earth* (Paulist Press, New York, 1963) has been heralded throughout the world for its moral and spiritual commitment to the establishment of a new structure of international relations in a manner conducive to peace, and for the acuteness and cogency of is analysis. Writing as the leader of the Roman Catholic Church, and taking full advantage of that institution's moral and spiritual heritage, Pope John discusses the various elements of human nature and social organization that he feels must coalesce if human society is to find a way to build a peaceful world. The encyclical is addressed not only to members of the Church, but to "all men of good will"; some translations have rendered this phrase as "addressed to all mankind." Pope John writes that the present international system is so constituted that the leadership exercised in the various nation-states is unable to provide for the security and peace of national populations and that some new system of international relations involving a supranational world authority must be brought into existence to accomplish these fundamental political purposes. It seems clear that Pope John does not write as though he is advocating a utopian or idealistic scheme. His encyclical seems rather to be in the vein of a practical proposal of what is presently needed and attainable.

The second selection is a speech given by Hugh Gaitskell, Leader of the opposition Labour Party in Great Britain who died in 1963. It is reprinted from a pamphlet published by the World Parliament Association (London, 1962). The speech was delivered October 25, 1962, at a time when Great Britain was negotiating entry into the Common Market; in the preceding months the Cuban missile crisis and the Chinese attack on India arising out of a boundary dispute had shaken international society badly.

The speech by Gaitskell constituted a serious and responsible political act by a party leader. Gaitskell's argument against using regional groupings to establish world order was undoubtedly related to the Labour Party's opposition to British membership in the Common Market; the view that a world order based upon such regional units would be unstable and unsatisfactory is nevertheless certainly worth taking seriously, especially as regionalism seems to be emerging so strongly in international politics. Like Pope John XXIII, Gaitskell puts himself on record as asking for a serious consideration of world government, not in the spirit of utopian speculation, but to carry out the practical needs of the day. Gaitskell's analysis of why world government is not taken more seriously, and the suggestions for what must be done about this, reflect his analysis of how to prevent war and express his experience as a political figure within his own society and on the international scene. The eight points listed as steps to be taken in the direction of world government demonstrate that those who practice the art of politics are likely to couple their advocacy of political goals with ideas about how to realize them, that is, about how to solve the transition problem. A practical politician will tend to respond to any proposal for change with the question "How shall we implement this?" It requires a superior imagination to conceive the implementation of any very radical change in the *status quo*. Very few people have the gift to comprehend or appraise the products of a superior imagination. This leads to the automatic deprecation of any proposal for sweeping change by those who are unimaginative, or who are caught up in daily routine. It requires too many steps between what exists and what is proposed to be seen as feasible. One of the real opportunities for peace research is to spell out these intervening steps so that it becomes easier to visualize and plan for the realization of proposals in the area of world order.

Pope John XXIII and Hugh Gaitskell managed to combine a political imagination capable of projecting long-range proposals with the practical sense to specify the intermediate behavior that is called for. It is significant that their diagnosis of our times convinced them that world government in some form was an urgent necessity. The Clark-Sohn plan for a limited world government gives us the kind of detailed presentation that makes it possible to think about life as it might be in such an altered political environment. On such a basis it becomes possible to determine whether we really want some form of world government, and whether it is worthwhile for individuals and nations to take risks and to make sacrifices to achieve it.

Pacem in Terris

PART IV

RELATIONSHIP OF
MEN AND OF POLITICAL COMMUNITIES
WITH THE WORLD COMMUNITY

Interdependence between Political Communities

130. Recent progress of science and technology has profoundly affected human beings and influenced men to work together and live as one family. There has been a great increase in the circulation of goods, of ideas and of persons from one country to another, so that relations have become closer between individuals, families and intermediate associations belonging to different political communities, and between the public authorities of those communities. At the same time the interdependence of national economies has grown deeper, one becoming progressively more closely related to the other, so that they become, as it were, integral parts of the one world economy. Likewise the social progress, order, security and peace of each country are necessarily connected with the social progress, order, security and peace of all other countries.

131. At the present day no political community is able to pursue its own interests and develop itself in isolation, because the degree of its prosperity and development is a reflection and a component part of the degree of prosperity and development of all the other political communities.

Existing Public Authority Not Equal to Requirements of the Universal Common Good

132. The unity of the human family has always existed, because its members were human beings all equal by virtue of their natural dignity. Hence there will always exist the objective need to promote, in sufficient measure, the universal common good, that is, the common good of the entire human family.

133. In times past, one would be justified in feeling that the public authorities of the different political communities might be in a position to provide for the universal common good, either through normal diplomatic channels or through top-level meetings, by making use of juridical instruments such as conventions and treaties, for example: juridical instruments suggested by the natural law and regulated by the law of nations and international law.

134. As a result of the far-reaching changes which have taken place in the relations within the human community, the universal common good gives rise to problems that are very grave, complex and extremely urgent, especially as regards security and world peace. On the other hand, the public authorities of the individual nations—being placed as they are on a footing of equality one with the other —no matter how much they multiply their meetings or sharpen their wits in efforts to draw up new juridical instruments, they are no longer capable of facing the task of finding an adequate solution to the problems mentioned above. And this is not due to a lack of good will or of a spirit of enterprise, but because their authority lacks suitable force.

135. It can be said, therefore, that at this historical moment the present system of organization and the way its principle of authority operates on a world basis no longer correspond to the objective requirements of the universal common good.

Relations between the Common Good and Public Authority in Historical Context

136. There exists an intrinsic connection between the common good on the one hand and the structure and function of public authority on the other. The moral order, which needs public authority in order to promote the common good in civil society, requires also that the authority be effective in attaining that end. This demands that the organs through which the authority is formed, becomes operative and pursues its ends, must be composed and act in such a manner as to be capable of furthering the common good by ways and means which correspond to the developing situation.

137. Today the universal common good poses problems of world-wide dimensions, which cannot be adequately tackled or solved except by the efforts of public authorities endowed with a wideness of powers, structure and means of the same proportions: that is, of public authorities which are in a position to operate in an effective manner on a world-wide basis. The moral order itself, therefore, demands that such a form of public authority be established.

Public Authority Instituted by Common Consent and Not Imposed by Force

138. A public authority, having world-wide power and endowed with the proper means for the efficacious pursuit of its objective, which is the universal common good in concrete form, must be set up by common accord and not imposed by force. The reason is that such an authority must be in a position to operate effectively; yet, at the same time, its action must be inspired by sincere and real impartiality: in other words, it must be an action aimed at satisfying the objective requirements of the universal common good. The difficulty is that there would be reason to fear that a supranational or world-wide public authority, imposed by force by the more

powerful political communities, might be or might become an instrument of one-sided interests; and even should this not happen, it would be difficult for it to avoid all suspicion of partiality in its actions, and this would take from the efficaciousness of its activity. Even though there may be pronounced differences between political communities as regards the degree of their economic development and their military power, they are all very sensitive as regards their juridical equality and their moral dignity. For that reason, they are right in not easily yielding in obedience to an authority imposed by force, or to an authority in whose creation they had no part, or to which they themselves did not decide to submit by conscious and free choice.

The Universal Common Good and Personal Rights

139. Like the common good of individual political communities, so too the universal common good cannot be determined except by having regard to the human person. Therefore, the public authority of the world community, too, must have as its fundamental objective the recognition, respect, safeguarding and promotion of the rights of the human person; this can be done by direct action when required, or by creating on a world scale an environment in which the public authorities of the individual political communities can more easily carry out their specific functions.

The Principle of Subsidiarity

140. Just as within each political community the relations between individuals, families, intermediate associations and public authority are governed by the principle of subsidiarity, so too the relations between the public authority of each political community and the public authority of the world community must be regulated by the light of the same principle. This means that the public authority of the world community must tackle and solve problems of an economic, social

political or cultural character which are posed by the universal common good. For, because of the vastness, complexity and urgency of those problems, the public authorities of the individual States are not in a position to tackle them with any hope of resolving them satisfactorily.

141. The public authority of the world community is not intended to limit the sphere of action of the public authority of the individual political community, much less to take its place. On the contrary, its purpose is to create, on a world basis, an environment in which the public authorities of each political community, its citizens and intermediate associations, can carry out their tasks, fulfill their duties and exercise their rights with greater security.[64]

Modern Developments

142. As is known, the United Nations Organization (UN) was established on June 26, 1945, and to it there were subsequently added Intergovernmental Agencies with extensive international tasks in the economic, social, cultural, educational and health fields. The United Nations Organization had as its essential purpose the maintenance and consolidation of peace between peoples, fostering between them friendly relations, based on the principles of equality, mutual respect, and varied forms of co-operation in every sector of human society.

143. An act of the highest importance performed by the United Nations Organization was the *Universal Declaration of Human Rights,* approved in the General Assembly of December 10, 1948. In the preamble of that Declaration, the recognition of and respect for those rights and respective liberties is proclaimed as an ideal to be pursued by all peoples and all countries.

144. Some objections and reservations were raised regarding certain points in the Declaration. There is no doubt,

---

[64] Cf. Pius XII's *Allocution* to youth of Catholic Action from the dioceses of Italy gathered in Rome, September 12, 1948, *A.A.S.,* XL, p. 412.

however, that the document represents an important step on the path towards the juridical-political organization of the world community. For in it, in most solemn form, the dignity of a person is acknowledged to all human beings; and as a consequence there is proclaimed, as a fundamental right, the right of free movement in the search for truth and in the attainment of moral good and of justice, and also the right to a dignified life, while other rights connected with those mentioned are likewise proclaimed.

145. It is Our earnest wish that the United Nations Organization—in its structure and in its means—may become ever more equal to the magnitude and nobility of its tasks. May the day soon come when every human being will find therein an effective safeguard for the rights which derive directly from his dignity as a person, and which are therefore universal, inviolate and inalienable rights. This is all the more to be hoped for since all human beings, as they take an ever more active part in the public life of their own political communities, are showing an increasing interest in the affairs of all peoples, and are becoming more consciously aware that they are living members of a universal family of mankind.

THE RT. HON. HUGH GAITSKELL, C. B. E., M. P.

An Eight Point Programme for World Government

A great debate is now taking place in Britian about our proposed entry into the E. E. C. I shall not continue it here. But I would like to remove one misunderstanding.

Because some of us hold that the terms so far negotiated do not adequately fulfil the conditions which we consider reasonable and necessary before we enter, this does not mean that we are hostile to Europe or wish to isolate ourselves from our continental neighbours.

Indeed the popular description of the controversy "Should Britain go into Europe or not?" is misleading. Britian is heavily involved—militarily, commercially and culturally—in Western Europe and will remain so whether or not we enter the E. E. C.

If the terms should be such that we do not feel able to enter the E. E. C., the alternative is not isolation, but a relationship with E. E. C. which would be even closer and friendlier than at present, accompanied by the special links we already have with the overseas Commonwealth and with the rest of Western Europe through EFTA.

But it is not about the Common Market that I wish to speak this evening. Indeed, I doubt whether the problems of disunity or unity in Western Europe are today among the greatest problems confronting the world. Fifty years ago, perhaps twenty-five years ago, this was true—though it was not from Western Europe but Europe as a whole, including Russia, that the danger of international conflict sprang. Since 1945, however, no one has seriously worried about the danger of war between Britain, France, Germany and Italy.

There are, of course, differences of opinion within the NATO alliance, but so there are within the Communist bloc. I doubt whether these differences have much connection with the formation of the E. E. C. or would be resolved by Britain's entry.

No, the really grave problems today are not the problems of part of a continent, however much we who live there may be absorbed by them, but those of the whole world. Their solutions can only be world solutions. Remedies which might have been suitable in a steam age half a century ago are not likely to be adequate in the days of rockets and astronauts.

It is trite but true to say that the world has become exceedingly small.

When one reflects that in a few years—if we survive—we shall probably all be sharing the excitement of celebrating the first voyage to the moon—regardless of who achieves it—it is clear that we are now more than ever before a single human society. It is the unity or disunity of this society which must be our principle concern.

Looked at in this light, the two greatest issues which face us are, on the one hand, the relations between the Communist bloc and the Western alliance from which springs the major danger of war, and, on the other hand, the problems of world poverty and the inequality between rich and poor nations. Both problems are world problems. Neither can be solved by local action alone.

There could be no more vivid proof of this than the two grave crises with which we are now confronted—the Chinese attack on the Indian frontier and Cuba. Their possible repercussions and the way in which they may each link up with other sources of conflict are very much in the minds of all of us. They are only the latest examples of the indivisibility of peace.

So also the major steps which are really necessary in dealing with the problem of world poverty—the stabilising of commodity prices, the opening up of markets for the products of the developing countries and the proper organisation and allocation of aid—unquestionably require world action.

But when we say world action, we do not mean some casual and temporary arrangement; for this would obviously not be sufficient. At best we should then still be staggering from one crisis to another. We mean, really, that we have got to set up and operate institutions which will mean nothing less than a major advance towards world government.

Global solutions of this kind which not long ago were dismissed as the cloudy fantasies of well-meaning cranks have today become the necessary conditions of our survival. Schemes for world government which were once just an academic exercise are now thrust upon us by the very logic of current international negotiations.

For example, both the United States and the Soviet Union propose in their disarmament plans the setting up of an international force. Indeed, it is now generally accepted that such a step is an essential part of a Disarmament Agreement. But if such a force is to be effective in providing security, it must have real power. If it is to have real power, the problem of who is to control it has to be solved. I do not see how this can be satisfactorily solved except through the establishment of a World Authority responsible to a World Legislature.

But how is the gap between the ideal of world government and the reality of the cold war to be closed? How do we move forward from the conflicting aims and ambitions of over 100 independent sovereign states to the creation of a system of international law and order?

Again, the Cuban crisis underlines the urgency of this matter. For it shows only too plainly the inherent instability in the balance of power and the danger of relying solely on this to prevent war.

Some say that the right path is by sacrificing sovereignty at the regional level. This, they hold, will lead in time to the breakdown of barriers at the global level. The idea is that larger and larger blocs are formed until at the end the last remaining blocs merge into one great world federation.

I understand and sympathise with those who take this view. Something like it seems to happen in industry. But I cannot find any evidence that it is likely in international politics.

The federation of one group designed to enhance the power and protect the interests of those who compose it may well lead to other countries following suit. But this will be out of fear and for self protection. For the continuing existence of a new state formed from several existing ones is too often dependent on the cult of a new nationalism. Moreover, while the whole process may seem admirable to those within, it is usually regarded as a threat by those who are left out. Thus, suspicion and fear, the chief barriers to disarmament and the sacrifice of sovereignty by the great powers are likely to be magnified rather than reduced. One must remember, too, that while a war between two small nations can be localised, this is scarcely possible if two super states are involved.

No doubt these objections would not apply if each merger remained open to other states to join or the grouping took the form not of new nation states but simply of loose associations. But, in practice, the first does not happen and the second would not, of course, involve the same sacrifice of sovereignty upon which the whole argument for a regional approach is based.

I conclude, therefore, with regret that there is no reason to think that a world divided into—say—a dozen great powers will necessarily be more peaceful than the world of a hundred nation states as we know it today.

As we must also reject the notion that world government should come about through world conquest—since in present circumstances this would also mean the end of civilisation, we are left, I believe, with only two other possibilities.

The first is the idea of a joint American-Russian domination which would retain a monopoly of nuclear weapons, refrain from attacking one another and impose peace on the rest of the world. For various reasons, however, I cannot believe that even if this were not so fanciful, it would be either a stable solution or be tolerated by the rest of the world.

The second is what I will describe inelegantly as the gradual, piecemeal approach on a global basis. I can explain this best by first considering what are the real obstacles in the way of the sacrifice of sovereignty necessary for the establishment of international authority. I call these obstacles "the four fears":—

1 The fear of nations—particularly the powerful ones—that they will lose an advantage which they believe their power still gives them in international relations.

2   The fear of nations that they will not be guaranteed the same security as would be provided by their own arms and alliances.

3   The fear that the decisions taken by the world authority will run counter to their national interests.

4   The fear that other nations will not observe or be compelled to observe the contract to accept world government.

How can these fears be overcome?   The answer, in general, is no doubt that they should be outweighed by the even greater fear of world war. Clearly, today, this is a greater factor than ever before in history.

More specifically, the first fear should count for much less because it is today much harder for the great nations to use their power effectively.   As my friend Denis Healey recently remarked—"You could do anything with bayonets but sit on them.   The only thing to do with the H bomb is to sit on it!"   The events of the last few days have not yet proved him wrong.

The nuclear stalemate has also had another effect.   It has increased the influence of less powerful, uncommitted nations.   For both super powers are anxious to preserve good relations with them.   The Soviet Union refrained from pressing its Troika proposal and its opposition to the U. N. operation in the Congo, because it did not wish to quarrel with the emergent states— especially in Africa.

For the rest I believe that these fears can be overcome gradually as the nations not only realise the disastrous dangers of the existing situation, but experience in one field after another the consequence of sacrificing sovereignty and realise that this is neither so dangerous nor so damaging as they supposed.

The fears are not indestructible.   Far from giving up, therefore, we should redouble our efforts, which should take two forms.

First there is a great need to increase enormously the educational and propaganda work of World Government.   I fully realise the almost insuperable difficulty of doing this in Communist States.   But we should not be deterred by this.   After all, we are not asking for any unilateral scrapping of defences.

Somehow we have got to get more and more people seriously considering the prospect of World Government, thinking about it as a real possibility, getting more and more accustomed to the idea.

Can we not have a single definitive plan on which we could all agree—all the various Associations who really accept the same ultimate aim?

Can we not have, for example, debates on the subject in the Assembly of the United Nations—leading up to the Charter Review Conference of 1965? Can we not now set about the task of creating a great and powerful Movement for World Government to enlist the maximum volume of support behind it?

But major institutional changes are a long term aim.   A Movement of this kind will only thrive if there are short term objectives as well.

In part these will be provided by the march of events.   It should be one of the functions of the Movement to take a stand on particular issues—in favour of action which clearly leads in the direction of World Government, against action which is opposed to this. Admittedly, not every case is straightforward, but there have been enough instances in recent years, about which there has surely been no doubt.

But there should also be, I suggest, a specific short term programme to which the Movement commits itself. In effect, this would contain the next steps towards World Government. All of them involve sacrifices of sovereignty, all of them involve greater support for international institutions.

Here are eight points which might be included in such a programme:

1 The establishment of the nucleus of a permanent international police force.

2 The creation of a World Development Organisation to ensure that this decade really is a decade of development with the necessary supervisory authority over the international economic agencies.

3 The setting up now by the United Nations of a Disarmament Agency not only to supervise the execution of a Disarmament Agreement but to help to secure it.

4 Reform of the United Nations financial arrangements so that member states are obliged to pay their allotted share of the U. N. operations whether or not they approve of particular projects.

5 Fullest support for the diplomatic activity of the Secretary General and his staff—and firm opposition to anything like the Troika proposals.

6 Reform of the Security Council and the Economic and Social Council so as to make them more representative—particularly of the large number of newer nations which have come into existence recently.

7 A greater effort to make the United Nations universal, including in particular the admission of the Peking Government of China.

8 The acceptance by member states of decisions of the Security Council and recommendations of the Assembly when carried by an overwhelming majority.

There is no short cut to World Government. Nor can we see the road all the way, but a Movement which advances on the two fronts—long term aims and short term objectives—would, I believe, command a great volume of support.

One last thought. The progress of this cause requires the active support of governments. It has been suggested by a distinguished American, Mr. Grenville Clark, that the British Government is well qualified to take the initiative—because of its political experience, because of its world-wide connections through the Commonwealth, because it is not a super power, because, though an important and loyal member of NATO, it is not fanatical in its attitude to Communism. Whether these qualifications are valid or appropriate, it is for others to say. In any case, the less individual nations arrogate virtues to themselves the better. But for my part I should be proud to see the British Government, in association with other like-minded governments, take a full part in this great enterprise. It is very much the kind of role I believe my country should play in the world today. I am sure that many others—in Western Europe and the Commonwealth and elsewhere— would gladly join with us.

We hear today of the various "blocs" in the United Nations Assembly. How encouraging if there were also a Pro-World-Government bloc!

Or if Party is a more attractive name to the supporters of World Parliament, why not make the first Party in the Assembly the Party for World Government?

It is even possible to detect in the recent history of the United Nations the beginning of such a group. What is needed now is to strengthen it, to clarify its principles and purposes and to put behind it the voices of millions of the world's citizens who see no other hope for humanity.

NOTES AND QUESTIONS

1. Pope John's emphasis upon the common good and more specifically on the Universal Declaration of Human Rights clearly associates him with those who believe that supranational authority is not desirable unless it is accompanied by minimal social and economic justice. However, Pope John does not state explicitly that these guarantees of social and political justice are the responsibility of the supranational authority.

2. In other parts of the encyclical Pope John makes a strong plea for general and complete disarmament and couples that plea with the obligation of the heavily industrialized states to aid the underprivileged of the world to achieve more satisfactory material living conditions. In these significant respects, then, Pope John's encyclical expresses a view of what is necessary for a stable peace system that resembles that developed in the Clark-Sohn plan.

The Causes of War and of Peace   2

This chapter is an introduction to the study of war. It surveys the main lines of explanation that have been given to account for past wars. No more than a minimum intellectual context can be given. The literature on war is vast. The subject of war has fascinated and perplexed man for centuries. Many heroic attempts have been made to give *the explanation* of why warfare is so prevalent in human history. None has proved to be entirely satisfactory. No single explanation of war has been accepted by a consensus of either scholars or statesmen. What exists is a bewildering variety of partial explanations, the better of which shed light on some aspects of the causative processes that eventuate in war. See Luther L. Bernard, *War and Its Causes* (Holt, New York, 1944); Morris Ginsburg, "The Causes of War," *Sociological Review*, vol. 31 (1939) p. 121.

We begin with a chapter from Quincy Wright's impressive work entitled *A Study of War* (unabridged ed., University of Chicago Press, 1965). This is probably the most authoritative, and certainly the most comprehensive, recent account of war. It is a great synthesis of all the thinking and experience on the subject. The short selection included here enumerates causal explanations for six great periods of warfare in human history. Wright also adds a helpful discussion of what it means to talk of the "cause" of war. Nothing is resolved by Wright's chapter, but the range of explanations that have been put forward to account for some of the great wars of the past are reviewed. Do these explanations "fit" the conditions of conflict today, so that if war breaks out it will be possible to choose from the stockpile of explanation assembled by Wright? Note that contemporary writing on the risk of nuclear war emphasizes accident, miscalculation, escalation, and catalytic agency. See Kahn, Chapter I. Does this suggest a shift in the causal basis of war in the nuclear age reflecting the awareness that major war is no longer likely to be a product of rational choice? Does this emphasis suggest a loss of human freedom and an acceptance of what might be called "technological determinism"?

QUINCY WRIGHT

Analysis of the Causes of War

Scientific method is a process involving definition of a problem through formulation of hypotheses, analysis of the problem through defining the constant and variable factors suggested by the hypotheses, solution of the problem through testing the various hypotheses and selecting the best, and formulation of the solution so that deductions can be drawn from it for application to actual conditions.[1]

It is difficult to apply this method in the social sciences because of the problems of contingency, purpose, universal change, and universal inter-relatedness, all stemming from the important role of man's expanding knowl-edge and increasing control of the conditions of his life.[2] This makes it necessary to consider not only variations in the phenomena meant (denoted) by a word but also variations in the meaning (connotation) of the word.[3]

---

[1] Scientific method as a logical activity may be distinguished from scientific technique, a manipulative activity. The latter consists of procedures of observation, measurement, and manipulation of the material phenomena involved in a problem in order to test hypotheses (see Abraham Wolf, "Scientific Method," *Encyclopaedia Britannica* [14th ed.], XX, 127).

[2] See chap. xvi above; Appen. XXV below.

[3] The relationship between phenomena, concepts, and words in applying scientific method in the social sciences may be illustrated by the word "liberty," which is defined in the *Standard Dictionary* as "the state of being exempt from the domination of others." Applying this con-ception, one can characterize different classes of people (slaves, serfs, freemen) as having increasing degrees of liberty, because they are in decreasing degree subject to the direction of people vested with authority over them by law. One can do this, however, only if the words in the definition are assumed to have a constant meaning. Suppose a society is so com-pletely co-ordinated by propaganda that people, instead of resenting direction of their lives by authority, welcome such direction because they believe that they can be assured security and livelihood only by the general acceptance of such direction. They resent failures of their neigh-bors to accept the orders of authority because they believe such failure will tend to deprive them of security and livelihood. Thus to them the words "domination by others" come to mean, not comprehensive direction of the individual's life by legal authority, but interference in his life without authority. People in such a society, reading the history of a society in which the law distinguishes slaves, serfs, and freemen, might decide that the freemen had the least liberty because their activities were continually interfered with by other freemen, who, without any explicit legal authority but because of free competition, deprived them of opportunities to sell and buy and make profits, while, on the other hand, the slaves might be considered to have the most liberty because their lives were entirely protected from outside interference by the masters vested with legal authority to direct them. See Pitirim Sorokin's distinction between "ideational" and "secular" freedom (*Social and Cultural Dynamics* [New York, 1937], III, 168); A. F. Pollard's discussion of the changing meaning of political terms (*Factors in Modern History* [3d ed.; London, 1932]); C. K. Ogden's distinction between words, thoughts, and things (*Bentham's Theory of Fictions* [New York, 1932], p. xii); and above, Vol. I, chap. vii, n. 38.

It has, therefore, been necessary to consider carefully the definition of war.[4]

War has been defined as the legal condition which equally permits two or more hostile groups to carry on a conflict by armed force. This definition suggests that the existence of a war at any time and place depends upon the social comprehension of certain concepts as well as upon their factual realization. War implies that both the participating and the nonparticipating members of the inclusive group within which war takes place understand the concepts "legal equality," "intergroup hostility," "conflict," and "armed force." Concepts are a social invention. Consequently, war in this sense is a social invention. People who do not utilize these concepts may have violent conflicts, but they do not have war.[5] The meaning of these concepts, however, has not been constant in history. International law has modified its criteria of "war" with changing political conditions.[6] Public opinion, with the development of new means of communication, has interpreted intergroup hostility by new signs. Governments, with the progress of social change, have altered their notions of the circumstances which imply an intergroup contention or conflict.[7] Few would agree with Bismarck today that economic strife is entirely compatible with diplomatic harmony.[8] The military profession has altered its conception of armed force with the progress of technical and social invention. Admiral Hussey recognized "the interdependence of the armed and the unarmed forces," suggesting that war today is a struggle of propagandas as well as of military forces.[9]

While it would be difficult enough to predict the future occurrence of war if the criteria for deciding what war is were constant, the solution becomes indeterminate when these criteria are changing. When the concepts, constituting the frame of reference of a problem, resemble rubber dollars or expanding yardsticks, they must be treated as parameters yielding indeterminate equations in any scientific formulation of the problem. This very changeability of the criteria, however, makes war even more controllable. The problem can be attacked from two sides: by changing the facts which

[4]See Chap. xvii above.

[5]Margaret Mead, "Warfare Is Only an Invention, Not a Biological Necessity," *Asia,* XL (August, 1940), 402 ff.

[6]William Ballis, *The Legal Position of War: Changes in Its Practice and Theory from Plato to Vattel* (The Hague, 1937); Luigi Sturzo, *The International Community and the Right of War* (New York, 1930); Quincy Wright, "Changes in the Conception of War," *American Journal of International Law,* XVIII (October, 1924), 755 ff.

[7]See, e.g., the varying attitudes taken by different governments as to utterances from foreign officials and writers which should be regarded as offensive: Vernon Van Dyke, "The Responsibility of States for International Propaganda," *American Journal of International Law,* XXXIV (January, 1940), 58ff.; H. Lauterpacht, "Revolutionary Activities by Private Persons against Foreign States," *American Journal of International Law,* XXII (1928), 105 ff.; Sidney Hyman, "State Responsibility for the Hostile Utterances of Its Officers" (manuscript thesis, University of Chicago Library, 1938).

[8]W. B. Harvey, "Tariffs and International Relations in Europe, 1860–1914" (manuscript thesis, University of Chicago Library, 1938), pp. 20 ff.

[9]C. R. Fish, N. Angell, and C. L. Hussey, *American Policies Abroad: The United States and Great Britain* (Chicago, 1932), p. 208.

have been called war and by changing the concepts which required that certain facts be called war. The latter process may appear analogous to the alleged practice of the ostrich in burying its head in the sand, but, because of the influence of ideas upon human behavior, this analogy is inaccurate. A formally arranged combat between two persons with fatal consequences was at one time recognized in many systems of law as a legitimate procedure of dueling. It is said that two thousand men of noble birth died from this form of activity in France between 1601 and 1609. The substitution of "murder" as the legal term applicable to this behavior has had important consequences. Events which in fact, if not in law, are duels still occur, but the casualties are less considerable.[10] The change in the legal designation of international hostilities found to have been undertaken contrary to legal obligation from "war" to "agression" may also in time have important practical results.[11]

To determine the causes of war it is, therefore, necessary to investigate possible changes in the meaning of the concepts by which war has been defined[12] and also to investigate probable changes in the circumstances denoted at the present time by these concepts.

The latter investigation, to be undertaken in this part of the study, will be facilitated by formulating hypotheses. Numerous hypotheses have been made on the subject by the various social disciplines, but none has been generally accepted by any of them.[13] What hypotheses are worth examination?

The most probable hypotheses on the causes of war may be ascertained by comparing propositions which appear in the literature with propositions resulting from an analysis of the history of actual wars.[14] The latter will be considered first. Six major conflicts in the West since the fall of Rome have been selected for study: the conquests of Islam (622–732), the Crusades (1095–1270), the Hundred Years' War (1339–1453), the Thirty Years' War (1618–48), the French Revolutionary and Napoleonic Wars (1793–1815), and World War I (1914–1920).

1. CAUSES OF SIX MAJOR WARS

The historians of each of these wars have usually distinguished idealistic, psychological, political, and juridical elements in their causation.[15] They have frequently referred to changes in climate, resources, economy, tech-

---

[10]See below, chap.xxiii, sec. 5.

[11]Such a change has been attributed to the Pact of Paris. One practical result has been the acknowledgment of the freedom of parties to the pact who are nonparticipants in a war to discriminate against the aggressor. See Q. Wright, "The Lend-Lease Bill and International Law," *American Journal of International Law,* XXXV (April, 1941), 305 ff.; Robert H. Jackson, attorney-general of the United States, "Address to Inter-American Bar Association, Havana, Cuba, March 27, 1941," *American Journal of International Law,* XXXV (April, 1941), 348 ff.

[12]Below, chaps. xxxiv and xxxviii.

[13]Above, chap. xviii.

[14]This process may be compared to that utilized in framing a definition of war. The definitions of war in the literature were compared with those suggested by a study of the actual phenomena of war (see above, chap. xvii).

[15]The historian Bishop William Stubbs thought social ideas, political forces, and legal rights had, respectively, accounted for recent, post-Renaissance, and medieval wars, but he

nology, and other material conditions, but they have usually assumed that such changes can cause war only in so far as they influence one or more of these socio-psychological patterns.

a) Moslem conquests.—Islam carried on wars of conquest in the seventh century. The new religion, by fixing attention upon common symbols, had inspired many of the Arabs with a missionary zeal.

Mohammed's preaching would probably not have been sucessful if the Arabs had been a contented people. They were harassed by pressures upon their frontiers from Persia to the east, Abyssinia and Yemen to the south, and the Eastern Empire to the west, by inter-tribal hostilities arising from traditional feuds, and by the increasing difficulties of making a living, perhaps due to a drying-up of the climate and to overpopulation.

A new idea, falling upon a soil fertilized by unrest and discontent, provided the opportunity for political leaders to create a state. Mohammed, Abu Bekr, Omar, and Othman, from A.D. 622 to 656, saw that internal strife could be stilled and political unity preserved by directing aggressive and acquisitive impulses externally. Their military ability, utilizing the technique of light cavalry, made it possible to use war as an instrument of political power until the area of the conquest became too large and the burdens of administration too great.

But with all their military ability they would not have succeeded had not the traditional thinking of the Arabs regarded war as a natural procedure, had not the doctrine of the jihad justifying wars for the spread of Islam been accepted, and had not adequate *casus belli* been sufficiently established by the refusal of the surrounding tribes, kingdoms, and empires to accept formal offers to become Moslem.[16]

b) The Crusades.—Historians of the Crusades have similarly emphasized the renewed enthusiasm for Christianity due to the preaching of Pope Gregory VII and Pope Urban II. These orators dwelt upon the indignities to which the Seljuk Turks were subjecting the holy places and the pilgrims after the capture of Jerusalem in 1071 and upon the appeals for help from the Eastern Empire.

Historians have also referred to the attitudes, receptive to distant adventure, provided by the widespread misery in the West caused by Norse invasions, depredations by feudal barons, and the serious pestilences of 1094 and 1095.

admitted that all played a part in all wars. He wrote before historians had joined the cult of economic and psychological determinism (*Lectures on the Study of Medieval and Modern History* [Oxford, 1886], p. 209). Historians have seldom used these words with much precision. Apparently "idealistic" includes social, religious, and other values springing from the group culture. "Psychological" includes economic, adventurous, and other motives springing from the individual's personality. "Political" includes defensive, aggrandizing, and other purposes springing from actual or potential governing authority. "Juridical" includes remedial, preventive, acquisitive, reformatory, and other claims springing from the prevailing ideas of law and justice (see below, n. 24). This classification of historic causes of war differs from the classification of individual motives for war (religious, political, cultural, and economic) discussed in Vol. I, chap. xi, n. 17, though the two are related. Historic causes result from the relatively permanent social patterning of certain individual motives in a given society.

[16]Majid Khadduri, *The Law of War and Peace in Islam* (London, 1940), pp. 19 ff., 23 ff.

The political ambitions of the pope to unify Christendom, of princes to gain prestige and territory, and of Italian towns to re-establish profitable trade routes were another factor.

Back of these lay the ideology of just war developed by theologians and legists since Augustine. This ideology recognized the justice of war under-taken to promote justice and came to consider the *bellum Romanum*, or war against the infidels, as a type of just war. To this juridical ideology, as well as to the idealism of Christian faith and the hope of political union of Christendom, Pope Urban successfully appealed at Clermont on November 26, 1095. "Let the truce of God be observed at home and let the arms of Christians be directed to conquering the infidels in an expedition which should count for full and complete penance."[17]   These factors—religious idealism, social unrest, political ambition, and accepted legal theory—which began the First Crusade in 1095 can be traced in the successive stages of these expeditions.[18]

c) The Hundred Years' War between Great Britain and France can be similarly analyzed. Here it was not religion but incipient national enthusiasm which inspired the British invaders of France. Until the later stages of the war, however, this idealistic element was less important than in the two instances already mentioned. In the latter part of the war French nationalism, stimulated by the leadership of Joan of Arc, inspired a people who had long endured the miseries of invasion to turn upon and drive out the English.

English economy, affected by the increasingly monopolistic tendency of the guilds and large landholders, did not distribute its benefits as equally in the fourteenth as it had in the thirteenth century. The Scotch wars added to the burdens of the people and the spirit of the army, thus creating a sentiment hospitable to adventure among many. The retaliations between Edward and Philip over the Flemish trade had injured economic interests both in England and in Flanders. The miseries of the Black Death, which began in 1348 soon after the Battle of Crècy, assisted in keeping the war alive.

Edward's political ambition to achieve glory, to unite his country, to prevent rebellion such as had forced the abdication of his father, to retain his feudal titles in France, and to add to his domain was doubtless the major factor originating the war. The successes of the technique of archery in the Scotch wars convinced him that the enterprise was practicable.

It was important, however, for Edward to find a *casus belli* which would justify war according to the legal conceptions of the time. This he did in 1338 by the discovery that Philip of France was helping his Scottish enemies and by the revival of ancient claims to the French crown. Defense against hostile acts and recovery of feudal titles were just causes of war according

[17]D. C. Munro, "Speech of Pope Urban II," *American Historical Review,* XI (1906), 239.

[18]Stubbs, *op. cit.,* p. 221; see above, Vol. I, chap. vii, n. 89.

to the Christian doctrine as expounded three-quarters of a century earlier by Thomas Aquinas.[19]

d) The Thirty Years' War found its idealistic basis in the religious revival stemming from the Reformation and dividing Europe into Catholic and Protestant camps, though Bohemian nationalism was a factor at its beginning, as were Dutch, Swiss, Danish, Swedish, and French nationalisms in later stages.

Its social background lay in the economic changes which had been deteriorating the relative position of agriculture and expanding trade and industry since the discoveries. These changes were manifested by a great increase in the use of coal in the sixteenth century. Many of the rich were getting poor and some of the formerly poor were becoming rich.

The political ambition of rising monarchs, rendered confident by their new type of disciplined armies, especially in France, Sweden, and Prussia, was a major factor in the later stages of the war. Beginning as a religious war, it ended as a war for territorial sovereignty.

International law had been changing since the secularism of the Renaissance had led to the rise of sovereign princes, substituting Machiavelli for Aquinas as their practical Bible. Reason of state was sufficient ground for intervention by France, England, Denmark, and Sweden in the later stages of the war, in a manner suggestive of the interventions in the Spanish civil war of 1937–38 by Italy, Germany, and Russia. In its origins, however, good medieval grounds for war were found in the contentions by the utraquists that the emperor's ecclesiastical interventions violated the Bohemian constitution and by the emperor Ferdinand that the Protestant revolt in Bohemia in 1618 impugned his authority and that Frederick of Austria was usurping the Bohemian throne. As in so many other wars, the increasing miseries brought on by the war provided human attitudes ready to believe that any fire would be better than the frying pan in which they found themselves—attitudes from which armies could be recruited and the war continued.[20]

e) The French Revolutionary and Napoleonic Wars were inspired by the idealism of the rights of man and the new religion of democratic nationalism with a missionary zeal to spread its benefits to mankind.

The miseries in France stemming from royal extravagance and debt which had led to dissatisfaction by provincial magnates and to inequitable taxation of the peasants and the city proletariat has been emphasized in literature such as Dickens' *Tale of Two Cities*. While this misery may not have been so great in France as in Germany, the people were more conscious of it

---

[19]David Hume (*History of England*, chap. XV) emphasizes the legal claims and political ambitions, G. B. Adams (*Civilization during the Middle Ages* [New York, 1903], pp. 332 and 335) emphasizes the nationalistic ideals, and E. P. Cheyney (*A Short History of England* [Boston, 1904], p. 231) emphasizes the economic and psychological motives behind this war.

[20]Stubbs, *op. cit.*, p. 230; C. V. Wedgwood, *The Thirty Years' War* (New Haven, 1939).

because they had known better times.[21]

The leaders of the Revolution saw the need to defend their newly acquired political power from the conservative, *émigré*-stimulated interventions from abroad. In later stages of the conflict the value of war as an instrument of international prestige, of internal solidarity, and of conquest was appreciated by Napoleon, whose military ability generally assured victory. For the governments of other states, from a political necessity to defend their institutions from the infection of revolutionary ideas, the war became an essential instrument to preserve the balance of power against Napoleon, who, utilizing new techniques to maintain morale and increase mobility, threatened their very existence.

In the international law of the time reason of state was now an adequate *casus belli*. The French declaration of war against Austria on April 20, 1792, signed by Louis XVI under pressure from a Girondist cabinet, was ostensibly based upon the refusal of the emperor Francis II to disavow the Declaration of Pilnitz (August 27, 1791), which had asserted the restoration of order and the maintenance of the monarchy in France to be a common interest of all sovereigns. The French thus justified war as a necessary resistance to foreign intervention in the internal affairs of France.[22]

f) World War I developed from nationalistic movements in the Balkans. The Allies fought to defend small nationalities such as Serbia and Belgium. The self-determination of nationalities, together with the organization of the world to prevent war and to make the world safe for democracy, was elaborated in the later stages after the entry of America. The idealism of democracy and nationalism had achieved general acceptance during the nineteenth century through the writings of Mazzini and the exploits of Bismarck, Cavour, and Lincoln.

There were economic difficulties and unrest in the Balkans brought on by two years of Balkan wars; the armament race which had been proceeding among the great powers for a decade had been generally augmenting taxes, and rising tariff barriers and more intense economic rivalries in backward areas were developing concern for the future in certain commercial circles. There was not, however, sufficient misery or fear to provide soil for widespread acceptance of radical doctrines until war itself had produced them. After three years of war, Wilsonian self-determination and Leninist communism gained widespread acceptance.

The primary causes for the war were political: the Austrian anxiety to preserve itself in the face of Yugoslav propaganda, the Russian fear of declining prestige in the other Slavic countries, the French hope to recover Alsace-Lorraine, and the German and British fear for the balance of power. Prussian military efficiency displayed in the Bismarckian wars and cultivated

---

[21]See Guy Stanton Ford, *Stein and the Era of Reform in Prussia* (Princeton, 1922), chap. i.

[22]Ferdinand Schevill, *A Political History of Modern Europe* (New York, 1907), pp. 349 ff., 365 ff.; F. M. Anderson, *The Constitutions and Other Select Documents Illustrative of the History of France, 1889–1901* (Minneapolis, 1904), p. 103.

since, loss of prestige by the central alliance in the Moroccan crises, and political disorders in France and the British Empire encouraged Germany to support the Austrian initiative.

The legal grounds in the early declarations of war emphasized defense against acts of aggression and assistance to enemies, violations of guaranties, and reasons of state. The later declarations referred to principles of justice, humanity, democracy, and international law. International law, except in the case of neutralized Belgium, imposed at this time no legal limits on the competence of states to initiate war, but the Hague Convention of 1907 required a statement of reason, and those given indicated the popular notion of just war prevailing at the time.[23]

Different as were many of the circumstances, each of these six great wars, scattered over thirteen hundred years, exhibit idealistic, psychological, political, and juridical causes. It appears that in these varying conditions of civilization individuals and masses have been moved to war (1) because of enthusiasm for ideals expressed in the impersonal symbols of a religion, a nation, an empire, a civilization, or humanity, the blessings of which it is thought may be secured or spread by coercion of the recalcitrant; or (2) because of the hope to escape from conditions which they find unsatisfactory, inconvenient, perplexing, unprofitable, intolerable, dangerous, or merely boring. Conditions of this kind have produced unrest and have faciliated the acceptance of ideals and violent methods for achieving them. Governments and organized factions have initiated war (3) because in a particular situation war appeared to them a necessary or convenient means to carry out a foreign policy; to establish, maintain, or expand the power of a govenment, party, or class within the state; to maintain or expand the power of the state in relation to other states; or to reorganize the community of nations; or (4) because incidents have occurred or circumstances have arisen which they thought violated law and impaired rights and for which war was the normal or expected remedy according to the jural standards of the time.[24]

2. OPINIONS ON THE CAUSES OF WAR

The phrase "causes of war" has been used in many senses. Writers have declared the cause of World War I to have been the Russian or the German mobilization; the Austrian ultimatum; the Sarajevo assassination; the aims and ambitions of the Kaiser, Poincaré, Izvolsky, Berchtold, or someone else; the desire of France to recover Alsace-Lorraine or of Austria to dominate the Balkans; the European system of alliances; the activities of the munition-makers, the international bankers, or the diplomats; the lack of an adequate European political order; armament rivalries; colonial rivalries; commercial policies; the sentiment of nationality; the concept of sovereignty;

---

[23]Bernadotte Schmitt, *The Coming of the War: 1914* (New York, 1930); Sidney B. Fay, *The Origins of the World War* (New York, 1928). For texts of declarations of war see United States Naval War College, *International Law Documents, 1917* (Washington, 1918).

the struggle for existence; the tendency of nations to expand; the unequal distribution of population, of resources, or of planes of living; the law of diminishing returns; the value of war as an instrument of national solidarity or as an instrument of national policy; ethnocentrism or group egotism; the failure of the human spirit; and many others.[25]

To some a cause of war is an event, condition, act, or personality involved only in a particular war; to others it is a general proposition applicable to many wars. To some it is a class of human motives, ideals, or values; to others it is a class of impersonal forces, conditions, processes, patterns, or relations. To some it is the entrance or injection of a disturbing factor into a stable situation; to others it is the lack of essential conditions of stability in the situation itself or the human failure to realize potentialities. These differences of opinion reflect different meanings of the word "cause." The three sentences, respectively, contrast causes of war in the historic and scientific senses, in the practical and scientific senses, and the historic and practical senses.[26]

In the scientific sense the cause of the changes in any variable is a change in any other variable in a proposition stating the relations of all the factors in a process or equilibrium.[27] Sometimes the statement itself is elliptically spoken of as the cause of variations in any of its factors. Thus it is sometimes said that heavenly bodies and falling apples behave as they do because of the law of gravitation or that rent is paid because of the law of dimin-

[24]These four types of causes of war may be classified according to their relative objectivity, concreteness, and historicity. Political and juridical causes are more objective than ideal and psychological causes because they develop from more completely institutionalized social patterns. Psychological and political causes are more concrete than ideal and juridical causes because they emphasize circumstances of the immediate time, place, and leadership rather than propositions deemed to have a wide validity. Psychological and juridical causes emphasize circumstances and conditions developed from the past while idealistic and political causes emphasize purposes and objectives of the future. See above, n. 15.

[25]Most of the concrete causes are discussed in a series of articles on "Assessing Blame for the World War" (*New York Times Current History,* May and June, 1924, reprinted in H. E. Barnes, *In Quest of Truth and Justice* [Chicago, 1928], pp. 84 ff.); see also n. 23 above. Most of the abstract causes are referred to in Conference on the Cause and Cure of War, *Findings* (Washington, 1925), pp. 1–2, and other articles reprinted in Julia E. Johnson (ed.), *Selected Articles on War—Cause and Cure* (New York, 1926), pp. 117 ff., 139 ff.

[26]See above, Vol. I, chap. ii, sec. 3. The term "causes of war" refers in this study to "efficient causes" which precede the outbreak of war. Confusion often arises because of the failure to distinguish such causes from "final causes" or purposes which may develop during the course of war. The efficient causes of a war are sometimes erroneously supposed to determine the purposes or war aims of the belligerents, and the purposes of the belligerents are sometimes erroneously supposed to have been the efficient causes of the war. The purposes of a belligerent, if formulated as an ideal, policy, or grievance before the war begins, may be an efficient cause of the war. It may happen, however, that the purposes of the belligerents have not been so formulated and exercise very little influence on the outbreak of war. Furthermore, the purposes of belligerents may change greatly during the course of the war. The purposes of the belligerents, particularly of the victor, are, however, of importance in understanding the peace after the war. A war usually gives the victor the opportunity to determine the shape of international relations for a time after the war; for how long a time depends on the wisdom with which this opportunity is utilized.

[27]See above, Vol. I, chap. ii, secs. 4 and 5; chap. xvi; below, Appen. XXV.

ishing returns.[28] A scientific statement usually asserts that if all factors can be ignored, except those observable, controllable, and presumptively measurable factors which it deals with as variables, parameters, or constants, a specified degree of change in any variable tends to be followed immediately or in a specified time by a specified degree of change in the other variables.

In the historic sense a cause is any event or condition figuring in the description of the relevant antecedents of an effect. Such a description is usually called a history and is confined to events within a time or space sufficiently near to the effect to be presumably related to it. Proximity in time or space thus establishes a presumption of causal relation, though this presumption ought to be confirmed by other evidence to avoid the *post hoc* fallacy. Evidence may indicate that proximate events were unrelated, and it may also indicate the transmission of influence from remote times and distant places.[29]

In the practical sense a cause is any controllable element in the statement of the origin, treatment, solution, or meaning of a problem or situation.   Such statements in medicine are called diagnoses, prognoses, prophylaxes, or treatments, and in social affairs, reports, interpretations, programs, policies, or plans. Such statements of social problems usually emphasize the human actions responsible for the situation and the human actions deemed to be the most effective for realizing desired ends in the circumstances of the time and place where the statement is made.[30]

It will be observed that in none of these cases is the word "cause" used as something which exists in phenomena but as something which exists in statements or propositions about phenomena. If one is convinced that a proposition is true,[31] he means that he is convinced that the proposition accurately describes the phenomena. Consequently, if the truth of a proposition has

[28]More accurate statements of these two propositions might be worded: "because motion has a relation to the masses of and the distance between bodies" and "because rent has a relation to the demand for land which arises because successive applications of capital and labor to a given piece of land yield a diminishing return."

[29]See Vol. I, chap. iii. The law considers direct and not remote causes in attributing responsibility, but "it is not merely distance of place or of causation that renders a cause remote. The cause nearest in order of causation, which is adequate without any efficient concurring cause to produce the result, may be considered the direct cause" (J. Bouvier, "Causa Proxima," *A Law Dictionary* [Philadelphia, 1872], I, 247, citing Thomas, J., 4 Gray, Mass. 412; Bacon, Max. Reg. 1; Story, J., 14 Pet. 99). The legal sense of causation resembles the practical rather than the historical sense of the term because causes are selected in legal proceedings to impute responsibility rather than to explain happenings (see below, nn. 50 and 52).

[30]See below, chap. xxxviii. Practical causation assumes evaluation, that is, a distinction between events or conditions which are pathological, undesirable, illegal, or immoral and those which are healthy, satisfactory, legal, or righteous. See G. K. K. Link, "The Role of Genetics in Etiological Pathology," *Quarterly Review of Biology,* VIII (June, 1932), 127 ff.; above, Vol. I, Appen. IV, n. 4. Stephen Taylor, a Voice in the Wilderness ("Grains and Scruples," *Lancet,* CCXXXV [1938], 909 ff.), treats war as a pathological condition of society. He presents the clinical picture, etiology, prognosis, prophylaxis, and treatment of this condition.

[31]Conviction of the truth of a proposition should arise from consideration of the cogency of the *evidence* supporting the proposition, the clarity of the *definition* of its terms, the reli-

been established, then the word "cause" can be considered either a term of the proposition or a phenomenon designated by the term. While superficially the scientific, historic, and practical senses of the word "cause" appear to be very different, fundamentally they are merely different approaches to the same concept. A cause of an entity, an event, or a condition is a term of a true proposition capable of explaining, predicting, or controlling its existence or changes.[32]

a) Scientific causes of war.—Scientists, in searching for the causes of phenomena, assume that the universal and the particular are aspects of one reality. They attempt to classify, combine, or analyze particular events into general concepts or ideas which represent measurable, controllable, repeatable, and observable phenomena capable of being treated as variables or constants in a formula.[33]

While scientists realize that there are events in any field of study which

ability of its *sources*, and the persuasiveness of its *assumptions*. The words "evidence," "definition," "source," and "assumption" have been confused with the word "cause," partly because of Aristotle's association of material, formal, first, and final causes with efficient causes. The latter is the sense in which the word is used here. "Evidence" refers to experiences or the records or testimony concerning experiences (observations, feelings, experiments) of the past which induce the belief that a proposition is true. "Definition" refers to the meaning of a word in a particular connection, that is, to the precise delimitation of a term. "Source" refers to the writing or document which first established the truth of a proposition to the satisfaction of a given society or discipline. Darwin's *Origin of Species* is in this sense the source of the doctrine of evolution and Newton's *Principia* of the law of gravitation. In law the word "source" usually refers to a class of written materials considered by the profession as credentials to the validity of a legal proposition, such as statutes, judicial precedents, treaties, custom, juristic writing, etc. "Assumption," or basis, refers to the axioms or postulates which persuade a given mind or society that the evidence demonstrates the truth of a proposition. In this sense the continuity of nature is the basis for most scientific laws, common sense is the basis for most historical laws, and general consent is today the basis of most practical and jural laws. In a broad sense the basis of a proposition is the sanction of its validity. As the sanction of geometry is the self-evident character of its axioms and postulates resting on the continuity of nature, so the sanction of jural law is the general belief that its basis—whether general consent, divine right, or natural law—gives assurance that the institutions of the society will have power to enforce the rules and orders legally promulgated. The fact that general consent is the basis for many propositions about society, and that this may be affected by the form in which the evidence and sources of the proposition and the definition of its terms are presented to the public, means that the truth of propositions in the social field may be influenced by propaganda. The distinction between the definition, the basis, the sources, the evidences, and the causes of international law are often discussed by writers on that subject. See L. Oppenheim, *International Law* (5th ed.; London, 1937) Vol. I, secs. 1, 5, 11, 15; A. S. Hershey, *The Essentials of International Public Law and Organization* (New York, 1927), chap. ii.

[32]In saying that "the cause of a certain effect is the totality of conditions that is sufficient to produce it," Abraham Wolf ("Causality," *Encyclopaedia Britannica* [14th ed.], V, 63) uses the term "cause" as equivalent to "total cause." Usage permits partial causes, conditions, or factors contributing to an effect to be referred to as causes of the effect, or even as the cause of the effect under circumstances which permit other factors in the total causation to be ignored. Strictly speaking, a factor contributing to or accounting for an effect is not its cause. The cause is the factor in relation to others, including the effect. Since relations are manifested in language rather than in phenomena, a cause should be thought of as a term in a proposition rather than as a factor in a situation, although, if the proposition is true, the two are equivalent.

[33]See Appen. XXV below.

have not yet been included in classes which can be precisely defined or measured, they are reluctant to believe that any factors are permanently "vague" and "imponderable"—a belief frequently held by practical men, historians, and poets.[34] In dealing with war, scientists prefer concepts such as military forces, public opinion, attitudes, population, and international trade, which have been measured, even though crudely, or concepts such as jurisdiction, arbitration, war, aggression, and right, which have a precise meaning in a body of law, rather than such concepts as personal influence, civilizing mission, imperialism, accidental events, and social potentialities, which have neither of these characteristics. They prefer concepts which denote things which can be manipulated and experimented with, though this is often difficult in the social sciences. They prefer concepts which represent series of events that appear continuously or in regular cycles or oscillations in history, so that interpolation or extrapolation is possible where data are lacking. They prefer concepts which represent classes of facts that are abundant in the records or in the contemporary world, so that the properties of these classes can be verified by the use of historical sources or observation.[35]

The scientifically minded have attempted to describe the normal functioning of the forces, interests, controls, and motives involved in international relations and to formulate abstract propositions relating, respectively, to the balance of power, to international law, to international organization, and to public opinion.[36] While they have sometimes included war as a periodic recurrence in such normal functioning, they have usually attributed war to the high degree of unmeasurability, uncontrollability, incompleteness, or uncertainty of the factors which they have studied. Thus they have attributed war (1) to the difficulty of maintaining stable equilibrium among the uncertain and fluctuating political and military forces within the state system;[37]

[34]Bismarck spoke of the importance of imponderables in politics. Historians recognize the important role of contingency in human affairs (Vol. I, Appen. IV, n. 8, above). Poets emphasize the significance of potentialities (chap. xxxviii, sec. 1, below).

[35]If language is taken into account, then we can distinguish science from other phases of human activity by agreeing that science shall deal only with events that are accessible in their time and place to any and all observers (strict behaviorism) or only with events that are placed in co-ordinates of time and space (*mechanism*), or that science shall employ only such initial statements and predictions as lead to definite handling operations (*operationalism*), or only terms such as are derivable by rigid definition from a set of everyday terms concerning physical happenings (*physicalism*). These several formulations, independently reached by different scientists, all lead to the same delimitation, and this delimitation does not restrict the subject matter of science but rather characterizes its method" (Leonard Bloomfield, *Linguistic Aspects of Science* ["International Encyclopedia of Unified Science," Vol. I, No. 4], p. 13). See also above, Vol. I, chap. ii, n. 20.

[36]See, e.g., David Hume, "Of the Balance of Power" (1st ed., 1751), in *Philosophical Works* (Boston, 1854), III, 364 ff.; Christian Wolff, *Jus genium methode scientifica pertractatum* (1st ed., 1749; Oxford, 1934); Immanuel Kant, *Eternal Peace* (1st ed., 1795; Boston, 1914); L. F. Richardson, *Generalized Foreign Politics* ("British Journal of Psychology: Monograph Series," Vol. XXIII [Cambridge, 1934]).

[37]C. J. Friedrich, *Foreign Policy in the Making* (New York, 1938), pp. 130 ff.; H. D. Lasswell, *World Politics and Personal Insecurity* (New York, 1935), pp. 57 ff. See below, chap. xx.

(2) to the inadequacy of its sources and sanctions continually to keep international law an effective analysis of the changing interests of states and the changing values of humanity;[38] (3) to the difficulty of so organizing political power that it can maintain internal order in a society not in relation to other societies external to itself;[39] and (4) to the difficulty of making peace a more important symbol in world public opinion than particular symbols which may locally, temporarily, or generally favor war.[40] In short, scientific investigators, giving due consideration to both the historic inertia and the inventive genius of mankind, have tended to attribute war to immaturities in social knowledge and control, as one might attribute epidemics to insufficient medical knowledge or to inadequate public health services.[41]

b) Historical causes of war.—Historians assume that the future is a development of the past which includes, however, forward-looking intentions and aspirations. They attempt to classify events into ideas which represent commonly observed processes of change and development.[42] Because of the common experience of small incidents releasing stored forces—the match and the fuse—they frequently distinguish the occasion from the causes of war.[43] Because people ordinarily think they are familiar with biological evolution, with psychological and sociological processes, with economic, political, and religious interests, historians have customarily classified the causes of war under such headings.[44]

This method may be illustrated by the causes of the Franco-Prussian War

---

[38]Sir J. F. Williams, *International Change and International Peace* (Oxford, 1932); H. Lauterpacht, *The Function of Law in the International Community* (Oxford, 1933); J. F. Dulles, *War, Peace and Change* (New York, 1939), pp. 29 ff.; Sterling E. Edmunds, *The Lawless Law of Nations* (Washington, 1925), pp. 3ff.; Q. Wright, "International Law and the World Order," in W. H. C. Laves (ed.), *The Foundations of a More Stable World Order* (Chicago, 1941), pp. 107 ff. See below, chap xxiii.

[39]Lasswell, *op. cit.*,p. 239; A. Maurois, *The Next Chapter: The War against the Moon* (London, 1927). See below, chap. xxvi.

[40]Norman Angell, *The Unseen Assassins* (London, 1937). See below, chap. xxx.

[41]J. J. Rousseau was convinced that the application of reason could produce peace ("Extrait du projet de paix perpetuelle," in W. E. Darby [ed.], *International Tribunals* [London, 1904], pp. 104 ff.; see above, Vol. I, Appen. III, n. 42). Kant believed that political improvement was only possible by the application of reason (*op. cit.,* p. 7) and that reason could only be applied to world-politics if statesmen followed the maxim, which to save their dignity they should keep secret, that "the maxims of the philosophers regarding the conditions of the possibility of a public peace shall be taken into consideration by the States that are armed for war" (*ibid.,* p. 100). See also W. E. Rappard, *The Quest for Peace* (Cambridge, Mass., 1940), pp. 497 ff.; I. W. Howerth, "Causes of War," *Scientific Monthly,* II (February, 1926), 118 ff.; Knight Dunlap, "The Causes and the Prevention of War," *Journal of Abnormal and Social Psychology,* XXXV (October, 1940), 479 ff. Scientific investigations of war have usually recognized the complexity of is causes and have seldom attributed war to a single cause as medical science sometimes attributes an illness to a specific germ. See below, n. 53.

[42]Above, Vol. I, Appen. IV, sec. 3.

[43]W. E. H. Lecky, *A History of the Rise and Influence of the Spirit of Rationalism in Europe* (London, 1870), II, 227; John Bakeless, *The Origin of the Next War* (New York, 1926), pp. 20 ff. They also distinguish the causes from the purposes of war (see above, n. 26).

[44]H. E. Barnes, *The Genesis of the World War* (New York, 1926), chap. i; Lecky, *op. cit.;* Conference on the Cause and Cure of War, *op. cit.*

set forth in Ploetz's *Manual of Universal History*.[45]   These are divided into "immediate causes," "special causes," and "general causes."   The first were said to be certain events which shortly preceded the war, including the election of the prince of Hohenzollern to the throne of Spain, the French demand that the Prussian king should never again permit the candidacy of the prince for the Spainish crown, and the Ems telegram from Bismarck announcing the king's refusal.   The special causes were said to be the internal troubles of the French government, the controversy concerning French compensation for the Prussian aggrandizement of 1866, and the news of new German infantry weapons threatening the superiority of the French chassepot.   The general causes were stated to be the French idea of natural frontiers as including the left bank of the Rhine and the long struggle of the German nation for unification, together with the French anxiety over it.

Historians have thus sought to demonstrate causes by drawing from a detailed knowledge of the antecedents of a particular war events, circumstances, and conditions which can be related to the war by practical, political, and juristic commonplaces about human motives, impulses, and intentions.   When they have written of the causes of war in a more general way, they have meant simply a classification of the causes of the particular wars in a given period of history.[46]   Thus certain of the causes of the Franco-Prussian War have been described by such words as "aggressive policies," "changes in military techniques," "domestic difficulties," "unsettled controversies," "dynastic claims," "aspirations for national unification," "historic rivalries," and "insulting communications."   Even broader generalizations have been made classifying the causes of war in the Western world as political, juristic, idealistic, and psychological.[47]

When generalization has reached this stage, the result is not unlike the scientific approach, for such words as "an ideal," "a psychological attitude," "a policy," or "a law" represent concepts which, though limited by the historian to a historic epoch, are universals which may be manifested in varying degrees in all times and places.   They are, in fact, variables susceptible, in theory, to mathematical treatment, however difficult it may be practically to measure their variations.

c) Practical causes of war.—Practical politicians, publicists, and jurists

---

[45]Karl Ploetz, *Manual of Universal History* (Boston, 1915), p. 513.

[46]Above, Vol. I, Appen. IV; Below, Vol. II, chap. xviii, sec. 1.

[47]Above, nn. 15 and 24.   This classification of the causes of war may be compared to the classification of the influence upon the frequency and magnitude of war of the development of civilization, discussed in Vol. I, chap. xv.   The fluctuations in the character of war were there related (1) to the development by the states in a balance-of-power system, of political, economic, social, and other contacts with outside communities (sec. 2b); (2) to the failure of legal and political centralization or decentralization among a group of states to keep pace with increases or decreases in their economic, social, or other contacts (sec. 2a); (3) to the tendency with the advance of a civilization for ideals, indicated by the pretexts for war, to become inconsistent with the actual motives or reasons for war (sec. 2d); and (4) to the variations in the intensity, homogeneity, and localization of pacifism and militarism in response to changes in the destructiveness of war (sec. 2e).

assume that changes result from free wills operating in an environment. They attempt to classify events according to the motives and purposes from which they seem to proceed.[48] Their assumptions have thus resembled those of the historians, though they have formulated their problems toward practical ends and have often excluded events and impersonal forces which the historian frequently considers. Because men like to rationalize their actions, publicists have often distinguished the pretexts from the causes of war.[49] Because they recognize that no free will ever really acts without antecedents, and therefore the origin of a series of causal events has to be determined arbitrarily, they have distinguished proximate from remote causes.[50] While they have sometimes attributed wars to the failure of society to adopt particular reforms or to modify certain conditions,[51] they have usually distinguished causes attributable to a responsible person from impersonal conditions and potential reforms.[52]   In the same way physicians more frequently attribute an illness to a germ rather than to the susceptibility of the patient because of a run-down condition or to his failure to take preventive or remedial precautions.[53]

Practical men have, then, usually thought of war as a manifestation of human nature with its complex of ambitions, desires, purposes, animosities, aspirations, and irrationalities.[54] They have insisted that the degree of consciousness or responsibility to be attributed to such manifestations is an important factor in devising measures for dealing with the problem. Classification of human motives from this point of view is familiar in law[55] and economics.[56] Publicists have often distinguished necessary, customary, rational, and capricious acts in the causation of war.[57] They suggest that

[48]The poets and idealists have had a similar point of view but have emphasized the potentialities rather than the actualities of human nature (see above, n. 34, and Vol. I, chap. iii, sec. I).

[49]See E. de Vattel, *The Law of Nations* (Washington, 1916), Vol. III, chap. iii, sec. 32, who also distinguishes "justifying grounds" from "motives" for war (*ibid.*, sec. 25).   See also H. W. Halleck, *International Law* (4th ed.; London, 1908), chap. xv.

[50]Above, n. 29.

[51]Q. Wright, "The Outlawry of War," *American Journal of International Law,* XIX (January, 1925), 76 ff.

[52]In mathematical terms a cause is a variable, a condition a constant, and a reform a parameter.

[53]This tendency has existed only since Pasteur; Claude Bernard took a more general view of the cause of disease; see also Link, *op. cit.*

[54]In legal pleading the word "cause" means the motives or reasons for an act (Bouvier, *op. cit.*).

[55]See J. W. Salmond, *Jurisprudence* (London, 1902), chap. xviii, for legal distinction of intention, motive, malice, negligence, etc.

[56]See "Economic Incentives," *Encyclopaedia of the Social Sciences.*   Z. Clark Dickinson ("The Relation of Recent Psychological Developments to Economic Theory," *Quarterly Journal of Economics,* XXXIII [May, 1929], 394 ff.) criticizes the familiar pleasure-pain classification of economic motives.

[57]See Vattel, *op. cit.*, chap. iii; Oppenheim, *op. cit.*, Vol. II, sec. 62.   Necessary and customary causes of war are usually considered just, while capricious or emotional causes are

wars arise in the following situations: (1) Men and governments find themselves in situations where they must fight or cease to exist, and so they fight from necessity.[58] (2) Men and governments have a custom of fighting in the presence of certain stimulae, and so in appropriate situations they fight.[59] (3) Men or governments want something—wealth, power, social solidarity— and, if the device of war is known to them and other means have failed, they use war as a means to get what they want.[60] (4) Men and governments feel like fighting because they are pugnacious, bored, the victims of frustrations or complexes, and accordingly they fight spontaneously for relief or relaxation.[61]

Thus among each class of writers, whether the effort has been to construct a formula relating measurable factors, to narrate a comprehensible process of change, or to describe the reactions by which the generally recognized human motives affect the environment, the process of generalizing from concrete events has developed similar categories. The historian, however, has usually kept closest to the events, and the scientists have been most bold in generalization, often resting to a considerable extent on the shoulders of

considered unjust. Rational causes may be just or unjust, according to the title to the interest served. War to reacquire a state's own territory may be just, while war to acquire another state's territory may be unjust.

[58]Military and sociological writers who emphasize the international struggle for existence and economists who emphasize overpopulation and the scarcity of resources as a cause of war take this position. See Friedrich Bernhardi, *On War of Today* (London, 1912); L. Gumplowicz, *Der Rassenkampf* (Innsbruck, 1909); F. C. Wright, *Population and Peace* (Paris: International Institute of Intellectual Cooperation, 1939); E. Van Dyke Robinson, "War and Economics," *Political Science Quarterly,* XV (December, 1900), 582 ff.

[59]This point of view is less characteristic of practical writers than of anthropologists, who find the causes of primitive warfare to be determined by the customs of the particular tribe (Meade, *op. cit.;* W. Lloyd Warner, "Murngin Warfare," *Oceania,* I [January, 1931], 417 ff.; cf. above, Vol. I, chap. vi, n. 18). Practical writers, however, while believing that war ought to be fought for rational objectives, sometimes consider that among average men both its initiation and its methods are often guided only by custom (Colonel J. F. C. Fuller, *The Reformation of War* [New York, 1923], Prologue). A. M. Carr-Saunders believes that war is neither a biological nor an economic necessity but arose from the instinct of pugnacity and developed into a custom. Among civilized peoples it is a mode of political action to achieve customary political ends (*The Population Problem* [Oxford, 1922], pp. 302–5). The Outlawry of War Movement was based on the assumption that war is an institution supported by custom (C. C. Morrison, *The Outlawry of War* [Chicago, 1927]).

[60]It is the usual assumption among military writers and publicists that war is an instrument of national policy. General Carl von Clausewitz (*On War* [1st ed., 1832; London, 1911], I, 121; III, 121) called war "a continuation of political intercourse with a mixture of other means." G. Lowes Dickinson (*War: Its Nature, Cause and Cure* [New York, 1923], p. 50) writes: "All states, in all their wars, have always had a double object: on the one hand, to keep what they have got; on the other, to take more. This, and this only, is the cause of all wars, other than civil wars." "Between two groups that want to make inconsistent kinds of worlds, I see no remedy except force" (Justice Oliver Wendell Holmes [February 1, 1920], in N. D. Howe [ed.], *Holmes-Pollock Letters,* II [Cambridge, Mass., 1941], 36). See above, Vol. I, chap. x, sec. 1.

[61]The opinion that pugnacity is a human trait is widespread, though opinions differ as to how easily it may be stimulated. See John Carter, *Man Is War* (New York, 1926); Bertrand Russell, *Why Men Fight* (New York, 1930), pp. 5 ff.; G. Lowes Dickinson, *op. cit.,* p. 57; above, Vol. I, chap. xi.

the historian and the publicist. (1) Scientists, historians, and publicists have each generalized about material forces in the state system, though they have referred to them, respectively, as the balance of power, political factors, and necessity. (2) So also each has generalized about ideological influences under the names of international law, juristic factors, and custom. (3) They have generalized concerning sociological structures, respectively, under the heads of international organization, idealism, and reason. (4) The reactions of personality have, finally, been generalized by the three classes of writers under the names of public opinion, psychological or economic factors, and caprice or emotion.

Whether evidence is sought in the study of wars themselves or in the study of competent generalizations about war, the same classification of the causes of war is suggested. War has politico-technological, juro-ideological, socio-religious, and psycho-economic causes. The following sections of this part of the study conform to this classification. They assume, respectively, that the belligerents are powers which become involved in war in the process of organizing political and material forces in ever larger areas, that they are states which became involved in war in the attempt to realize more complete legal and ideological unity, that they are nations which became involved in war in the effort to augment the influence of particular political, social, and religious symbols, and that they are peoples which become involved in war through behaving according to prevailing psychological and economic patterns. These four points of view emphasize, respectively, the technique, the law, the functions, and the drives of war.[62]

[62] Above, Vol. I, chap. ii, sec. 5.

Kenneth Waltz, our next author, has also written a major book on war entitled *Man, The State, and War* (Columbia University Press, 1959). It concentrates on describing and classifying the types of explanations of war by a careful analytical study of the inherited wisdom of the past. The short extract from an essay written by Waltz summarizes his scheme of classification. Waltz is of the opinion that the corpus of thought on war clusters about three basic images of why conflict arises in international relations. Theorists of the first image emphasize the aggressive nature of man. Theorists of the second image emphasize the aggressive nature of certain states seeking to advance their power, prestige, and wealth. And theorists of the third image emphasize the anarchic character of international society with its lack of an effective machinery of social control. Of course, Waltz is talking of the emphasis in a thinker's approach. He acknowledges in his book that most great thinkers combine the three images in their thought, but tend to give prominence to one.

We include this piece by Waltz because it develops a useful set of categories for the discussion of war and its prevention. For, as must be evident, the causal explanation of war that is adopted influences the choice of remedial approach. Which of Waltz's three images do Clark and Sohn hold?

Both Waltz and Wright are convinced that the history of past wars is relevant to the study of war in the nuclear age. Would you want to alter the causal account of war in view of the development of nuclear weapons and automated delivery systems?

(Excerpt from)

POLITICAL PHILOSOPHY AND THE STUDY OF INTERNATIONAL RELATIONS

BY KENNETH N. WALTZ

According to one view of international relations, the locus of the major causes of war is found in the nature and behavior of man. Wars, according to this image of the world, result from selfishness, from misdirected aggressive impulses, from stupidity, from lack of information; other causes are secondary and have to be interpreted in the light of these factors. If these are the primary causes of war, then an end to war must come through uplifting and enlightening men or securing their psychic-social readjustment. This estimate of causes and possible cures has been dominant in the writings of many serious students of human affairs from Confucius to present-day pacifists. It is the leitmotif of many modern-day behavioral scientists as well. Clyde Kluckhohn, to cite one example from the many available, has identified "the central problem of world peace" as one of minimizing and controlling "aggressive impulses." [20] W. Fred Cottrell, to cite another, defines the presently remaining prerequisite for peace as "a clear understanding on the part of all elites that war is inferior to

20. Clyde Kluckhohn, *Mirror for Man* (New York, 1949), p. 277.

peace in pursuit of their values." [21] One may, however, agree with the first-image analysis of causes without admitting the possibility of meaningful prescription for their removal. St. Augustine attributes to man's love for "so many vain and hurtful things" a long list of human tribulations, ranging from quarrels and robberies to murders and war.[22] The explanation is for him an unbreakable one, going beyond any man-made remedy. Man's sin explains both the necessity of political constraints and the necessarily defective quality of all political institutions. With many states, he once wrote, we have wars among them; given a world state, we would have wars within it.[23] The thought finds its echo in the present when George Kennan defines the conduct of government as a "sorry chore . . . devolving upon civilized society, most unfortunately, as a result of man's irrational nature, his selfishness, his obstinacy, his tendency to violence." [24] There is here an attractive world-weary wisdom as well as a valuable caution against expecting too much from changes in forms and institutions. Yet the first image, if rigidly held, becomes sterile. The search for causes is an attempt to account for differences. If men were always at war, or always at peace, the question of why war, or why peace, would never arise. What does account for the alternation of periods of war and peace? Human nature no doubt plays a role in bringing about war. Human nature, however, cannot by itself explain both war and peace, except by the simple statement that man's nature is such that sometimes he fights and sometimes he does not. And this statement leads inescapably to the attempt to explain why he fights sometimes and not others. The partial quality of the first image leads us to go beyond it in seeking the understanding that enables one to account for differences.

In a second image of international relations the basic causes of war are found in the political structures and social, economic conditions of the separate states. The initial argument is that all wars can be attributed to defects in some or in all states. The statement is then often reversed: If bad states make wars, good states would live at

21. W. Fred Cottrell, "Research to Establish the Conditions for Peace," *The Journal of Social Issues,* XI (1955), p. 20.
22. St. Augustine, *The City of God,* tr. Marcus Dods, Bk. XXII, ch. xxi.
23. *Ibid.,* Bk. XIX, ch. vii.
24. George F. Kennan, *Realities of American Foreign Policy* (Princeton, 1954), p. 48.

peace with one another. With varying degrees of justification this view has been attributed to Plato and Kant, to nineteenth-century liberals and revisionist socialists. Differing in their descriptions of good states as well as on the problem of bringing about their existence, they agree on the principle involved. Thus Thomas Hill Green, liberal-idealist of the mid-nineteenth century, saw no reason why states, as they improve internally, "should not arrive at a passionless impartiality in dealing with each other. . . ." [25] But how good would good states have to be before most occasions for conflict among them would disappear and those remaining could consistently be settled by cold reason? This question endures even if one can imagine a process by which the generalization of a single pattern of the state could take place.

In a third image, the locus of major causes is found neither in men nor in states but in the state system itself. The first and second images are criticized not so much as being wrong but as being incomplete. Their partial qualities drive one to seek the more inclusive nexus of causes. The old problem of political philosophy — do men create the societies and states in which they live or do those societies and states, so to speak, remake the men who live in them? — here appears in a different form. Rousseau has argued that the sources of conflict are not so much in men as they are in society. In asking if a man would not be a fool to enclose and cultivate a piece of land when the first comer may rob him of the fruits of all his toil, he puts his point negatively.[26] In commenting upon "the most perfect society imaginable" that would presumably exist among "a people of true Christians," he notes that "all the citizens without exception would have to be equally good Christians; if by ill hap there should be a single self-seeker or hypocrite . . . he would certainly get the better of his pious compatriots." [27] He thus implies a criticism that, with terms changed, applies to the second as well as the first image. One cannot begin to behave decently unless he has some assurance that others will not be able to ruin him. This thought Rousseau develops and applies

---

25. Thomas Hill Green, *Lectures on the Principles of Political Obligation,* par. 175.
26. Jean Jacques Rousseau, *A Discourse on the Origin of Inequality* in *The Social Contract and Discourses,* tr. G. D. H. Cole (New York, 1950), p. 212.
27. *The Social Contract,* pp. 135-136. I have added to the English translation the word "equally" in order to render the French text more accurately.

to states existing in a condition of anarchy in his fragmentary essay on "The State of War" and in his commentaries on the works of the Abbé de Saint-Pierre. A state may want to behave peacefully; it may have to consider undertaking a preventive war, for the nations of Europe are willful units in close juxtaposition with rules neither clear nor enforceable to guide them. This is his basic explanation for the behavior of all of them, though with Alexander Hamilton he would add that to presume a lack of hostile motives among states is to forget that men are "ambitious, vindictive, and rapacious." A monarchical state may go to war because the vanity of its king leads him to seek glory in military victory; a republic may go to war because of the folly of its assembly or because of its commercial interests. That the king be vain, the assembly foolish, or the commercial interests irreconcilable: none of these is inevitable. However, so many and so varied are the causes of war among states that "to look for a continuation of harmony between a number of independent, unconnected sovereigns in the same neighborhood, would be to disregard the uniform course of human events, and to set at defiance the accumulated experience of the ages." [28] The third image while not excluding the first and second, places them in a defined perspective. This perspective is especially well developed in Rousseau, though one finds it in Hobbes, Hamilton and others as well.

Each image may be taken, optimistically, as a clue to necessary and sufficient prescriptions for peace or, more realistically, as a description of crucial difficulties under which men must live. The third image, moreover, makes clear why, in the absence of tremendous changes in the factors included in the first and second images, war will be perpetually associated with the existence of separate sovereign states.

28. *The Federalist Papers,* No. 6. Cf. No. 4 (Jay) and No. 7 (Hamilton).

Our next selection is by Werner Levi, "On the Causes of War and the Conditions of Peace," *Journal of Conflict Resolution*, vol. IV, no. 4 (December, 1960) pp. 411–420. It uses an ahistorical approach to classify the causes of war. Levi's mode of classification supplements Waltz's mode and aids in the task of thinking systematically about war and its prevention.

What is striking, however, about Levi's piece is his suggestion that we should try to explain peace as well as war. This is unusual. Intellectual attention is usually given only to the comprehension of the problematic in human affairs. The philosopher John Dewey goes so far as to suggest that all human thought is problem-oriented, that, in fact, the impulse to think only arises when man is confronted with an obstacle that blocks the attainment of his goals. Even if one accepts an extreme view such as Dewey's, Levi nevertheless indicates that one way to grasp the problematic is to study the unproblematic; he contends that we should study the causes of peace as well as the causes of war. Note the emphasis at the end of the article upon the development of a sense of community as essential to the maintenance of world peace. For a fuller treatment, see Werner Levi, *International Organization: The Fundamentals of World Organization* (University of Minnesota Press, 1953).

Levi's article also usefully connects an analysis of the causes of war with the establishment of the conditions of peace. This conceives of the relation between a war-prone and a peaceful world to be itself a form of social process. In this regard the recent attention to conflict resolution is helpful. It is also helpful to consider how various domestic societies have been able to eliminate violence from various sectors of conflict—for example, disputes between labor and management. Amitai Etzioni generalizes even further this line of inquiry by suggesting that we might improve the quality of international society by studying how economic firms learn to transform wasteful and mutually destructive competition into constructive competition. He uses the shift from price wars to quality competition in the automobile industry as a principal example. See Amitai Etzioni, "On Self-Encapsulating Conflicts," *Journal of Conflict Resolution*, vol. 8 (September, 1964) p. 242.

On the causes of war and the conditions of peace[1]

WERNER LEVI

One of man's fundamental problems is to live in peace with his fellow men. He cannot live alone. Yet, in coexistence with others, conflicts inevitably arise. It is therefore characteristic of individuals, alone or organized in groups, to seek power for the satisfaction of their interests. Lest this lead to an eternal state of war, men organize themselves to reap the greatest benefit from cooperation and to reduce as much as possible conflict and strife. In particular, it is the minimum goal of social organization that the satisfaction of vital interests—usually bodily integrity and survival—should not lead to violent conflict but should, rather, be assured by peaceful methods or, failing these, by the application of supreme coercive power which is socially organized and usually vested in a central authority.

The social organization of the state[2] is intended to provide adequate means for peaceful adjustment of conflicts and to obviate the need for individual violence. Even when the means prove inadequate, the state simply does not permit violence—except as a matter

of self-defense. The individual's person cumulation of power is limited to most of power short of physical force. As a pensation the state guarantees, as a mum, the physical integrity and surviv the contestants in a conflict. This arr ment rests upon a habitual way of life mental attitudes of the citizens indic the existence of a community. The complete the integration of the men into the community, the more successf

In the international society, that association of states, the situation is bas different. Relations between states ar dered by routine practices and a vast work of international organizations pro ing and regularizing the satisfaction o tional interests. Much expedient coc tion exists between states, with well-lished rules, regulations, and institution numerable conflicts of interest are res by accommodation and adjustment, mutual or one-sided, depending upo power relationship of the states inv But this possibility is severely restricte cause the society of states lacks an ized authority endowed with the legi supreme coercive power to guarante integrity and survival of each state, wh in turn merely 'an indication of the ab of any sense of solidarity among the p of the world. Every state is the guardia guarantor of all its own interests. It m ready to defend them at all times a this purpose must possess power. In co

---

[1] This article is a chapter in a forthcoming book, tentatively entitled *Principles of International Relations*.

[2] It should be understood throughout this article that "state" is used as a shorthand expression. It does not refer to any organism but rather, depending upon the context in which the word is used, to those making decisions on behalf of the people, those influencing these decisions, or all the citizens.

intrastate conditions, the possession of power cannot be limited to the non-physical and because national interests may be threatened which a state wishes to defend force. The time when such a vital threat may arrive is unpredictable, and the nature the threat is unknown. Therefore, the quest for power becomes inevitably permanent, though not for this reason all-consuming. It is conditioned by its relation to the goals the state pursues, by its relation to the power of other states, by the capabilities the state, by the intensity of the state's will to survive integer, and by the results of the interrelations of these factors.

The quest for power becomes a major occupation of the state and a standard by which most aspects of its life and activities are measured, no matter how relative the magnitude of the desired power may be. It can be granted that, as states usually assert the diplomatic record, they do not seek power for its own sake; they do so merely as means to the end of satisfying their needs. For the nature of power, they can argue with cogency up to a point, like that of money, allows it to be accumulated and stored, to be expended for a great variety of unforeseeable ends at a time of need (25, 7). But whatever the end of the search for power and whatever its qualifications and limitations, the possibility remains that it can itself lead to violent conflict. States may become rivals in vying for elements of power in one attempting to become more powerful than the other. The paradox here is that the search for power, even if only to have it available for a future conflict of interests, may itself become a source of violent conflict. This is an unending process because power as such has become a vital interest to some states. The search for it becomes necessary to guard against the consequences this search.[3] Thus, until another way is found to guarantee satisfaction of a state's interest, especially those it considers vital (or until states disappear), the possibility of violent conflict is a built-in feature of the nation-state system in the modern world (16, 22).

This fact can easily enough explain the mutual suspicion among states and their potential hostility. Here is genuine conflict. No amount of good will among nations, understanding among peoples, elimination of stereotypes, or clarification of semantic difficulties can obliterate it. Better knowledge of each other among peoples may gradually lead to greater integration on the way to a community and thereby reduce the chances of violence as a solution of conflict; but it cannot abolish conflict (4). It is therefore quite erroneous to assume, as has often been done, that states have violent conflicts because their citizens are aggressive, militaristic, and nationalistic. It is often the other way around: citizens assume these characteristics or are being prepared for warfare because there are real conflicts between states which may have to be solved with violence. The vicious circle is that a potential threat to their state makes citizens bellicose, and their bellicosity makes them appear as a threat to other states. Under the prevailing system the citizen must live in anticipation of violence and take the necessary precautions, including readiness for war. Polls in many European and some American states showed that anywhere from one-third to three-quarters of the people consulted did

---

[3] The general ideas outlined here in regard to the role of power in international relations are old, although judging by recent debates raging around this subject, one may not think so. That states seek power to satisfy their interests was not discovered in the United States in the middle of the twentieth century. It was discussed in the pre-Christian era by such men as Kautilya in India and Mo Ti in China.

not think it was possible to live in peace (8, pp. 125–216, question 3*a*).

This expectation of war does not, however, have to lead to war in accord with the assertion that "expectations determine behavior" (9, p. 15). For the expectation may produce behavior which either leads to its fulfilment or to its frustration. History is full of proof that governments have genuinely tried to avoid wars, knowing their potential existence. One of the reasons why they have sometimes failed is that they did not or could not choose the right means to avoid it. In a nation-state system, with the close identification of the citizen with his state, the anticipation of violence regularly leads the citizen to turn to his own community for increased security rather than to attempt integration with the threatening state for the sake of reducing the chance of violence (15, p. 19).

There are relations between states to which this general description does not apply. Not all states are hostile to each other, or, at any rate, not all consider every other state a potential threat to vital interests. Albania and Honduras are not anticipating violent conflict, nor are Norway and Great Britain, nor Canada and the United States. Such states either are not rivals for interests or power; or there is enough sentiment of community between them to obviate violence; or they repress violence for the sake of unity against a common enemy. They may still have conflicts of interest, but for a variety of reasons, including possibly the technical inability to be violent with each other or much simultaneous cooperation, they do not consider the use of violence. Such reasons may change, of course, or new causes may produce violence. Colombia was engaged in violent conflict with North Korea under United Nations action in the name of collective security. There was no reason for this in the direct relations be-

tween the two states, but for reasons su[ffi]cient to the Colombian government the vi[o]lent conflict between the two states exist[ed] nevertheless, and very likely North Korea[n] such had very little to do with these reaso[ns]. As peace becomes increasingly indivisib[le] and as technical developments enable—[in] the future—even small states to posse[ss] weapons which can reach any point on t[he] globe and wipe out any state in the wor[ld] the chances for violent conflict between t[wo] states hitherto geographically, political[ly] and in every other way remote from ea[ch] other, increase; just as—a compensating v[ir]tue—the chances for their integration a[nd] growth into a community also become gre[at]er. With such a community come the p[at]terns of behavior facilitating peaceful so[lu]tion of conflict and making the applicati[on] of coercive power by the supreme author[ity] only one of the means of conflict soluti[on] and an increasingly rare one.

In the meantime, while states continue [to] fight each other, almost all conceivable a[nd] some inconceivable reasons have been giv[en] why they use violence in the solution [of] some of their conflicts. Supernatural powe[r] the state-system, social institutions, t[he] character of groups, and the nature of m[an] have been named as the causes of war (8[,] 5, 17, 33, 12, 7, 18). If supernatural caus[es] are disregarded, the common denominat[or] of the rest is, sooner or later in the arg[u]ment, man. But whether, as the constituti[on] of UNESCO asserts, it is the mind of m[an] or some other part, is a matter of debate— [as] is whether it is man as an individual or [as] member of a group.

The number of natural traits held respo[n]sible as the cause of war is almost unlimite[d]. As so often with psychological explanatio[ns] of personal or social phenomena, any tr[ait] can somehow be made to serve as expla[na]tion. A man with an inferiority complex m[ay] either become a dictator or a mouse! Th[e]

many reasons for these kinds of alterna-
es: the same natural trait can find many
ferent outlets, depending upon the op-
rtunities which the environment offers;
n is a complex of psychological factors
m whose interaction behavior results, so
.t no one factor can be singled out; many
chological factors which appear mutual-
exclusive in the abstract can nevertheless
practice produce the same action. If the
lanations of all psychologists are accepted
valid, the whole spectrum of natural traits
man is covered as cause of war—which is
explanation at all, for it is obvious that
nature of human beings is responsible
human actions. In most cases, therefore,
y certain natural traits or psychological
tors are singled out by various authors to
count primarily for the existence of war.
One group of these factors can be classi-
l as destructive: aggressiveness, hostility,
alry, bias and prejudice, hatred, sadism,
jection of one's own shortcomings upon
enemy. Another group contains factors
ing for balancing or compensation, such
boredom, thirst for adventure, social frus-
tion, insecurity, to which war offers the
ernative of excitement and personal li-
se. A third group refers to ego fulfilment:
d for prestige, status, and recognition;
ire to be wanted, wish for possessions.
ere is, finally, the not very frequently
ed group of constructive factors allegedly
sing people to go to war: sense of sacri-
, neighborly love, contribution to the
mmunity, sense of mission.

The protagonists of the theory that these
chological factors are the causes of war
intain that they can find particularly good
ression in war and, without further ado,
y jump to the conclusion that they are
cause. As one author put it, "eventually
growing hostility and the military prepa-
ion do lead to war, each side believing
t the war was made necessary by the ac-

tions of the other" (13, p. 132). Unfortunately, things are not so simple. Even as a description of events this statement is not
borne out by the facts, for there are innumerable instances in history of states being both hostile and militarily prepared without war breaking out between them. Things
become even more complicated when the
causes of war are sought in group conflict,
regardless of one's concept of the group.[4]

Depending upon that concept, various explanations have been given to make the
peculiar characteristics of the group responsible as the cause of war: in a group the
individual loses the customary social restraints, so that he can act aggressively
against the enemy as he would not against
a fellow member of his community; or, in
joining a group, the individual's destructive
drives become magnified and war offers itself as an outlet. Tensions between states,
which can exist in the absence of concrete
conflicts, have been blamed for the outbreak
of violence (24, pp. 427–30). Or, it has
been claimed, tensions and conflicts within
a state are externalized for the sake of maintaining the national community and war
results. Psychonalysts blame unconscious
remnants of man's earliest past which survive in the group and perpetuate war as an
institution.

Some value cannot be denied to these attempts at explaining wars through psychological factors since it is men who are making wars. But they are not the whole explanation. Indeed, they leave many crucial

----

4 Some differing conceptions of the nature of
groups are: a group is the sum total of its individuals, no more, no less; a group is something
more than the sum total of its individual members, it becomes a new, independent creature
(what Morris Cohen, opposed to this idea, called
the "Communal Ghost"); the "group mind" is
part of the psychic equipment of each individual
(explains Edward Glover [14, p. 183]).

questions unanswered. When for instance, will certain natural traits or psychological drives find outlets in war, and when in something more peaceful? Why did German fight German before the political unification of Germany, and why has such a contingency been practically unthinkable since? How are these traits and drives of millions of individual citizens suddenly crystallized into a state of war against a specific enemy at a given moment? What these explanations fail to do is to indicate how these human factors are translated into violent conflict involving all citizens, regardless of their individual nature, and performed through a highly complex machinery constructed over a period of years for just such purpose.

There is always the missing link in these fascinating speculations about the psychological causes of war between the fundamental nature of man and the outbreak of war. It is fairly easy to understand how a conflict of interest can lead to personal violence in a face-to-face situation between two or a very few people. But this situation is vastly different from conflict between two states, each possibly composed of hundreds of millions of individuals. It then becomes evident that the natural traits of the citizenry cannot, by themselves, directly be related to international violence and adequately explain the origin of wars. Even on the assumption that the cause of war lies somehow in the total population of a state, these explanations need qualifications and refinements and amplifications whose character becomes clearer when psychological factors are more closely related to the nature of modern wars and the citizen's role in them.

In this connection the distinction between the causes and the conditions of war is of relevance (22, p. 224; 32, epilogue). In practice such a distinction may not be easily feasible, and there is danger that its definition may deteriorate into semantics. Never-

theless, there is good purpose in separati as has often been done, the circumstan which are necessary prerequisites for v (sometimes called the "deeper" or "und lying" causes) and those which are dire resulting in war. The possession of weap for instance, is an indispensable condition modern war, but not necessarily its ca The occupation of an enemy's territory the enemy resists, is a cause of war, and is the enemy's resistance. Usually, the p chological factors and human traits can classified as conditions of war more corr ly than as causes.

The example of the invading ene brings to mind another distinction wh might be equally difficult to make in p tice, but which nevertheless raises questi unanswered by the theories on psycholog causes of war. There are aggressive v and defensive wars. Regardless of what parties themselves claim, it is objectiv possible for a government to start a wa the conviction that its country is about to attacked and that its action is truly fensive. It would seem that the differing tivation behind these two types of wars quires different psychological explanat even though the wars will all look alike (pp. 43–47).

In fact, the failure of most psycholog explanations of war to distinguish betw different kinds of wars is another one their weaknesses. Contrary to the usual sumption, wars are not always the s thing. In addition to being different reg ing the aggressor and defender, wars differ in regard to the kind of violence u the weapons employed, the number types of people involved, and several o things. Although the actual soldiers d the fighting may have certain characteris in common, from the standpoint of expl ing on psychological grounds the origi wars, it makes a basic difference whe

ian tribes fight, or armies hired by princes
et in battle, or the German people fight
French people in a total war.

he juxtaposition of these types of war
ws clearly that each provides quite a
erent "environment," meaning: supplies
te different outlets for human traits and
chological drives. In modern wars there
never enough "aggressive" men flocking
he recruiting stations, while on the home
it attractive salaries for war work seem
ave greater attraction than the psychic
ards of a contribution to the war effort.[5]
rywhere men are drafted into armies.
ir and the general public's fighting spirit
roused by government effort at great ex-
se and not always successfully. How, for
ance, can these explanations fit into their
eme Britain's war on Egypt in 1956
ch had to be stopped because (among
er reasons) a large section of the British
lic did not want to fight it? In some
ies more than half the men who were
posed to shoot did not pull the trigger.
home from ten to twenty people are re-
red in order to maintain one man at the
t lines, most often continuing to do their
tine work. In future push-button wars,
psychic satisfaction in war at the home
t will be even further reduced. Usually,
mass at home has to be stirred up by an
rmous propaganda campaign to become
icose—after the war has started or is
ut to start—and the stimulus of revenge
lefense of the fatherland soon has to be
aced by "war aims" conjuring up visions
a beautiful, peaceful future world. In
f: in the long run, the more effective
eals to keep people in a fighting spirit

It must be recognized, though, that such psy-
satisfactions exist. Fred Blum discovered
ng factory workers that they began to enjoy
, which they had found dull and monoto-
, as soon as it contributed to the war effort

are not to aggressiveness and hatreds but to
the desire for lasting peace and greater welfare. This is no conclusive argument against
the possibility that people may yearn for war
for other reasons. But, first, it is not likely
that people switch their attitudes so radically from pro to con regarding war so
quickly; second, it is, historically, extremely
rare to find before modern wars appeals
arousing sentiments designed directly to
cause a war (19, p. 199; 27, p. 34); and,
third, when preparation for war is compared, chronologically, to warlike appeals to
the public, it will be found that the appeals
begin at a considerably later moment, if not
after the outbreak of the war; just as stereotypes of one people about another are often
adjusted to suit the demands of the war.[6]

The long and complex preparations needed
for modern wars make it quite inconceivable
that they result from some sudden, collective
impulse of the state's citizenry. Whatever
destructiveness and aggressiveness may be
part of man's nature, "it is not a part of his
native behavior to combine these into strategy and tactics, into armies and sea power
and air forces, all controlled for the purposes
of the State" (31, p. 254). This is all the
more true as the majority of citizens, even
in the best-educated countries, are notoriously uninterested in foreign affairs and un-
informed about the course of international
events. When polled, these citizens may express a phobia against foreigners in general
or against a particular people, but there is
no evidence that this has ever been strong
enough to lead them to demand war or prepare for it. Indeed the relative insignificance
of such phobias and stereotypes about other
peoples as causes of war can best be discov-

---

[6] "How Nations See Each Other" is a very
variable matter. This was strikingly demonstrated, for instance by the stories about the Soviet Union in the popular journals during World
War II and after the war.

ered in the fact that a people has found itself allied with another people in war about
which it had worse ideas than about the
common enemy. A *Fortune* poll in 1939, for
instance, showed that 6.9 per cent of American pollees considered themselves most
friendly to the Germans, while only 0.9
per cent considered themselves friendly to
the Russians (8, p. 117). Similarly, Great
Britain was at war with Germany twice in
modern times, although the British people
consistently show a sentimental preference
for Germans over Frenchmen.

The weaknesses in attempts to give individual psychological or natural traits as
causes of war can be found, *mutatis mutandi,*
in group psychology. Whatever the accepted
theory about group behavior and group tensions, the need remains to explain how these
characteristics of the group are organized
and translated into war (27, p. 44; 28, p.
83). For it should be clear that, while man
is endowed with certain psychological qualities, the environment of every individual
man determines how these qualities become
effective and what results they will produce.
What may be said about psychological contributions to the outbreak of war, if "man in
general" is considered, is that the institution-
alization of war does indeed provide numerous and convenient outlets for psychological
drives which might otherwise be channeled
into different directions or be sublimated to
produce different results. To some citizens
the outbreak of war might thus become a
pleasant prospect and lead to emotional
readiness for it. But this is, essentially, a
passive readiness, which is, besides, produced in almost every citizen in modern
times by his civic training and his habitual
way of life. This is an indispensable condition for war as long as it remains a mass war.
Such readiness is, however, not the same
thing as being a cause of war. It will be
even less relevant when the perfection of

missile warfare might conceivably lead
the ending of a war before anybody has
a chance to develop any feelings about

The relevance of psychological or nat
traits upon war becomes greater with a
ter differentiation among groups and i
viduals in a state and the role they pla
the shaping of the state's destiny (18
47–50; 11, p. 32). Since obviously s
citizens are more important than other
relation to the decision to make war,
failure to distinguish between them has
of necessity to such a generalization of
planations in psychological terms that t
are not very fruitful. The nature of tl
making decisions within a state and of tl
prominently influencing these decision
not only of importance in uncovering
origin of wars but may also be easier of
vestigation than the people as a whole. E
then, however, personal natural factors
likely to be only among the condition
war. Even the most powerful dictator
modern state cannot determine policy,
of all policy directed toward war, ent
according to his whims. Like all po
makers, he is dependent upon many co
tions over which he has no or little con
He too is part of the environment in w
he lives and which contributes to the sha
of his personal character, though he may
be very conscious of this, while conscic
many elements of the situation in which
must make his decision will enter into
calculations.

This brings into focus a possible cau
war which has been too often neglecte
the preoccupation with finding psycholo
reasons: the use of war deliberately a
instrument of foreign policy. It is true
anyone considering war today as a pol
means must be, in a manner of spea
"insane." Yet historical evidence is
vincing in demonstrating that modern
did not result from emotional outburs

ccumulated frustrations by either decision-makers or the general public. Instead, they were preceded by long and cool-headed preparations and finally started after carefully calculated decisions. Mr. Anthony Eden's memoirs—to take only a very recent example—show quite clearly that military action against Egypt in the Suez crisis in 1956 was much discussed by the British cabinet and in contacts with the United States Department of State and was eventually undertaken on the basis of a fairly unemotional conclusion that British interests in the Suez Canal made it worthwhile.

It is quite possible that the motivations of those who wish to use war as a means to reach certain goals are irrational,[7] also that non- or irrationality affects the judgment of the instrumental usefulness of war in the particular situation. The decision-maker can hardly help seeing the world through his own eyes. This is natural and therefore unavoidable. But this is merely saying that there are limits to man's rationality and that these limits are among the conditions for peace and war which must be studied. Nevertheless, the decision to go to war has usually been made, as history shows, upon careful deliberation of the usefulness of war as an instrument and can largely be understood as such. Indeed, since usually many individuals contribute to the making of the war decision, the chances are very good that the variations and peculiarities of their natural traits have canceled out each other and that the decision has been arrived at upon the merits of war as a desirable instrument (1, 10). That decision-makers take war into their calculations at all will remain true as long as war

remains as an institution. Only as the use of violence between contesting parties becomes suppressed as it has been, generally, within many states, will this possibility change.

The fundamental difficulty in discovering the cause of war is that any fact, to be the cause, requires a particular conjunction of conditions not any one of which may itself be directed toward war. War is a social situation, a complex of relationships developing out of the interplay of a great many factors (27, p. 33; 34, II, p. 1284; 20, p. 45). This interplay is unique and many different variations can be responsible for some fact or facts becoming causes of war. Hence the impossibility of specifying what particular facts may cause wars. Hence, also, the experience that roughly similar historical situations may in one case end in war and in another not. One and the same factor in a number of situations will not always have the same result. The possession of weapons, for instance, is a condition always present in situations leading to war and may therefore appear as co-responsible. Yet, in other situations (Switzerland during World War II) it not only fails to lead to war but may contribute to the preservation of peace. Obviously the context in which the possession of weapons occurs is of decisive importance. The conclusion appears inevitable that no generally valid specifiable factor causes war but that, instead, only a particular constellation of factors can produce the conditions of war in which a factor or factors can become effective as causes. To overlook this nature of war has been a shortcoming in most of the attempts to look to the nature of man as the cause of wars. What most of these attempts have done is to search for all possible elements present in the situation to explain the origin of war. What they have usually not done is to try to discover whether there are missing elements whose presence would lead to the avoidance of the use of violence.

---

[7] The concepts of rationality and irrationality have been avoided here as much as possible, mostly for methodological reasons. Where the concept is used, it should be understood according to the definition given to it by Felix B. Oppenheim (26).

Yet this discovery is not difficult when states are considered, in which the use of inter-group violence has become a rarity and the exception for the solution of conflicts. It will then be found that the relative peacefulness within states was not achieved by changing human nature, altering human psychology, or eliminating conflict. It was not even achieved by eliminating hatreds between groups, discrimination, false stereotypes, prejudices, bias, rivalry, or competition—all of which continue in some of the most peaceful (internally) states with an intensity matching that of nationalism. Only the use of violence as a normal and accepted pattern of social relations has disappeared. To the extent that it has so disappeared, it did so by the addition of new behavior patterns, that is to say institutions, leading to the integration of hitherto separated groups into a community.[8]

Once a group has grown into a community (20, pp. 1–27; 2, pp. 205–06; 29, pp. 12–14; 23, p. 28), its members habitually act in conformity with a sense of solidarity, unity, and cohesion which normally excludes violence as a means for the solution of conflicts between them. An organization has evolved which reinforces from without the habit of peaceful relations originating in the attitudes within the members, with a continual interaction between the two. Thus a community possesses the ideological and material restraints necessary to make warfare among its members practically unthinkable. It provides outlets for personality factors in the great variety of its institutions, such as legislatures, public opinion media, plurality of interest groups with overlapping memberships, which in their totality guarantee peaceful change and perform fundamen-

----

[8] Among the first men to emphasize the nature of community and discover its relevance for peace were Confucius, Marcus Aurelius, and Jesus Christ.

tal peace-preserving functions. The mono oly of coercion by a central authority—i. force and violence—is largely a result these institutions and exists primarily f emergency situations. But also, its existen provides the citizen with that sense of sec rity which makes him trust in the success these peace-preserving institutions. In community, conflicts of interest are adjust without violence for the sake of higher i terests in the preservation of the communi which the contestants share. The use of vi lence is simply not considered either becau of a common higher loyalty to the comm nity, or because of learned habitual behavi and inner compulsion of social responsibilit because of fear of effective sanction again antisocial behavior made possible by t creation of the community or because of these and possibly other reasons.

Unfortunately for the peace of the worl the growth of groups into such a communi is a slow process. Many of the organizatio calling themselves states in Asia and Afri today can hardly be described as commur ties in this sense, for they lack, above a the peace-preserving plurality of intere groups which allows them to develop a cor mon loyalty toward the state as such ar therewith that sense of security which is or of the foundations of peaceful behavior (2 pp. 25–29). The development of a comm nity requires high frequency and great i tensity of contact between its members, c rectly or indirectly through shared exper ences of almost any kind. The more th have things spiritual and material in cor mon, the greater is the chance that a cor munity will develop (30, pp. 18–74). It for this reason (and not for reasons of elin nating conflict) that all those enterprises u dertaken for the sake of bringing abo "better understanding" among nations ma in the long run, have the effect of diminis ing the use of violence in international rel s (3, p. 40). There may be a faster and -complicated way to stop violence. The ins of war may become such that their will guarantee the destruction of the : as well as the enemy. Then the useless-; of war as an instrument might lead to elimination of war.

REFERENCES

ABEL, T. "The Element of Decision in the Pattern of War," *American Sociological Review*, VI (1941), 853–59.

ANGELL, ROBERT C. "Discovering Paths to Peace." In International Sociological Association, *The Nature of Conflict*. Paris: UNESCO (1957), 204–23.

———. "Government and Peoples as Foci for Peace-Oriented Research," *Journal of Social Issues*, XI (1955), 36–41.

BERNARD, JESSIE. "The Sociological Study of Conflict." In International Sociological Association, *The Nature of Conflict*. Paris: UNESCO (1957), 33–117.

BERNARD, L. L. *War and Its Causes*. New York: Henry Holt & Co., 1944.

BLUM, FRED. *Toward a Democratic Work Order*. New York: Harper & Bros., 1953.

BOUTHOUL, G. *Les guerres, éléments de polémologie*. Paris: Payot, 1951.

BUCHANAN, WILLIAM, and CANTRIL, HADLEY. *How Nations See Each Other: A Study in Public Opinion*. Urbana: University of Illinois Press, 1953.

CANTRIL, HADLEY (ed.). *Tensions that Cause Wars*. Urbana: University of Illinois Press, 1950.

DEUTSCH, KARL W. "Mass Communications and the Loss of Freedom in National Decision-making," *Conflict Resolution*, I (1957), 200–211.

FARBER, MAURICE L. "Psychoanalytic Hypothesis in the Study of War," *Journal of Social Issues*, XI (1955), 29–35.

Findings of the Conference on the Cause and Cure of War, Washington, D.C., 1925.

GLADSTONE, ARTHUR. "The Conception of the Enemy," *Conflict Resolution*, III (1959), 132–37.

GLOVER, EDWARD. *War, Sadism and Pacifism*. London: George Allen & Unwin, 1946.

HAAS, ERNST B., and WHITING, ALLEN S., JR. *Dynamics of International Relations*. New York: McGraw-Hill Book Co., 1956.

16. INTERNATIONAL SOCIOLOGICAL ASSOCIATION. *The Nature of Conflict*. Paris: UNESCO, 1957.

17. JOHNSEN, JULI E. *Selected Articles on War—Cause and Cure*. New York: H. W. Wilson Co., 1926.

18. KELMAN, HERBERT C. "Societal, Attitudinal and Structural Factors in International Relations," *Journal of Social Issues*, XI (1955), 42–56.

19. KLINEBERG, OTTO. *Tensions Affecting International Understanding*. New York: Social Science Research Council, 1950.

20. LEVI, WERNER. *Fundamentals of World Organization*. Minneapolis: University of Minnesota Press, 1950.

21. ———. "The Fate of Democracy in South and Southeast Asia," *Far Eastern Survey*, XXVIII (1959), 25–29.

22. MACK, RAYMOND W., and SNYDER, RICHARD C. "The Analysis of Social Conflict—Toward an Overview and Synthesis," *Conflict Resolution*, I, (1957), 212–48.

23. MAY, MARK A. *A Psychology of War and Peace*. New Haven, Conn.: Yale University Press, 1943.

24. MORGENTHAU, HANS J. *Politics among Nations*. New York: Alfred A. Knopf, 1960.

25. NITZE, PAUL M. "Necessary and Sufficient Elements of a General Theory of International Relations." In WILLIAM T. R. FOX, *Theoretical Aspects of International Relations*. Notre Dame: University of Notre Dame, 1959.

26. OPPENHEIM, FELIX E. "Rational Choice," *Journal of Philosophy*, L (1953), 341–50.

27. RÖPKE, WILHELM. *Internationale Ordnung*. Erlenbach-Zürich: Eugen Rentsch, 1945.

28. RÜSTOW, ALEXANDER. "Zur soziologischen Ortsbestimmung des Krieges," *Friedenswarte*, XXXIX (1939), 81–94.

29. SCHWARZENBERGER, GEORG. *Power Politics*. London: Stevens & Sons, 1951.

30. SMEND, RUDOLF. *Verfassung und Verfassungsrecht*. München: Duncker & Humblot, 1928.

31. STRATTON, GEORGE M. *Social Psychology of International Conduct*. New York: D. Appleton & Co., 1929.

32. TOLSTOY, LEO. *War and Peace*.

33. WALTZ, KENNETH N. *Man, the State, and War*. New York: Columbia University Press, 1959.

34. WRIGHT, QUINCY. *A Study of War*. Chicago: University of Chicago Press, 1942.

The final selection in this chapter is a provocative essay by H. L. Nieburg entitled "Uses of Violence," *The Journal of Conflict Resolution*, vol. VII, no. 1 (December, 1960) pp. 43–54. The author argues that conflict resolution and social change are crucially dependent upon violence and its threat. He argues that most major progressive steps in domestic society have been the consequence of the constructive use of violence. And finally, Nieburg contends that law, stability, and change in international society are inevitably bound up with the possibility of violence. This leads the essay to attack as naive and sentimental those proponents of world government who identify the good society with a world without violence.

This is a line of argument that a book studying the transition to a warless world must take into serious account. One may disagree with Nieburg's thesis that all social order must rest upon the potentiality for violence, or one may contend that the prospect of a warless world has no relation to Nieburg's analysis. It has no relation, it can be maintained, because a world is warless in our sense when nations give up the capacity to wage war with national defense establishments against one another. As Millis points out in Chapter 1, this relinquishment does not require the elimination of violence, but only the drastic reduction of its scale. Is this a satisfactory answer to Nieburg? Do Clark and Sohn acknowledge the constructive uses of violence?

Nieberg's argument is not novel. Several writers, including Marx, have stressed the constructive role of social violence and conflict. See Lewis A. Coser, *The Functions of Social Conflict* (Free Press of Glencoe, New York, 1956).

Uses of violence

L. NIEBURG

The threat of violence, and the occasional
break of real violence (which gives the
eat credibility), are essential elements
conflict resolution not only in interna-
nal, but also in national communities.[1]
lividuals and groups, no less than nations,
ploit the threat as an everyday matter.
is fact induces flexibility and stability in
mocratic institutions and facilitates peace-
social change.

refer not only to the police power of the
te and the recognized right of self-defense,
also to private individual or group vio-
ce, whether purposive or futile, deliber-
or desperate. Violence and the threat of
lence, far from being meaningful only in
ernational politics, is an underlying, tacit,
ognized, and omnipresent fact of domes-
life, of which democratic politics is some-
es only the shadow-play. It is the fact
t instills dynamism to the structure and
wth of the law, the settlement of dis-
es, the processes of accommodating in-
sts, and that induces general respect for
verdict of the polls.

n effort by the state to obtain an abso-
monopoly over violence, threatened or
d on the behalf of private interests, leads
orably to complete totalitarian repression
ll activities and associations which may,
ever remotely, create a basis of anti-
e action. A democratic system preserves

"Violence" is defined as direct or indirect
on applied to restrain, injure, or destroy
ons or property.

the right of organized action by private
groups, risking their implicit capability of
violence. By intervening at the earliest possible point in private activities, the totalitarian state increases the chance that potential violence will have to be demonstrated
before it is socially effective. On the other
hand, by permitting a pluralistic basis for
action, the democratic state permits potential violence to have a social effect with only
token demonstration, thus assuring greater
opportunities for peaceful political and social
change. A democratic system has greater
viability and stability; it is not forced, like
the totalitarian, to create an infinite deterrent to all nonstate (and thus potentially
anti-state) activities. The early Jeffersonians
recognized this essential element of social
change when they guaranteed the private
right to keep and bear arms (Second Amend-
ment). The possibility of a violent revolution once each generation acts as a powerful
solvent of political rigidities, rendering such
revolutions unnecessary.

The argument of this essay is that the
risk of violence is necessary and useful in
preserving national societies.[2] This specifically includes sporadic, uncontrolled, "irrational" violence in all of its forms. It is true
that domestic violence, no less than interna-

---

[2] The role of violence in political organizations is vividly demonstrated by a recent event
among a group of elks at the Bronx Zoo. A 4-
year-old bull elk, Teddy, had his magnificent
antlers sawed off to one-inch stumps. He had
reigned as undisputed boss of a herd of six cow

tional violence, may become a self-generating vortex which destroys all values, inducing anarchy and chaos. However, efforts to prevent this by extreme measures only succeed in making totalitarian societies more liable to such collapses. Democracies assume the risk of such catastrophes, thereby making them less likely.

Violence has two inextricable aspects: its actual use (political demonstrations, self-immolation, suicide, crimes of passion, property, politics, etc.), or its potential use. The actual demonstration of violence must occur from time to time in order to give credibility to its threatened outbreak; thereby gaining efficacy for the threat as an instrument of social and political change. The two aspects, demonstration and threat, cannot be separated. The two merge imperceptibly into each other. If the capability of actual demonstration is not present, the threat will have little effect in inducing a willingness to bargain politically. In fact, such a threat may provoke "pre-emptive" counter-violence.

The "rational" goal of the threat of violence is an accommodation of interests, not the provocation of actual violence. Similarly, the "rational" goal of actual violence is demonstration of the will and capability of action, establishing a measure of the credibility of future threats, not the exhaustion of that capability in unlimited conflict.[3]

---

elks and one younger bull. But the breeding season was on, and he was becoming "a bit of a martinet." With his antlers off, he gets a new perspective on his authority and becomes a tolerable leader. A younger bull may try to take over as paramount leader of the herd, but if he does, the veterinarian will saw off his antlers, too (New York Times, September 26, 1962, p. 35).

[3] By "rational" here is meant: having a conceptual link to a given end, a logical or symbolic means-ends relationship which can be demonstrated to others or, if not demonstrable, is accepted by others (but not necessarily all) as proven.

Political Systems and Consensus

An investigation of the function of v lence begins with an outline of concep We assume that all human relationships, b individual and institutional, are involved a dynamic process of consensus and comp tion. These are opposites only as concept poles of a continuum. In real relationsh it is often difficult to distinguish objectiv between the two. The distinction is sh only subjectively, for the participant, his perception of consensus or competit may change from moment to moment, pending on his political role and objec circumstances.[4] A political role is defi in terms of the many political systems which the individual objectively or sub tively (by identification of interests) p a part. A political system operates thro a hierarchy of authority and values. E system constitutes a complex structure leadership and influence but, because of nature of its task (maximizing and alloca certain values), decision-making powe usually vested in one or a few roles (the e at the top of a pyramid of authority relat ships. Formal and informal political syst exist at all levels of group life (childr play groups, families, lodges, gangs, w groups, nation-states, international al ments, etc.), interpenetrating each o among and between levels. Each isola system has an interdependent structure roles, involving loyalty to certain val symbols, leaders, and patterns of beha according to system norms. The disc individual, part of many different syste must structure his own hierarchy of com ment to meet the simultaneous dema made upon him by many different role

---

[4] Essentially, the perception by an indivi of his relationship to others within a framew of hostility or cooperation is the subjective of "ideology" (Mannheim, 1957, pp. 265–6

Vithin the individual, the conflicting de-
ıds of these roles create tension. Similarly,
ıin each system there are conflicting val-
among members which are constantly
ısted as roles change, maintaining a state
ension. Political systems have an objec-
, dynamic interrelationship, structured
the hierarchy of macrosystems. Within
latter, each subsystem has a role much
that of the individual in smaller constel-
ıns. Each subsystem may be part of
ʀal macrosystems, imposing conflicting
ıands upon it. Consequently, within
rosystems there is maintained a state of
ʈant tension between subsystems. This
ctive tension, existing on all levels, is
. subjectively in terms both of competi-
and consensus, depending on the com-
ʈive degrees of collaboration and con-
which exist in the situation at any given
ıent.

ny two or more systems may appear as
ile at any given time. From the view-
t of the participants, the conceptual
ework of competition overrides under-
ʒ consensus. Decisions and policies of
ʀival elites are rationalized in terms of
ility to the values and leaders of the
ʀ system. However, if events conspire to
e a higher value on a hostile tactical sit-
ın involving the macrosystem of which
smaller systems are a part, their rela-
hip will be transformed quickly to a
eptual framework of consensus which
override and mute the unresolved com-
ive elements. Such an event may also
ʒ about internal leadership changes in
subsystems, if the elites were too firmly
led to the requirements of the now-
vant competitive situation.

ıjectively, tension is always present
ıg all roles and systems; that is, there is
ys present both elements of competi-
and consensus. The subjective emphasis
h each pole of the continuum receives

depends on the value which the tactical
situation places on acts and attitudes of hostility or collaboration among the various systems at various times. Degrees of hostility
and collaboration are structured by a hierarchy of values within and among all roles
and systems all the time. All are involved in
a dynamic process.

Conflict, in functional terms, is the means
of discovering consensus, of creating agreed
terms of collaboration. Because of the individual's personal role in the macrosystem of
nation-states, he tends to view the Cold War
in terms of competition. Similarly, because
of his role in the subsystem of the family,
he tends to view family problems in terms
of consensus (until the system breaks down
completely).

One can reverse these conceptual fields.
The Cold War can be viewed in terms of
the large areas of consensus that exist between the two power blocs, for example,
the wish to prevent the spread of nuclear
weapons to each other's allies; the wish to
avoid giving each other's allies the power of
general war and peace between the main
antagonists; the common interest in reducing accidental provocations; the common
interest in establishing certain norms of predictability in each other's behavior; etc.
Conflict can be considered merely as the
means of perfecting these areas of consensus.
In the same way, one can view the family
situation negatively in terms of competition
and hostility. As in an O'Neill drama, one
would dwell on all of the things that divide
the family members and interpret all actions
in terms of maneuvers to subdue each other's
will. Consensus becomes a residual category
hors de combat, and therefore of no importance. One might dwell upon the collaborative aspects of international affairs or the
disruptive aspects of family affairs. A policy-
maker should do both in the former area,
just as a psychiatrist does both in the latter.

The collaborative view of the Cold War should not, however, induce euphoria about the nature of the relationship (as it unfortunately does for some), since a high percentage of crimes of violence occur in families, or between lovers or ex-lovers (Frankel, 1938–39, pp. 687–8).

In performing this exercise, the relativistic nature of the concepts of consensus and competition becomes evident. It is impossible to reach any consensus without competition and every consensus, no matter how stable, is only provisional, since it represents for all of its members a submerging of other values. There is a constant effort by all collaborating individuals, groups, or nations to exploit any favorable opportunity to improve their roles or to impose a larger part of their own value structures upon a larger political system. In an important sense, all individuals, groups, or nations desire to "rule the world," but are constrained to collaborate with others on less desirable terms because of the objective limits of their own power.

The commitment required by a credible threat of violence, able to induce peaceable accommodation, is one of a very high order. Not all individuals nor all political systems are capable of credibly using the threat of violence in order to induce greater deference by others to their values. There is general recognition by all of the kinds of values which can and cannot elicit the high degree of commitment required to make the threat credible.

By and large, all violence has a rational aspect, for somebody, if not for the perpetrator. All acts of violence can be put to rational use, whether they are directed against others or against oneself. This is true because those who wish to apply the threat of violence in order to achieve a social or political bargaining posture are reluctant to pay the costs or take the uncertain risks of an actual demon-

stration of that threat. Many incoherent a of violence are exploited by insurgent e as a means of improving their roles or posing a larger part of their values upo greater political system. The greater logical connection between the act and ends sought, the easier it is to assimilate act and claim it as a demonstration of threat available to the insurgents if t demands are ignored. The rapidity v which insurgent movements create mart often from the demise of hapless bystand and the reluctance of governments to martyrs to the opposition, are evidence this.

Nations, Laws, and Ballots

The nation is a highly organized, for political system, whose structure is defined by law and custom, reinforced sanctions legally imposed by the p power of the state. The central problem lawful societies is to develop principles, cedures, institutions, and expectations create conditions of continuity and pre ability in the lives of its members. The l system is an abstract model of the soci designed to crystallize relationships of status quo, maintain their continuity in midst of political and social change, pro lawful methods of resisting or accommo ing change. Law itself, however, tend maintain the status quo and, with the in ments of state power, to resist change. relationships in organized societies cha anyway. The process for codifying chan conditions and relationships is called " tics." Formal political systems legiti certain kinds of potential violence w controlled limits.[5] However, law al

---

[5] The distinction between "violence" "force" (one controlled, the other uncontrol was common in pre-Lasswellian literature. are often difficult to distinguish object Assessments of controllability may be almos

r serves the interests of all equally.
ner, it protects some against others or
s advantages to some over others. By
ing the violence of the state behind the
ests of some, law serves to neutralize
potential violence behind the demands
thers. In a sense, it thus raises the
shold of violence required to make so-
protests against the law efficacious.
fact guarantees that the law cannot be
ged easily or quickly by any group,
giving it greater permanence and sta-
.

essures for political and social change
be substantial before the threat of vio-
and the fear of the breakdown of law
order rises above the threshold set by
eserves of force held by the state. While
threat and fear remain below the
hold, the status quo often responds to
enges against the law by more severe
cement, augmented police and enlarged
ns. Just as soon as the threat and fear
or cross the threshold, there is a gen-
tendency toward nonenforcement of the
The status quo interests begin to share
the disaffected groups a desire to evade
to change the law.

vate demonstrations of violence are
l in all domestic societies. Toleration
corded to threats of potential violence,
ver, to the extent that the laws and
utions are democratic. In all systems,
tate must apply adequate force to con-
all outbreaks of actual violence by
te sources. If the state power is not
to a private threat, the government in
r ceases to rule. The private threat of
nce becomes in fact the last resort of

ideological. I prefer to use "force" to
ate the objective capabilities, i.e., the
te means or instruments for violence.

authority in the system.[6] Why do governments fall when there is a general strike, or
a street demonstration? Governments fall
when their capabilities for dealing with
threatened violence fail. The emerging
political system which proves itself capable
of raising a higher threshold of violence becomes *de facto* the highest authority, and
de jure the new government.

Laws are not merely the rules of a game
of economic and political competition. They
can also be a means of winning the game,
if some of the players can, as they do in
fact, write the laws. The ideal system is
one in which the rules are written with
perfect dispassion, so that they accord no
special advantages to anyone. This ideal
is never realized. The process of politics
which underlies the making and unmaking
of laws is not dispassionate. Indeed, it is
one of the most passionate of the affairs of
men. No matter how scrupulously fair may
be the original constitution and the representation of governing institutions, the
tensions of political systems soon intrude
historical hierarchies of advantage. Whom-
ever enjoys early advantages in the game
soon enjoys more by law, with the heightened threshold of the state to vouchsafe
them.

Thus, the law tends always to become to
some extent the instrument of the status

---

[6] There are many areas outside the jurisdiction of formal governmental authority, as, for
example, "off-limit" slum areas where police
seldom penetrate, or the Mafia areas of Sicily.
Such areas represent political subsystems which
possess a high degree of sovereignty, tolerated,
for one reason or another, by the general government. Within such areas, the *de facto*
authority is often the elite able to maintain the
highest threshold of potential violence, not the
formal government. In such areas, there is
usually an unwritten law making it a severely
punished offense to call upon the authority of
the general government.

quo and an instrument for resisting change.

However, in democratic societies the law also guarantees the rights of voluntary association, political liberties, and restrains (by a constitutional distribution of authority) arbitrary use of the police power. These permit opponents of the status quo to establish and maintain a formidable base of political action. It is difficult for the regime to find legal pretexts for controlling this base while its potential for anti-state violence is still within the state's control capability. Once the insurgent capability of demonstrating violence is equal or greater than that of the state, there is no realistic prospect of repressing it. Changing the law gains precedence over enforcing it, even for status quo leaders, who wish to preserve what control remains over informal political systems whose elite they are. Once the process of peaceful political change has been successfully established, all political elites, both emerging and declining, have a high interest in maintaining general freedom to threaten violence without initiating or provoking it, either on the part of the state or by other groups. For the insurgent elites, there is usually more to be gained in preserving the continuity of the laws than in appealing to the uncertain results of violence.

In democratic systems, the ballot becomes the nonprovocative symbol by which the elites may measure their capabilities for threatening direct action. In a real sense, voting is an approximation of picking sides before a street fight. Once the sides are picked, the leaders are able to gauge their bargaining strengths and make the best possible deal for themselves and their cohorts. The appeal to actual battle is not only unnecessary, but also, for the weaker side (the only side with an interest in challenging the results of the count), does not promise to change the results, and may

in fact undermine the authority of the p as a method of reversing one's position the future.

The threat of violence implicit in counting of heads is an ambiguous mea of the power available to the political tems into which people group themselv election time. The extent of voter com ment in these systems is uncertain probably, in most cases, unequal to mands for supporting action. There very few national elections in the Un States, although many elsewhere, in w the results prefigure a plausible threa civil war as the means by which the feated candidates can gain concessions appointments from the winning side. general, democratic political leaders s a common interest in resolving disp without invoking real violence. Ne side is confident that the loyalty of v will stand the test of a demonstratio strength. Voting is a very imperfect reg of loyalty, but rather conveys a miscel of emotions, difficult to penetrate c order rationally. Strenuous efforts are n by defeated candidates to restrain a sho violence by one's own followers. P concessions of defeat, homiletic congra tions, and avowals of support for the ner, are designed to communicate to voters the finality of the verdict at the p which is subject to revision, not by a der stration of violence, but by renewed p ful efforts in the next election.

In 1960, after the close and some questionable result of the Kennedy-N election, what dangers could have beer leased if Nixon had publicly repudiate poll and openly supported minority e to hold recounts in California and Illi In a situation of this kind, it is clear close to the surface lies the threat of lence implicit in the voting process.

e International Process

Many people blithely argue for law as a
bstitute for violence, as though there were
choice between the two. They call for
ernational law and world government to
minate war. This point of view reveals
blissful ignorance of the functions of vio-
ace in domestic legal systems. A viable
stem based on law protects the conditions
group action. Law always rests on vio-
ace. The threat of violence and the fear
the breakdown of law and order act to
derate demands and positions, thereby
ting into peaceful motion the informal
litical processes of negotiation, conces-
n, compromise, and agreement. Although
ere is no centralized police power in the
ernational forum, the processes of medi-
on and negotiation operate in much the
ne way. The credible threat of violence
the hands of the nations has a similarly
bilizing effect, providing statesmen are
entive to maintaining their national capa-
ity for demonstrating violence, and pro-
ding their ambitions are commensurate to
bargaining position which their arma-
nts achieve. More comprehensive legal
des and a world government may not
prove the stability of the world commu-
ty in any case, since the possibility of civil
nflict exists in all political systems. Civil
rs are frequently bloodier and more un-
giving than wars between sovereign
tions.

In international politics, the threat of
lence tends to create stability and main-
n peace. Here the threat is more di-
tly responsive to policy controls. The
tion-state has greater continuity than the
ormal political systems that coalesce and
solve in the course of domestic social
ange. The threat of violence can be
erted much more deliberately and can be
monstrated under full control, as in "good

will" navy visits, army manuevers near a
sensitive border, partial mobilization, etc.
Because of the greater continuity of these
macro-systems, the national leaders must
strive to maintain the prestige of a nation's
might and will. If the reputation of a nation's military power is allowed to tarnish,
future bargaining power will be weakened.
It may be forced to reestablish that prestige
by invoking a test of arms, as a means of
inducing greater respect for its position
from other nations. All strong nations are
anxious to demonstrate their military power
peaceably in order that their prestige will
afford them the bargaining power they deserve without a test of arms.

Because the threat of violence is a conscious instrument of national policy, it generally lacks the random character which
violence has domestically. This means that
if the armaments of nations fall out of
balance, if the prestige of nations is no
longer commensurate with their ambitions,
if the will to take the risks of limited military conflicts is lacking, if domestic political
considerations distort the national response
to external threat, then the time becomes
ripe for the outbreak of violence, escalating
out of control.

In general, the dangers of escalating
international conflict induce greater, not
lesser, restraint on the part of national
leaders in their relations with each other.
Attempts to achieve infinite security for the
nation are as self-defeating as such attempts
are for domestic regimes.

The functioning of consensus and competition between nations is not fundamentally
different from that of domestic politics. The
most striking difference is that in domestic
politics the level of centralized violence
available to the state creates a high threshold of stability against the threats brought
to bear within the system by private groups.
In the international forum, the closest ap-

proximation to such a threshold is the decentralized forces available to the Great Powers. A power interested in modifying the status quo must raise the level of its threat of violence, in order to induce other powers to choose between concessions to its demands or the costs and risks of an arms race. To the extent that the status quo powers are capable and willing to pay the costs and take the risks, their own levels can be raised, depriving the challenger of any political advantages from his invest- ment. When all of the great powers are attentive to the equations of potential vio- lence, no nation can hope to gain conclusive political advantages from an arms race. This situation makes possible international agreements for stabilizing arms and bring- ing about political settlements.

Diplomatic ceremonials, like the cere- monials of personal relations which we call "manners," serve to minimize the dangers of provocation and threat in the day-to-day relations between nations. Conversely, man- ners tend to minimize the dangers of pro- vocation and threat in relations between people.

The Domestic Process

Underneath all of the norms of legal and institutional behavior in national societies lies the great beast, the people's capability for outraged, uncontrolled, bitter, and bloody violence. This is common to totali- tarian as well as democratic societies. Any group whose interests are too flagrantly abused or ignored is a potential source of violent unrest. This fact is a major restraint against completely arbitrary government. Even totalitarian regimes can hope for sta- bility only if they reflect the changing currents of political interest of the people and if they are willing to recruit new elites from the potentially disaffected groups which they rule. Even totalitarian states

must purvey some concept of fairness and flexibility, an ability to change in response to the changing internal and external de- mands put upon it. In fact, to the extent that a totalitarian regime permits the threat of violence to be raised against it in the form of political pressure, it has ceased to be totalitarian and has become, for substantive purposes, pluralistic. However, the dynamics of totalitarianism generally make this kind of evolution difficult, if not impossible. Dictatorships of one or a few raise the level of official terror to offset or deter the threat of violence from below. The terror and counter-terror may escalate until the whole system collapses in an orgy of violence. The prospects for raising any- thing but another such dictatorship out of the wreakage are remote. Dictators may seek an escape from this iron logic by ex- ternal adventures which unite the country behind the leader, postponing issues of in- ternal dissension.

The threat to carry political dissent out- side peaceable channels can distract the government from the pursuit of other val- ues, can impose upon the government as a first and major responsibility the establish- ment of domestic peace and order, and can force the government into shortsighted measures to suppress violence, which may widen the base of opposition and increase the occasions for anti-government protest.

The mere threat of private violence di- rected against the government has very great power over government actions. By causing reallocations of the resources of the society into the essentially negative goals of internal security, the opposition is in a po- sition to defeat or cripple the positive goals whose accomplishment might legitimize and strengthen government authority. To avoid this predicament, even totalitarian govern- ments may go out of their way to appease

r critics. The alternative to reform is
less suppression not only of the sources
he threat, but also of every symptom of
ed social action. Bowling clubs, as-
blies of three or more people on street
ers—there is no rational way to identify
first links of the chain which leads to
al action. All must be broken up, and
y symptom, however innocuous, must
stamped out. The hopeless search for
ite security begins in this way and
n ends with the downfall of the regime.
Vith this choice before it, it is easy to
why social and political reform are the
erred reactions to the threat of violence.
s is why so many kings and tzars, rather
destroying their opposition, sent them
enforced vacations and educational tours
ad. In more recent cases, the State
artment arranged scholarships in United
es colleges for a number of leading anti-
kee student agitators in Panama.

democratic societies this sharp di-
ma is avoided far short of infinite de-
ence. The institutional distribution of
ority (checks and balances, federalism,
rights, etc.) precludes unilateral at-
pts to centralize all the police powers in
hands of one agent. Also, the law
cribes the overt threat of private vio-
e and the existence of para-military
es, although it tolerates and protects the
licit threat of pluralistic political activi-
Violence is demonstrated, not in
nized forms, but rather in sporadic out-
ts. Those disgruntled elites who possess
lear capability for causing a planned
onstration, i.e., they have organized
ps with a deep sense of moral outrage
injustice, avoid incriminiating them-
es and avoid provoking counteraction
nst themselves. Instead, they carry out
ceable demonstrations" designed to re-
their numbers and the intensity of their
mitment. These are likely to have the

bonus effect of provoking violent action
against them, causing government intervention, and/or causing their more inflammable
followers to ignite into unplanned outbursts
of violence. This potential exists implicitly
in the situation.

The reformist leader is placed in a
position of minimum risk and maximum
effectiveness, that of playing the role of "responsible leader." He can bargain with
formal authorities and with all the other
members of the society in this way: "You
must accept our just complaints and you
must deal with us; otherwise, we will not
be able to control our people." While playing this role, the reformist leader is not
unhappy to have his prophesies fulfilled by
a few psychotic teenagers. Events which
demonstrate violence (and thus induce
other elites to make concessions) do not
have to be planned. Once the emotions of
a real social movement are churned up, the
problem is to keep them from happening.

The irresponsible elements are, of course,
disowned, but the bargaining power of the
responsible leaders is enhanced. In the
bargaining process, the moderate leaders
often accept concessions which fall short of
those demanded by some of their more extremist followers. Opportunists or "realists"
often inherit the benefits wrought by the
blood of martyrs. This is a healthy mode of
exploiting the demonstration of violence
without condoning it, enabling compromises
to be reached which isolate the extremists
and render them less dangerous to the body
politic. The bulk of followers in social
movements will follow responsible leadership through the gives-and-takes of compromise, because they share the general
fear of unlimited violence and counter-
violence, with their unpredictable results
and the defeat of all rational goals. Accom-
modations can be reached, even if only
provisionally, which preserve the general

consensus in maintaining the form and continuity of society and law.

Some Concrete Examples

Let us turn to some concrete examples of how this process works in practice.

A classical case of the actual demonstration of violence against the legality of existing authority is that of the founding of the state of Israel in 1949. The Irgun, an underground terror organization, created conditions in Palestine which made further British government occupation impossible. There is some doubt that the British government would have honored their commitment to the Jewish Agency or honored it when they did, had it not been for the Irgun's role. Yet it was the Jewish Agency, the responsible and moderate leadership, which negotiated the partition of Palestine and which played the major role in the founding of the new state, all the while disavowing the terrorist acts and methods of the Irgun. Before the launching of Irgunist terror, the British government stalled the Jewish Agency and accorded it little respect.

More instructive are cases of domestic violence where the actual demonstration is minimal and where the implicit threat is all, as in the current fight for Negro rights. Until the last decade, there has been little sustained pressure to improve the Southern Negro's position by governmental action. Even with the growth of Negro voting power in the big cities of the North, the Federal Administration has always shown great respect for the implicit capabilities of violence of well-organized White Supremacists. Partly because of the great power of the White South in the Congress, in Democratic National Conventions, and in the Electoral College, presidents have acted with restraint in protecting the rights of Southern Negroes. So long as the possibility of violence was asymmetrical, the Whites

well-organized and armed, the Neg apathetic, intimidated, and disorgani Negro attempts to register to vote, to test lynchings and other injustices, co easily be tranquillized by the County S iffs, the local police, and the KKK. In last decade, the Negroes have been in throes of a new self-consciousness, co dence, organization, and leadership. Black Muslims, the Committee on Ra Equality, the National Association for Advancement of Colored People, etc., b now demonstrated that the Southern Ne is capable of social action and of organi demonstrations of strength. As the ca bility grows for effective counter-viole against White Citizen Council provocat or, what is more significant, nonvic demonstrations which invoke violence the extremist Whites, the Negro will increasing consideration for his dema increasing support from "moderate" W leaders, and increasing attention and s port from the Federal authorities. Jus the existence of the White Citizens Cour strengthened the hand of southern mo ates in trying to restrain civil rights ac from Washington, so the existence of Black Muslims and Core now strengthen position of the NAACP in seeking con sions from Southern Whites and action the Justice Department. The threat of controlled violent outbursts, hovering beneath the surface, acts as a modera influence, maintaining the institutions peaceful process, inducing status quo gro to a greater readiness to yield some pr leges, and restraining the responsible lea of the insurgent Negroes from extre demands.[7]

---

[7] The recent violence at Oxford, Mississi involving the registration of Negro James M dith at the State University, is likely to expe Negro integration throughout the South. precipitating violence (which resulted in

he strategy of nonviolent social action
sive resistance or pacifism) does not
don the threat of force as an instrument
cial change. Rather, it is designed to
ate within a civilized society by its
ocative effects. By provoking the use
rce by others, it forces the government
tervene on the behalf of the nonviolent
onstrators, while evoking the sym-
ies of those less intensely involved. As
nternational ideology, pacifism or uni-
al nonviolence, may fail to achieve its
ctives. Unless those who pursue it suc-
in invoking some force in their behalf,
will be destroyed with impunity by
enemies.

he Douhabor Sons of Freedom (of Van-
er, British Columbia) have adopted a
l tactic of demonstrating violence as
conduct their immemorial campaign
nst compulsory public education. They
ire to their own homes and barns, standby and watching the blaze. They also
de naked down the center of city
ts. The significance of these demon-
ions is plain. Their religion forbids
to threaten or use violence against
rs. Instead, they symbolically demon-
e their discipline and passionate
mitment to their own way of life by
ting violence upon their own property.
naked marches provoked arrests and
isonment and the house-burnings
d the welfare agencies to provide
orary shelter. Both actions impose on

the government responsibilities it is ill-pre-
pared to carry out, especially if such
demonstrations were to continue indefinitely
and involve the entire Douhabor settlement.
In addition, the demonstrations invoke public attention and sympathy for the believers.
All of this may well give the local authorities
incentive to ignore Douhabor defiance of
school attendance laws. In fact, this is
what has happened. Efforts to enforce the
laws are spasmodic and half-hearted, while
the law is generally evaded.

The relations of suicide and crime to
social change are too large a subject for
treatment here (Henry and Short, 1954,
pp. 69–81). Durkheim studied these phenomena as an indicator or measure of social
disorganization. They might be studied in
terms of demonstrating violence as an instrument of political and social change.
When teenagers commit crimes, the legitimate grievances which they have get more
attention. When someone commits suicide,
all those who may sense the circumstances
that drove him to it reexamine their own
lives, are strengthend in convictions concerning the society in which they live. A
suicide of an over-extended installment
buyer in Chicago led to efforts to reform
state and national laws governing interest
rates and collection of unpaid installment
debts. A suicide, apart from its real motives, will be quickly exploited by those
with a social cause. In effect, a suicide resembles a resignation from a government:
it challenges values and institutions, evoking
from all survivors a sense of the unresolved
tensions which surround them, threatening
the prospects for their own survival.[8] Suicides and crimes, however obscure and

---

s), the White Extremists may have
gthened the ranks of the Moderates. Fear-
recurrence, white leadership in future situ-
s may be more concerned with controlling
irebrands than in using them to force con-
ns from the Justice Department. Gunnar
al put his finger on this when he referred
e "positive" aspect of the riots. "The riots
people think," he declared (*New York*
s, October 4, 1962, p. 10).

[8] According to numerous press reports, the
suicide of Marilyn Monroe led within a few
days to a flurry of suicides by women. In the
same manner, it may also have led to many
decisions to live, which were not recorded.

ambiguous, threaten the world and thus change it.

Some Concluding Remarks

There are several points that might be made in conclusion. Demonstrations of domestic violence serve to establish the intensity of commitment of members of the political system. The more intense the commitment, the greater the risks which the system will take in challenging the status quo. Accordingly, the greater will be the bargaining efficacy of future threats. Social change often occurs legalistically. Rationalization in terms of the continuity of abstract legal models is a useful means of stressing consensus over competition, adding to the stability of the whole society. However, it is obvious that a legal or ideological syllogism is meaningless except in terms of the emotional force which members of the society attach to the first principle. The infinite regress of syllogistic reasoning ends somewhere with a commitment of self. Such commitments cannot be explained or understood by reasoning alone. Efforts to adduce rational principles for explaining social and political change are futile unless one grapples with the often irrational and illogical intensity of self-commitment which marks social movements.

No system can hope to survive unless it can live with and adjust itself to the multitudinous threats of violence which are the basis of social change. Democracies have

shown a greater ability to do this. Howe this is not to rule out the possibility even within totalitarian forms, substa democracy can be achieved. On the hand, democratic forms can be subve to become totalitarian in substance, if search for infinite security in the inte tional forum is reflected internally by search for infinite deterrence of th against the social and political status Major social changes have major s causes; they are not the result of iso conspiracies and plots. They canno arrested by an effort to stamp out all spiracies and plots.

"Reason," as understood by Eighte Century Rationalists, Nineteenth Cer Positivists, and Twentieth Century I matists, plays an important role in co resolution as a means of gauging the sibilities of potential violence in barga situations. But conflicts cannot be res as merely legalistic, academic, or ide cal abstractions. The dimensions of mitment and potential violence cons the real substratum which give the r of consensus reality.

REFERENCES

FRANKEL, E. "One Thousand Murderers," nal of Criminal Law and Criminology, in MARSHALL B. CLINARD, Sociology o viant Behavior. New York: Rinehart, I

HENRY, ANDREW F., and SHORT, JR., JAM Suicide and Homicide. Glencoe, Illinois Free Press, 1954.

The Nature of International Society

3

This chapter completes the task of establishing a setting appropriate for the study of how international society might be transformed to reduce the risks of the outbreak of World War III. The selections in Section A depict the main attributes and tendencies of international political life at the present time. In particular, emphasis is put upon the relative roles played in world politics by such varied actors as states, blocs, regional organizations, and the United Nations. This helps to clarify some of the connections between the locus of power and the structure of order in the international system. It also reflects a belief that it is necessary to comprehend and transform power, rather than ignore it, if the study of war prevention is to be responsibly carried forth.

In Section B, the selections discuss the character and contribution of disciplined inquiry into the more descriptive material covered by the authors read in Section A. In the social sciences it is common to identify such concerns as "methodology." The objective is to relate method to the substantive concerns of the book—namely, patterns of interstate conflict, the regulation of violence, and the enhancement of world order. In the background of these considerations lurks the skeptical question concerning the degree to which what we think and what we know can be brought to bear significantly upon what we do. There is also present the question of whether the acquisition of knowledge is a cumulative, and not only an accumulative, process; do we in fact know more today about international conflict than we did some centuries ago when Machiavelli, or even longer ago, when Thucydides lived, analyzed, and prescribed? We have more information, of course, but do we have any better grasp of the bases of political behavior or of how to use our knowledge to promote our goals? In a book investigating a proposal for a drastic change in the character of world order it is very important to face honestly and directly both the limits of our knowledge and the limits of our ability to translate knowledge into behavior. Some clarification of the philosophic issue involved is to be found in Stuart Hampshire's *Thought and Action* (Viking Press, New York, 1960); a quite different view of the relation of thought to action is found in both Marxist and Existentialist writing. For a grand, if unsuccessful, attempt at synthesis, see Jean-Paul Sartre, *Critique de la Raison Dialectique* (Gallimard, Paris, 1960); for assessments, see Wilfred D. Desan, *The Marxism of Jean-Paul Sartre* (Doubleday, New York, 1965); Walter Odajnyk, *Marxism and Existentialism* (1965).

A. Differing Views of the World

To solve a problem it is important to have a sense of the causes that seem to account for its existence. Hence, Chapter 2 dealt with the causes of war. But it is essential also to have a sense of the specific milieu in which the problem (the danger of major war) manifests its present form. For this reason it is useful to make reference to the relevant aspects of "the world." When this is done it becomes immediately clear that different observers see the world differently, and for this reason, propose to deal with it differently. The obvious explanation of these differences is the differing constellations of values that give to men, even those living peacably together in a society, distinct, and often antagonistic, policy orientations. But values are not the only cause of differences in outlook. Observers also differ about what is actually going on and how to assess the significance of specific developments. In international affairs the unevenness and inadequacy of our access to authoritative knowledge is especially serious. Even sophisticated and trained observers resident in free societies are victims of managed news and suffer from a modern phenomenon that has been aptly described as "the nationalization of truth." We cannot, of course, hope to avoid these difficulties. It may encourage more useful analysis to call attention to some of the prominent modes of thought about contemporary international society and ask what difference it makes whether one adopts this or that mode of analysis.

The first selection is by Roberto Ducci, an Italian diplomat and scholar, whose brief essay sketches the major developments in international life since the end of World War II, and on this basis, suggests some of the implications for the future of world order in the years directly ahead of us.

In "The World Order in the Sixties," *Foreign Affairs*, vol. 42, no. 3 (April, 1964) pp. 379–390, Ducci describes the breakdown of the wartime alliance, the start of the cold war, the emergence of two blocs each led by a superpower, and the growth of an

important new political force in the third world composed of
states receiving their independence since 1945.   He then examines some more recent developments and finds that defec-
tions within the blocs point toward the actual disappearance of
the bipolar world.   He suggests that we are now entering a
period of gradual "atomization."   Although Ducci is not very
specific about the duration or extent of this atomization, he does
find it plausible to speculate about a system of international
relations in which 125 to 135 nation-states pursue their various
interests without regard for "bipolarization."   Ducci favors "the
formation of units larger than the traditional nation-state," and
gives as an example a United Europe.   He also appears to favor
the expansion of other regional organizations.   Ducci, however,
considers that the prospects for world peace continue to depend
primarily upon the efforts of the Great Powers, and especially
upon their capacity to work out standards and practices for
some level of permanent cooperation.   For this reason, he suggests that the Charter of the United Nations be revised to give
the more powerful states greater relative authority in the
Organization than they now possess.   Such a suggestion leads
one back to the image of the United Nations that prevailed at
the preliminary drafting sessions held at Dumbarton Oaks
during the closing months of World War II.   This view leads
Ducci to advocate the retransfer of authority for the maintenance of international peace back from the General Assembly to
the Security Council, and especially back to the five permanent
members.   The permanent members were expected to establish
under Articles 41 and 42 of the Charter a military arm to be
available to the United Nations Organization to enable it to
carry out its peace-keeping missions.   See further in **III 4-5,
9-10**.

In contrast to Ducci, Kenneth N. Waltz doubts whether
international society will experience any significant atomization, even to the extent of suggesting that analysts will be led
to substitute multipolarity for bipolarity as the dominant
image expressive of the distribution of world power.   Waltz, in
his article, "The Stability of a Bipolar World," *Daedalus*, vol.
93, no. 3 (Summer, 1964) pp. 881–907, takes note of the decline
of inter-bloc rivalry and the weakening of intra-bloc cohesion,
but insists nevertheless, that the superpowers will retain their
preeminence because only they have both the productive
capacity and the wealth needed to produce the expensive new
varieties of nuclear weapons systems.   As a consequence of this
military preeminence, Waltz argues that the superpowers will
remain by far the most influential poltical actors in world

affairs. By reaching this conclusion Waltz maintains in his analysis the traditional link between relative military power and relative international influence. Waltz does not believe that France or China have the capacity to challenge the super-powers, and for this reason does not think that they will emerge as significant rival centers of international power. It is this notion of rival centers of power that underlies the anticipation of a multipolar world. Waltz's analysis virtually omits reference to the relative power of the newly independent states of Asia and Africa, but this omission is consistent with the correlation of power and influence with wealth, income, and industrial capacity. It is also consistent with giving relatively little attention to the relevance of international institutions, and giving no attention to the role of the United Nations as a source of effective authority. Waltz states the case imaginatively for looking beneath certain dramatic evidence of atomization and taking account of the more conventional constituents of power (wealth and force) in political life. His prediction that bipolarity will not vanish is coupled with some indication of confidence in the capacity of the system of mutual deterrence to maintain international peace. It certainly would seem to follow that a portrayal of international society in terms of bipolarity leads to an emphasis on existing and prospective ordering arrangements that have been worked out explicitly or tacitly between the Soviet Union and the United States.

Yalem's piece on regionalism does not quite agree with the other two selections in the section. He does not suggest that regional actors form the existing or prospective basis of world order. His claim is more modest. Yalem is content merely to suggest that the relevance of regionalism to world order warrants careful analysis. Part of the value of his discussion is to clarify the concept of what constitutes a region for purposes of asserting formal competence. Is it primarily a matter of territorial contiguity or primarily a matter of ideological affinity? Yalem finds difficulty accepting either notion in unalloyed form.

Yalem also relates regional organizations to the United Nations. He discusses, first of all, the status of regional organizations within the framework of the United Nations Charter in "Regionalism and World Order," *International Affairs*, vol. 38, no. 4 (October, 1962) pp. 460-471. Yalem contends that unless regional actors are made subordinate to the United Nations their existence and growth will be detrimental, rather than a benefit to the maintenance of stability and peace in international relations. For a fuller discussion, see Yalem, *Regional and World Order* (Public Affairs Press, Washington, D.C., 1965).

Throughout this first section it is useful to consider how national, regional, and global actors interact in contemporary international society and to ask what pattern of interaction seems most consistent with the realization of the overriding objective of war prevention. Most thought about international society has been devoted to analyzing the relations among states. International law developed in a political environment within which states were the only significant actors. We will be concerned in a later chapter about how to adapt our habits of thought and our structures of authority to accommodate the presence of such other significant actors as regional, bloc, and global entities.

THE WORLD ORDER IN THE SIXTIES

By Roberto Ducci

W E live, no doubt, in a period of accelerating history, though what precisely we can expect from this acceleration nobody dares predict. The end of World War II is still not 20 years away, yet there already is little resemblance between the blueprint for world order drawn in 1944 and the world of 1964. A world order after a war which caused 30,000,000 casualties should last somewhat longer than that. The *Pax Romana* after the civil wars fought just before the birth of Christ lasted, on and off, a couple of centuries. The *Pax Anglica* after the Napoleonic Wars lasted a century. The *Pax Americana* (nobody can deny that the United States has kept the peace since VJ-Day, with some tacit coöperation from Russia) has now lasted nineteen and a half years, but thanks only to several changes in the organization of the world, some of them improvised under the pressure of events.

This article will attempt to peer into the darkness of the future and imagine how peace can be kept in the sixties and the early seventies. Is the present world order (if any) going to last? What forces and what ideas are pressing for a change? Where are the centers of resistance? What sort of new equilibrium (if needed) will be established, and by whom?

II

The blueprint for peace at the end of World War II was simple and therefore had a certain harmonious elegance. Five main powers were to be responsible for assuring the peace of the globe, and they were given juridical sanction for this in the United Nations Charter, which accorded them permanent seats and veto rights in the Security Council. The United Kingdom was to be responsible for northwest Europe, the Mediterranean, the Near and Middle East, southern Asia and Oceania; the Soviet Union for its own enormous mainland and for Eastern Europe; France for the bulk of Africa, north and south of the Sahara; China (the China of Chiang Kai-shek) for the Far East. The United States, having brought peace back to the earth and the boys back home, could safely withdraw to its front porch overlooking Latin America, except for giving a hand in the establishment of democracy in

Germany and Japan and generally supervising the state of affairs in the four other continents.

This idyllic dream of San Francisco and Yalta was shattered within a year or so of F.D.R.'s death. The United Kingdom was unable to bear such a heavy burden in four continents; having wisely let India go, it tried with scant or no success to hold the Near and Middle East, and was forced to put the defense of the eastern Mediterranean and of Australasia in the lap of President Truman. France kept her colonies for a time, thanks to the ability and devotion to her *corps d'élite;* but then the retreat had to be sounded. China surprised most people by going Communist, and thereby subverting the balance of the world: for Russia had in the meantime converted the whole of Eastern Europe into a fortified encampment and had brought her weight to bear all along the provisional border with the West. The American boys, 400,000 of them, had to be sent back to Europe in a hurry.

The forces which were active in international society in those years and which changed the face of it in an amazingly short time were not always identified correctly. At the beginning, the nature and the strength of the world-wide revolt against the white race was much underrated. The capacity of glorious old countries like Britain and France to play a world role was, on the contrary, much overestimated. Most people saw Communism in terms of aggressiveness, and few in terms of weakness: yet weak it certainly was until 1950 at least, during the period in which there was little the Soviet Union could do against the American nuclear monopoly. For the Kremlin, those were the years of the Great Fear: the fear of Capitalism using its military superiority to blow Communism out of existence; the miserable fear that Marx and Lenin had been wrong after all and the bourgeoisie right. One of the two blocs into which the world split itself in the late forties was created out of that weakness and that fear: for Stalin's iron hand imposed the Soviet yoke on the young countries of Eastern Europe, ruthlessly suffocating their nationalistic pride and their pathetic invocation of independence, in order to establish the widest possible *glacis* between the American bases in Germany and the main Russian industrial and population centers. While even old guard Communists were sent to their death or placed in solitary confinement, all vestiges of national identity in Eastern Europe, except in Tito's Jugoslavia, were pursued and as far as possible suppressed.

Thus, the Soviet response to the challenge presented by the American nuclear monopoly was the forcible integration into the U.S.S.R. of those parts of Europe which were within reach of the Soviet Army. When shortly afterward the American monopoly was broken, the general impression (probably a very hasty one) was that, conditions of parity having been reëstablished in the nuclear field, the superiority now rested with whoever had the biggest conventional forces, namely, the Soviet bloc. The art of nuclear deterrence being in its infancy, people's minds and even generals' thoughts were conditioned by the old doctrines of conventional warfare. This was a powerful incentive to integration among the Western European states and to the integration of them all with the United States in a single political and military system.

III

The Western bloc, of course, was never really similar to the Stalinist bloc, except in the sense that there was one leading power which, however, did not need to threaten or use force to be recognized as leader. This is shown, among other ways, by the Western bloc's parallel development in the direction of Atlantic integration and in the direction of European integration. (Stalin had violently forbidden any attempt at union among his satellites.) There were psychological reasons for evoking the rise of a united Europe from the ashes of the defeated and impoverished old continent, once suzerain of the world. There was idealistic aspiration toward a general reconciliation of the European peoples, putting an end to three thousand years of strife. But this might not have been transferred to the realm of practical politics had it not been for the necessity of solving a seemingly unsolvable problem: how to call upon the potential might of Germany (a few years after her defeat and destruction) to help in the defense of the West, without making her again the dominant country in Europe.

There were two schools of thought. The first, mostly English, held that Germany could safely be contained only in a political and military system guaranteed by the United States and the United Kingdom. The other school, prevailingly French, thought that no real security could be obtained unless Germany were merged along with some other European countries in a new supranational system. In the latter system there would be equality among the participating countries, but France would be a little more equal than her partners (she would not renounce atomic weapons, would not be subject to legal limits in conventional forces, would receive financial aid for her colonial policy or for her nuclear research, and so on)—though not enough more equal to please Charles de Gaulle's vision of French equality. This second school got the encouragement and support of the United States, but could not totally prevail over the first.

These two patterns of organization therefore coexist in the Western world, not hampering, but strengthening each other. One is intended to maintain the balance of military power in the world, and therefore inside Europe itself, through the absolute superiority of the United States in nuclear weapons; the other is to maintain the balance of political and economic power inside Europe. But this double scheme may continue only so long as no participant questions how the military equilibrium in the world is to be kept. Since one of the conditions of the equilibrium is the nuclear monopoly of the United States, the questioning of that monopoly will not permit the double scheme to survive for long.

John Foster Dulles was, if not the author (because he must share that honor with Jean Monnet), at least the most powerful sponsor of the Western political system just described and of the system of world order founded upon it. It has become fashionable nowadays to pass negative judgments upon Dulles' achievements and designs; his credo is branded as reactionary, his effort to establish a world-wide net of military pacts is described as a form of mania, his diplomacy of brinkmanship is labeled as warmongering. His stern and disciplinary vision of reality, his habit of telling blunt truths, his massive and rather dominating personality did not endear him to statesmen or to the masses. Still, the objective historian will acclaim him as a man who possessed a supreme capacity for weighing exactly the forces present in the world arena. He was the first man in America and probably in the world to understand the political implications of nuclear weapons and the advantages that diplomacy could get from even a temporary superiority in that field. The doctrine of massive retaliation, which the West is now correctly abandoning, was in Dulles' days the right application to the diplomatic struggle of the military superiority then enjoyed by the United States, since it could devastate the heart of the Soviet Union while the Russians could not do the same to the United States. The doctrine gave better results in a defensive posture (as in the Quemoy-Matsu case) than in an offensive one (although the fact that it was not invoked to help the insurgent workers and students of Budapest may be charitably explained by the state of utter confusion into which the West had worked itself over the Suez affair). But normally, since brinkmanship was based on an exact evaluation of the opposing forces, it was able to keep the status quo and peace. When the first Sputnik showed that the balance of power was about to be redressed in favor of the U.S.S.R., Dulles was quick to perceive it and to start the slow retreat toward a different military and political posture.

Through the menace of massive nuclear retaliation, and while it was credible, Dulles had consolidated a world order which looked and was rational. It was jointly administered by the two blocs, one of which was deterred from making war if not from exporting subversion, while the other had renounced war except in self-defense (as the autumn of 1956 crudely showed). Communist propaganda attacked the "imperialistic policy of blocs" as a menace to world peace. The reverse was true: it was the existence of two solid and balanced blocs that kept the peace. Probably this was silently recognized even in the Kremlin.

Was Khrushchev sincere when at the end of 1958 he suggested fixing a legal frontier between East and West by a legal partition of Germany, implying that this would establish peace firmly on the Continent? Probably he had in mind the advantages of a truce with the West while the Soviet Union consolidated its economic and political situation. It is not likely, however, that the whole content of the Berlin ultimatum of 1958 can be explained in a conservative way, even though other acts and gestures of Khrushchev's reveal that a thread of conservatism runs through his policies corresponding to the present situation of the U.S.S.R. in the world. The insistence that war is not inevitable, the recent emphasis on the sanctity of frontiers—be they Tsarist frontiers in Asia or Potsdam frontiers in Europe—and above all the support given to the plan for limiting the possession of nuclear weapons to the "haves" reveal the Soviet interest in perpetuating the present state of the world—one in which, on more or less Dulles' lines, each of the two Great Powers would continue maintaining order in its third of the world, while the other third remain the object of their mutual competition, short of war.

IV

The perpetuation of the two-bloc system as a basis for world order might not be a bad thing, though hardly one that the Chinese would call revolutionary. The question is whether the changing face of society has not already made it obsolete.

In the last five years it has become apparent that a gradual process of erosion is at work in each of the two opposing blocs. Owing to various reasons which will be examined later, the leader of each bloc does not seem to have the same authority as before. There have been cases of overt rebellion, France in one camp and China plus Albania in the other, as well as a number of minor acts of insubordination in both. The two apparently monolithic constructions of the fifties now have more resemblance to boiling underground magmas, from which come rumbles indicating the formation of deep and wide crevices. This fluidity is reflected in the internal situation in several states of the Western Alliance. Ideological and party divisions which until a few years ago used to be very sharp, and which mostly coincided with the dividing line between friends of the United States and friends of the U.S.S.R., have become less precise and even tend to disappear. The corresponding phenomenon in the East, though less visible, is the emergence of revisionist or of pro-Chinese factions in the Communist parties. There is a continuous interaction, further, between these new trends and others which are at work in a different sphere: Roman Catholicism under the leadership of the Popes themselves is breaking out of its medieval fortress, seeking union for the Christian churches and admitting tolerance toward other religions (including, it would seem at times, the Communist religion). In such a syncretistic and conciliatory atmosphere it becomes more difficult, in turn, to enforce the dogmatic creeds as of old; and Yevtushenko can fight in the East the battle for intellectual liberty which has become a bit stale in the West.

Let me now try to indicate the motives, more or less common to the Western and Eastern societies, which may have prompted these visible transformations. Starting with the less important, the first motive can be found in the fact that the difference in economic and technical capacity between the leading nation and the other nations of a bloc is decreasing; for short periods, indeed, the leading nation may even be the one to experience an economic crisis. Thus what was once a powerful force for the unity of each bloc is now less effective. Financially and economically, Western Europe is on its own. The same cannot be said of the smaller Comecon countries; yet present-day Russia, in the grip of a severe agricultural crisis and begging for long-term credits, is certainly not in a position to supply capital in the amounts necessary for their further industrial development (not to speak of China).

The second main cause of the erosion of both blocs is that the effectiveness of the nuclear protection afforded by each of the two leading nations is diminishing and the fear of nuclear reprisal against political misbehavior is vanishing. De Gaulle's thesis on the first point is well known. Without going so far as he has in his reasoning, all eyes now can see that the threshold for nuclear intervention is being set higher and higher, so that only the most vital interests would trigger the deterrent. The growing appreciation of this has certainly had a considerable influence on China's rift with the Soviet Union. What assurance can Peking have that, in case China were threatened with nuclear weapons, the Soviet Union would willingly run the risk of being itself wiped out? The Peking leaders must be convinced that China needs her own nuclear arsenal in order to survive; and if they cannot get it from the U.S.S.R., they will do everything possible to procure it by their own efforts. (If this analysis is correct, there is no chance of China subscribing to a treaty against the dissemination of atomic weapons. And if this treaty were applied only to the mainland of Europe—France excepted—and to underdeveloped continents, what useful purpose could it serve? Nations that have accepted the lower status do not need to take such engagements; others, whenever able, will pay no heed to them.)

On the other hand, there has been ample proof by now that even a weak country can sever itself from a bloc, and either change sides or remain isolated, without suffering more than economic hardship. Jugoslavia, Cuba and Albania are cases in point. Why this should be possible, and in what limits (the U.S.S.R. rapidly intervened against Hungary's attempt to leave the Warsaw Pact), may be explained by the fact that in the nuclear era Great Powers need allies much less than before. Allies may have a psychological, economic or propaganda value; they have very little military value now, and even the importance which their geographic position might have had for the establishment of nuclear bases has been reduced to practically nil by the development of intercontinental and sea-based missiles. On purely strategic grounds, allies and therefore blocs have more and more a marginal value.

The third reason for the erosion of the bloc system is found in a series of psychological factors. After 15 years of tension, the ruling groups on both sides of the Iron Curtain no longer find it possible to keep their peoples in a state of active ideological mobilization. The measures taken for diminishing tension have a multiplier effect. "Imperialistic encirclement" ceased to be an excuse for crop failures or for the paucity of consumer goods in the Soviet Union once the United States began to be impersonated by Kennedy's smile. In the same fashion, the "threat of Soviet aggression" is ceasing to be an effective electoral device for rightist parties since Stalin's deadly sarcasm began to be replaced by Khrushchev's parables and jokes. It is now permissible for a member of the bourgeoisie to be "American" or "Gaullist" and for a member of a Communist party to be "Russian" or "Chinese" (though not in the East), even though Gaullism and China are not yet really credible alternatives. In the sphere of individual conscience, a new urge is growing not just to move toward an ill-defined "peace" (which might also be the peace of the dead), but to ensure wider possibilities to express one's personality, to meet and understand one's neighbor, to communicate with him in some new endeavor, to establish a measure of fraternity somewhere else than in war cemeteries, to make the whole world one's home.

Above all, fear—that great cement of alliances—is beginning to vanish, both in the internal relations between members of each bloc and in the relations between the two blocs. Big Brother has ceased to be feared because of his bigness, or to be loved because of his brotherhood. Die-hard capitalism and intransigent Communism are both becoming obsolete and out of fashion. All this presages something new—for something has to fill the void which will be created.

v

Just as in internal politics people are fleeing extremes, so in international society new positions are becoming fashionable. These positions could be called neo-nationalism and neo-neutralism (similar to but not identical with nineteenth- and early twentieth-century nationalism and neutralism). Some neo-nationalistic countries, like de Gaulle's France, have chosen to remain for the time being members of a bloc; and nearly all neo-neutralist countries feel sooner or later the barrenness of their position and try to coalesce in a "non-bloc" in order to increase their influence on world affairs. But fundamentally the position of both is sustained by the faith that in our changing world a nation can find its salvation best by relying upon its own efforts and resources. This trend points therefore, if we are not grossly mistaken, to a gradual "atomization" of international society.

Before considering its implications, we should ask whether this trend is not something fleeting, whether the old system will not in the end be reëstablished without too great difficulty. If I sincerely doubt this, notwithstanding what I had to say on the advantages of the two-bloc system, it is because in order to have once again a bipolar world we would have to find a way of convincing ourselves that China does not exist: an exploit which may still be possible for a while on the East River but is certainly impossible everywhere else. The leading powers of the two blocs enjoyed a remarkable and very rare combination of three faculties. They had exclusive control of the "final" weapons. They had economic resources which permitted them to extend aid to the nations of their group. They enjoyed positions of ideological superiority deserved as a result of victory in war and/or revolution, so that the ideology each sponsored had no difficulty in becoming the ideology of the group. These three conditions are obsolescent, and in combination are obsolete. A treaty may try to keep control of nuclear weapons in the hands of *beati possidentes:* it will mean nothing for China, nor probably for France, nor even for those nations or groups of nations which will invoke the Chinese and French precedents. Economic aid from the leading nation of a bloc will be required in decreasing quantities. Finally, the ideological leadership will be challenged more and more often (as it already is beginning to be): people who cease to be afraid or in need do not remain convinced of the ideological superiority of others.

All signs seem therefore to point to an alteration of the world order. The movement is led, as always, by real revolutionaries. In our day the role is played by de Gaulle and Mao, who have revolted openly against the established order. But what really signals that the wind is set to blow in another direction is the recognition by the World Establishment itself of the change in the psychological, if not yet in the political, climate. In different fields, obeying different pressures, aiming at different goals,

John F. Kennedy and John XXIII and Nikita Khrushchev have given a powerful impulse toward transforming the order which had prevailed in the world since 1947.

VI

In a way it is comforting that in such a short time and over such a vast surface of mankind's geographical and spiritual domain the trend toward a new state of affairs has been given favorable recognition. The risks accompanying a prolonged period of changes are evident. As Walpole, Metternich and Salisbury, among others, saw in their times, hardly any modification of a given international equilibrium can take place without involving the possibility of war. In our day such a possibility might produce so much more terrible destruction and misery that the period of change should, if possible, be reduced to a minimum.

The first and most risky effect of the weakening of the two-bloc system is or will be, as I said, the "atomization" of international society. The compound effect of nationalism and neutralism, the two forces which are wearing down the blocs, will be felt not only in South America and Africa, in the Middle East and Asia, but in Europe itself, both Eastern and Western. The example of Hungary will not be reproduced easily or soon; but the example of Jugoslavia or Albania might well find imitators, in forms and circumstances which cannot be foreseen. The political posture of Sweden and Finland, as well as that of Switzerland and Austria, may have a larger appeal in the context of world-wide ideological and political détente. Neutral-nationalism (the theory of salvation through one's own efforts or, one might say, the modern political Protestantism) will cross the barriers of color, race and geography; unity might be sought in this faith, as suggested by Tito and others, instead of in geographical-racial factors, as suggested by Sukarno. And properly so, because ideas, as missiles, do not stop at state borders. We shall indeed witness more and more frequent attempts (not always crowned with success) by certain powers to act beyond what would be considered their normal range of influence—China in South America, Cuba in Africa, France in the region of Asia from which she was forcibly expelled ten years ago.

The battle between good and evil continues to be fought, though with softer trumpets and more sedate alarums. But official neutrality in that battle is no longer considered a bad thing. Dulles was often accused, in office and after, of wanting to brand neutrals as immoral. In effect, he might have adopted the words *Hors de l'Eglise pas de salut*—outside the Church there is no salvation—a very justified precept for the Roman Church in pitched battle against the Reform, but less correct, leaders of the Ecumenical Movement feel, in a situation of religious stalemate. Still, it may well be that Dulles, consistent with his conception of world order, was against neutrality not so much because he considered it immoral as because he found it infectious.

In the same way, it is not to be concluded from the likely atomization of international society that the freedom of movement which it will offer to small and big powers is a bad thing in itself; it may even be, under certain aspects, a valuable thing. But this freedom of movement, if left to its natural operation, carries with it the danger of frequent collisions. In the world political system of the fifties the risk of war was limited. It was unlikely that a global conflict could happen by accident and there were no possible *agents provocateurs*. In Berlin, Korea, Viet Nam and Egypt escalation was prevented by a tacit agreement between the two world powers. It seems doubtful that this could remain true in a world where five or more nuclear powers existed and where, moreover, nearly every state's lack of responsibility could create innumerable occasions for conflict.

I shall not presume to show on what lines the new international order should be erected if the worst is to be avoided, but merely point out that the main responsibility for a peaceful and rapid transition rests with the present great powers. It is for them to realize that the first-priority requirement is to reduce the number of unknown factors in the international equation. They should encourage, whenever and wherever possible, the formation of units larger than the traditional nation-state (or than the artificial countries created in Africa and Latin America). The benefit which a really united Europe could be for the stabilization of peace and the prevention of adventures in one of the most sensitive regions of the world is now evident to many. Let us hope that one day it may become as evident in Moscow as it is now in Washington. Similar solutions should be attentively considered as the eventual aim of a gradual evolution in the Middle East, or in certain regions of Africa, or in the area stretching from Malay to New Guinea to the Philippines.

Pending the formation of such wider and more responsible

political units, encouragement should be given to regional organizations, of the type recognized by the U.N. Charter. They
should be strengthened so as to make them able to keep the
peace in their respective areas: NATO in the North Atlantic and
the Council of Europe in the European regions, O.A.S. in the
Americas, O.A.U. in Africa, SEATO in Southeast Asia. Nobody,
looking back to the events in Cyprus, can fail to see, for instance,
how useful a strong European regional organization might have
been for solving both the short- and the long-term crisis.

Realistically, however, one must recognize that the effort to
concentrate power and therefore responsibility in several groupings of nations, thereby reducing the margin of anarchy in the
world, has evident limits. Could the United Nations help to put
some order into the residual anarchy? The answer must be, as
Secretary of State Rusk pointed out in his address at Columbia
University last January, that the present United Nations, being
founded on the juridical fiction of equal rights and responsibilities
for every single member state, without possessing ways and
means to enforce some sort of order, in practice reinforces the
anarchy natural to a society based on a multiplicity of irresponsible states.

The effort to improve the peace-keeping machinery of the
United Nations, as suggested by Secretary Rusk, is therefore
going to be vital. It is indeed difficult to see how the world order
is to be kept in the late sixties and early seventies unless the
United Nations undergoes a thorough overhaul. Not incon-
ceivably the two present superpowers may one day agree that
the strengthening of the United Nations might be in the interest
of both, so that it might help them carry the responsibility of
peace which they will not be able to shoulder any longer. It
might well be to their advantage (as shown by Mr. Rusk's proposal to enhance the prestige and power of the Security Council,
and particularly of the countries having permanent seats) to
delegate some functions to other countries or groups, and have
them share the burden of the superpowers in the world arena—
though probably not their real strength as measured by the yardstick of the missile age. If that happens, the future organization
of the world might not be very dissimilar in principle from the one
which was drafted in Dumbarton Oaks 20 years ago by the victors
of World War II.

KENNETH N. WALTZ

The Stability of a Bipolar World

THERE is a conventional wisdom, accumulated over the centuries, upon which statesmen and students often draw as they face problems in international politics. One part of the conventional wisdom is now often forgotten. Many in Europe, and some in America, have come to regard an alliance as unsatisfactory if the members of it are grossly unequal in power. "Real partnership," one hears said in a variety of ways, "is possible only between equals."[1] If this is true, an addendum should read: Only unreal partnerships among states have lasted beyond the moment of pressing danger. Where states in association have been near equals, some have voluntarily abdicated the leadership to others, or the alliance has become paralyzed by stalemate and indecision, or it has simply dissolved. One may observe that those who are less than equal are often dissatisfied without thereby concluding that equality in all things is good. As Machiavelli and Bismarck well knew, an alliance requires an alliance leader; and leadership can be most easily maintained where the leader is superior in power. Some may think of these two exemplars as unworthy; even so, where the unworthy were wise, their wisdom should be revived.

A second theorem of the conventional wisdom is still widely accepted. It reads: A world of many powers is more stable than a bipolar world, with stability measured by the peacefulness of adjustment within the international system and by the durability of the system itself. While the first element of the conventional wisdom might well be revived, the second should be radically revised.

Pessimism about the possibility of achieving stability in a two-power world was reinforced after the war by contemplation of the character of the two major contenders. The Soviet Union, led by a possibly psychotic Stalin, and the United States, flaccid, iso-

lationist by tradition, and untutored in the ways of international relations, might well have been thought unsuited to the task of finding
a route to survival. How could either reconcile itself to coexistence
when ideological differences were great and antithetical interests
provided constant occasion for conflict? Yet the bipolar world of
the postwar period has shown a remarkable stability. Measuring
time from the termination of war, 1964 corresponds to 1937. Despite
all of the changes in the nineteen years since 1945 that might have
shaken the world into another great war, 1964 somehow looks and
feels safer than 1937. Is this true only because we now know that
1937 preceded the holocaust by just two years? Or is it the terror
of nuclear weapons that has kept the world from major war? Or
is the stability of the postwar world intimately related to its bipolar
pattern?

Stability Within a Bipolar System

Within a bipolar world, four factors conjoined encourage the
limitation of violence in the relations of states. First, with only two
world powers there are no peripheries. The United States is the
obsessing danger for the Soviet Union, and the Soviet Union for
us, since each can damage the other to an extent that no other state
can match. Any event in the world that involves the fortunes of the
Soviet Union or the United States automatically elicits the interest
of the other. Truman, at the time of the Korean invasion, could not
very well echo Chamberlain's words in the Czechoslovakian crisis
and claim that the Koreans were a people far away in the east of
Asia of whom Americans knew nothing. We had to know about them
or quickly find out. In the 1930's, France lay between England and
Germany. England could believe, and we could too, that their frontier and ours lay on the Rhine. After World War II, no third power
could lie between the United States and the Soviet Union, for none
existed. The statement that peace is indivisible was controversial,
indeed untrue, when it was made by Litvinov in the 1930's. It became a truism in the 1950's. Any possibility of maintaining a general peace required a willingness to fight small wars. With the
competition both serious and intense, a loss to one could easily appear as a gain to the other, a conclusion that follows from the very
condition of a two-power competition. Political action has corresponded to this assumption. Communist guerrillas operating in
Greece prompted the Truman doctrine. The tightening of Soviet

control over the states of Eastern Europe led to the Marshall Plan and the Atlantic Defense Treaty, and these in turn gave rise to the Cominform and the Warsaw Pact. The plan to form a West German government produced the Berlin blockade. Our response in a two-power world was geared to Soviet action, and theirs to ours, which produced an increasingly solid bipolar balance.

Not only are there no peripheries in a bipolar world but also, as a second consideration, the range of factors included in the competition is extended as the intensity of the competition increases. Increased intensity is expressed in a reluctance to accept small territorial losses, as in Korea, the Formosa Strait, and Indo-China. Extension of range is apparent wherever one looks. Vice President Nixon hailed the Supreme Court's desegregation decision as our greatest victory in the cold war. When it became increasingly clear that the Soviet economy was growing at a rate that far exceeded our own, many began to worry that falling behind in the economic race would lead to our losing the cold war without a shot being fired. Disarmament negotiations have most often been taken as an opportunity for propaganda. As contrasted with the 1930's, there is now constant and effective concern lest military preparation fall below the level necessitated by the military efforts of the major antagonist. Changes between the wars affected different states differently, with adjustment to the varying ambitions and abilities of states dependent on cumbrous mechanisms of compensation and realignment. In a multipower balance, who is a danger to whom is often a most obscure matter: the incentive to regard all disequilibrating changes with concern and respond to them with whatever effort may be required is consequently weakened. In our present world changes may affect each of the two powers differently, and this means all the more that few changes in the national realm or in the world at large are likely to be thought irrelevant. Policy proceeds by imitation, with occasional attempts to outflank.

The third distinguishing factor in the bipolar balance, as we have thus far known it, is the nearly constant presence of pressure and the recurrence of crises. It would be folly to assert that repeated threats and recurring crises necessarily decrease danger and promote stability. It may be equally wrong to assert the opposite, as Khrushchev seems to appreciate. "They frighten us with war," he told the Bulgarians in May of 1962, "and we frighten them back bit by bit. They threaten us with nuclear arms and we tell them: 'Listen, now only fools can do this, because we have them too, and they are not smaller than yours but, we think, even better than yours. So why do you do foolish things and frighten us?' This is the situation, and this is why we consider the situation to be good."[2] Crises, born of a condition in which interests and ambitions conflict, are produced by the determination of one state to effect a change that another state chooses to resist. With the Berlin blockade, for example, as with Russia's emplacement of missiles in Cuba, the United States decided that to resist the change the Soviet Union sought to bring about was worth the cost of turning its action into a crisis. If the condition of conflict remains, the absence of crises becomes more disturbing than their recurrence. Rather a large crisis now than a small war later is an axiom that should precede the statement, often made, that to fight small wars in the present may be the means of avoiding large wars later.

Admittedly, crises also occur in a multipower world, but the dangers are diffused, responsibilities unclear, and definition of vital interests easily obscured. The skillful foreign policy, where many states are in balance, is designed to gain an advantage over one state without antagonizing others and frightening them into united action. Often in modern Europe, possible gains have seemed greater than likely losses. Statesmen could thus hope in crises to push an issue to the limit without causing all the potential opponents to unite. When possible enemies are several in number, unity of action among states is difficult to secure. One could therefore think —or hope desperately, as did Bethmann Hollweg and Adolph Hitler—that no united opposition would form.

In a bipolar world, on the other hand, attention is focused on crises by both of the major competitors, and especially by the defensive state. To move piecemeal and reap gains serially is difficult, for within a world in confusion there is one great certainty, namely, the knowledge of who will oppose whom. One's motto may still be, "push to the limit," but *limit* must be emphasized as heavily as *push*. Caution, moderation, and the management of crisis come to be of great and obvious importance.

Many argue, nonetheless, that caution in crises, and resulting bipolar stability, is accounted for by the existence of nuclear weapons, with the number of states involved comparatively inconsequent. That this is a doubtful deduction can be indicated by a consideration of how nuclear weapons may affect reactions to crises. In the postwar world, bipolarity preceded the construction of two opposing atomic weapons systems. The United States, with some success, substituted technological superiority for expenditure on a conventional military system as a deterrent to the Soviet Union during the years when we had first an atomic monopoly and then a decisive edge in quantity and quality of weapons. American military policy was not a matter of necessity but of preference based on a calculation of advantage. Some increase in expenditure and a different allocation of monies would have enabled the United States to deter the Soviet Union by posing credibly the threat that any Soviet attempt, say, to overwhelm West Germany would bring the United States into a large-scale conventional war.* For the Soviet Union, war against separate European states would have promised large gains; given the bipolar balance, no such war could be undertaken without the clear prospect of American entry. The Russians' appreciation of the situation is perhaps best illustrated by the structure of their military forces. The Soviet Union has concentrated heavily on medium-range bombers and missiles and, to our surprise, has built relatively few intercontinental weapons. The country of possibly aggressive intent has assumed a posture of passive deterrence vis-à-vis her major adversary, whom she quite sensibly does not want to fight. Against European and other lesser states, the Soviet Union has a considerable offensive capability.** Hence nuclear capabilities merely reinforce a condition that would exist in their absence: without nuclear technology both the United States and the Soviet Union have the ability to develop weapons of considerable destructive power. Even had the atom never been split, each

---

    * The point has been made by Raymond Aron, among others. "Even if it had not had the bomb, would the United States have tolerated the expansion of the Soviet empire as far as the Atlantic? And would Stalin have been ready to face the risk of general war?" Raymond Aron, *The Century of Total War* (Boston: Beacon Press, 1955), p. 151.

    ** Hanson W. Baldwin, from information supplied by Strategic Air Command headquarters, estimates that Russian intercontinental missiles are one-fourth to one-fifth as numerous as ours, though Russian warheads are larger. The Russians have one-sixth to one-twelfth the number of our long-range heavy bombs, with ours having a greater capability (*New York Times*, November 21, 1963). In medium range ballistic missiles Russia has been superior. A report of the Institute of Strategic Studies estimated that as of October, 1962, Russia had 700 such missiles, the West a total of 250 (*New York Times*, November 9, 1962). British sources tend to place Russian capabilities in the medium range higher than do American estimates. Cf. P. M. S. Blackett, "The Real Road to Disarmament: The Military Background to the Geneva Talks," *New Statesman* (March 2, 1962), pp. 295–300, with Hanson W. Baldwin, *New York Times*, November 26, 1961.

would lose heavily if it were to engage in a major war against the other.

If number of states is less important than the existence of nuclear power, then one must ask whether the world balance would continue to be stable were three or more states able to raise themselves to comparable levels of nuclear potency. For many reasons one doubts that the equilibrium would be so secure. Worries about accidents and triggering are widespread, but a still greater danger might well arise. The existence of a number of nuclear states would increase the temptation for the more virile of them to maneuver, with defensive states paralyzed by the possession of military forces the use of which would mean their own destruction. One would be back in the 1930's, with the addition of a new dimension of strength which would increase the pressures upon status quo powers to make piecemeal concessions.

Because bipolarity preceded a two-power nuclear competition, because in the absence of nuclear weapons destructive power would still be great, because the existence of a number of nuclear states would increase the range of difficult political choices, and finally, as will be discussed below, because nuclear weapons must first be seen as a product of great national capabilities rather than as their cause, one is led to the conclusion that nuclear weapons cannot by themselves be used to explain the stability—or the instability—of international systems.

Taken together, these three factors—the absence of peripheries, the range and intensity of competition, and the persistence of pressure and crisis—are among the most important characteristics of the period since World War II. The first three points combine to produce an intense competition in a wide arena with a great variety of means employed. The constancy of effort of the two major contenders, combined with a fourth factor, their preponderant power, have made for a remarkable ability to comprehend and absorb within the bipolar balance the revolutionary political, military, and economic changes that have occurred. The Soviet Union moved forward and was checked. Empires dissolved, and numerous new states appeared in the world. Strategic nuclear weapons systems came into the possession of four separate countries. Tactical nuclear weapons were developed and to some extent dispersed. The manned bomber gave way to the missile. Vulnerable missiles were hardened, made mobile, and hidden. A revolution in military technology occurred on an average of once every five years and at an accelerating

pace.[3] Two "losses" of China, each a qualified loss but both traumatic, were accommodated without disastrously distorting—or even
greatly affecting—the balance between America and Russia.

The effects of American-Soviet preponderance are complex. Its
likely continuation and even its present existence are subjects of
controversy. The stability of a system has to be defined in terms of
its durability, as well as of the peacefulness of adjustment within it.
In the pages that follow, some of the effects of preponderance will
be indicated while the durability of the system is examined.

The End of the Bipolar Era?

In a bipolar world, by definition each of two states or two blocs
overshadows all others. It may seem that to write in 1964 of bipolarity is merely to express nostalgia for an era already ending. Richard Rosecrance, referring to the period since the war, describes
the world as "tripolar."[4] Walter Lippmann, in a number of columns
written in late 1963 and early 1964, assesses the recent initiatives
of France and Communist China, their ability to move contrary to
the desires of the United States and the Soviet Union, as marking
the end of the postwar world in which the two superpowers closely
controlled the actions of even their major associates.* Hedley Bull,
in a paper prepared for the Council on Foreign Relations in the fall
of 1963, tentatively reaches the conclusion that between now and
1975 "the system of polarization of power will cease to be recognizable: that other states will count for so much in world politics
that the two present great powers will find it difficult, even when
cooperating, to dominate them."[5]

If power is identical with the ability to control, then those who
are free are also strong; and the freedom of the weak would have
to be taken as an indication of the weakness of those who have
great material strength. But the weak and disorganized are often
less amenable to control than those who are wealthy and well disciplined.** The powerful, out of their strength, influence and limit

---

* See, for example, Walter Lippmann, "NATO Crisis—and Solution: Don't
Blame De Gaulle," *Boston Globe*, December 5, 1963, p. 26: "The paramount
theme of this decade, as we know it thus far, is that we are emerging from a
two-power world and entering one where there are many powers."

** Cf. Georg Simmel, "The Sociology of Conflict, II," *The American Journal
of Sociology*, IX (March, 1904), 675: "when one opposes a diffused crowd of
enemies, one may oftener gain isolated victories, but it is very hard to arrive
at decisive results which definitely fix the relationships of the contestants."

each other; the wealthy are hobbled by what they have to lose. The weak, on the other hand, bedevil the strong; the poor can more easily ignore their own interests. Such patterns endure and pervade the relations of men and of groups. United States Steel enjoys less freedom to vary the price of its products than do smaller producers. The United States government finds it easier to persuade large corporations and the great labor unions to cooperate in an anti-inflationary policy than to secure the compliance of small firms and independent unions. The political party in opposition is freer to speak irresponsibly than is the government. Power corrupts *and* renders its possessors responsible; the possession of wealth liberates *and* enslaves. That similar patterns are displayed in international relations is hardly surprising. It is not unusual to find that minor states have a considerable nuisance value in relation to states greatly their superiors in power. A Chiang Kai-shek, a Syngman Rhee, or a Mossadegh is often more difficult to deal with than rulers of states more nearly one's equal in power.

The influence and control of the two great powers has stopped short of domination in most places throughout the postwar period. The power of the United States and of the Soviet Union has been predominant but not absolute. To describe the world as bipolar does not mean that either power can exert a positive control everywhere in the world, but that each has global interests which it can care for unaided, though help may often be desirable. To say that bipolarity has, until recently, meant more than this is to misinterpret the history of the postwar world. Secretary Dulles, in the middle 1950's, inveighed against neutralism and described it as immoral. His judgment corresponded to a conviction frequently expressed in Communist statements. P. E. Vyshinsky, in a 1948 issue of *Problems of Philosophy*, declared that "the only determining criterion of revolutionary proletarian internationalism is: are you for or against the U.S.S.R., the motherland of the world proletariat?. . . The defense of the U.S.S.R., as of the socialist motherland of the world proletariat, is the holy duty of every honest man everywhere and not only of the citizens of the U.S.S.R."[6] The rejection of neutralism as an honorable position for other countries to take is another example of intensity of competition leading to an extension of its range. By coming to terms with neutralism, as both the United States and the Soviet Union have done, the superpowers have shown even their inability to extend their wills without limit.

Bearing in mind the above considerations, can we say whether the recent independent action of France and Communist China does in fact indicate the waning of bipolarity, or does it mean merely the loosening of bipolar blocs, with a bipolar relation between the United States and the Soviet Union continuing to dominate? By the assessment of those who themselves value increased independence, the latter would seem to be the case. The Earl of Home, when he was Secretary of State for Foreign Affairs, thought he saw developing from the increased power of the Soviet Union and the United States a nuclear stalemate that would provide for the middle states a greater opportunity to maneuver.[7] De Gaulle, in a press conference famous for other reasons, included the statement that uncertainty about their use "does not in the least prevent the American nuclear weapons, which are the most powerful of all, from remaining the essential guarantee of world peace."[8] Communist China's calculation of international political and military forces may be highly similar. "Whatever happens," Chou En-lai has said recently, "the fraternal Chinese and Soviet peoples will stand together in any storm that breaks out in the world arena."[9] Ideological disputes between China and Russia are bitter; their policies conflict. But interests are more durable than the alliances in which they sometimes find expression. Even though the bonds of alliance are broken, the interest of the Soviet Union could not easily accommodate the destruction of China if that were to mean that Western power would be poised on the Siberian border.

That strategic stability produces or at least permits tactical instability is now a cliché of military analysis. The axiom, transferred to the political realm, remains true. Lesser states have often found their opportunity to exist in the interstices of the balance of power. The French and Chinese, in acting contrary to the wishes of their principal partners, have certainly caused them some pain. Diplomatic flurries have resulted and some changes have been produced, yet in a more important respect, France and China have demonstrated not their power but their impotence: their inability to affect the dominant relation in the world. The solidity of the bipolar balance permits middle states to act with impunity precisely because they know that their divergent actions will not measurably affect the strength of the Soviet Union or the United States, upon which their own security continues to rest. The decisions of Britain, France, and China to build nuclear establishments are further advertisements of weakness. Because American or Soviet military might provides adequate protection, the middle powers need not participate in a military division of labor in a way that would contribute maximally to the military strength of their major associates.

The United States is inclined to exaggerate the amount of strength it can gain from maintaining a system of united alliances as opposed to bilateral arrangements. The exaggeration arises apparently from vague notions about the transferability of strength. Actually, as one should expect, the contribution of each ally is notable only where it believes that its interests require it to make an effort. In resisting the invasion of North Korean and, later, Chinese troops, roughly 90 per cent of the non-Korean forces were provided by the United States.[10] In South Vietnam at the present time the United States is the only foreign country engaged. British and French military units in West Germany, under strength and ill equipped, are of little use. Western Europe remains, to use the terminology of the 1930's, a direct consumer of security. The only really significant interest of the United States, as is nicely conveyed by Arnold Wolfers' dubbing us "the hub power,"[11] is that each country that may be threatened by Soviet encroachment be politically stable and thus able to resist subversion, be self-dependent and thus less of an expense to us, and be able at the outset of a possible military action to put up some kind of a defense.

On these points, the American interest in Western Europe is precisely the same as its interest in the economically underdeveloped countries. In the case of the European countries, however, losses are harder to sustain and there are advantages clearly to be gained by the United States where our interests and theirs overlap. It would be difficult to argue that the foreign-aid programs undertaken by Britain, France, and West Germany transcend a national purpose or have been enlarged in response to our insisting upon their duty to share the military and economic responsibilities that the United States has assumed. The protection of persons, property, and the pound sterling required Britain to resist Communist guerrillas in Malaya, which was after all still her dependency. In such a case, the bearing of a heavy burden by another country serves its interests and ours simultaneously. If anything, the possibility of a transfer of strength has decreased in the past fifteen years, along with a decline in usable military power in Britain. Britain had in her army 633,242 men in 1948; by 1962 she had 209,500, with further reductions anticipated. The comparable figures for France are 465,000 and 706,000.[12] France, with a system of conscription for a comparatively long term and at relatively low pay, has maintained military forces impressively large when measured as a percentage of her population.* As France takes the first steps along the route followed by England, her military planning runs parallel to the earlier English calculations; she will seek to cope with the pressures of large money requirements by making similar adjustments. According to present French plans, the total of men under arms is to be reduced by 40 per cent.**

To compensate for the loss of *influence* that once came from making a military contribution outside their own borders, the one country has tried and the other is now attempting to build nuclear establishments that supposedly promise them some measure of *independence*. The British effort remains dependent on American assistance, and the French effort to build an effective nuclear weapons system is in its infancy. The independence of recent French policy cannot have been grounded on a nuclear force that barely exists. It is, rather, a product of intelligence and political will exercised by President de Gaulle in a world in which bipolar stalemate provides the weak some opportunity to act. Independence of action by France and by the People's Republic of China is at once a product of loosening alliances—the lesser dependence of principals upon their associates—and a protest against it.

In the wake of the war, the countries of Western Europe derived a considerable influence from their weakness and our inability to let them succumb to internal difficulties or external pressures without thereby disadvantaging ourselves in relation to Russia. We were less free then because they were so dependent upon our support. The Soviet challenge made it important to recreate strength in Western Europe, a purpose that could best be achieved cooperatively. From about 1960 onward, the dependence of each of the nuclear giants upon its associates lessened. The earlier postwar pattern was one of interdependence with consequent influence for junior partners. More recently a lesser interdependence has permitted and produced assertions of independence, which must be understood in part as efforts to recapture influence once enjoyed.

---

* In 1960, 1.5% of total population for France; 1.01% for the United Kingdom; 1.39% for the United States. M. R. D. Foot, *Men in Uniform* (London: Weidenfeld and Nicolson, for the Institute for Strategic Studies, 1961), pp. 162, 163.

**The reduction is figured from the level of military manpower in 1960. Ministre des Armées, Pierre Messmer, "Notre Politique Militaire," *Revue de Défense Nationale* (May, 1963), p. 754.

The Durability of the Bipolar World

Bipolarity as a descriptive term remains appropriate as long as there is a great gap between the power of the two leading countries and the power of the next most considerable states. When one looks in this light at Communist China, he is likely to be mesmerized by the magic of numbers. Surely 750 million Chinese must enable their Communist government to do some things very damaging to the United States or the Soviet Union, or to both of them. When one considers the West European states, he may be struck by their rapid movement from economic and military dependence upon the United States to positions of some independence. It is natural to ask whether this is part of a trend that will continue, or simply a movement from nearly zero on the scale of independence to a threshold that can hardly be passed. It is easy to think that the trend will continue until, again in the words of Hedley Bull, "over the next decade the Soviet Union and the United States will find themselves still the principal powers in opposed systems of alliances, but, like Britain and Germany 1907–1914, aware that their allies are not irrevocably committed to their cause and able to cooperate themselves against their lesser allies on particular issues."[13] But this is an analogy that can mislead. The allies of Britain and of Germany were of an order of power, as measured by a combination of territory, population, and economic capability, similar to that of their principals. That many important changes have occurred in the past fifteen years is obvious. That the changes that have occurred and others that are likely will lift any present state to the level of Soviet or American capabilities is all but impossible.

In 1962, the gross national product of the Soviet Union was $260 billion, of the United States $555 billion, of West Germany $84 billion, and of Communist China roughly $50 billion. If one projects from these figures, the following picture emerges: the Soviet Union, at an assumed growth rate of 5 per cent, will have in the year 2004 a gross national product of $2,080 billion; the United States, at a growth rate of 3 per cent, will have by 2000 a gross national product of $2,220 billion; West Germany, if it grows at a sustained rate of 6 per cent yearly, will have by 1998 a gross national product of $672 billion, and Communist China, projected at 7 per cent, will have a gross national product in 2002 of $800 billion.* The growth rates assumed are unlikely to be those that

* To complete the picture, Britain in 1962 had a gross national product of

actually prevail. The rates chosen are those that will narrow the gap between the greatest and the middle powers to the largest extent presently imaginable. Even on these bases, it becomes clear that the Soviet Union and the United States to the end of the millenium will remain the preponderant powers in the world unless two or more of the middle powers combine in a way that gives them the ability to concert their political and military actions on a sustained and reliable basis.

The gap that exists can be described in other ways which are more fragmentary but perhaps give a still sharper picture. The United States has been spending on its military establishment yearly an amount that is two-thirds or more of the entire West German or British or French gross national product. In 1962, the Europe of the Six plus Great Britain spent on defense less than a quarter of the military expenditure of the United States.[14] The United States spends more on military research and development than any of the three largest of the West European countries spends on its entire military establishment.

The country that would develop its own resources, military and other, in order to play an independent role in the world, faces a dreadful problem. It is understandably tempting for such countries to believe that by developing nuclear weapons systems, they can noticeably close the gap between themselves and the superpowers. The assumption that nuclear weapons will serve as the great equalizers appeared early and shows an impressive persistence. "The small country," Jacob Viner wrote in 1946, "will again be more than a cipher or a mere pawn in power-politics, provided it is big enough to produce atomic bombs."[15] Stanley Hoffmann, writing in the present year, reflects a similar thought in the following words: "True, the French nuclear program is expensive; but it is also true that conventional rearmament is not cheaper, and that a division of labor that would leave all nuclear weapons in United States hands and specialize Europe in conventional forces would earmark Europe for permanent dependence (both military and political) in the cold war and permanent decline in the international competition."[16]

$79 billion and France of $72 billion. Gross national product figures for all of the countries mentioned, except China, are from the New York Times, January 26, 1964, E8. The figure of $50 billion for China in 1962, though it is a figure that is widely given, is necessarily a crude estimate. As a close and convenient approximation, I have taken 3, 5, 6, and 7% as doubling in 24, 14, 12, and 10 years, respectively.

It is difficult to know just what is meant by saying that "conventional rearmament is not cheaper" than a nuclear program, but it is clear that nuclear programs are very expensive indeed.* France and Britain now spend about 7 per cent of their gross national products on defense. If this were increased to the American level of approximately 10 per cent, or even if it were doubled, the defense spending of each country would remain comparatively small. The inability to spend large sums, taken together with the costs of research, development, production, and maintenance, leads one to the conclusion that the French government is betting that Kahn's revolution in military technology every five years will no longer take place. The French might then hope that Polaris submarines, with their missiles, would remain invulnerable. It is doubtful that they are truly invulnerable even now.

The point is a complicated one. By confusing the tracking mechanism of a hunter-killer submarine, an easy accomplishment, one submarine can escape from another. A Soviet submarine, however, may be able to meet and quietly destroy a French submarine as it comes out of port. It is unlikely that the French would in such an event say anything at all; surely they would not wish to draw attention to the loss of what might be one-third of their strategic nuclear system.** To prevent this, France could choose to operate her submarine fleet entirely from the Mediterranean, a sea from which the Soviet Union is militarily excluded. But limiting the direction from which missiles may come will make it easier for the Soviet Union to defend against them. Khrushchev's claim that the Soviet Union's rockets can hit a fly in the sky, which strikes Americans as an irrelevant boast, has an important implication for the country that would build a small nuclear force.[17] Missile defenses, almost useless against large numbers, may be highly successful against the approach of only a few missiles. Furthermore, a single command and control system can easily be obliterated. Middle powers will have to concentrate on a single system or a very small number of systems, and thus deny to themselves the invul-

---

* Albert Wohlstetter has estimated that the first one hundred Polaris missiles manufactured and operated for five peacetime years will cost three to five times as much as the cost of the first one hundred B-47s ("Nuclear Sharing: NATO and the N+1 Country," *Foreign Affairs*, XXXIX [April, 1961], 364).

** France plans to have three nuclear submarines of sixteen missiles each, the first to be operating in 1969, the others following at two-year intervals (Messmer, "Notre Politique Militaire," p. 747).

nerability gained by the United States from dispersion of the weapons of any one system and the existence of multiple systems. Were military innovation to cease, a force such as that projected by France could gradually be built up to a level of military significance. If, however, a future French Polaris force should begin to look dangerous to the Soviet Union, the increased French capability would itself become an incentive for Russia to move faster. And if Russia does, so must we too. Far short of America or Russia using nuclear weapons for the surgical excision of any country's embryonic nuclear capability, the opportunity to develop a nuclear force to a level of usefulness exists, if it is present at all, only on sufferance of the two nuclear giants.

To look upon nuclear weapons systems as the great equalizers is to see them as causes of the increased power of states. It is more accurate and more useful to look upon them as the products of great scientific and economic capability. The railway age brought a great increase in military mobility, which the elder von Moltke brilliantly exploited in the wars for German unification. So long, however, as war power took the form of great masses of men and material, railways were not able to deliver the whole force of a nation to a front or concentrate it upon a point. Even in transporting a portion of a country's military power, railways were not able to cross the front. Thus in 1914, German armies *marched* through Belgium.[18] In World War II, the wedding of high explosives and air transport still did not make it possible to aggregate a nation's whole power and deliver it suddenly and decisively to designated military targets. World War II was won slowly and largely on the ground. Nuclear technology produced a change decisive in one respect. The power of a nation can now be distilled. Like the French chef who boils down a pig for three days until he has a pint of liquid that represents the very essence of pig, the country that produces nuclear warheads and the requisite delivery systems is distilling the power of a whole nation. But the power has to be there before it can be distilled. The stills of such countries as Britain, France, and Communist China are simply not large enough.

Nuclear weapons systems are not the great equalizers, but they are, rather, in all of their complexity and with all of their tremendous cost, outward signs of the Soviet and American ability to outstrip all others. If other countries should nevertheless be able to build nuclear systems capable of doing great damage on second strike to any attacker, they would then, as the Soviet Union and

United States now do, participate in a nuclear stand-off. Competition would shift to other means, which to some extent has already happened, and traditional criteria of power, including economic and military capability, would once again take on their old significance.

This is not to say that nuclear diffusion makes no difference. It is useful to consider briefly some of the possibilities. (1) A threat by Britain, France, or Communist China to use nuclear force in order to deter a conventional attack launched by a great nuclear power is a threat to do limited damage to the invading state at the risk of one's own annihilation. It is a radically different way of assuming the deterrent-defensive posture of Switzerland and should be interpreted as a move to bow out of the great-power picture. In part the desire for an independent nuclear deterrent derives, as the late Hugh Gaitskell put it, "from doubts about the readiness of the United States Government and the American citizens to risk the destruction of their cities on behalf of Europe."[19] The nuclear superiority enjoyed by America in the early 1950's created in Europe a fear that the United States would too easily succumb to a temptation to retaliate massively. The arrival of strategic stability has produced the opposite worry. In the words of a senior British general: "McNamara is practically telling the Soviets that the worst they need expect from an attack on West Germany is a conventional counterattack."[20] Behind the difference on strategy lies a divergence of interest. A policy of strategic nuclear threat makes the United States the primary target. A policy of controlled response would shift some of the danger as well as additional burdens to Europe. The countries of Europe, separate or united, have an incentive to adopt destabilizing military programs. Where Britain has led, France now follows. While it is understandable that lesser powers should, by threatening or using nuclear weapons, want to be able to decide when the United States or the Soviet Union should risk their own destruction, it is also easy to see that both the United States and the Soviet Union would resist such an outcome. The more badly a country may want to be able to trigger someone else's force, the more difficult it becomes to do so, which is another way of saying that the Soviet Union and the United States have something close to invulnerable second-strike systems.

(2) If a middle power were engaged in a conventional military action against a state of comparable or lesser size, the Soviet Union or the United States might threaten a nuclear strike in order to

bring about a withdrawal. It is sometimes thought that the possession of a small nuclear force by the middle power would make such a threat ineffective. In the Suez adventure, for example, military action by Britain and France called forth Soviet rocket threats against them. Against states having no strategic nuclear forces, such threats would be more readily credited, and thus more likely to exert pressure successfully against the conventional action itself. A small military action, however, is not worth and does not require nuclear interference by a great power, for it can be stopped in other ways. The onus of threatening to use nuclear weapons first, in order to interdict conventional interference, is then placed upon the smaller power. Such a threat would not be credible.

Both the first and second uses presuppose the adequacy of the small country's nuclear threat when directed against the United States or the Soviet Union. A capability that is small compared to America's or Russia's may be adequate to its task; a certain minimum, doubtfully achievable in the foreseeable future, is nevertheless required. When Hedley Bull says that the French ambition is "to become strong enough to choose deliberately to act alone,"[21] he may have in mind the second use mentioned above, or the one following, which is seldom discussed.

(3) As the United States and the Soviet Union have opened up a gap in military power between themselves and all others, so Britain, France, the People's Republic of China, and states who may follow them can differentiate themselves from non-nuclear nations. Great Britain has placed nuclear weapons in the Middle and Far East. Let us suppose Indonesia were to move militarily against Malaysia. A British threat to use nuclear weapons could conceivably follow, which might cause Indonesia to stop short or might persuade the United States to offer the support of the Seventh Fleet and American Marines in order to avoid the use of nuclear weapons.

The effects of nuclear diffusion are necessarily uncertain, but one point can sensibly be made: Building a small nuclear force is an unpromising way of seeking to maintain the integrity of one's state, even though it may enable that state to act positively against equal or lesser powers.

There can be approximate equality among states even where there is considerable disparity in the material bases of their power. Whether or not effective power is fashioned from the material available depends upon adequacy of national organization, wisdom of policy, and intensity of effort. In the 1920's, France sought to maintain a greater military strength than Germany in order to compensate for a lesser French productivity and smaller population. Where the material differences are relatively small or where countries of immensely larger capacity are quiescent, it may be possible to "mobilize" a nation in peacetime in order to build on a lesser material base a superior military strength. Germany and Japan in the 1930's began to play the game from which France was withdrawing. The Soviet Union, since the war, has been able to challenge the United States in many parts of the world by spending a disproportionately large share of her smaller income on military means. There is in the West a quiet nightmare that the People's Republic of China may follow such a path, that it may mobilize the nation in order to increase production rapidly while simultaneously acquiring a large and modern military capability. It is doubtful that she can do either, and surely not both, and surely not the second without the first, as the data previously given clearly indicate. As for France and Great Britain, it strains the imagination to the breaking point to believe that in a world in which scientific and technological progress has been rapid, either of them will be able to maintain the pace.* Unable to spend on anywhere near the American or Russian level for work in research, development, and production, middle powers will, once they have gained an initial advantage, constantly find themselves falling behind. France and Britain are in the second-ranking powers' customary position of imitating, with a time lag, the more advanced weapons systems of their wealthier competitors.**

From the above analysis, it is clear that the time when other states can compete at the highest levels of power by a superiority of effort in mobilizing their resources lies far in the future. Unless

---

* It is not wholly absurd for British and French governments to proclaim, as they frequently do, that an embryonic capability brings an immediate increase of strength; for further expenditures are not likely to bring much of an additional payoff. Cf. President de Gaulle's message to his minister-delegate at Reggane upon the explosion of France's first atomic device: " 'Hurrah for France! From this morning she is stronger and prouder!' " Leonard Beaton and John Maddox, *The Spread of Nuclear Weapons* (London: Chatto & Windus, 1962), p. 91.

** The experiences of Chinese Communists prior to 1949 and of the People's Republic of China since that date suggest that attempts to outflank may bring a greater success than efforts to imitate! Or, applying an economist's term to military matters, would-be Nth-countries would do well to ask, where do we have a comparative advantage?

some states combine or others dissolve in chaos, the world will remain bipolar until the end of the present century.

Some Dissenting Opinions

The fact remains that many students of international relations have continued to judge bipolarity unstable as compared to the probable stability of a multipower world. Why have they been so confident that the existence of a number of powers, moving in response to constantly recurring variations in national power and purpose, would promote the desired stability? According to Professors Morgenthau and Kaplan, the uncertainty that results from flexibility of alignment generates a healthy caution in the foreign policy of every country.[22] Concomitantly, Professor Morgenthau believes that in the present bipolar world, "the flexibility of the balance of power and, with it, its restraining influence upon the power aspirations of the main protagonists on the international scene have disappeared."[23] One may agree with his conclusion and yet draw from his analysis another one unstated by him: The inflexibility of a bipolar world, with the appetite for power of each major competitor at once whetted and checked by the other, may promote a greater stability than flexible balances of power among a larger number of states.

What are the grounds for coming to a diametrically different conclusion? The presumed double instability of a bipolar world, that it easily erodes or explodes, is to a great extent based upon its assumed bloc character. A bloc improperly managed may indeed fall apart. The leader of each bloc must be concerned at once with alliance management, for the defection of an allied state might be fatal to its partners, and with the aims and capabilities of the opposing bloc. The system is more complex than is a multipower balance, which in part accounts for its fragility.* The situation

* Morton A. Kaplan, *System and Process in International Politics* (New York: Wiley, 1957), p. 37; and "Bipolarity in a Revolutionary Age," in Kaplan, ed., *The Revolution in World Politics* (New York: Wiley, 1962), p. 254. The difficulties and dangers found in a bipolar world by Kaplan are those detected by Hans J. Morgenthau in a system of opposing alliances. It is of direct importance in assessing the stability of international systems to note that Morgenthau finds "the opposition of two alliances . . . the most frequent configuration within the system of the balance of power" (*Politics Among Nations* [3d ed.; New York: Knopf, 1961, part 4], p. 189). Kaplan, in turn, writes that "the

preceding World War I provides a striking example. The dissolution of the Austro-Hungarian Empire would have left Germany alone in the center of Europe. The approximate equality of alliance partners, or their relation of true interdependence, plus the closeness of competition between the two camps, meant that while any country could commit its associates, no one country on either side could exercise control. By contrast, in 1956 the United States could dissociate itself from the Suez adventure of its two principal allies and even subject them to pressure. Great Britain, like Austria in 1914, tried to commit, or at least immobilize, its alliance partner by presenting him with a *fait accompli*. Enjoying a position of predominance, the United States could, as Germany could not, focus its attention on the major adversary while disciplining its ally. The situations are in other respects different, but the ability of the United States, in contrast to Germany, to pay a price measured in intra-alliance terms is striking.

It is important, then, to distinguish sharply a bipolarity of blocs from a bipolarity of countries. Fénelon thought that of all conditions of balance the opposition of two states was the happiest. Morgenthau dismisses this judgment with the comment that the benefits Fénelon had hoped for had not accrued in our world since the war, which depends, one might think, on what benefits had otherwise been expected.*

The conclusion that a multipower balance is relatively stable is reached by overestimating the system's flexibility, and then dwelling too fondly upon its effects.** A constant shuffling of alliances would be as dangerous as an unwillingness to make new combinations. Neither too slow nor too fast: the point is a fine one, made finer still by observing that the rules should be followed not merely out of an immediate interest of the state but also for the sake of preserving the international system. The old balance-of-power system here looks suspiciously like the new collective-security system of the League of Nations and the United Nations. Either system

---

most likely transformation of the 'balance of power' system is to a bipolar system" (*System and Process*, p. 36).

* Kaplan, though he treats the case almost as being trivial, adds a statement that is at least suggestive: "The tight bipolar system is stable only when both bloc actors are hierarchically organized" (*System and Process*, p. 43).

** Kaplan, e.g., by the fourth and sixth of his rules of a balance-of-power system, requires a state to oppose any threatening state and to be willing to ally with any other (*System and Process*, p. 23).

depends for its maintenance and functioning upon a "neutrality of alignment" at the moment of serious threat. To preserve the system, the powerful states must overcome the constraints of previous ties and the pressures of both ideological preferences and conflicting present interests in order to confront the state that threatens the system.[24]

In the history of the modern state system, flexibility of alignment has been conspicuously absent just when, in the interest of stability, it was most highly desirable.[25] A comparison of flexibility within a multipower world with the ability of the two present superpowers to compensate for changes by their internal efforts is requisite, for comparison changes the balance of optimism and pessimism as customarily applied to the two different systems. In the world of the 1930's, with a European grouping of three, the Western democracies, out of lassitude, political inhibition, and ideological distaste, refrained from acting or from combining with others at the advantageous moment. War provided the pressure that forced the world's states into two opposing coalitions. In peacetime the bipolar world displays a clarity of relations that is ordinarily found only in war. Raymond Aron has pointed out that the international "système depend de ce que sont, concrètement, les deux pôles, non pas seulement du fait qu'ils sont deux."[26] Modifying Aron's judgment and reversing that of many others, we would say that in a bipolar world, as compared to one of many powers, the international system is more likely to dominate. External pressures, if clear and great enough, force the external combination or the internal effort that interest requires. The political character of the alliance partner is then most easily overlooked and the extent to which foreign policy is determined by ideology is decreased.

The number of great states in the world has always been so limited that two acting in concert or, more common historically, one state driving for hegemony could reasonably conclude that the balance would be altered by their actions. In the relations of states since the Treaty of Westphalia, there have never been more than eight great powers, the number that existed, if one is generous in admitting doubtful members to the club, on the eve of the First World War. Given paucity of members, states cannot rely on an equilibrating tendency of the system. Each state must instead look to its own means, gauge the likelihood of encountering opposition, and estimate the chances of successful cooperation. The advantages of an international system with more than two members can at best be small. A careful evaluation of the factors elaborated above indicates that the disadvantages far outweigh them.

Conclusions That Bear upon Policy

If the preceding explanations are correct, they are also of practical importance. Fixation upon the advantages of flexibility in a multipower balance has often gone hand in hand with an intense anxiety associated with bipolarity: the fear that a downward slide or a sudden technological breakthrough by one great state or the other would decisively alter the balance between them. Either occurrence could bring catastrophic war, which for the disadvantaged would be a war of desperation, or world domination from one center with or without preceding war. The fear is pervasive, and in American writings most frequently rests on the assumption that, internally dissolute and tired of the struggle, we will award the palm to the Soviet Union. Sometimes this anxiety finds a more sophisticated expression, which turns less upon internal derangements. In this view, the United States, as the defensive power in the world, is inherently disadvantaged, for the aggressive power will necessarily gain if the competition continues long enough. But a conclusion derived from an incomplete proposition is misleading. One must add that the aggressive state may lose even though the state seeking to uphold the status quo never take the offensive. The Soviet Union controls no nation now, except possibly Cuba, that was not part of its immediate postwar gains. It has lost control in Yugoslavia and the control it once seemed to have in China. The United States, since the time it began to behave as a defensive power, has seen some states slip from commitment to neutralism, but only North Vietnam and Cuba have come under Communist control. One would prefer no losses at all, but losses of this magnitude can easily be absorbed. On balance, one might argue that the United States has gained, though such a judgment depends on the base line from which measurement is made as well as upon how gains and losses are defined.

That the United States and the Soviet Union weigh losses and gains according to their effect upon the bipolar balance is crucial, but there are many changes in Africa, or Asia, or Latin America that are not likely to be to the advantage of either the Soviet Union or the United States. This judgment can be spelled out in a number of ways. The doctrine of containment, for example, should be amended to read: defend, or insulate so that one loss need not lead to another. The habits of the cold war are so ingrained and the dangers of a bipolar world so invigorating that the defensive country is easily led to overreact. In Southeast Asia, since no gain for Communist China is likely to benefit the Soviet Union, American concern should be confined to maintaining its reputation and avoiding distant repercussions. If one goes further and asks how great a gain will accrue to the People's Republic of China if it extends its territorial control marginally, the answer, in any of the areas open to it, must be "very little." Neutralization moves by President de Gaulle, if they can obscure the responsibility for unwanted events, may in fact be helpful. It is important to realize that the bipolar world is continuing lest we worry unnecessarily and define the irrelevant gesture or even the helpful suggestion of lesser powers as troublesome.

A 5 per cent growth rate sustained for three years would add to the American gross national product an amount greater than the entire gross national product of Britain or France or West Germany. Even so, the accretion of power the Soviet Union would enjoy by adding, say, West Germany's capabilities to her own would be immensely important; and one such gain might easily lead to others. Most gains from outside, however, can add relatively little to the strengths of the Soviet Union or the United States. There are, then, few single losses that would be crucial, which is a statement that points to a tension within our argument. Bipolarity encourages each giant to focus upon crises, while rendering most of them of relative inconsequence. We might instead put it this way: Crisis is of concern only where giving way would lead to an accumulation of losses for one and gains for the other. In an age characterized by rapidity of change, in many respects time is slowed down—as is illustrated by the process of "losing" Indo-China that has gone on for nineteen years without a conclusive result. Since only a succession of gains could be decisive, there is time for the losing state to contrive a countering action should it be necessary to do so.

Intensity and breadth of competition and recurrence of crises limn a picture of constant conflict verging on violence. At the same time, the relative simplicity of relations within a bipolar world, the great pressures that are generated, and the constant possibility of catastrophe produce a conservatism on the part of the two greatest powers. The Soviet Union and the United States may feel more comfortable dealing à deux than in contemplating a future world in which they vie for existence and possible advantage with other superpowers. While there is naturally worry about an increase of tensions to intolerable levels, there is also a fear that the tensions themselves will lead America and Russia to seek agreements designed to bring a relaxation that will be achieved at the expense of lesser powers. The French general, Paul Stehlin, commenting on American opposition to Nth-country nuclear forces, which he interprets as part of an American-Russian effort to maintain a bipolar world, asks wistfully: "Does Europe have less political maturity than the Big Two credit each other with?" With some bitterness he criticizes America for placing "more faith in the ability of the Russians to control their tremendous stockpiles of offensive weapons than they do in my country's capacity to use with wisdom and moderation the modest armaments it is working so hard to develop for purely deterrent purposes."[27]

Worries and fears on any such grounds are exaggerated. The Soviet Union and the United States influence each other more than any of the states living in their penumbra can possibly hope to do. In the world of the present, as of the recent past, a condition of mutual opposition may require rather than preclude the adjustment of differences. Yet first steps toward agreement have not led to second and third steps. Instead they have been mingled with other acts and events that have kept the level of tension quite high. The test ban was described in the United States as possibly a first great step toward wider agreement that would increase the chances of maintaining peace. In almost the same breath it was said that we cannot lower our guard, for Soviet aims have not changed.[28] Larger acts than agreement to halt testing under the sea and above the ground are required to alter a situation that congealed long ago. The Soviet Union and the United States remain for the foreseeable future the two countries that can irreparably damage each other. So long as both possess the capability, each must worry that the other might use it. The worry describes the boundaries that have so far limited both the building up of tensions and the abatement of competition.

Where weapons of horrible destructive power exist, stability necessarily appears as an important end. It will not, however, be everyone's highest value. One who accepts the analysis of bipolarity and the conclusions we have drawn may nevertheless prefer a world of many powers. The unity and self-dependence of Europe may, for example, rank higher as goals than international stability. Or, one may think of European unity as a means of melding American power with the strength of a united Europe in order to achieve Western hegemony. Unipolarity may be preferable, for those peoples who then become dominant, to a competition between two polar states. It may even promise a greater stability. The question is too complicated to take up at the moment, but some words of caution are in order.

The United States has consistently favored the unification of Europe, for adding the strength of a united Europe to the existing power of America would be sufficient to establish a world hegemony. But there is a confusion in American rhetoric that accurately reflects a confusion in thought. We have wanted a Europe united and strong and thus able to share our burdens with us, but a Europe at the same time docile and pliant so that it would agree on which burdens are to be assumed and how duties should be shared. The enchanting dream of Western hegemony has many implications, some of them possibly unpleasant. A Europe of the Seven, or even the Six, could, given time to put its combined resources to work, become a third power in the world on the largest scale. President de Gaulle has entertained the fear that such a Europe, if it were to be born under Anglo-Saxon auspices, would serve as an instrument of American foreign policy. One may have doubts of what would necessarily follow.[29] De Gaulle is a useful instructor. If we find the weak troublesome, will the strong be more easily controlled? A united Europe would represent a great change in the world; because the change would be great, its effects are difficult to foresee. If Europe were to be stable, strong, and cooperative, one might be delighted; but surely it would be dangerous to predict that a new Europe would rapidly find internal stability and develop political maturity. It would be more dangerous still to assume that the old American and the new European state would find their policies always in harmony. It is seemingly a safe assumption that a clear and pressing interest of a new state of Europe would be to stand firm against any Soviet attempts to move forward. But interests must be taken in relation to situations. In a world of three great powers, identical interests may logically lead and in the past have led to dangerously disparate policies. European history of the twentieth century makes optimism difficult. Nor could one be serene about America's reaction. Typically, Americans have insufficiently valued the prize of power. The yearning for a Europe united and thus strong enough to oppose the Soviet Union unaided is but one example. The pressures of bipolarity have helped to produce responsibility of action. A relaxation of those pressures will change the situation to one in which it will no longer be clear who will oppose whom. Two considerations then should give one pause: the necessarily unpredictable quality of the third power and the greater instability of a multipower world.

A system of small numbers can always be disrupted by the actions of a Hitler and the reactions of a Chamberlain. Since this is true, it may seem that we are in the uncomfortable position of relying on the moderation, courage, and rationality of men holding crucial positions of power. Given the vagaries of men and the unpredictability of the individual's reaction to events, one may at this point feel that one's only recourse is to lapse into prayer. We can, nonetheless, take comfort from the thought that, like other men, those who are elevated to power and direct the activities of great states are not wholly free agents. Beyond the residuum of necessary hope that men will respond sensibly lies the possibility of estimating the pressures that encourage and constrain them to do so. In a world in which two states united in their mutual antagonism far overshadow any other, the incentives to a calculated response stand out most clearly, and the sanctions against irresponsible behavior achieve their greatest force. Not only how the leaders will think but also who they may be will be affected by the presence of pressures and the clarity of challenges. One may lament Churchill's failure to gain control of the British government in the 1930's, for he knew what actions were required to maintain a balance-of-power system. Churchill did come to power, it is interesting to note, as the world began to assume the bipolar form familiar in wartime. If a people representing one pole of the world now indulges itself by selecting inept rulers, it runs clearly discernible risks. Leaders of the United States and the Soviet Union are presumably chosen with an eye to the tasks they will have to perform. Other countries can enjoy, if they wish, the luxury of selecting leaders who will most please their peoples by the way in which internal affairs are managed. The United States and the Soviet Union cannot.

It is not that one entertains the utopian hope that all future Premiers of the Soviet Union and Presidents of the United States will combine in their persons a complicated set of nearly perfect virtues, but rather that the pressures of a bipolar world will strongly encourage them to act in ways better than their characters might otherwise lead one to expect. It is not that one possesses a serene confidence in the peacefulness, or even the survival of the world, but rather that cautious optimism may be justified as long as the pressures to which each must respond are so clearly present. Either country may go beserk or succumb to inanation and debility. That necessities are clear increases the chances that they will be met, but there can be no guarantees. Dangers from abroad may unify a state and spur its people to heroic action. Or, as with France facing Hitler's Germany, external pressures may divide the leaders, confuse the public, and increase their willingness to give way. It may also happen that the difficulties of adjustment and the necessity for calculated action simply become too great. The clarity with which the necessities of action can now be seen may be blotted out by the blinding flash of nuclear explosions. The fear that this may happen has reinforced the factors and processes described in the preceding pages.

By making the two strongest states still more powerful and the emergence of third powers more difficult, nuclear weapons have helped to consolidate a condition of bipolarity. It is to a great extent due to its bipolar structure that the world since the war has enjoyed a stability seldom known where three or more powers have sought to cooperate with each other or have competed for existence.

REFERENCES

1. Henry Kissinger, "Strains on the Alliance," *Foreign Affairs*, XLI (January, 1963), 284. Cf. Max Kohnstamm, "The European Tide," *Dædalus*, XCIII (Winter, 1964), 100–102; McGeorge Bundy's speech to the Economic Club of Chicago, *New York Times*, December 7, 1961; John F. Kennedy, "Address at Independence Hall," Philadelphia, July 4, 1962, *Public Papers of the Presidents of the United States* (Washington, D. C.: Government Printing Office, 1963), pp. 537–539.

2. Quoted in V. D. Sokolovskii, ed., *Soviet Military Strategy*, Herbert S.

Dinerstein, Leon Gouré, and Thomas W. Wolfe, translators and English editors (Englewood Cliffs: Prentice-Hall, 1963), p. 43.

3. Herman Kahn, *On Thermonuclear War* (Princeton: Princeton University Press, 1960), p. 315.

4. Richard N. Rosecrance, *Action and Reaction in World Politics* (Boston: Little, Brown, 1963), pp. 210–211.

5. Hedley Bull, "Atlantic Military Problems: A Preliminary Essay." Prepared for the Council on Foreign Relations meeting of November 20, 1963, p. 21. Quoted with permission of the author.

6. P. E. Vyshinsky, "Communism and the Motherland," as quoted in *The Kremlin Speaks* (Department of State publication, 4264, October, 1951), pp. 6, 7.

7. National Union of Conservative and Unionist Associations, *Official Report*, 81st Annual Conference, Llandudno (October 10–13, 1962), p. 93.

8. Ambassade de France, Speeches and Press Conferences, No. 185 (January 14, 1963), p. 9.

9. In a statement taped in Peking before his African trip in January of 1964, *New York Times*, February 4, 1964, p. 2. Cf. the message sent by Communist China's leaders to Premier Khrushchev upon the occasion of his seventieth birthday. After referring to differences between them, it is stated that: "In the event of a major world crisis, the two parties, our two peoples will undoubtedly stand together against our common enemy," *New York Times*, April 17, 1964, p. 3.

10. Leland M. Goodrich, "Korea: Collective Measures Against Aggression," *International Conciliation*, No. 494 (October, 1953), 164.

11. "Stresses and Strains in 'Going It With Others,'" in Arnold Wolfers, ed., *Alliance Policy in the Cold War* (Baltimore: Johns Hopkins Press, 1959), p. 7.

12. *The Statesman's Year-Book*, S. H. Steinberg, ed. (London: Macmillan, 1948), p. 50. *Ibid.* (1951), p. 991. *Ibid.* (1963), pp. 103, 104, 1003. The figures for Great Britain exclude the women's services, Territorial Army, and colonial troops. Those for France exclude the gendarmes.

13. Bull, "Atlantic Military Problems," p. 24.

14. Alastair Buchan and Philip Windsor, *Arms and Stability in Europe* (New York: Praeger, 1963), p. 205.

15. Jacob Viner, "The Implications of the Atomic Bomb for International Relations," *Proceedings of the American Philosophical Society*, XC (1946), 55.

16. Stanley Hoffmann, "Cursing de Gaulle Is Not a Policy," *The Reporter*, XXX (January 30, 1964), 40.

17. Cf. Malcolm W. Hoag, "On Stability in Deterrent Races," in Morton A.

Kaplan, ed., *The Revolution in World Politics* (New York: Wiley, 1962), pp. 408, 409.

18. Cf. a forthcoming book by Victor Basiuk, Institute of War and Peace Studies, Columbia University.

19. *House of Commons, Parliamentary Debates* (March 1, 1960), cols. 1136–1138. Compare Hugh Gaitskell, *The Challenge of Co-Existence* (London: Methuen, 1957), pp. 45–46.

20. Quoted by Eldon Griffiths, "The Revolt of Europe," *The Saturday Evening Post*, CCLXIII (March 9, 1963), 19.

21. Bull, "Atlantic Military Problems," p. 29.

22. Hans J. Morgenthau, *Politics Among Nations* (3d ed.; New York: Knopf, 1961), part 4. Morton A. Kaplan, *System and Process in International Politics* (New York: Wiley, 1957), pp. 22–36. I shall refer only to Morgenthau and Kaplan, for their writings are widely known and represent the majority opinion of students in the field.

23. Morgenthau, *Politics Among Nations*, p. 350. Cf. Kaplan, *System and Process*, pp. 36–43; and Kaplan, "Bipolarity in a Revolutionary Age," in Kaplan, ed., *The Revolution in World Politics* (New York: Wiley, 1962), pp. 251–266.

24. The point is nicely made in an unpublished paper by Wolfram F. Hanrieder, "Actor Objectives and International Systems" (Center of International Studies, Princeton University, February, 1964), pp. 43–44.

25. For a sharp questioning of "the myth of flexibility," see George Liska's review article "Continuity and Change in International Systems," *World Politics*, XVI (October, 1963), 122–123.

26. Raymond Aron, *Paix et Guerre entre les Nations* (Paris: Calmann-Lévy, 1962), p. 156.

27. Gen. Paul Stehlin, "The Evolution of Western Defense," *Foreign Affairs*, XLII (October, 1963), 81, 77.

28. See, for example, Secretary Rusk's statement before the Senate Foreign Relations Committee, *New York Times*, August 13, 1963.

29. Ambassade de France, Speeches and Press Conferences, No. 175 (May 15, 1962), p. 6.

REGIONALISM AND WORLD ORDER

RONALD J. YALEM

THE proliferation of regional organizations since 1945 is one of the most significant developments of contemporary international relations. Certainly it was not foreseen by the framers of the United Nations' Charter who believed that regionalism must be subordinated to the universal approach to peace and security. What then is the relationship between such organizations and the United Nations in terms of the maintenance of peace and security? Is regionalism a symptom or a cause of international disorder? Assuming the continued growth of regional organizations, what possibilities are there of eventually promoting world order? Do regional organizations reflect a movement away from exclusive reliance on the nation-state as the basic unit in international relations?

These questions are suggested by the increasing prominence of regional groups in world affairs today. This article attempts to suggest tentative answers by examining the reasons for the growth of contemporary regionalism, the lines of compatibility and conflict between regional and universal forms of international organization, and the relationship between regionalism and the concept of a world order; and these answers are based on the assumption that the growth of regionalism has been more a pragmatic response to the changing dynamics of international politics than the outcome of a conviction that regionalism was theoretically superior to universalism as a form of international cooperation.

Regionalism as an institutional form of international cooperation is often identified with the number of security agencies that have developed since 1945 such as N.A.T.O., S.E.A.T.O., and the Warsaw Pact. But there are numerous examples of regional economic and social organizations, especially in Western Europe. The European Economic Community, European Coal and Steel Community and the Organization for Economic Cooperation and Development are important regional agencies. In the Latin American area a new Inter-American Development Bank has recently been formed as well as a Free Trade Association between nine of the republics.[1] In South Asia the Colombo Plan organization, comprising both economically advanced and under-developed States, serves to channel important economic aid and technical assistance into the area. It seems

---

[1] Lincoln P. Bloomfield, 'The United States, the United Nations, and the Creation of Community,' *International Organization*, Vol. XIV, No. 4, 1960, p. 511.

likely that as the newly independent States of Africa gain political maturity, regional organizations to promote the economic and social well-being of that continent may be developed. Already a customs union involving seven former dependencies of French West Africa has been formed.[1]

The development of such organizations is certainly a phenomenon of the years since the second World War. However, it is possible to look back to the inter-war period to find precedents for regional cooperation although these, such as the Little Entente, were mainly of a defensive nature. While the League of Nations represented the first attempt to universalize peace and security, Article 21 of the Covenant provided that regional understandings for securing peace were legitimate. This article, inserted at the request of President Wilson to safeguard the integrity of the Monroe Doctrine, could be interpreted as implicit recognition of the principle of regionalism. Even so there were many statesmen who opposed it for fear that it would jeopardize the operations of the League by undermining universalism.

The experience of the inter-war period, however, revealed little if any direct antagonism between the various regional arrangements of the time and the League of Nations. The eventual collapse of the universal approach to peace and security was attributable much more to the unwillingness of the leading members of the League to accept the demands of collective security than to the existence of regional organizations. In fact these were formed largely to supplement what were thought to be the inadequate security guarantees of the Covenant.

When the San Francisco Conference met in 1945 to draft a charter for a new international organization for the maintenance of peace and security, the prevailing sentiment again favoured the universal rather than the regional approach to the problem, and this view was reflected in those articles of the U.N. Charter giving to the Security Council the dominant responsibility for enforcing peace and security. On the other hand, the Charter contained more explicit recognition of regionalism than had the Covenant, for Chapter VIII was devoted to provisions governing the relationship between so called regional arrangements and the United Nations. These provisions were inserted at the insistence of certain Latin American and Middle Eastern delegations whose countries had just concluded regional agreements in the form of the Act of Chapultepec and the Arab League. Article 33 of the Charter also implicitly recognized regionalism by exhorting member States to resort first to regional agencies in seeking the peaceful settlement of disputes before submitting them to the United Nations, while Article 51 legalized the right of collective self-defence against armed aggression.

Nevertheless, Articles 52, 53, and 54 of the Charter definitely establish

[1] *Op. cit.*

the subordination of regional arrangements to the United Nations. Article 52 establishes the legality of such arrangements if consistent with the purposes and principles of the United Nations. Article 53 stipulates that regional enforcement action is subject to the prior approval of the Security Council except in cases involving enemy States of the second World War. Article 54 obliges regional arrangements to keep the Security Council informed of any action they may contemplate for the maintenance of peace and security.

The subordinate position thus clearly relegated to regional security agencies in the Charter is in sharp contrast to their actual relationship with the United Nations today. To the great disappointment of many ardent supporters of universalism, regional security agencies have assumed a significance that overshadows the United Nations. Although this development is primarily the result of political factors for the most part unforeseen in 1945, the existence of such agencies in increasing numbers has been morally justified on the ground that they are consistent with the purposes and principles of the United Nations. Indeed, it is asserted that these purposes and principles are identical in that regional security agencies, like the United Nations, are designed to keep the peace.

This view is based on Article 51 of the Charter which permits the right of individual or collective self-defence '. . . if an armed attack occurs against a Member of the United Nations, until the Security Council has taken the measures necessary to maintain international peace and security.' While the Western Powers have maintained that N.A.T.O., S.E.A.T.O., and the Rio Treaty do not conflict with the paramount position of the United Nations as regards the enforcement of peace, it could be argued that Article 51 was designed to permit the *ad hoc* organization of collective force to meet specific situations rather than as the basis for the establishment of permanent security organizations, for which provision is made in Chapter VIII of the Charter in respect of regional arrangements. The fact that these agencies are based on Article 51 means that they have escaped regulation and control by the Security Council. Although such control would have obviously interfered with the efficacy of these agencies because of the veto power of the Soviet Union, this does not alter the view that they fall more properly under Chapter VIII rather than under Article 51 of the Charter.

Since the legal relationship of such agencies to the United Nations has not been clarified by an advisory opinion from the International Court of Justice, it seems likely that in the event of future military action they will be required only to inform the Security Council or the General Assembly of action taken; and as both the super-Powers on the Council have a right of veto over any enforcement action by the Council, it would be virtually impossible for the United Nations to act even though such action is provided for under Article 51. The net effect of this situation has been to exempt both the Western and Soviet regional security systems from effective control by the United Nations.

*   *   *

Basic to any assessment of regionalism and world order is an examination of the major causes for the disproportionate influence of regionalism in contemporary world politics. Such an examination must not be limited solely to political factors but must also take account of the fact that regionalism is a response to what Professor John Herz has called 'the decline of the territorial State' in which changing technological conditions have rendered the State more penetrable and less secure than at any other period in modern history.[1] First, therefore, I will examine some political explanations for the emergence of regional security organizations and I will then examine regionalism as a response to the possible obsolescence of the nation-State.

It is a truism to assert that hopes for the restoration of a stable world order after the second World War rested on the continuation of wartime cooperation among the major Powers. Yet a recognition of this fact is a necessary prerequisite to an awareness of the steady disintegration of universalism since 1945 and the consequent rise of regionalism. Given the extent and nature of the disparity of power between States in the modern world, peace must always rest on some minimum degree of consensus among the most powerful States. Such a consensus pervaded the era of *Pax Britannica* in the nineteenth century. However, it must be admitted that the prospects for such consensus and stability were much less in 1945 than in 1815. In the earlier period the existence of a complex balance of power involving several States of approximately equal strength, and the stabilizing factor of Great Britain as the 'balancer,' contributed to political order. But by 1945 the structure of the balance of power had so altered that peace no longer depended on a consensus among several Powers but only on the United States and the Soviet Union. While the change in the balance of power must thus be adduced as a reason for the failure to restore an effective universalism, perhaps the most important cause for the failure lay in the increasing ideological conflict between the United States and the Soviet Union manifested in and out of the United Nations. Amicable relations even between two States that shared a common ideology would have been subject to severe strain. The bipolar structure of power would have made them potential if not actual competitors since no third State was powerful enough to act as a 'balancer' in any conflict that might arise. Nevertheless, it was assumed that the United States and the

---

[1] *International Politics in the Atomic Age* (New York, Columbia University Press, 1959), pp. 96–108.

Soviet Union would be able to cooperate to maintain the peace, and this assumption rested in turn on another: that they shared a common view of what was to be defended or what constituted the territorial *status quo*. When it soon appeared that there were divergent interpretations of the *status quo* revealed by Soviet aggrandizement in Eastern Europe and attempts to engulf Western Europe as well, all hopes for a universal order under the aegis of the United Nations began to fade. It became apparent that international organization for peace and security could not be divorced from the dynamics of international politics which began to set limits on the possibilities that the United Nations could achieve.

The repeated use of the veto by the Soviet Union in the Security Council, her menacing attitude toward Iran, and generally uncooperative behaviour in negotiating the various European peace treaties, prompted the United States and her allies to search for alternatives to a system of universal peace and security. In 1949 the North Atlantic Treaty Organization was created to deter further Soviet expansion, particularly in Europe. In 1954 the Southeast Asia Treaty Organization was formed to block Soviet, and especially Communist Chinese influence in that area. The United States also concluded numerous bilateral treaties involving American commitment to protect such allies as Nationalist China, South Korea, Japan and the Philippines in the event of these States being attacked by Communist aggressors.

Although it may be argued that the United States-sponsored Uniting for Peace Resolution of 1950 constituted evidence of a willingness to endorse universal collective security, possible action under this resolution is limited by the nature of the obligation that it imposes on members of the United Nations—in contrast to the various regional commitments which involve heavier obligations. Under this Resolution the General Assembly can only recommend military or non-military sanctions against an aggressor. It is therefore doubtful if, in the event of Communist armed aggression, the General Assembly could bring about resistance to the extent that would be achieved by either N.A.T.O. or S.E.A.T.O. which are directly designed for such a purpose.

The Suez crisis of 1956 provides an interesting example of the limitations of the Uniting for Peace Resolution. The General Assembly responded to the vacuum created in the Security Council by the vetoes of Britain and France by passing a resolution calling for a cease-fire and the withdrawal of British, French and Israeli forces from the Suez Canal. But there was no recommendation that military sanctions should be imposed. The General Assembly resolution constituted an effective expression of world public opinion condemnatory of Britain and France, but it in no sense amounted to a collective security action. In fact it was influences exerted outside the United Nations, in the shape of diplomatic pressures from the United States and the Soviet Union that helped to bring about a cessation of hostilities.

*   *   *

It is customary to attribute the growth of regionalism since 1945 to the disintegration of the universal security system of the United Nations. Yet this does not adequately explain the reasons for the growth of non-military regional agencies reflecting the desires of various States to raise standards of living and accelerate industrial development. The tremendous regionalization of Western Europe evidenced in the European Economic Community, the European Coal and Steel Community, the European Atomic Community and the Council of Europe is only partially explained by the threat of Soviet expansion and the decline of Western Europe as a centre of world power. It would be naïve to underrate these facts for they have been important influences in the creation of these groupings. A greater degree of unity in Europe has been necessary as a protection against Soviet penetration through divisive tactics. Many Europeans also believe that greater unity will provide compensation for the weakness of individual European States and so make it possible for the continent to exert more influence in world politics than would otherwise be possible.

In the same way the newly independent States of Africa and Asia could be more immune to Soviet subversion, and could exert more power in world politics, through regional unity. The fact that such unity is not forthcoming in those areas suggests that circumstances within nation-states must be considered no less than external factors if the dynamics of regional integration are to be understood. What are these circumstances and what do they reveal regarding the adequacy of the nation-State to satisfy the changing needs and demands of its citizens?

Part of the answer may lie in the 'decline of the territorial State' as a result of technological developments that have created a situation in areas such as Western Europe where nations can no longer function effectively as self-contained military, economic or political units but must seek wider cooperation to solve common problems. If this growth of regionalism has been faster there it has been due not only to the Soviet threat but also because the area, artificially fragmented economically, in reality constitutes a natural economic unity in terms of the exchange of goods and services.

The growth of regionalism in Western Europe was also hastened by the recognition by Europe's leading statesmen that they could avoid permanent dependence on the United States, and regain their full economic potential and independence, by a form of economic union that might also provide a basis for political union. Underlying this view was a certain disillusionment with the excessive nationalism of the past, and the feeling that this must be ended if Western Europe was to regain a semblance of its former importance in world affairs. This could only mean that nationalism must yield to internationalism.

Such awareness presupposes, however, a degree of political maturity and stability missing in most of the States that have gained their independence from colonial rule since 1945. These nations are still too intoxicated with the emotion of freedom and self-determination to be willing to subordinate aspects of their newly-acquired national sovereignty to transnational control. We must conclude, therefore, that regionalism as an approach to world order is not automatically transferable from one geographical area to another, but is contingent for its success on a complex of internal factors as well as external conditions.

This is not to imply that the movement away from the nation-State is a one-way process. Regional integration depends upon a certain degree of shared economic, political, and ideological interests before it can be successfully launched. Yet the impact of regional institutions upon the evolving process of unification should not be minimized. For example, while the Council of Europe in no way possesses the substantive powers of a European parliament or European executive, it has provided an institutional setting for discussion by European statesmen of various integration schemes. Similarly, the Assembly that serves the three functional Communities of continental Europe acts as a permanent organizational structure for continuous contact among the member States as well as an important symbol of a rapidly evolving regional unity.

While the preceding discussion may have implied the inevitability of political integration among the States of continental Europe, it would be imprudent to predict such a development without qualification. The process of unification beyond the nation-State is apt to be marked by setbacks as well as by progress, as the stillborn European Defence Community revealed.

*   *   *

We are now in a position to raise some important questions regarding regionalism and the United Nations. To what extent have regional security agencies served as successful replacements for the disintegrated United Nations security system? Have they brought the world any closer to peace and order? Does the creation of non-military regional agencies complement or conflict with the economic and social functions of the United Nations and its specialized agencies? Finally, to what extent do regional agencies constitute genuine departures from a system of international relations based on the nation-State, and what are the prospects that regionalism will continue to flourish in the future as an alternative to global cooperation? These are difficult questions to answer, but the task must be attempted so that a preliminary assessment of the relationship between regional and universal approaches to peace and security may be made.

Proponents of regional security organizations argue that such arrangements have not only filled in the gap caused by the weakness of the United Nations but that, in Europe, they have prevented the Soviet Union from achieving any significant new territorial gains. They maintain that such agencies were the only alternatives to further insecurity for the United States and its allies.

In considering this argument, it is necessary to examine critically the assumption that such organizations have provided adequate substitutes for the United Nations security system. Admittedly, the United Nations has failed to develop in the way envisaged by its supporters, but is it possible to assert that the pragmatic response to this failure in the formation of regional alliances has contributed to a stabilization of international tensions? Quite the contrary. In many respects the creation of multilateral and bilateral mutual security treaties by the United States and the Soviet Union marks a return to the period before the first World War, a period of competing alliances which Woodrow Wilson believed to be the primary cause of war. Regional security systems are not only viewed by the major antagonists in the cold war as a threat to their own security, but they have also incurred the resentment and hostility of many newly independent States who see such arrangements as exacerbating rather than relieving world tensions.

With regard to N.A.T.O. it is difficult to make assessments. Probably the establishment of that organization served as an important psychological warning to the Soviet that the West was prepared to resist any further encroachment in Europe. To some extent N.A.T.O. has proved to be useful as a means by which the United States has shared defence burdens with her allies. But is the absence of further Soviet aggression in Western Europe and elsewhere attributable to the presence of N.A.T.O. forces in numerical inferiority to Soviet troops or, more plausibly, to the delicate balance of nuclear weapons that renders any military excursion too costly? To the extent that N.A.T.O. may achieve a collective nuclear capability this conclusion would have to be modified. Whether such a development would contribute to a lowering of tensions is, however, extremely doubtful.

Elsewhere the elaborate network of mutual security treaties developed by the United States contains numerous gaps. This is particularly noticeable in the Middle East where the C.E.N.T.O. organization is weakened by the absence of Iraq and Afghanistan. Similarly, the S.E.A.T.O. organization is hampered by the absence of the key States of India, Ceylon, and Burma. It has been ineffective in preventing the aggression in Laos and is militarily incapable of mobilizing sufficient forces if Communist China were to launch a full scale attack on vulnerable Thailand or the Philippines.

The preceding discussion does not imply that the various regional alliances should be dissolved. Rather, it emphasizes some of their serious limitations as instruments of security in a world devoid of an effective universal organization to enforce the peace. Ideally, the solution to the problem of world peace requires the subordination of regional agencies to a universal agency for the maintenance of peace. Such a restatement of this maximalist approach to peace, however, only underlines the extent to which the world has strayed from the ideal of collective security suggested by Wilson—although that ideal perhaps presupposed conditions of international solidarity that are impossible to realize in a world bifurcated into conflicting political ideologies.

The restoration of a more normal equilibrium between global and regional security agencies is not in sight. The present imbalance is a symptom more than a cause of international disorder. As suggested earlier, the immediate causes of that imbalance may be traced to the change from a relatively stable to a highly unstable balance of power system, and to the appearance of divisive ideological forces. But would the normalization of relations between the Soviet Union, Communist China and the United States and the return to a complex balance of power system restore an equilibrium between universalism and regionalism? A modification of the present imbalance in world order might be realized, but the prospects of that happening appear very remote.

A more fundamental analysis by Professor Kenneth Waltz suggests that international conflict is the result of three factors that may be difficult if not impossible to modify: the nature of man; the nature of the State; and the nature of the state system.[1] Until harmony can be achieved among these three elements the possibilities for world order are not optimistic. In the meantime, it is likely that, with their success in Western Europe, non-military regional forms of international cooperation will continue to flourish, subject to appropriate internal conditions in the underdeveloped areas.

A seldom explored question is the extent to which such agencies operating in economic and social spheres oppose or complement similar activities of the United Nations and its specialized agencies. Only a tentative answer may be given in view of the absence of research on this particular issue. In theory there need be no conflict between universal and regional approaches to economic and social development. Cooperation is often more readily forthcoming in regions where common economic and social problems present opportunities for collaboration not so easily available on a world level.

[1] *Man, the State, and War* (New York, Columbia University Press, 1959).

Where such regional economic integration has taken definite shape the possibility of conflict between the purposes of the regional and the universal organization is likely. Although the European Economic Community represents a substantial advance toward free trade, such an arrangement is discriminatory in States outside the Common Market area and so conflicts with the universalist ideal of expanded world trade. The creation of additional common market arrangements in Latin America, Africa, and Southeast Asia involves the threat of intensified economic protectionism unless satisfactory concessions can be worked out on an inter-regional basis. Unfortunately, the United Nations has no control over such developments and therefore cannot function as a coordinator where coordination is so vitally needed.

On the other hand, the United Nations through its technical assistance and economic development programmes has involved itself in activities embracing several distinct regions of the world. The same thing is true of the various specialized agencies operating in the fields of health, sanitation, agriculture, and education. The fact that in many of the underdeveloped areas regional cooperation has not developed to any appreciable degree has meant that States in such areas have been anxious to obtain the assistance of the United Nations and its specialized agencies.

On balance it may be said that regional economic arrangements constitute an improvement over the economic nationalism that has been a feature of international economic relations for several years, but that they represent something less than universal economic internationalism. The failure to achieve this ideal through the establishment of the International Trade Organization has in fact prompted the movement toward economic regionalism first in the prosperous and now in the underdeveloped areas. Nevertheless, the progress achieved through the International Bank and Monetary Fund, and by the G.A.T.T., in developing a multilateral framework for investments, currency stabilization and lower tariff barriers should not be underestimated.

* * *

There remains the question whether the development of regional agencies, of a military and non-military nature, marks a departure from the nation-State as the traditional unit of international relations. If so, does that development necessarily imply, as proponents of regionalism assert, that regionalism will inevitably tend toward the creation of a supranational global order?

Although it is still too early to assess the impact of regional military and non-military agencies on the traditional system of nation-States, certain conclusions appear justifiable. Trends towards regional union cannot be arbitrarily separated into military and non-military categories.

The process of integration is likely to begin with cooperation in relatively narrow spheres and, where such efforts are successful, to spill over into other areas and ultimately embrace some form of political union. Thus the experience of Western Europe since 1945 demonstrates that transnational cooperation developed first in the military area, involving a gradual standardization of weapons systems and armed forces, without however culminating in a European Army. Then the trend towards integration spread into a relatively specialized sector of economic production with the creation of the European Coal and Steel Community. It has since spread further to include the gradual removal of all national tariff barriers and immigration restrictions, and the development of common monetary and investment policies under the European Economic Community.

Though critics assert that the degree of transnational cooperation so far attained in Western Europe still leaves the national sovereignty of the States pretty much intact, loyalties extending beyond the narrow confines of the member States have been slowly building up. Whether this tendency will culminate in the development of supranational legislative and executive organs, with powers binding upon the member units without their unanimous consent, is still uncertain. The acceleration of European unity will no doubt be affected by the intensity of Soviet hostility toward the West. As such hostility does not appear likely to abate, pressures for further unification are likely to continue. The main point is that precedents for cooperation have been established that reveal that, if the process of interdependence cannot find institutional expression on the world level in the reduction of nationalism and sovereignty, it is possible for parochial nationalism to be gradually superseded by a regional internationalism.

The appearance of greater regional unity in the under-developed areas must await a greater political maturity and stability of the States located there. In many areas intra-regional rivalries act as divisive forces while nationalism also provides a deterrent to wider unity. But even in these areas regional cooperation is being advanced. The activities of the Organization of American States have been expanded into the economic field with the creation of the Inter-American Development Bank and the Free Trade Association foreseen by the Montevideo Treaty. In West Africa several States have entered into a customs union.

It is not to be expected, however, that in these areas the movement towards regional unity will proceed at the same pace as in Western Europe. Each of the under-developed regions is affected by political instability in varying degrees—an instability resulting not only from the post-independence problem of maintaining law and order but also from the lack of adequately trained civil servants, marked gaps in standards of living between the élites and the masses, and rising populating pressures that threaten economic growth. Before regional cooperation can become effective, these problems will have to be solved, or at least a start must be made towards their improvement. Finally, since regionalism presupposes a willingness to dilute nationalism with internationalism, important changes in the attitude of most of these States will be required. Many are caught up in such a wave of rising expectations for their peoples that nationalism rather than internationalism is apt to be dominant at least in the short run. All of these factors lead to the conclusion that while regional co-operation for economic and social development is under experiment in the under-developed areas, its rate of growth will be much slower than in Western Europe.

Altogether, then, it is doubtful whether regional entities are mainly towards the formation of a supranational global order, or that the nation-State is being superseded by regional federations or confederations throughout the world. Only in Western Europe can this be said to be happening.

* * *

To the extent that regional cooperation provides for an increase in stability within regions by removing historical rivalries, settling intra-regional disputes, and promoting economic and social cooperation, it serves as a catalyst for regional peace and order. But in itself regionalism as an approach to world order is incomplete. Unless regional units are subordinated to a universal agency, regional self-sufficiency can only be damaging to inter-regional relations. It is only necessary to cite the tense inter-regional or inter-bloc conflict existing between the North Atlantic region and the Communist world of Russia, Eastern Europe, and Com-munist China.

In the final analysis, the world needs cooperation at both the global and regional levels. But acceptance of the need for simultaneous universal and regional cooperation, and for the existence of adequate coordinating links between the two levels, does not bring them about. A world trisected into three weakly coordinated segments, of which two are deadly hostile to each other, is not an orderly world. A revival of universalism presupposes elements of consensus and cohesion that have been notably lacking since 1945. Unless and until international politics evolves into a system in which the three great political and ideological forces of Communism, Democracy and Neutralism can function cooperatively, it is likely that the present disequilibrium between universal and regional organization will continue.

NOTES AND QUESTIONS

1. Distinguish between bipolarity, multipolarity, regionalism, and atomization. Consider the relevance of each pattern of organization to the objectives of war prevention. Does the distribution of power and authority in international society influence the degree of war-proneness (in Boulding's sense) of the system?

2. Ducci refers to the feeling of Walpole, Metternich, and Salisbury that any change in the existing international equilibrium creates the possibility of war. See also, Emmerich de Vattel, *Law of Nations* (Oceana, Dobbs Ferry, N.Y., 1964) Chapter I. Does this tend to support Waltz's argument that prospects for peace will worsen if the bipolar organization of international society is upset? Is the Clark-Sohn plan a change in the international equilibrium that might actually raise the risks of major war? How can one answer this sort of question?

3. The atomistic system that Ducci anticipates is not very clearly delineated. It could be a world in which the 130 or so nation-states behave as the nation-states in Western Europe did during the 19th century. This pattern of international relations might lead to the emergence of some vastly complicated form of a balance of power system. For a useful discussion of the various forms that the organization of international society has taken, see Inis L. Claude, *Power and International Relations* (Random House, New York, 1962); see also George Liska, *International Equilibrium* (Harvard University Press, 1957). From the perspective of the history of legal thought, see Walter C. Schiffer, *The Legal Community of Mankind* (Columbia University Press, 1954). On the other hand, these many states might find it convenient or necessary to use various patterns of semi-centralized and fully centralized structure as a framework for both their cooperative and competitive activities. See Inis L. Claude, *Swords into Ploughshares* (rev. ed., Random House, New York, 1964) for a useful discussion. It could even be argued, although Ducci refrains from doing so, that atomization is a necessary prerequisite to the development of world structure. In fact, Ducci seems to feel that, despite atomization, various forms of supranationalism should be encouraged. Ducci is not optimistic about the capacity of regional organizations to provide a stable world order unless accompanied by a reinvigoration of the peace-keeping capacities of the United Nations. There is some irony implicit in Ducci's conclusion.

For within the original concept of the United Nations was the idea that the big powers would form a world police force by exercising the powers in Chapter VII of the United Nations Charter. Would not this produce a world structure that is more akin to Waltz's preference for bipolar management than to the notions of Clark and Sohn? It would be a world in which the Great Powers would accept responsibility for maintaining the peace. See Peter Calvocoressi, *World Order and New States* (Praeger, New York, 1962) for analysis of implications of this loss of function by the Great Powers and its bearing on the role of the United Nations. This would presuppose a degree of harmony among the Great Powers that is certainly not present at this time.

4. While we have been discussing bipolarization, atomization, and regionalism as though they were different views of the existing empirical system of international relations, Ducci, Waltz, and Yalem each make clear their awareness that the present system is a mix of all three. How do you account for their differing

appraisals of the significance of atomization? What kind of information would you need to be in a position to choose the more correct of the appraisals? Certainly part of an answer would involve a judgment about the capability—actual and potential—of China, and perhaps France, Germany, and Japan. What factors are crucial? Population, size of armies, size of military budget, nuclear weapons, delivery systems, aggressive intentions, diplomatic skill, gross national product, per capita income, rate of economic growth, geopolitical position?

5. There has been very little theoretical work done on whether a system in which regions were the prime agents or units of international relations would be more or less stable than the present system, an atomistic system, or a world law system. Yalem suggests that a regional international system would be unstable. What arguments are there for saying that it would become or could be made to become stable?

It interesting to note that the constitution drafted by the Committee for the Drafting of a World Constitution chose nine regions as their basic units. Does territorial regionalism make more sense than ideological regionalism? An argument against territorial regionalism has been that various states in permanent conflict would be lumped together. For full discussion, see the Introduction in **III-4** relevant to the debates on the expansion of the Security Council. For example, Israel would be part of the Middle East, whereas Malaysia, Taiwan, China, and Indonesia would become part of the Southeast Region. It could also be contended that it would facilitate accommodation to place these hostile states together in the various regional units, on the theory that since the unity of the region would increase its influence on the world level, the acceptance of regional units would increase the incentive to abolish intra-regional dissension. Any prospect of regional harmonization certainly must face formidable obstacles.

6. What would be the probable effects of the growth of regional organizations upon the chances for the adoption of the Clark-Sohn plan?

7. The Troika was proposed by the Soviet Union to assure that the United Nations would act to advance the three main groups of states active in international society: the West, the states associated with Soviet leadership, and the non-aligned. Any action by the Secretary-General, according to the Soviet proposal, must be supported by representatives of each of these three political groupings. Given the rivalry of the cold war it was felt, especially by the West, that an acceptance of the Troika would virtually paralyze the United Nations in any situation of international conflict. What do you think? Is ideological affinity as crucial as power in the description of international society? Is the world "bipolar" for Waltz because the Soviet Union and the United States are dominant military powers, or because they are the main propagators of the most salient ideologies?

8. What is the connection between ideological antagonism and political solidarity in domestic political systems? How is it relevant to an analysis of international society? Twenty to thirty-five per cent of the vote in France and Italy have gone to the Communist Party in each election since the end of World War II. Both national societies have been governed with reasonable effectiveness during this period by non-Communists without even the participation of more than a very few Communists at the cabinet level. Some would discount the relevance of the French and Italian experience; they argue that much of the voting strength of the Communist Party arises from a spirit of reformist protest, or from the contribution made by the Communist Party in these two countries to the bread and

butter aspirations of workers, rather than from any kind of real desire for Marxism or for an external affiliation with the international Communist movement, or even for a revolution in their own society.

Compare the veto idea incorporated into the Troika proposal with the veto given to the five permanent members of the Security Council. Would an ideological veto be more detrimental to effective action by the Organization than a right of veto bestowed on the Great Powers as of 1945? Both conceptions emphasize the need for a certain kind of consensus as a prerequisite to effective action on the part of the United Nations. The Troika implies a tripolar authority structure. Is this a realistic alternative to the choice between bipolarity and multipolarity?

9. It might be useful to compare a return to the original conception of the United Nations with both the Clark-Sohn scheme and with Waltz's conception of a continuation of a bipolar world. Is a world policed by the Great Powers more akin to the bipolar world of Waltz or to the fully disarmed world that is proposed by Clark and Sohn? In what way would a world body consisting of regional units be compatible with the thinking of Clark and Sohn, Ducci, or Waltz?

10. Even when formal organizational structure may be said to have an independent impact upon political processes, underlying political processes will continue. See, in this respect, the article by Inis Claude in **II-3** that argues that the United Nations has been an arena within which the old balance of power system has, by and large, operated.

11. Does one explain differences in the way the world is viewed primarily as a consequence of differing interpretations of the same facts, or primarily as a series of interpretations that correspond to sets of different facts? To what extent is the interpretation affected by different values held by the interpreter? How do you distinguish between facts and values in your own view of the world? Should the values of an author be made explicit? Should a responsible author seek to repress his values when analyzing the subject of war prevention? Do you detect any significant differences in the values of the authors represented in this section of readings? What are the relevant values of Clark and Sohn? Is it generally more useful to discuss differences in the rankings or priority table of values, rather than differences in values? That is, both X and Y may believe in values A and B, but X may think A is more important than B, and Y may think B more important than A in situations where one must promote one and subordinate the other.

12. Finally is should be noted that each of the three authors are from Western society and that whatever differences exist among them about the way the world is or ought to be ordered, these differences are not as great as those that exist between them and certain non-Western scholars and statesmen. The most striking of these differences at this time (Fall, 1965) is the way in which the political elite of the Chinese People's Republic apparently view the world. See, for example, the excerpt from a major policy statement made by Defense Minister, Marshall Lin Piao, published in the September 4, 1965 issue of the *New York Times*. Of special significance is his view on the role of violence to achieve a desired world order. How important these differences are in terms of the twin problems of understanding world political processes and of achieving a more peaceful world order is a theme running through these volumes. Of course, for the full range of world views, you will have to supplement the materials contained herein.

B.   Differing Methods of Viewing the World

It is perhaps trivial to emphasize the extent to which assumptions about the proper method to study the world shape the way we view the world. Some background for these matters is to be found in Karl Mannheim, *Ideology and Utopia* translated by L. Wirth and E. Shils, (Harcourt, Brace, New York, 1959). Matters of method are usually kept implicit and hidden. In this section we explore some key methodological questions for their own sake and to make evident the relevance of methodological choices to substantive outcomes. Therefore, these selections are a natural complement to the readings of Section A.

Our more ambitious objective here is to encourage readers to think throughout the book about whether the methods of inquiry used by various authors are adequate for their stated purposes. And in particular, whether there are any methodological conclusions about the proper way to study proposals for drastic change in international society. Clark and Sohn do not devote much attention to explaining their method. Could this account for their failure to devote sufficient attention to the refractory nature of the transition problem? What methodological assumptions must be introduced so that adequate attention could be given to the processes of social and structural transformation in international society? Note that what we seek to investigate is a new system of world order established in the near future. What do we know about system change? Is it more likely to come about slowly through time or all at once? Some have said that a drastic change in the character of world order can only come about as the aftermath of catastrophe. It is obviously in the interest of mankind to make whatever changes are necessary without the persuasiveness of a catastrophe itself.

The typically skeptical view of proposals for system change in international society has been recently expressed by Thornton Read in *Military Policy in a Changing Political Context*, Policy Memorandum no. 31 (Center for International Studies, Princeton University, 1964) pp. 4–5:

Whatever may be the ultimate prospect of a radical change in the international system and the emergence of a World Federal Government, a radical change in the distribution of power in the short term would surely be either the cause or the consequence of a disaster. The social-political world is in this respect analogous to the world of living organisms: degeneration may take place either gradually or suddenly, but healthy growth is always gradual.

Read goes on to quote Herman Kahn's pungent complaint

that "we have access to more than a five-foot shelf of books and studies about the possibilities of evolutionary change, but not one really definitive study of the revolutionary routes to radical change." Read responds that our knowledge about radical change is discouraging rather than deficient. In fact, Read goes so far as to conclude:

Some thought should no doubt be given to how to pick up the pieces after a not quite fatal catastrophe, but in that case the problem would be not how to build a better world on the ruins of the old, but how to mitigate the harshness of the inevitable regression to a more primitive and oppressive soical order. In short, radical planning should be concerned with moderating a disastrous regression; planning for an improved world should envision marginal changes and gradual evolution.

It should be noted that Read advances very little evidence in support of his strong views aside from a questionable analogy between the character of biological change and the proper forms of political change. He seems confident enough of his conclusion to give fairly dogmatic counsel against the intellectual venture that underlies this book. For we feel that radical change is an apt subject for study, that we are able to plan for the radical reordering of international society, and that it is not *necessarily* the case that radical change can only be the cause or consequence of disaster. We feel somewhat encouraged in this view by the course of revolutionary experiences in domestic societies, as well as by the inherent rationality of engaging in an enterprise of thought devoted to specifying the altered conditions for the survival of mankind in an altered world environment. However, at the root of methodological discussions of this question raised so sharply by Read is the question whether or not a radical improvement in the character of world order can be brought about by a reliance on peaceful means in the short term.

Our first selection is an article by J. David Singer, "The Level-of-Analysis Problem in International Relations," *The International System*, edited by Klaus Knorr and Sidney Verba (Princeton University Press, 1961) pp. 77-92. It raises a central question of method—what is the most effective strategy of inquiry into the phenomena of international society? Singer argues that it is necessary consciously to discipline inquiry into the subject matter of international relations. Such discipline is the condition for intellectual progress. Singer is especially concerned with distinguishing between what he calls "the levels of analysis." In his essay Singer shows the difference in understanding and explanation that results from examining a particular problem from the perspective of a national actor and from the perspective of the international system taken as a whole. He recognizes the advantages of each for a total understanding of the subject and the need for a reconciliation of the two levels in a single coherent body of knowledge. While reading Singer, it might be useful to consider the relevance of his approach to the study of the central problems of war prevention and system change. How shall we take the varying levels of analysis into account? At least Singer helps put us on our guard against the acceptance of any single perspective as productive of sufficient knowledge about the subject. We need the knowledge that is acquired by recourse to a series of perspectives.

Singer's piece stresses the various functions of an analytical model: description, explanation, and prediction. Singer raises another important methodological problem in the social and behavioral sciences by discussing the relationship between "phenomenological" factors and "objective" factors. Here "phenomenological" means the perceptions of the actors or the meanings that actors place on or find in situations, whereas the objective factors are the elements, variables, and patterns that the researcher or observer posits as present from his more detached vantage point.

The article by Anatol Rapoport, "Systemic and Strategic Conflict," *The Virginia Quarterly Review,* vol. 40, no. 3 (Summer, 1964) pp. 337-368, continues the line of inquiry commenced in general terms by Singer, and applies it to the more specific context of international conflict and the prevention of violence. Rapoport contrasts the two dominant modes of thought operating on war-peace issues: the systemic view and the strategic view. The systemic view stresses the presence of deterministic elements in international life that operate independently of *"rationally designed actions or consciously conceived goals."* A systemic thinker tries to demonstrate the kind of political determination relevant to the particular system under scrutiny. In contrast, the strategic view, epitomized by game theory, tries to examine participation in international society from the point of view of a player seeking to maximize his pay-offs. Rapoport is upset that the strategic view prevails in diplomatic and military settings, because of its tendency to force upon us an emphasis on self-interest, so conceived, as the basis for rational action in world affairs. In a manner paralleling Singer's portrayal of the levels of analysis, Rapoport calls for a merging of the strategic with the systemic mode in our thinking about international politics. Rapoport wants to orient thought in terms of what he calls "the survival value of the species." How can we learn to recognize our communality of interests and cooperate for the promotion of these interests, rather than stressing our antagonism of interests and our tendency to calculate how we might gain at the other's expense? This viewpoint opposes that earlier one attributed to Read on the same issue, as Rapoport asks us to think in the manner appropriate for our survival whatever the radical consequences such thought may entail. In Boulding's article, "The Prevention of World War III," reprinted in Chapter I, we see the advocacy of a system change as a consequence of adopting a starting point for speculation that seems to accord with Rapoport's prescription. On many of the issues raised here, see Ranyard West, *Conscience and Society* (Emerson Books, New York, 1945).

The third selection is Harold Lasswell's Presidential address to the American Political Science Association in 1956 calling for a mobilization of knowledge in the interests of achieving an improved social environment. Lasswell is explicitly optimistic about the capacity of man to think his way through to solutions that reflect policy preferences. See Chapter 3B. In Lasswell's judgment, consistent with Singer's plea, the proper forms of disciplined inquiry can improve our ability to cope with "the horizon of the unfolding future." In fact it is a matter of the highest social responsibility to make full use of this ability.

In selecting armament, production, and evolution as subjects of his analysis for developing the argument that political scientists must become more familiar with physical and biological sciences in order to be prepared to assist policy-makers to make appropriate choices, Lasswell skillfully blends an appraisal of past events with futuristic thinking. We call special attention to his discussion of overcoming the inadequate relation between thought and action that he finds present in our decision to drop atomic bombs on the populated cities of Hiroshima and Nagasaki at the close of World War II. Lasswell's four suggestions for improving the contribution of academicians to the decision process are valuable to bear in mind when considering how much it is reasonable to expect from the future. As we shall see in **II-1B**, these suggestions when translated into a frame of reference of goals, trends, factors and projections seem especially helpful for our efforts to assess the feasibility and desirability of the Clark-Sohn plan.

Finally, there seems to be a confrontation between Read's pessimism and Lasswell's optimism about the ability of man to adapt to the future. How do you choose?——by recourse to history, common sense, belief-system, logic, psychoanalysis, technological progress, or international conflict?——or by some

judgment of the whole context within which a particular proposal for action is made? Among philosophers who have dealt
with these issues none is more illuminating than Alfred North
Whitehead. See, in particular, *The Function of Reason* (Beacon
Press, Boston, 1962); see also Michael Polanyi, *The Logic of
Liberty* (University of Chicago Press, 1951) and *Personal Knowledge* (University of Chicago Press, 1958).

THE LEVEL-OF-ANALYSIS PROBLEM
IN INTERNATIONAL RELATIONS

By J. DAVID SINGER

IN any area of scholarly inquiry, there are always several ways in which the phenomena under study may be sorted and arranged for purposes of systemic analysis. Whether in the physical or social sciences, the observer may choose to focus upon the parts or upon the whole, upon the components or upon the system. He may, for example, choose between the flowers or the garden, the rocks or the quarry, the trees or the forest, the houses or the neighborhood, the cars or the traffic jam, the delinquents or the gang, the legislators or the legislative, and so on.[1] Whether he selects the micro- or macro-level of analysis is ostensibly a mere matter of methodological or conceptual convenience. Yet the choice often turns out to be quite difficult, and may well become a central issue within the discipline concerned. The complexity and significance of these level-of-analysis decisions are readily suggested by the long-standing controversies between social psychology and sociology, personality-oriented and culture-oriented anthropology, or micro- and macro-economics, to mention but a few. In the vernacular of general systems theory, the observer is always confronted with a system, its sub-systems, and their respective environments, and while he may choose as his system any cluster of phenomena from the most minute organism to the universe itself, such choice cannot be merely a function of whim or caprice, habit or familiarity.[2] The responsible scholar must be prepared to evaluate the relative utility—conceptual and methodological—of the various alternatives open to him, and to appraise the manifold implications of the level of analysis finally selected. So it is with international relations.

But whereas the pros and cons of the various possible levels of analysis have been debated exhaustively in many of the social sciences, the issue has scarcely been raised among students of our emerging

[1] As Kurt Lewin observed in his classic contribution to the social sciences: "The first prerequisite of a successful observation in any science is a definite understanding about what size of unit one is going to observe at a given time." *Field Theory in Social Science*, New York, 1951, p. 157.

[2] For a useful introductory statement on the definitional and taxonomic problems in a general systems approach, see the papers by Ludwig von Bertalanffy, "General System Theory," and Kenneth Boulding, "General System Theory: The Skeleton of Science," in Society for the Advancement of General Systems Theory, *General Systems*, Ann Arbor, Mich., 1956, I, part I.

discipline.[3] Such tranquillity may be seen by some as a reassuring indication that the issue is not germane to our field, and by others as evidence that it has already been resolved, but this writer perceives the quietude with a measure of concern. He is quite persuaded of its relevance and certain that it has yet to be resolved. Rather, it is contended that the issue has been ignored by scholars still steeped in the intuitive and artistic tradition of the humanities or enmeshed in the web of "practical" policy. We have, in our texts and elsewhere, roamed up and down the ladder of organizational complexity with remarkable abandon, focusing upon the total system, international organizations, regions, coalitions, extra-national associations, nations, domestic pressure groups, social classes, elites, and individuals as the needs of the moment required. And though most of us have tended to settle upon the nation as our most comfortable resting place, we have retained our propensity for vertical drift, failing to appreciate the value of a stable point of focus.[4] Whether this lack of concern is a function of the relative infancy of the discipline or the nature of the intellectual traditions from whence it springs, it nevertheless remains a significant variable in the general sluggishness which characterizes the development of theory in the study of relations among nations. It is the purpose of this paper to raise the issue, articulate the alternatives, and examine the theoretical implications and consequences of two of the more widely employed levels of analysis: the international system and the national sub-systems.

I. The Requirements of an Analytical Model

Prior to an examination of the theoretical implications of the level of analysis or orientation employed in our model, it might be worthwhile to discuss the uses to which any such model might be put, and the requirements which such uses might expect of it.

Obviously, we would demand that it offer a highly accurate *description* of the phenomena under consideration. Therefore the scheme must present as complete and undistorted a picture of these phenomena as is possible; it must correlate with objective reality and coincide with our empirical referents to the highest possible degree. Yet we know that

[3] An important pioneering attempt to deal with some of the implications of one's level of analysis, however, is Kenneth N. Waltz, *Man, the State, and War*, New York, 1959. But Waltz restricts himself to a consideration of these implications as they impinge on the question of the causes of war. See also this writer's review of Waltz, "International Conflict: Three Levels of Analysis," *World Politics*, xii (April 1960), pp. 453-61.

[4] Even during the debate between "realism" and "idealism" the analytical implications of the various levels of analysis received only the scantiest attention; rather the emphasis seems to have been at the two extremes of pragmatic policy and speculative metaphysics.

such accurate representation of a complex and wide-ranging body of phenomena is extremely difficult. Perhaps a useful illustration may be borrowed from cartography; the oblate spheroid which the planet earth most closely represents is not transferable to the two-dimensional surface of a map without *some* distortion. Thus, the Mercator projection exaggerates distance and distorts direction at an increasing rate as we move north or south *from* the equator, while the polar gnomonic projection suffers from these same debilities as we move *toward* the equator. Neither offers therefore a wholly accurate presentation, yet each is true enough to reality to be quite useful for certain specific purposes. The same sort of tolerance is necessary in evaluating any analytical model for the study of international relations; if we must sacrifice total representational accuracy, the problem is to decide where distortion is least dysfunctional and where such accuracy is absolutely essential.

These decisions are, in turn, a function of the second requirement of any such model—a capacity to *explain* the relationships among the phenomena under investigation. Here our concern is not so much with accuracy of description as with validity of explanation. Our model must have such analytical capabilities as to treat the causal relationships in a fashion which is not only valid and thorough, but parsimonious; this latter requirement is often overlooked, yet its implications for research strategy are not inconsequential.[5] It should be asserted here that the primary purpose of theory is to explain, and when descriptive and explanatory requirements are in conflict, the latter ought to be given priority, even at the cost of some representational inaccuracy.

Finally, we may legitimately demand that any analytical model offer the promise of reliable *prediction*. In mentioning this requirement last, there is no implication that it is the most demanding or difficult of the three. Despite the popular belief to the contrary, prediction demands less of one's model than does explanation or even description. For example, any informed layman can predict that pressure on the

[5] For example, one critic of the decision-making model formulated by Richard C. Snyder, H. W. Bruck, and Burton Sapin, in *Decision-Making as an Approach to the Study of International Politics* (Princeton, N.J., 1954), points out that no single researcher could deal with all the variables in that model and expect to complete more than a very few comparative studies in his lifetime. See Herbert McClosky, "Concerning Strategies for a Science of International Politics," *World Politics*, viii (January 1956), pp. 281-95. In defense, however, one might call attention to the relative ease with which many of Snyder's categories could be collapsed into more inclusive ones, as was apparently done in the subsequent case study (see note 11 below). Perhaps a more telling criticism of the monograph is McClosky's comment that "Until a greater measure of theory is introduced into the proposal and the relations among variables are specified more concretely, it is likely to remain little more than a setting-out of categories and, like any taxonomy, fairly limited in its utility" (p. 291).

accelerator of a slowly moving car will increase its speed; that more or less of the moon will be visible tonight than last night; or that the normal human will flinch when confronted with an impending blow. These *predictions* do not require a particularly elegant or sophisticated model of the universe, but their *explanation* demands far more than most of us carry around in our minds. Likewise, we can predict with impressive reliability that any nation will respond to military attack in kind, but a description and understanding of the processes and factors leading to such a response are considerably more elusive, despite the gross simplicity of the acts themselves.

Having articulated rather briefly the requirements of an adequate analytical model, we might turn now to a consideration of the ways in which one's choice of analytical focus impinges upon such a model and affects its descriptive, explanatory, and predictive adequacy.

II. THE INTERNATIONAL SYSTEM AS LEVEL OF ANALYSIS

Beginning with the systemic level of analysis, we find in the total international system a partially familiar and highly promising point of focus. First of all, it is the most comprehensive of the levels available, encompassing the totality of interactions which take place within the system and its environment. By focusing on the system, we are enabled to study the patterns of interaction which the system reveals, and to generalize about such phenomena as the creation and dissolution of coalitions, the frequency and duration of specific power configurations, modifications in its stability, its responsiveness to changes in formal political institutions, and the norms and folklore which it manifests as a societal system. In other words, the systemic level of analysis, and only this level, permits us to examine international relations in the whole, with a comprehensiveness that is of necessity lost when our focus is shifted to a lower, and more partial, level. For descriptive purposes, then, it offers both advantages and disadvantages; the former flow from its comprehensiveness, and the latter from the necessary dearth of detail.

As to explanatory capability, the system-oriented model poses some genuine difficulties. In the first place, it tends to lead the observer into a position which exaggerates the impact of the system upon the national actors and, conversely, discounts the impact of the actors on the system. This is, of course, by no means inevitable; one could conceivably look upon the system as a rather passive environment in which dynamic states act out their relationships rather than as a socio-political entity with a dynamic of its own. But there is a natural tendency to endow that upon which we focus our attention with somewhat greater potential than it might normally be expected to have. Thus, we tend to move, in a system-oriented model, away from notions implying much national autonomy and independence of choice and toward a more deterministic orientation.

Secondly, this particular level of analysis almost inevitably requires that we postulate a high degree of uniformity in the foreign policy operational codes of our national actors. By definition, we allow little room for divergence in the behavior of our parts when we focus upon the whole. It is no coincidence that our most prominent theoretician— and one of the very few text writers focusing upon the international system—should "assume that [all] statesmen think and act in terms of interest defined as power."[6] If this single-minded behavior be interpreted literally and narrowly, we have a simplistic image comparable to economic man or sexual man, and if it be defined broadly, we are no better off than the psychologist whose human model pursues "self-realization" or "maximization of gain"; all such gross models suffer from the same fatal weakness as the utilitarian's "pleasure-pain" principle. Just as individuals differ widely in what they deem to be pleasure and pain, or gain and loss, nations may differ widely in what they consider to be the national interest, and we end up having to break down and refine the larger category. Moreover, Professor Morgenthau finds himself compelled to go still further and disavow the relevance of both motives and ideological preferences in national behavior, and these represent two of the more useful dimensions in differentiating among the several nations in our international system. By eschewing any empirical concern with the domestic and internal variations within the separate nations, the system-oriented approach tends to produce a sort of "black box" or "billiard ball" concept of the national actors.[7] By discounting—or denying—the differences among nations, or by

---

[6] Hans J. Morgenthau, *Politics Among Nations*, 3rd ed., New York, 1960, pp. 5-7. Obviously, his model does not preclude the use of power as a dimension for the differentiation of nations.

[7] The "black box" figure comes from some of the simpler versions of S-R psychology, in which the observer more or less ignores what goes on within the individual and concentrates upon the correlation between stimulus and response; these are viewed as empirically verifiable, whereas cognition, perception, and other mental processes have to be imputed to the individual with a heavy reliance on these assumed "intervening variables." The "billiard ball" figure seems to carry the same sort of connotation, and is best employed by Arnold Wolfers in "The Actors in International Politics" in William T. R. Fox, ed., *Theoretical Aspects of International Relations*, Notre Dame, Ind., 1959, pp. 83-106. See also, in this context, Richard C. Snyder, "International Relations Theory—Continued," *World Politics*, XIII (January 1961), pp. 300-12; and J. David Singer, "Theorizing About Theory in International Politics," *Journal of Conflict Resolution*, IV (December 1960), pp. 431-42. Both are review articles dealing with the Fox anthology.

positing the near-impossibility of observing many of these differences at work within them,[8] one concludes with a highly homogenized image of our nations in the international system. And though this may be an inadequate foundation upon which to base any *causal* statements, it offers a reasonably adequate basis for *correlative* statements. More specifically, it permits us to observe and measure correlations between certain forces or stimuli which seem to impinge upon the nation and the behavior patterns which are the apparent consequence of these stimuli. But one must stress the limitations implied in the word "apparent"; what is thought to be the consequence of a given stimulus may only be a coincidence or artifact, and until one investigates the major elements in the causal link—no matter how persuasive the deductive logic—one may speak only of correlation, not of consequence.

Moreover, by avoiding the multitudinous pitfalls of intra-nation observation, one emerges with a singularly manageable model, requiring as it does little of the methodological sophistication or onerous empiricism called for when one probes beneath the behavioral externalities of the actor. Finally, as has already been suggested in the introduction, the systemic orientation should prove to be reasonably satisfactory as a basis for prediction, even if such prediction is to extend beyond the characteristics of the system and attempt anticipatory statements regarding the actors themselves; this assumes, of course, that the actors are characterized and their behavior predicted in relatively gross and general terms.

These, then, are some of the more significant implications of a model which focuses upon the international system as a whole. Let us turn now to the more familiar of our two orientations, the national state itself.

III. THE NATIONAL STATE AS LEVEL OF ANALYSIS

The other level of analysis to be considered in this paper is the national state—our primary actor in international relations. This is clearly the traditional focus among Western students, and is the one which dominates almost all of the texts employed in English-speaking colleges and universities.

Its most obvious advantage is that it permits significant differentiation among our actors in the international system. Because it does not require the attribution of great similarity to the national actors, it encour-

---

[8] Morgenthau observes, for example, that it is "futile" to search for motives because they are "the most illusive of psychological data, distorted as they are, frequently beyond recognition, by the interests and emotions of actor and observer alike" (*op.cit.*, p. 6).

ages the observer to examine them in greater detail. The favorable results of such intensive analysis cannot be overlooked, as it is only when the actors are studied in some depth that we are able to make really valid generalizations of a comparative nature. And though the systemic model does not necessarily preclude comparison and contrast among the national sub-systems, it usually eventuates in rather gross comparisons based on relatively crude dimensions and characteristics. On the other hand, there is no assurance that the nation-oriented approach will produce a sophisticated model for the comparative study of foreign policy; with perhaps the exception of the Haas and Whiting study,[9] none of our major texts makes a serious and successful effort to describe and explain national behavior in terms of most of the significant variables by which such behavior might be comparatively analyzed. But this would seem to be a function, not of the level of analysis employed, but of our general unfamiliarity with the other social sciences (in which comparison is a major preoccupation) and of the retarded state of comparative government and politics, a field in which most international relations specialists are likely to have had some experience.

But just as the nation-as-actor focus permits us to avoid the inaccurate homogenization which often flows from the systemic focus, it also may lead us into the opposite type of distortion—a marked exaggeration of the differences among our sub-systemic actors. While it is evident that neither of these extremes is conducive to the development of a sophisticated comparison of foreign policies, and such comparison requires a balanced preoccupation with both similarity and difference, the danger seems to be greatest when we succumb to the tendency to overdifferentiate; comparison and contrast can proceed only from observed uniformities.[10]

One of the additional liabilities which flow in turn from the pressure to overdifferentiate is that of Ptolemaic parochialism. Thus, in overemphasizing the differences among the many national states, the observer is prone to attribute many of what he conceives to be virtues to his own nation and the vices to others, especially the adversaries of the moment. That this ethnocentrism is by no means an idle fear is borne out by perusal of the major international relations texts published

[9] Ernst B. Haas and Allen S. Whiting, *Dynamics of International Relations*, New York, 1956.

[10] A frequent by-product of this tendency to overdifferentiate is what Waltz calls the "second-image fallacy," in which one explains the peaceful or bellicose nature of a nation's foreign policy exclusively in terms of its domestic economic, political, or social characteristics (*op.cit.*, chs. 4 and 5).

in the United States since 1945. Not only is the world often perceived through the prism of the American national interest, but an inordinate degree of attention (if not spleen) is directed toward the Soviet Union; it would hardly be amiss to observe that most of these might qualify equally well as studies in American foreign policy. The scientific inadequacies of this sort of "we-they" orientation hardly require elaboration, yet they remain a potent danger in any utilization of the national actor model.

Another significant implication of the sub-systemic orientation is that it is only within its particular framework that we can expect any useful application of the decision-making approach.[11] Not all of us, of course, will find its inapplicability a major loss; considering the criticism which has been leveled at the decision-making approach, and the failure of most of us to attempt its application, one might conclude that it is no loss at all. But the important thing to note here is that a system-oriented model would not offer a hospitable framework for such a detailed and comparative approach to the study of international relations, no matter what our appraisal of the decision-making approach might be.

Another and perhaps more subtle implication of selecting the nation as our focus or level of analysis is that it raises the entire question of goals, motivation, and purpose in national policy.[12] Though it may well be a peculiarity of the Western philosophical tradition, we seem to exhibit, when confronted with the need to explain individual or collective behavior, a strong proclivity for a goal-seeking approach. The question of whether national behavior is purposive or not seems to require discussion in two distinct (but not always exclusive) dimensions.

Firstly, there is the more obvious issue of whether those who act on behalf of the nation in formulating and executing foreign policy consciously pursue rather concrete goals. And it would be difficult to deny, for example, that these role-fulfilling individuals envisage certain specific outcomes which they hope to realize by pursuing a particular

---

[11] Its most well-known and successful statement is found in Snyder *et al., op.cit.* Much of this model is utilized in the text which Snyder wrote with Edgar S. Furniss, Jr., *American Foreign Policy: Formulation, Principles, and Programs,* New York, 1954. A more specific application is found in Snyder and Glenn D. Paige, "The United States Decision to Resist Aggression in Korea: The Application of an Analytical Scheme," *Administrative Science Quarterly,* III (December 1958), pp. 341-78. For those interested in this approach, very useful is Paul Wasserman and Fred S. Silander, *Decision-Making: An Annotated Bibliography,* Ithaca, N.Y., 1958.

[12] And if the decision-making version of this model is employed, the issue is unavoidable. See the discussion of motivation in Snyder, Bruck, and Sapin, *op.cit.,* pp. 92-117; note that 25 of the 49 pages on "The Major Determinants of Action" are devoted to motives.

strategy. In this sense, then, nations may be said to be goal-seeking organisms which exhibit purposive behavior.

However, purposiveness may be viewed in a somewhat different light, by asking whether it is not merely an intellectual construct that man imputes to himself by reason of his vain addiction to the free-will doctrine as he searches for characteristics which distinguish him from physical matter and the lower animals. And having attributed this conscious goal-pursuing behavior to himself as an individual, it may be argued that man then proceeds to project this attribute to the social organizations of which he is a member. The question would seem to distill down to whether man and his societies pursue goals of their own choosing or are moved toward those imposed upon them by forces which are primarily beyond their control.[13] Another way of stating the dilemma would be to ask whether we are concerned with the ends which men and nations strive for or the ends toward which they are impelled by the past and present characteristics of their social and physical milieu. Obviously, we are using the terms "ends," "goals," and "purpose" in two rather distinct ways; one refers to those which are consciously envisaged and more or less rationally pursued, and the other to those of which the actor has little knowledge but toward which he is nevertheless propelled.

Taking a middle ground in what is essentially a specific case of the free will vs. determinism debate, one can agree that nations move toward outcomes of which they have little knowledge and over which they have less control, but that they nevertheless do prefer, and therefore select, particular outcomes and *attempt* to realize them by conscious formulation of strategies.

Also involved in the goal-seeking problem when we employ the nation-oriented model is the question of how and why certain nations pursue specific sorts of goals. While the question may be ignored in the system-oriented model or resolved by attributing identical goals to all national actors, the nation-as-actor approach demands that we investigate the processes by which national goals are selected, the internal and external factors that impinge on those processes, and the institutional framework from which they emerge. It is worthy of note that despite the strong predilection for the nation-oriented model in most

[13] A highly suggestive, but more abstract treatment of this teleological question is in Talcott Parsons, *The Structure of Social Action*, 2nd ed., Glencoe, Ill., 1949, especially in his analysis of Durkheim and Weber. It is interesting to note that for Parsons an act implies, *inter alia*, "a future state of affairs toward which the process of action is oriented," and he therefore comments that "in this sense and this sense only, the schema of action is inherently teleological" (p. 44).

of our texts, empirical or even deductive analyses of these processes are conspicuously few.[14] Again, one might attribute these lacunae to the methodological and conceptual inadequacies of the graduate training which international relations specialists traditionally receive.[15] But in any event, goals and motivations are both dependent and independent variables, and if we intend to explain a nation's foreign policy, we cannot settle for the mere postulation of these goals; we are compelled to go back a step and inquire into their genesis and the process by which they become the crucial variables that they seem to be in the behavior of nations.

There is still another dilemma involved in our selection of the nation-as-actor model, and that concerns the phenomenological issue: do we examine our actor's behavior in terms of the objective factors which allegedly influence that behavior, or do we do so in terms of the actor's *perception* of these "objective factors"? Though these two approaches are not completely exclusive of one another, they proceed from greatly different and often incompatible assumptions, and produce markedly divergent models of national behavior.[16]

The first of these assumptions concerns the broad question of social causation. One view holds that individuals and groups respond in a quasi-deterministic fashion to the realities of physical environment, the acts or power of other individuals or groups, and similar "objective" and "real" forces or stimuli. An opposite view holds that individuals and groups are not influenced in their behavior by such objective forces, but by the fashion in which these forces are perceived and evaluated, however distorted or incomplete such perceptions may be. For adherents of this position, the only reality is the phenomenal—that which is discerned by the human senses; forces that are not discerned do not exist

---

[14] Among the exceptions are Haas and Whiting, *op.cit.*, chs. 2 and 3; and some of the chapters in Roy C. Macridis, ed., *Foreign Policy in World Politics*, Englewood Cliffs, N.J., 1958, especially that on West Germany by Karl Deutsch and Lewis Edinger.

[15] As early as 1934, Edith E. Ware noted that ". . . the study of international relations is no longer entirely a subject for political science or law, but that economics, history, sociology, geography—all the social sciences—are called upon to contribute towards the understanding . . . of the international system." See *The Study of International Relations in the United States*, New York, 1934, p. 172. For some contemporary suggestions, see Karl Deutsch, "The Place of Behavioral Sciences in Graduate Training in International Relations," *Behavioral Science*, III (July 1958), pp. 278-84; and J. David Singer, "The Relevance of the Behavioral Sciences to the Study of International Relations," *ibid.*, VI (October 1961), pp. 324-35.

[16] The father of phenomenological philosophy is generally acknowledged to be Edmund Husserl (1859-1938), author of *Ideas: General Introduction to Pure Phenomenology*, New York, 1931, trans. by W. R. Boyce Gibson; the original was published in 1913 under the title *Ideen zu einer reinen Phänomenologie und Phänomenologischen Philosophie*. Application of this approach to social psychology has come primarily through the work of Koffka and Lewin.

for that actor, and those that do exist do so only in the fashion in which they are perceived. Though it is difficult to accept the position that an individual, a group, or a nation is affected by such forces as climate, distance, or a neighbor's physical power only insofar as they are recognized and appraised, one must concede that perceptions will certainly affect the manner in which such forces are responded to. As has often been pointed out, an individual will fall to the ground when he steps out of a tenth-story window regardless of his perception of gravitational forces, but on the other hand such perception is a major factor in whether or not he steps out of the window in the first place.[17] The point here is that if we embrace a phenomenological view of causation, we will tend to utilize a phenomenological model for explanatory purposes.

The second assumption which bears on one's predilection for the phenomenological approach is more restricted, and is primarily a methodological one. Thus, it may be argued that any description of national behavior in a given international situation would be highly incomplete were it to ignore the link between the external forces at work upon the nation and its general foreign policy behavior. Furthermore, if our concern extends beyond the mere description of "what happens" to the realm of explanation, it could be contended that such omission of the cognitive and the perceptual linkage would be ontologically disastrous. How, it might be asked, can one speak of "causes" of a nation's policies when one has ignored the media by which external conditions and factors are translated into a policy decision? We may observe correlations between all sorts of forces in the international system and the behavior of nations, but their causal relationship must remain strictly deductive and hypothetical in the absence of empirical investigation into the causal chain which allegedly links the two. Therefore, even if we are satisfied with the less-than-complete descriptive capabilities of a non-phenomenological model, we are still drawn to it if we are to make any progress in explanation.

The contrary view would hold that the above argument proceeds from an erroneous comprehension of the nature of explanation in social science. One is by no means required to trace every perception, transmission, and receipt between stimulus and response or input and output in order to explain the behavior of the nation or any other human group. Furthermore, who is to say that empirical observation—subject

---

[17] This issue has been raised from time to time in all of the social sciences, but for an excellent discussion of it in terms of the present problem, see Harold and Margaret Sprout, *Man-Milieu Relationship Hypotheses in the Context of International Politics*, Princeton University, Center of International Studies, 1956, pp. 63-71.

as it is to a host of errors—is any better a basis of explanation than informed deduction, inference, or analogy? Isn't an explanation which flows logically from a coherent theoretical model just as reliable as one based upon a misleading and elusive body of data, most of which is susceptible to analysis only by techniques and concepts foreign to political science and history?

This leads, in turn, to the third of the premises relevant to one's stand on the phenomenological issue: are the dimensions and characteristics of the policy-makers' phenomenal field empirically discernible? Or, more accurately, even if we are convinced that their perceptions and beliefs constitute a crucial variable in the explanation of a nation's foreign policy, can they be observed in an accurate and systematic fashion?[18] Furthermore, are we not required by the phenomenological model to go beyond a classification and description of such variables, and be drawn into the tangled web of relationships out of which they emerge? If we believe that these phenomenal variables are systematically observable, are explainable, and can be fitted into our explanation of a nation's behavior in the international system, then there is a further tendency to embrace the phenomenological approach. If not, or if we are convinced that the gathering of such data is inefficient or uneconomical, we will tend to shy clear of it.

The fourth issue in the phenomenological dispute concerns the very nature of the nation as an actor in international relations. Who or what is it that we study? Is it a distinct social entity with well-defined boundaries—a unity unto itself? Or is it an agglomeration of individuals, institutions, customs, and procedures? It should be quite evident that those who view the nation or the state as an integral social unit could not attach much utility to the phenomenological approach, particularly if they are prone to concretize or reify the abstraction. Such abstractions are incapable of perception, cognition, or anticipation (unless, of course, the reification goes so far as to anthropomorphize and assign to the abstraction such attributes as will, mind, or personality). On the other hand, if the nation or state is seen as a group of individuals operating within an institutional framework, then it makes perfect sense to focus on the phenomenal field of those individuals who participate in the policy-making process. In other words, *people* are capable of experiences, images, and expectations, while insti-

[18] This is another of the criticisms leveled at the decision-making approach which, almost by definition, seems compelled to adopt some form of the phenomenological model. For a comprehensive treatment of the elements involved in human perception, see Karl Zener *et al.*, eds., "Inter-relationships Between Perception and Personality: A Symposium," *Journal of Personality*, xviii (1949), pp. 1-266.

tutional abstractions are not, except in the metaphorical sense. Thus, if our actor cannot even have a phenomenal field, there is little point in employing a phenomenological approach.[19]

These, then, are some of the questions around which the phenomenological issue would seem to revolve. Those of us who think of social forces as operative regardless of the actor's awareness, who believe that explanation need not include all of the steps in a causal chain, who are dubious of the practicality of gathering phenomenal data, or who visualize the nation as a distinct entity apart from its individual members, will tend to reject the phenomenological approach.[20] Logically, only those who disagree with each of the above four assumptions would be *compelled* to adopt the approach. Disagreement with any one would be *sufficient* grounds for so doing.

The above represent some of the more significant implications and fascinating problems raised by the adoption of our second model. They seem to indicate that this sub-systemic orientation is likely to produce richer description and more satisfactory (from the empiricist's point of view) explanation of international relations, though its predictive power would appear no greater than the systemic orientation. But the descriptive and explanatory advantages are achieved only at the price of considerable methodological complexity.

IV. Conclusion

Having discussed some of the descriptive, explanatory, and predictive capabilities of these two possible levels of analysis, it might now be useful to assess the relative utility of the two and attempt some general statement as to their prospective contributions to greater theoretical growth in the study of international relations.

In terms of description, we find that the systemic level produces a more comprehensive and total picture of international relations than does the national or sub-systemic level. On the other hand, the atomized and less coherent image produced by the lower level of analysis is somewhat balanced by its richer detail, greater depth, and more intensive portrayal.[21] As to explanation, there seems little doubt that the sub-

[19] Many of these issues are raised in the ongoing debate over "methodological individualism," and are discussed cogently in Ernest Nagel, *The Structure of Science*, New York, 1961, pp. 535-46.

[20] Parenthetically, holders of these specific views should also be less inclined to adopt the national or sub-systemic model in the first place.

[21] In a review article dealing with two of the more recent and provocative efforts toward theory (Morton A. Kaplan, *System and Process in International Politics*, New York, 1957, and George Liska, *International Equilibrium*, Cambridge, Mass., 1957), Charles P. Kindleberger adds a further—if not altogether persuasive—argument in favor

systemic or actor orientation is considerably more fruitful, permitting as it does a more thorough investigation of the processes by which foreign policies are made. Here we are enabled to go beyond the limitations imposed by the systemic level and to replace mere correlation with the more significant causation. And in terms of prediction, both orientations seem to offer a similar degree of promise. Here the issue is a function of what we seek to predict. Thus the policy-maker will tend to prefer predictions about the way in which nation x or y will react to a contemplated move on his own nation's part, while the scholar will probably prefer either generalized predictions regarding the behavior of a given class of nations or those regarding the system itself.

Does this summary add up to an overriding case for one or another of the two models? It would seem not. For a staggering variety of reasons the scholar may be more interested in one level than another at any given time and will undoubtedly shift his orientation according to his research needs. So the problem is really not one of deciding which level is most valuable to the discipline as a whole and then demanding that it be adhered to from now unto eternity.[22] Rather, it is one of realizing that there *is* this preliminary conceptual issue and that it must be temporarily resolved prior to any given research undertaking. And it must also be stressed that we have dealt here only with two of the more common orientations, and that many others are available and perhaps even more fruitful potentially than either of those selected here. Moreover, the international system gives many indications of prospective change, and it may well be that existing institutional forms will take on new characteristics or that new ones will appear to take their place. As a matter of fact, if incapacity to perform its functions leads to the transformation or decay of an institution, we may expect a steady deterioration and even ultimate disappearance of the national state as a significant actor in the world political system.

However, even if the case for one or another of the possible levels of analysis cannot be made with any certainty, one must nevertheless maintain a continuing awareness as to their use. We may utilize one level here and another there, but we cannot afford to shift our orientation in the midst of a study. And when we do in fact make an original

---

of the lower, sub-systemic level of analysis: "The total system is infinitely complex with everything interacting. One can discuss it intelligently, therefore, only bit by bit." "Scientific International Politics," *World Politics,* xi (October 1958), p. 86.

[22] It should also be kept in mind that one could conceivably develop a theoretical model which successfully embraces both of these levels of analysis without sacrificing conceptual clarity and internal consistency. In this writer's view, such has not been done to date, though Kaplan's *System and Process in International Politics* seems to come fairly close.

selection or replace one with another at appropriate times, we must do so with a full awareness of the descriptive, explanatory, and predictive implications of such choice.

A final point remains to be discussed. Despite this lengthy exegesis, one might still be prone to inquire whether this is not merely a sterile exercise in verbal gymnastics. What, it might be asked, is the difference between the two levels of analysis if the empirical referents remain essentially the same? Or, to put it another way, is there any difference between international relations and comparative foreign policy? Perhaps a few illustrations will illuminate the subtle but important differences which emerge when one's level of analysis shifts. One might, for example, postulate that when the international system is characterized by political conflict between two of its most powerful actors, there is a strong tendency for the system to bipolarize. This is a systemic-oriented proposition. A sub-systemic proposition, dealing with the same general empirical referents, would state that when a powerful actor finds itself in political conflict with another of approximate parity, it will tend to exert pressure on its weaker neighbors to join its coalition. Each proposition, assuming it is true, is theoretically useful by itself, but each is verified by a different intellectual operation. Moreover—and this is the crucial thing for theoretical development—one could not add these two kinds of statements together to achieve a cumulative growth of empirical generalizations.

To illustrate further, one could, at the systemic level, postulate that when the distribution of power in the international system is highly diffused, it is more stable than when the discernible clustering of well-defined coalitions occurs. And at the sub-systemic or national level, the same empirical phenomena would produce this sort of proposition: when a nation's decision-makers find it difficult to categorize other nations readily as friend or foe, they tend to behave toward all in a more uniform and moderate fashion. Now, taking these two sets of propositions, how much cumulative usefulness would arise from attempting to merge and codify the systemic proposition from the first illustration with the sub-systemic proposition from the second, or vice versa? Representing different levels of analysis and couched in different frames of reference, they would defy theoretical integration; one may well be a corollary of the other, but they are not immediately combinable. A prior translation from one level to another must take place.

This, it is submitted, is quite crucial for the theoretical development of our discipline. With all of the current emphasis on the need for more empirical and data-gathering research as a prerequisite to theory-building, one finds little concern with the relationship among these separate and discrete data-gathering activities. Even if we were to declare a moratorium on deductive and speculative research for the next decade, and all of us were to labor diligently in the vineyards of historical and contemporary data, the state of international relations theory would probably be no more advanced at that time than it is now, unless such empirical activity becomes far more systematic. And "systematic" is used here to indicate the cumulative growth of inductive and deductive generalizations into an impressive array of statements conceptually related to one another and flowing from some common frame of reference. What that frame of reference should be, or will be, cannot be said with much certainty, but it does seem clear that it must exist. As long as we evade some of these crucial *a priori* decisions, our empiricism will amount to little more than an ever-growing potpourri of discrete, disparate, non-comparable, and isolated bits of information or extremely low-level generalizations. And, as such, they will make little contribution to the growth of a theory of international relations.

NOTES AND QUESTIONS

1. How does Singer's discussion of the requirements of an analytical model apply to our choice of the Clark-Sohn plan as a model of the warless world? Does it facilitate *explanation* of the relationships under investigation? Does it have any bearing upon our capacity for *prediction*? Does it assist in the process of *description*? Should any special considerations apply when our model seeks to portray preferences about the *future* rather than to present an interpretation of the *present*?

2. According to Singer, what are the strengths and weaknesses of choosing the international system as the proper level of analysis? ——of choosing the nation-state? What other levels of analysis might be adopted?

3. What does it mean to possess a systemic orientation? How does it differ from being, in Singer's sense, "systematic"? Is it helpful to conceive of international society as a "system"? Why? How would you define "the international system"?

4. What is meant by "the phenomenological issue"? To what extent is it helpful to emphasize the *perceptions* of national actors rather than strive to rely upon an *objective account* of phenomena? Consider the relevance of your answer for the study of war-peace issues. Are Waltz and Ducci sensitive to the discrepancy between perceptions and actualities in world affairs? Is there such a discrepancy?

5. To what extent are Soviet and American perceptions of the dangers of war different from one another? Is one more accurate than the other? How can one identify inaccuracies? How can we structure international relations to reduce the distance between perceptions and actualities? Does this last question have any bearing upon the wisdom of excluding China from the United Nations? Are perceptions likely to be distorted by the isolation and exclusion of a nation from diplomatic intercourse? See Urie Bronfenbrenner's article, "Mirror-Image in Soviet

American Relations: A Social Psychologist's Report," *Journal of Social Issues,* vol. 17 (1961) p. 45; see J. David Singer's "Threat-Perception and the Armament-Tension Dilemma," *Journal of Conflict Resolution,* vol. 2 (1958) p. 90; see also Urie Bronfenbrenner, "Social—Psychological Factors Affecting Soviet Reactions to Arms Control Proposals" (Institute for Defense Analyses, 1962).

SYSTEMIC AND STRATEGIC CONFLICT

What Happens When People Do Not Think—and When They Do

By ANATOL RAPOPORT

IN the year when World War II broke out, there appeared in the Monograph Supplements of the British Journal of Psychology a long article entitled "Generalized Foreign Policy." There is no evidence that the article attracted any attention at the time it appeared. Those who could follow the logic of its argument were not among those who were competent to judge its content, while those who were versed in matters with which the article was concerned were for the most part ignorant of the logic on which the arguments were constructed. The author applied a method of reasoning which had been developed in one context to an entirely different context.

Lewis F. Richardson, the author of the article, was a physicist and a meteorologist; the method of reasoning he used—the mathematical hypothetico-deductive method—dominates the physical sciences. In "Generalized Foreign Policy," Richardson offered an illustration of how the mathematical method could be used in a context far removed from its natural habitat: namely, in constructing a theory of international politics.

Long ago Thucydides argued that a primary cause of the Peloponnesian War was the mutual fear that Athens and Sparta had of each other. Being afraid of Sparta, Athens kept increasing its armed might, which, in turn, convinced Athens that its fears were justified. Under these circumstances, according to Thucydides, a clash became inevitable. Evidently Thucydides was espousing a theory that an arms race and, by implication, war are self-sustaining processes of the sort now familiar to us in some self-catalyzing chemical reactions. There are, of course, other theories of international conflict; for example, those that place the sources of arms races and wars in economic or political dynamics. One may well ask how any such theories can be supported by evidence.

Arguments about "what causes what" can sometimes be resolved if they occur in a context where controlled observations can be made. For instance, specific diseases are attributed to specific pathogenic organisms on the basis of experimental results. Obviously, no such controlled observations can determine the "causes of wars." Ideas about such matters are backed by personal convictions rather than by objective evidence. No doubt such convictions sometimes stem from observations and their interpretations, but the line of reasoning which leads from hypothesis to observation to conclusion is never sharp. The mathematico-deductive method is specifically designed to sharpen this reasoning and to set clearer limits as to what may or must or may not be inferred from available evidence.

The foundation of the mathematico-deductive method is the so-called mathematical model—a statement in mathematical language of the assumptions underlying a theory. If, for example, one speaks about levels of armaments, one has to specify how these levels are to be measured. More generally, if one espouses an idea that the "hostility" of one nation toward another elicits (or inhibits) reciprocal hostility, one must specify how "hostility" is manifested in measurable quantities. Also one must specify what one means by eliciting (or inhibiting) hostility.

Mathematical models have the remarkable advantage that in them several ideas of this sort can be combined. For example, the effects of both chronic "grievances" and of acute mutual stimulation on the rates of growth of armament expenditures can be expressed in a single system of equations. In his equations, Richardson also included the *inhibitory* effects of the arms race on the participants (as an economic burden). The system then became a representation of the dynamics of an arms race between two potentially hostile nations or blocs. The system combined several factors proposed by various political theorists as components of inter-nation conflict.

When the equations were solved, Richardson was able to plot a *theoretically* derived course of increasing armament levels of two rival blocs. He then compared this theoretical plot with the actual levels of armament expenditures of two rival blocs (the Entente vs. the Central Powers) and got an excellent agreement between the theoretically derived and the actual levels.

What is one to think of this achievement? Richardson faithfully followed the steps listed in science text books, as comprising the "scientific method." He noted a process in international affairs which our modern strategists have since christened "escalation," namely, a crescendo of mutual threats and an increase in destructive capacity (referred to by each side as self-defense). He made a generalization from these observations that escalation is characteristic of international relations under certain conditions. He proposed a hypothesis, bearing on the mathematical relation between armament levels of one nation (or bloc) and those of a potential rival. He derived by mathematical reasoning the theoretical consequences of the hypothesis, related to the time course of armament expenditures. He compared his deductions with actually observed yearly expenditures in the period preceding World War I (1908-1914) and found that the observations agreed with the predictions. Such an agreement, according to the "rules of evidence" in the Court of Scientific

Validation constitutes a "confirmation" of the hypothesis from which the deductions had been made.

Does this mean that the issue is settled, that arms races have been "proved" to be results of a mutually stimulating escalating process? It means nothing of the sort, because a confirmation of a hypothesis is very far from being a "proof." Contrary to our courts of justice, where the benefit of doubt is supposed to be in favor of the defendant, the Court of Scientific Validation operates on the opposite principle. No amount of evidence can ever vindicate a hypothesis beyond all doubt. On the contrary, a single discrepancy between the conclusions of a hypothesis and the observations is, in principle, sufficient to refute the hypothesis.

In practice, of course, these rules are not rigid. Evidence in favor of some hypotheses sometimes becomes so overwhelming that the hypothesis is considered established beyond reasonable doubt. Correspondingly, discrepancies between deduction and observation do not always imply that the hypothesis is doomed. The discrepancies are often attributed to some unforeseen complications, extraneous influences, or errors of observation.

And so the degree of belief in a scientific hypothesis remains, as in ordinary affairs, pretty much a personal subjective matter, depending on how much weight the investigator chooses to assign to various lines of evidence. Moreover, it is not the belief in a specific hypothesis which determines the complexion of a scientist's outlook. Hypotheses are not proposed helter-skelter. They fit into a system of thought, *i.e.*, a philosophical system, which is much more resistant to radical changes than individual hypotheses. Often when a hypothesis turns out to be untenable, the investigator will reject it in favor of another one basically of the same kind, that is, one which fits into the same philosophical system.

For this reason, in evaluating a broad scientific theory, it is not the fate of a particular hypothesis that must be examined, but rather of a whole complex of such hypotheses. In extreme cases, an entire system of thought must come under scrutiny together with its philosophical (or metaphysical) foundations. When this results in a fundamental restructuring of a system of thought, a scientific revolution occurs. These revolutions mark the great scientific advances. Examples are the Copernican, the Newtonian, the Relativity, and the Quantum Revolutions in the physical sciences, the Darwinian and, possibly, the Mendelian in biological science. One is tempted to include also the Marxian Revolution in social science and the Freudian in psychology, but here one treads on more shaky ground. A system of thought relating to the nature of human society must of necessity be much looser (in our present stage of intellectual development) than one relating to the nature of the physical world, and a system of thought relating to the nature of man must be still looser. Not only are social and mental phenomena vastly more complex than physical or even biological ones but they are also much more difficult to approach in a spirit of detachment—a necessary component of the scientific attitude.

Still, with due regard to reservations, we can speak with some justification of the Marxian and the Freudian Revolutions and of the systems of thought which have grown out of them. In spite of the chasm between the content areas with which these systems of thought are concerned and in spite of the possibly diametrically opposite conceptions of man implied in the two systems, they nevertheless have one vital feature in common. The appreciation of this feature is important for understanding the underpinnings of Richardson's theory of arms races and of war and for differentiating between the two widely different approaches to the study of international relations, which constitute the theme of this article.

The Systemic View

The basic *philosophical* assumption which underlies the thought of Marx, of Freud, of Richardson (and of many other thinkers, for example, Adam Smith, Pareto, Tolstoy, Spengler, and Toynbee) is the following: *There are determinants in human affairs which operate independently of any one's rationally designed actions or consciously perceived goals.* Notions of where these determinants originate and how they are manifested differ in the minds of the different proponents of this basic idea. For example, Freud thought of the determinants as originating in instincts or suppressed drives and in rationalizations of actions. The principal conclusion was that the stated or perceived reasons for action were not the real reasons and that man was far less "rational" than he imagined himself to be. The classical "free enterprise" economics, derived from the ideas of Adam Smith and Ricardo, postulates an "invisible hand," which insures certain optimal equilibria in the operation of the economy, even though individual entrepreneurs seem to be pursuing their own private goals. Marxian ideas, too, stem from the notion that global socio-economic forces operate regardless of individuals' presumably purposeful actions and that these forces *drive* human society toward a predetermined outcome (the Proletarian Revolution). Tolstoy's determinism first becomes manifest in "War and Peace," where he argues that the forces of history are resultants of innumerable individual acts and that these forces are relentless and cannot possibly depend on the wills or purposes of apparent leaders.

Richardson's theory of arms races is developed in the same spirit. He places at the center of attention not a maze of goals, purposes, cross-purposes, and strategies, which in historical accounts and in the writings of political analysts constitute international relations, but instead a system of equations of the sort that govern the motions of planets or of air currents, chemical reactions, and possibly the ebb and flow of animal populations in the struggle for existence. These are "global" or "systemic" equations. They describe the behavior of large systems. The systems may be composed of myriads of small particles (molecules, genes, individual organisms) and the detailed behavior of these particles may be governed by different factors (chemical affinities, mutations, instincts, even "rational decisions"), but there are so many of these particles that the *emergent* phenomena are only statistical resultants, quite independent of what the individual particles do or what happens to them.

Such is the underlying philosophical basis of Richardson's theory. It deserves attention quite apart from the success or the failure of any particular model of a sector of human affairs (such as arms races) which Richardson might have proposed.

How seriously are we to take "determinism" in large-scale human affairs? Richardson himself gives a clear indication of his own attitude.

"The equations," he wrote, "are only indications of what would happen if people did not stop to think."

Here, then, is no commitment to a specific theory of international relations; not what actually happens, but what *would* happen if the blind forces of interaction were the only ones operating, if intelligent intervention were not possible. Because of the way his quantitative deductions, related to the 1908-1914 arms race, agreed with data, Richardson did suspect that something of this nature might have been happening. To his way of thinking, the Great Powers with their rivalries constituted a quasi-mechanical system. The fate of systems is governed by dynamic laws. Self-perpetuating inter-nation rivalry in an arms race exploding into a war was, Richardson thought, evidence of the operation of such laws.

Could World War I have been avoided? Richardson thought it could. This opinion was also based on his conception of systemic laws and on a modified conception of determinism. Besides the time course of the 1908-1914 arms race, Richardson derived another conclusion from his mathematical investigation, namely, that the systems governed by his equations could be either stable or unstable, depending on the value of the parameters of the system (*i.e.*, the constant quantities in the equations). These parameters were of three kinds: (1) those representing the mutually stimulating factors of the rival blocs (in the currently fashionable jargon of cybernetics, these are called the "positive feedback" parameters); (2) those representing the inhibiting factors (*i.e.*, the economic restraints on the armament budgets—the "negative feedback" parameters); and (3) those representing the supposedly constant or chronic "grievances" considered as stimulants to armaments. With the latter, the so-called "reservoirs of good will" can also be lumped as "grievances with a negative sign." Richardson showed mathematically that the grievance and the good-will factors played no part in determining the stability or the instability of the system. Only the relations among the magnitudes of the positive and negative feedback factors determine whether the system is stable or unstable. When a stable system is in equilibrium, small deviations from this equilibrium set forces in motion which tend to restore the equilibrium. This state of affairs is reminiscent of the "balance of power" theory espoused by nineteenth-century political theorists. An unstable system, on the contrary, cannot persist in an equilibrium state even if there is one. The smallest deviation from such a state sets forces in motion which *magnify* the deviation. Such a system tends to move away from its (theoretical) equilibrium position. The direction of the departure depends on the direction of the initial deviation.

By examining the rate of Britain's disarmament following World War I and the rate of Germany's rearmament prior to World War II, Richardson was able to make rough estimates of the parameters which characterized his model of the European system of power blocs. He concluded that even allowing a large margin of error, the system was evidently unstable. Moreover, at the start of the arms race in 1908, the system seemed to be very near its (unstable) equilibrium but somewhat displaced from it in the direction of a mutually stimulating arms race. Had this displacement been in the other direction, Richardson's theory would have predicted an opposite self-stimulating process resulting in ever-increasing international trade and co-operation instead of ever-increasing armament budgets. In effect, Richardson concluded that if the inter-bloc yearly trade volume between the Entente and the Central Powers had been just £5,000,000 greater (or equivalently, had the armament expenditures been smaller by the same amount), the whole process might have gone in reverse toward a United Europe.

Such a conclusion is hard to take seriously. However, the method used by Richardson is not to be judged in terms of its specific conclusions (especially since there is no way to verify what would have been). The chief value of the method is in the potentialities it opens up for viewing large-scale human affairs from a point of view very different from the conventional ones, in which specific goals and strategies of nation states are assumed to be the prime movers of their behavior.

Richardson's global view does not categorically dismiss the rôle of specific goals or strategies. It only calls attention to the limitations within which the decision makers may be operating. It may be quite as necessary for them to know these limitations as it is for an engineer to know the laws of mechanics and thermodynamics. Knowledge of these laws does not incapacitate the engineer in the task of designing serviceable systems. On the contrary, by revealing to him the constraints under which he must operate, the knowledge of what is determined by physical laws enables the engineer to think fruitfully about what is possible and how to put the laws to work in the service of his goals. It is in the absence of the knowledge of constraints (*i.e.,* of the laws of nature) that man's efforts to better his lot were largely wasted, as in the pursuit of magic, preoccupation with astrology, et cetera. Knowledge of natural laws is often knowledge of what is impossible (*e.g.,* the creation of matter or energy from nothing, getting information about the future from the positions of the stars). With the knowledge of what is impossible comes also knowledge of what is possible (*e.g.*, transformations of matter and energy, deriving from astronomical observations information about the nature of the physical universe). It is in this spirit that men like Adam Smith, Karl Marx, Sigmund Freud, and Lewis F. Richardson sought the hitherto unsuspected determinants in human affairs.

Richardson devoted thirty years of his life to the study of war, deliberately eschewing all the standard political explanations. Having examined the dynamics leading up to World War I, the course of the war itself (in terms of the ebb and flow of "war moods") and of its aftermath, he turned to the period of 1933-1939 and found the same general pattern. He virtually predicted World War II on the basis of what he found. After that war he started an analysis of the East-West arms race which began in 1948. Richardson died in 1953 without having come to any conclusion concerning the outcome of the current arms race. His total effort was directed to calling attention to the relentless mechanical forces operating in international relations, forces which would be the only determining factors "if men did not stop to think." His avowed purpose was to induce people to stop and think, to alert them to the possibilities of bringing the blind forces of history under control, just as the blind forces of physical nature were brought under control in the service of man.

The Strategic View

Eleven years before Richardson's "Generalized Foreign Policy" appeared in print, another paper was published in the German mathematical journal Mathematische Annalen, entitled "Zur Theorie der Gesellschaftspiele" ("On the Theory of Parlor Games") by John von Neumann. Like Richardson's paper, von Neumann's also went unnoticed at the time of publication. However, this was not because it was addressed to a readership unable to cope with the technicalities. Von Neumann wrote on a mathematical subject in a mathematical journal. Nor was the content inappropriate. Mathematics, specifically the theory of probability, had been successfully applied to the analysis of games of chance. The result of those earlier applications was something which could be called a rational theory of gambling—a set of principles according to which one can decide whether it is advantageous or not to accept or offer bets under given sets of conditions. Von Neumann's paper was apparently an extension of mathematical reasoning to games which were predominantly not games of chance but games of strategy. Outstanding examples of such games are chess and checkers. The more sophisticated card games, like bridge and poker, also fall into this category; for although chance does take a part in these games (for example in "determining" the arrangement of the cards), still the outcomes depend to a large extent also on the strategic skill of the players.

We all have an idea of what is involved in strategic skills. Roughly these skills have to do with the ability to anticipate a large range of possible future situations, which can arise in the course of the game and to realize the logical connections among one's own choices of action (the "moves" of the game), the opponent's correspondent choices, and the joint outcomes of these choices. The chess player is constantly calculating in this fashion: If I do this, he has a choice of these alternatives. If he should choose that alternative, I shall, in turn, have the following choices; if, however, he should choose this other alternative, then I will have the following courses of action open, et cetera.

A "game," then, in von Neumann's conceptualization, is essentially a situation in which two or more "players" make choices among available alternatives of action. Their *joint* choices determine a sequence of situations, each of which, in turn, makes certain alternatives possible. A "termination rule" brings the game to a close in one of several possible "outcomes." Associated with each outcome is a set of "pay-offs," one to each player. These pay-offs may be in money or simply in the satisfaction of having "won the game." Whatever the actual nature of the pay-offs, it seems natural to assign numerical values to them, representing what the outcomes are "worth" to the player in question. For example, we could symbolize the worth of winning the game of chess by $+1$, its loss by -1, and a draw by 0.

This assignment of quantities opens the way for a mathematical theory whose goal is the development of finding the "best way" to play a given game. The best way is defined as one which gives to the player in question the largest pay-off possible under the constraints of the situation.

Game theory differs from the earlier gambling theory in that in the latter the player, strictly speaking, does not face a rational opponent. To be sure, the outcomes of a gamble are determined by Chance, but Chance has no real interest in the matter. She does not play *against* the player. In a game of strategy, on the contrary, the player has at least one "rational" opponent. If the opponent's interests are opposed to one's own, he will deliberately make choices calculated to minimize one's own pay-offs so as to maximize his own.

It may seem superfluous to say "if the other's interests are opposed to one's own," for this seems to be always the case in parlor games: what one player wins, the other or others must lose. However, there is no logical necessity for this restriction. One can well conceive of situations in which the interests of the players at least partially coincide.

Whether or not the interests of the players are diametrically opposed or partially coincident makes a fundamental difference in the theory, as we shall see. For the moment, we shall summarize the principal result of von Neumann's 1928 paper, the first theoretical investigation of games of strategy.

The 1928 paper dealt with the logical structure of "two-person zero-sum games." As the name implies, these are the games in which there are two players, whose gains and losses cancel each other. If losses are designated by negative numbers, the sum of the pay-offs of the respective players is always zero, regardless of the outcome.

It would seem that there is a vast number of such games, and it is difficult to see how one could say anything which would apply to them all. But von Neumann found a way to do this. The crucial concept in the theory of games is that of a strategy. A strategy is roughly a plan which prescribes what a player will do in every conceivable situation in which he can find himself in the course of the game with a given set of rules. In practice, it is out of the question to list all the available strategies of even very simple games. However, game theory is concerned not with examining individual strategies of particular games but rather with the way such strategies are logically related to each other. For this reason, it suffices for the purpose of illustrating the principles of game theory to discuss artifically constructed games with very few strategies. As an example, consider the logical structure of the game shown in Matrix 1.

	A_2	B_2	C_2
A_1	-3, 3	-6, 6	12, -12
B_1	-1, 1	5, -5	2, -2
C_1	-6, 6	10, -10	-8, 8

Matrix 1.

The rules of this game require player 1 to choose one of three strategies, represented by the horizontal rows of the matrix (as the rectangular arrays of this sort are called) and player 2 to choose a vertical column. The pair of choices determine the outcome, i.e., one of the boxes of the matrix. The numbers in the box show the pay-offs to player 1 and to player 2 respectively.

The question before us is now how a rational Player 1 would choose. There is no row which is in every respect better than either of the other two rows. For instance, the top row may seem more attractive than the second row because it contains the biggest pay-off (12) to Player 1, but the other two pay-offs are worse for him than the corresponding ones in the second row. Similarly the second row may seem more attractive than the third, because the pay-offs in the first and third columns are better than the corresponding ones in the third row, but the pay-off in the middle column is worse. The situation is quite as ambivalent for Player 2.

One might think that this is a situation involving a calculated risk, and indeed it would be if each player could assign certain probabilities to the choices of the other. However, there is no basis for doing this. The other player cannot be assumed to leave his choices to chance, for he too is rational. He will guide his choices by what will give him the greatest pay-off under the constraints of the situation.

After some reflection, we can discern a principle of rational choice in this situation. Suppose Player 1 is guided by the principle of the greatest prudence. Instead of asking what is the greatest amount he can win, he asks instead what is the smallest amount he needs to lose. If he chooses the first row, he *may* in the worst case lose 6 (column 2); if he chooses the second row, he may lose 1 (column 1); if he chooses the last row, the worst that can happen to him is a loss of 8 (column 3). Of these outcomes, the loss of 1 is clearly the best (the best of the worst outcomes in each eventuality, that is). Next, Player 1 can ask whether he can do better than that. He knows that Player 2 is rational. Therefore, if Player 2 were sure that Player 1 would choose row 2, he would certainly choose column 1, for that is the best outcome for him in that row. Now, knowing that Player 2 will choose column 1, what should Player 1 do? Clearly choose row 2, for that is the best outcome for him in that column. It follows that neither player can do better than choose respectively row 2 and column 1. If Player 1 departs from this choice, he will only lose more; similarly if Player 2 departs from this choice he will do worse. The outcome is a genuine equilibrium representing a sort of "balance of power" or a stalemate. And so the outcome of this game can be discovered in advance without playing the game.

This situation is known in some real games. For instance, the outcome of the children's game of tic-tac-toe is known in advance. It will be a draw whenever both players play "rationally." It is a simple matter to discover the "rational strategy" of each player in tic-tac-toe, and once it is discovered the game is "solved" and, incidentally, becomes completely uninteresting as a game. Games like chess are too complex to yield to a complete analysis and so have not been solved. But frequently the end games in chess can be completely analyzed. For instance, it sometimes becomes evident that White can force a mate in so many moves or can queen a pawn, which insures his win. In such cases the game is usually broken off. The end game becomes analogous to a solved game.

Not all games are determined in the sense just described. Consider the game shown in Matrix 2.

	A_2	B_2	C_2
A_1	-3, 3	-6, 6	12, -12
B_1	6, -6	5, -5	2, -2
C_1	-6, 6	10, -10	-8, 8

Matrix 2.

It differs from the previous game in only one outcome (row 2, column 1). Let us see what happens now if Player 1 makes the "most prudent" choice. Of the three outcomes worst for him in the respective rows, clearly a win of 2 (in row 2) is the best. Therefore, as in the previous game, he might decide on row 2, which contains the "best of the worst" or the "minimax," as it is called in game theory. Knowing this, Player 2 would choose column 3, for this minimizes his loss. But now if Player 1 knew that column 3 would be Player 2's choice, he would play row 1, where his pay-off is the biggest. However, Player 2 could figure this out too and so would play column 2, giving Player 1 a loss of 6. But if Player 1 figured this out, he would choose row 3 for a gain of 10, in which case Player 2 should choose column 3, which drives Player 1 to row 1, and so on around the clock.

Formulated in this way there seems to be no "rational way" of playing a game such as this one. Whatever choice one makes, on further thought another one seems to be better. The remarkable result obtained by von Neumann in his 1928 paper was that there *is* a rational way of playing games like the one represented by Matrix 2. To explain this result an additional concept is necessary, namely, that of a "mixed strategy." Instead of choosing a particular one of the three available strategies, each player lets chance decide for him which one shall be chosen. However, the *probabilities* which each player assigns to the choice of each of the strategies are calculated in a certain way (prescribed by game theory). This procedure insures a maximum *expected gain* (in the actuarial sense) to each player. Neither can do better in the sense of increasing this expected gain.

Thus a chance element is brought into games of strategy. However, the rôle of chance here is quite different from that in gambling theory. In a gambling situation, probabilities of outcomes are either given or estimated. The player remains passive with respect to these probabilities. He can do nothing to change them, and can only adjust his decisions to what the probabilities are or are believed to be. In the case of two-person games, probabilities are imposed by each player on his own choices. The purpose of this deliberately introduced uncertainty is to deny to the other player knowledge of what one is going to do on a particular play of the game. (Incidentally, this knowledge could not be denied to the other in the game represented by Matrix 1, where each player can deduce exactly what the other is going to do.)

Games represented by Matrix 1 are called games with a saddle point. Those represented by Matrix 2 are called games without a saddle point. Every two-person zero-sum game is either of the one or of the other sort. Having "solved" the general two-person zero-sum game both with and without a saddle point, von Neumann solved all such games "in principle." That is to say, given enough computing facility and enough time, one could on the basis of the generalized minimax theory find "the" best way of playing any two-person zero-sum game whatsoever.

The Dominance of the Strategic View in Diplo-Military Theory

As we have said, like Richardson's 1939 paper, von Neumann's fundamental paper on the theory of games went practically unnoticed. To my knowledge nothing on this subject was published for sixteen years thereafter. Then in 1944 suddenly an extensive treatise appeared in the United States under the authorship of John von Neumann and Oskar Morgenstern, entitled "Theory of Games and Economic Behavior." The treatise was founded on the results of the 1928 paper. In it the theory was extended to games with more than two players and to non-zero-sum games, in which bargaining becomes an important factor.

In 1947 a second even more extensive edition of the work appeared and was promptly hailed in mathematical circles as a major achievement of the century. Thereafter game theory attracted world-wide attention.

In the 1928 paper, the context in which the mathematical theory was developed was that of parlor games. In the 1944-47 treatise, the context was extended to "economic behavior," *i.e.,* to a context in which economic units compete with each other and form coalitions in order to compete more effectively with other coalitions. It seems, however, that the keen interest and enthusiasm with which the theory was received stems not from its possible applications to economics and business but from the realization that here at last was a rigorous and general theory of rational conflict. The "humble" beginnings of the theory not only did not detract from but, on the contrary, emphasized its stature. The English philosopher R. B. Braithwaite wrote:

No one today will doubt the intensity, though he may dislike the color, of the (shall I say) sodium light cast by statistical mathematics, direct descendant of games of chance, upon the social sciences. Perhaps in another three hundred years' time economic and political and other branches of moral philosophy will bask in radiation from a source—theory of games of strategy—whose prototype was kindled round the poker tables of Princeton.

Trail-blazing scientific theories receive acclaim when they arrive at especially propitious times, that is, when the intellectual climate is just ready for a radically new approach to some field of inquiry. It seems to me that the theory of games, ushered in at the close of World War II on the threshold of the atomic age, found itself in the fortunate position of answering a sharply felt intellectual need. What this need was and how game theory fitted in with it is admittedly little more than a conjecture on my part, and I offer it to the reader for what it is worth.

The paramount fact of our lives today is the dilemma of "defense." There was a time when "defense" was practically synonymous with "national security." One aimed to discourage military attack on one's country by possessing fortifications and armies. Whether militarily strong nations were actually more immune to attack than weak ones is open to argument, but at least it seemed reasonable to identify national security with military strength. If one could not be sure that one could prevent an attack by being prepared for it, one could at least hope to "win" a war if it did occur.

Nuclear weapons have made the victory argument for military strength vacuous. In some circles, there is still talk about "winning" a nuclear war ("prevailing" is the fashionable term), but not many people care to contemplate the fruits of such a victory. It is no longer unpatriotic to assert that with the advent of nuclear weapons military victory has become impossible or meaningless. To some extent this situation means that war has become obsolete as an instrument of national policy. Some go still further and conclude that military strength has lost all the advantages it may have had and that therefore general and complete disarmament might be the primary goal of international diplomacy. This, however, appears to be a minority view. The majority of those who make or influence or attempt to influence national policy still view military strength as an indispensable factor in national security.

Among those in the United States who have come to realize the fact that victory and defeat are meaningless in the context of a nuclear war, the rationale for military strength is developed along two main lines of thought. One of these deplores the overwhelming emphasis placed by the United States defense policy on nuclear weapons to the neglect of conventional armaments. People who think this way emphasize the importance of being prepared for a "limited" (nonnuclear) war. The other line of thought, although recognizing the absurdity of "nuclear victory" emphasizes the importance of nuclear weapons as "deterrents."

The difference between these two views, then, is the following: the deterrence people would like to make the most of the *threat* of war (including nuclear war) as an instrument of national policy; the limited-war people would like to include war itself (but excluding nuclear war, if possible) as an instrument of national policy. There is no sharp line dividing these two camps, and many advocates of preparedness see no reason why both the use of actual limited war and of the threat of nuclear war cannot be combined into an effective diplo-military policy. Therefore, it does not do either group an injustice to lump them together into a single power-oriented camp. These are the people who believe, as Machiavelli and Clausewitz and Metternich and Bismarck believed, that the content of politics is the struggle for and the use of power. Moreover, competence in politics appears to these people (as it did to their mentors) as the *rational* use of power. In particular, they decry the use of violence for its own sake. War or the threat of war is justified only as a means to gain some end (it being understood that the increase of one's own power at the expense of that of others is always a legitimate end). They subscribe wholeheartedly to Clausewitz' famous dictum, "War is the continuation of politics by other means" (which could just as well have been stated as "Politics is the continuation of war by other means"). Their admiration for Clausewitz is explicit. For example, H. A. Kissinger, an outstanding strategist, writes:

War, argued Clausewitz, can never be an act of pure violence because it grows out of the existing relations of states, their level of civilization, the nature of their alliances, and the objectives in dispute. War would reach its ultimate form only if it became an end in itself, a condition which is realized only among savages and probably not even among them. For war to rage with absolute violence and without interruption until the enemy is completely defenseless is to reduce an idea to absurdity.

Herman Kahn, another strategist, called his magnum opus "On Thermonuclear War," an obvious tribute to Clausewitz, whose classical treatise was entitled simply "On War."

Now Clausewitz wrote, be it noted, in the first decades of the nineteenth century. The "ideal" of eighteenth-century warfare had been strategic elegance and limited objectives. Who was to succeed to the throne of Spain may have been a *casus belli,* but certainly the existence of Spain or any other monarchy as a sovereign state was never an issue. The monarchs were mostly cousins and had respect for each other's divine rights. Napoleon, who was nobody's cousin, had entirely different conceptions about war and of the diplomilitary game. He played for keeps.

To us, in retrospect, the Napoleonic wars seem like a foretaste of our own age with its total wars, in which entire populations instead of just the professionals participate and in which destruction of civilians and of their means of livelihood has become a frequent objective. Napoleonic wars must have been viewed by Clausewitz and his contemporaries as regressions to a barbaric state or to the religious wars of the seventeenth century or as harbingers of a day when wars would become intolerable. It is not unreasonable to interpret Clausewitz's treatise as an attempt to restore war to respectable status—to defend it as an activity worthy of man's highest intellectual effort and commitment, like science, art, and religion.

It seems to me that the modern strategists have set for themselves a similar task. Appalled by the senselessness of "total war" in which the traditional objective of international politics (namely the accumulation of power within the existing inter-state framework) has been lost sight of, they seek a way out of the impasse. Robert E. Osgood asks bluntly in the opening sentence of his book, entitled "Limited War": "How can the United States employ military power as a rational instrument of foreign policy when the destructive potentialities of war exceed any rational purpose?"

This dilemma, I believe, reveals the reason why the theory of games which in 1928 appeared as an abstruse branch of mathematics, suddenly at the end of the 1940's found itself in the limelight. For here was the theoretical formulation of a genuine science of *rational* conflict, of conflict stripped of its emotional baggage. It does not help a chess player to hate his opponent and the object of chess is not to harm the person of the opponent. "Bravery" in chess is equally irrelevant. Even "cunning," although popularly conceived to be an asset in games of strategy, is of questionable value in really sophisticated chess. For cunning manifests itself in the exploitation of the opponent's naïveté, but profound chess strategy does not stoop to trickery, because the opponent is always conceived to be completely aware of all potentialities. Here, then, is truly a noble way of thinking, as noble as one finds in the profoundest scientific analysis, and yet a way of thinking entirely geared to conflict—to rational conflict, that is, in its purest form. For these reasons, game theory must have appeared as a magnificent intellectual accomplishment, not only to those who appreciate the profoundness of its mathematical insights, but also to those who were seeking a philosophical anchorage for the power-oriented world view.

It should be noted that for men of sufficient intellectual power, it is not necessary to be versed in the technical intricacies of a theory to understand its spirit and significance. Thus very few of our modern strategists are game theoreticians in the technical sense, and many are quick to point out that none of their concepts or conclusions derive from game-theoretical analysis. Nevertheless, a great deal of modern diplo-military thinking is conceived in the spirit of game theory. Here and there the characteristic mode of thought and occasionally the terminology of game theory reveal themselves in the writings of the strategists. At any rate, it is not maintained here that game theory provided the impetus to contemporary strategic thinking. It is merely noted that both sprang into existence at a time when it seemed to many that war would never be respectable again.

One might venture to guess that game theory restored nobility and glamor to war in the guise of profound intellectual exercises (when war had lost its traditional glamor of bravery, gallantry, and self-negation) and that revived war-mindedness put game theory at the focus of attention of many people whose business is thinking.

A Tactical Problem

Let us now see how the ideas of game theory could be applied in solving a military problem. Consider Matrix 3, which you will note is identical with Matrix 2 except that the rows and columns are now interpreted as tactical choices.

	Defend Sector 1	Defend Sector 2	Defend Sector 3
Attack Sector 1	-3, 3	-6, 6	12, -12
Attack Sector 2	6, -6	5, -5	2, -2
Attack Sector 3	-6, 6	10, -10	-8, 8

Matrix 3.

Imagine that you, the row chooser, are a military commander who must choose one of three sectors in which to attack the enemy, while the column chooser is the enemy commander who knows that you are going to attack one of these three sectors and must decide which one to defend most heavily. The outcome of the battle depends both on what you choose to do and what your enemy chooses to do. What each outcome is "worth" to you depends on many factors, the strategic importance of victory or defeat in each of the sectors, losses of men and matériel, possibly some intangibles like morale in the field and at home, even your own personal ambitions. It is not the business of game theory to estimate all these potential gains and losses. Before the game-theorist can start his calculations, the entries in the game matrix must be given. One might object that these estimates are the very essence of strategic science or art and that a theory that by-passes these problems cannot claim the status of the mathematical foundation of such a discipline. I agree that there is much substance in this objection. However, even after the above calculations have been made and the numbers entered into the matrix, there is still a serious problem to solve: how to choose. Game theory steps in at this point.

And so suppose the numbers (the "utilities," as the game theorists call them) are given. Let us suppose that they are given by Matrix 3, and let us interpret their possible meanings. For example, the entry 5 in row 2, column 2 means that if you attack sector 2 while the enemy is defending the same sector, the outcome is worth 5 "utiles" to you, possibly because the terrain is favorable to your forces in that sector, so that victory is fairly certain. Calculating the "utility" of that victory, modified, perhaps by its probability and by the estimated losses (to you and to the enemy), you assign 5 utiles to that outcome. On the other hand, if you choose to attack sector 3, and the enemy chooses to defend the same sector (row 3, column 3), the outcome will be the worst possible for you, perhaps because that is the sector most favorable to his forces. Consider now the case when you attack sector 3, while he defends sector 1 (row 3, column1). The outcome is again bad for you (—6). It may happen that if you break through in sector 3, the enemy, who is concentrated in sector 1, can launch a devastating counter-attack on your flank. On the other hand, if you attack sector 3, while he defends sector 2 (row 3, column 2), the outcome is very favorable for you (+10), because you will be in an extremely favorable position vis-à-vis his forces.

Again, we ask, how ought you as a "rational" commander to choose? Should you choose sector 2, because all of the outcomes associated with this choice are positive? But if you make this choice, and the enemy figures it out (because he is rational and knows that you too are rational), he may defend sector 3, in which case you will get only 2, if you attack sector 2, while you might have gotten +12 if you attacked sector 1 (while he defends sector 3)! But he, too, is rational and can make you lose 6, if he defends sector 2 (while you attack sector 1). It is not hard to see that we are going around in circles exactly as we did when we tried to solve this problem in the abstract.

As we said above, a way out of this impasse was shown by von Neumann in his 1928 paper. The "solution" of the tactical problem is as follows. The attacking commander lets chance decide for him which sector to attack. However, he sees to it that the chances that each of the three sectors are chosen are in proportion 1:6:0. The defending commander does the same thing, except that he arranges the "lottery" in such manner as to give the three sectors chances in proportion 0:10:11.

This is a "solution" in the sense that each commander gets the maximum "expected gain" (in utiles as given), which the situation allows. It is basically the same sort of solution as in the game with a saddle point (Matrix 1), except that here the pay-offs are in "expectations" rather than in actual utiles. The *actual* pay-off is, of course, going to be one of the pairs of entries in the matrix. For all we know, one of the parties may actually draw the worst possible pay-off, but he will at least have the satisfaction of knowing that under the circumstances he could not have done better. His situation is like that of the gambler who chose "rationally," *i.e.,* the bet with the biggest expected gain, but lost as luck would have it.

The Limitations of the Strategic View

It is most important to realize that this solution of the two-person zero-sum game is entirely theoretical and in no sense practical. Its importance was in having provided a conceptual framework for a theory of rational conflict. Whether it is possible or feasible to derive practical rules of conducting real conflicts (or for that matter for playing real games) on the basis of this conceptual framework remains an open question, since the formulation of a real conflict (or game) in terms of all available strategies (let alone the calculation of optimal strategies) is in most cases of interest a problem of unimaginable complexity. However, the importance of the conceptual framework is not to be underestimated. By clarifying the meaning of a "strategy" in mathematically rigorous terms and by stating the conditions under which it is at all meaningful to speak of "optimal" strategies, game theory has cleared the way for a rational approach to rational conflict. Among those who extol the rôle of rational conflict in human affairs, those who understand the true meaning of the theoretical achievement of game theory are justified in hailing the theory as an outstanding intellectual feat of the century. Those who expect game theory to provide handbook answers on how to conduct business competition or diplo-military conflict are deluded.

However, our concern here is not with the "practical" value of game theory but precisely with the conceptual value of the game-theoretical framework of thought, in particular with the question of how far-reaching is the method of game theory in analyzing rational conflict, with a view of providing insights into its *logical structure*.

The limitations of game theory and of its underlying strategic view of conflict becomes apparent once we leave the realm of the two-person zero-sum game.

Let us return to our two opposing military commanders, who now, let us assume, find themselves in a somewhat different situation. Each sits behind a fortified position. Neither has orders to attack the other; their job is simply to hold the position. However, neither knows that the other's objective is merely a defensive one. Each reasonably fears that the other may initiate a surprise attack. The question before each is now whether to initiate a surprise attack or not. To formulate this problem as a game, we need to know the pay-offs. Let us assign the simplest reasonable pay-offs to each of the four possible outcomes.

Outcome 1. Neither initiates a surprise attack. In this case, both have discharged their assigned obligations (to defend the position); consequently we assign a gain of 1 unit to each commander.

Outcome 2. Commander A initiates a surprise attack against B. We shall assume that a surprise attack means a victory to the attacker. If this outcome obtains (since he went "beyond the call of duty"), we assign a win of 2 units (+2) to A and a loss of 2 units (—2) to B.

Outcome 3. Commander B initiates a surprise attack against A. Here, of course, the situation is the reverse of the preceding one, so that A gets —2 while B gets +2.

Outcome 4. They attack each other. We shall assume that a simultaneous attack by both is indecisive. But the losses suffered by both sides must be taken into account. Accordingly we assign a loss of 1 unit (—1) to each.

Let us now put ourselves into A's position. Should he attack? If B is about to attack, A certainly should attack to avoid a loss of —2. If B does not attack, it is still to A's advantage to attack, since he can get the bonus pay-off of 2 instead of settling for 1. Therefore, it is to A's advantage to attack *no matter what B does*. Putting ourselves in B's shoes, we come to a similar conclusion, namely, that it is to B's advantage to attack, no matter what A does. Consequently, a strategic analysis of the situation prescribes "attack" to both commanders. But (by our hypothesis) if they attack each other, they only waste personnel and matériel; whereas if they had sat behind their fortified positions, they would have achieved the same result (status quo) without such expenditure. How does it happen that strategic analysis, apparently derived from game theory, prescribes a pair of strategies which are by no means optimal (the optimal pair being for neither to attack)?

The crucial feature of this situation is that it is not a zero-sum game. Indeed, if we examine the sums of the pay-offs, we find that they add up to zero in outcomes 2 and 3, but not in outcomes 1 and 4. In outcome 1 the pay-offs add up to +2, in outcome 4 to —2. We can only surmise that game-theoretical solutions may at times be at variance with common-sense solutions of non-zero-sum games.

Let us now approach the problem of the two commanders from a common-sense point of view. To bring out a salient feature consider a somewhat different situation. The commanders are assigned to their positions for one week, after which both will be relieved. Both know this from their intelligence reports. We now assume that the attacks are on a small scale and so not decisive. However, the advantage is still with the attacker, in the sense that the attacker inflicts losses on the enemy and does not suffer losses himself unless the attack is reciprocated. The pay-offs are as before and are calculated for each day separately.

Common-sense reasoning might now prescribe the following strategy to each commander: assume that the other will not attack and do not attack him. If he attacks, attack in retaliation. We shall also make an additional somewhat artificial assumption that retaliation can follow only on the day following the attack on one's own position (say because the other's initiative disrupts communications so that it becomes disadvantageous to launch a counter-attack until they are re-established).

Suppose now commander A receives the following intelligence: B has decided on a tit-for-tat strategy, namely, to refrain from attacking unless A attacks and to retaliate on the next day should A attack.

If A believes this intelligence report, what should he do? Examining the pay-offs, he can easily see that the best strategy for him to follow is to refrain from attacking on the first six days of the week and then to attack on the seventh, taking advantage of the fact that B will not attack on the last day (since A did not attack on the next to last day). This last-day attack (on Saturday) can be undertaken with impunity because A will be relieved from his post on the following day.

Now we shall suppose that B has deliberately let the information concerning his intentions leak to A. In doing so, his intention was not by any means to doublecross A by lulling him into a false sense of security and then launching a surprise attack. On the contrary, B intends to stick to his plan, because if A believes the intelligence, *it is in A's interest* to refrain from attacking at least on the first six days, which is also in B's interests. The interests of both commanders would be jeopardized if either broke faith in this tacit agreement to refrain from attack.

If this is as far as the analysis goes, the plan may work. B will refrain from attacking, and he has let A know that he will refrain if A will refrain. Any breach of faith on A's part will be followed by retaliation by B, and A knows this and consequently will not jeopardize the arrangement. We see, then, that a tacit agreement seems possible; moreover, it is a tacit agreement based not on "good will" (which is difficult to assume under the circumstances) but strictly on self interest.

However, *we have not gone far enough in our analysis.* Or rather we have assumed that the commanders have not gone far enough. We have not pursued the consequences of the fact that it is to A's advantage to attack on Saturday (the last day) *and that B knows that it is so.*

If B is to do what is "best for him in this circumstance"

he must attack A on Saturday, thus reducing his loss from
—2 to —1. But A, being rational, is aware of this conclusion
on B's part (he needs no intelligence reports to figure this
out). Consequently, A knows that no matter what happens,
B will attack on Saturday. It appears, then, that it is to A's
advantage to attack on Friday (since he cannot prevent an
attack on Saturday by refraining from attacking on Friday).
But B, being rational, has figured this out too. So he too
decides to attack on Friday, which makes it imperative for
A to attack on Thursday, et cetera.

Strategic analysis has led us to the conclusion that the
only stable "solution" of this game is for both commanders
to attack each other on each of the seven days, which results
in a loss of 7 units for each of them. Had they not stopped
to figure out this "solution," they might have won 7 units.
Had B done nothing to anticipate A's attack on Saturday
and had A known that B would do nothing about it, the
result would have been a win of 8 units for A and 4 units
for B. This may seem unfair to B, but it is still better than
losing 7 units, which is the inexorable result of a complete
strategic analysis of this situation.

Are There Other "Rational" Approaches to Conflict?

We have described two views of conflict, the systemic and
the strategic. Recall that the first systemic analysis led to
theoretical conclusions about what is likely to happen when
people *do not* stop to think (the runaway arms race). Strategic analysis leads to certain theoretical conclusions about
what is likely to happen when people *do* stop to think. From
both of these analyses it appears that if people do not stop
to think, the results are bad and if they stop to think hard
enough, the results are still bad. Can it be that there is an
"optimal" amount of thinking, neither too little nor too
much, that leads to best results? No, the answer is not in
regulating the amount of thinking. The answer is to be sought
in distinctions between different *modes* of thinking. Game

theory presupposes thinking in the strategic mode, which places at the center of attention the interests of the isolated individual "player," who may be a person, an institution, a nation, or any entity with well-defined interests. These interests are pitted against those of other players. To be sure, game theory treats also of coalitions, in which players pool their interests, and has also been extended to the analysis of coalition formation (bargaining theory). But the basic tenets of strategic thinking are preserved in all these contexts— the ultimate reference point remains the smallest acting unit —the player who must rationalize his actions in terms of his self-interest immediate or ultimate. This outlook has a long tradition. It stems from classical economics, where the individual producer or consumer has been put at the foundation of the conceptual system. These competing, bartering, bargaining "atoms" constituted the economic system of the classical theory. It is noteworthy that nineteenth-century economics has earned the epithet of "The Dismal Science" because of its inexorable conclusions that the poor must forever stay poor—a conclusion rationalized by a vulgarized version of the Darwinian notion of the struggle for existence and survival of the fittest.

In our day, the epithet "dismal" can be appropriately transferred to political science, at least that portion of it which is profuse with neo-Hobbesian ideas. Like the ideas of primitive economics, those of primitive political theory also stem from a crude interpretation of the struggle for existence and also lead to inexorable conclusions about the inevitability and hence the justification of power struggles.

A more profound understanding of the natural selection principle, however, has revealed that the individual is by no means the most important competing unit. A whole species may be a competing unit and one of the most significant advantage-conferring traits of such a unit is the extent of co-operation among the individuals comprising it. Moreover, natural selection operates on units much larger than species. Groups of widely separated species may constitute co-operating units, for example, flowering plants and the insects which effect their pollination. Even predators and prey may be said to co-operate, in that predation functions as a population control for the prey which could not survive without such control. Thus the argument by analogy with "the struggle for existence" is a lame one if it aims to establish competition and conflict as an "inexorable fact of life." With equal conviction, one can argue that co-operation is an inexorable fact of life and that units which fail to merge their "interests" with other units are doomed to extinction, whatever short-run successes they may enjoy. For example, the Age of Reptiles was supplanted by the Age of Mammals, in spite of the fact that the newborn reptile can survive without parental care while a newborn mammal cannot. It is precisely the helplessness of the newborn mammal which conferred superior survival potential on the mammalian way of life by making parental care (and by extension co-operative groups of individuals) necessary.

Now strategic thinking cannot by itself lead to the merging of interests. True, interests of "players" are often merged for strategic reasons, but this can happen only if the parties (1) recognize the communality of interests and (2) suspend strategic thinking at least long enough to accomplish the merging. As an example, consider two gunmen who are equally quick on the draw. Both draw and now each has the other "covered." A minute movement may mean death for both, since each must (in self defense) put the worst interpretation on any faintly suspicious movement of the other. It is clear to any onlooker that these two men have a *common* problem. The recognition of this problem is not an "answer," *i.e.,* a result of a strategic calculation, but an insight. And even the insight is worthless unless a disengagement can be managed. But to drop one's guard is impossible! The other is sure to take advantage! This is again a consequence of the strategic axioms and leads inexorably into an impasse from which double murder is the only way out. What can one do? There is no answer to this question as long as the subject of "do" is "one." *One* cannot do anything. But both can. They can lower their guns. They can, but will they? Some will, and some won't. The former will survive; the latter will die. "Natural selection" here will be operating on pairs, not on individuals. Members of surviving pairs will also survive as individuals, but paradoxically only because they were able to forget that they were "individuals" and consequently were able to forget that one must always be calculating one's "self-interest." The surviving individuals will be those who transcend the strategic framework of thought and think something like this: "I can survive only if the pair of which I am a member will survive. Those pairs will survive whose members lower their guns. Therefore I ought to lower my gun."

The reasoning is offered here as an example of reasoning which has survival value, but certainly not as a paragon of logic. The conclusion can be immediately refuted by a strategist who will be quick to point out that any relaxation on the part of one will immediately force the other to press for advantage, because his self-interest dictates it. This argument is irrefutable *within the framework of strategic thinking* just as the argument that Achilles can never overtake the tortoise was irrefutable within the framework of the Eleatic's logic. The Achilles paradox could be resolved only when it was shown that the Eleatic's logic was inadequate for reasoning about space and time. Similarly, the paradox of the balance of terror can be resolved only when understanding dawns that strategic logic is inadequate for reasoning about problems of human beings as distinguished from "players."

In short, passing from the realm of necessity (as exemplified by global "systemic" types of conflict) into the realm of rational decision (as exemplified by the development of strategic science) has not appreciably improved the survival chances of our species. At least one more step is needed— transcending the limitations of strategic thinking and recognizing the indivisibility of the vital interests of the human race as a whole.

NOTES AND QUESTIONS

1. Distinguish between the systemic and strategic modes of conceiving conflict.   Does the leadership of any nation indicate a willingness to subordinate strategic considerations to systemic constraints?   How does one persuade policy-makers to reorient thought in light of the survival of the species?   Note that this reorientation leads to more than caution in a world filled with nuclear weapons.   It tends to support policies designed to achieve a safer world; that is, specific policies are adopted so as to have a system-transforming impact.

2. Is there present in Rapoport an ambiguity or vagueness about the relation between the creative potential of human thought and the deterministic effect of systemic forces?   How would you reconcile freedom and determinism in Rapoport's piece? Is man free to transform that which determines?

3. How does Rapoport's presentation of the systemic mode differ from Singer's presentation of the systemic level of analysis?   Is the strategic-game theoretical mode necessarily descriptive of thought on the sub-systemic national level of analysis?   Rapoport argues for a wider horizon of awareness on the national level.   Does Singer share his viewpoint?

4. Note that Singer is concerned about the discrepancies between perceptions and actualities in international society.   How does this concern relate to Rapoport's plea for a wider frame of conceptual reference?

THE POLITICAL SCIENCE OF SCIENCE:

An Inquiry into the Possible Reconciliation of Mastery and Freedom*

HAROLD D. LASSWELL

My intention is to consider political science as a discipline and as a profession in relation to the impact of the physical and biological sciences and of engineering upon the life of man. I propose to inquire into the possible reconciliation of man's mastery over Nature with freedom, the overriding goal of policy in our body politic.

In the interest of concreteness I shall have something to say about past and potential applications of science in three areas: armament, production, and evolution.

I. POLITICAL SCIENCE AND ARMAMENT

It is trite to acknowledge that for years we have lived in the afterglow of a mushroom cloud and in the midst of an arms race of unprecedented gravity. Here I shall support a proposition that may at first evoke some incredulous exclamations. The proposition is that our intellectual tools have been sufficiently sharp to enable political scientists to make a largely correct appraisal of the consequences of unconventional weapons for world politics.

We have correctly understood the strength of the factors that perpetuate a feeble international order even in the face of recent technoscientific developments. The traditional tools at our disposal for the analysis of politics prepare us to regard a voluntary relinquishment of power as much less likely than efforts to perpetuate power. In a divided world it is not surprising to find that more elites expect to be in a better position by continuing the current system than by taking the risks involved in consenting to a new structure of power. But we have not dis-

* Presidential address delivered at the annual meeting of the Association in Washington, D. C., September 6, 1956.

missed as altogether hopeless the prospects of a more perfect union, achieved by measures short of general war. On the occasions when power is relinquished those who make the seeming sacrifice actually expect to be better off eventually in terms of power (and other values) than if they fail to pay the price.

For at times voluntary confederation, federation or integration does take place. Steps toward unity occur when elites perceive an external threat or obstacle to the preservation or fuller realization of commonly interpreted values. It occurs when elites perceive a common internal threat or obstacle. When atomic weapons appeared on the scene it required no great acumen to see that they were introduced under circumstances in which factors of division were heavily loaded against factors favoring a new structure of unity. Nuclear weapons were introduced unilaterally by one member of a wartime coalition. It is noteworthy that the innovating member did not feel sufficiently bound to allied and associated powers to share the new weapons with the coalition. When the enemy was defeated incentives to share were reduced. They were further reduced by the estrangement that promptly set in to separate the partners in a coalition that had been unable to achieve a high level of trust and cooperation even under the provocation of war.

It was easy to recognize that the active political elite of the largest potential rival of the United States had more inducements to procrastinate than to make the immediate sacrifices that would have been necessary for a global system of security. Moscow leaders were not faced by an ultimatum, but by an inspection proposal that in the beginning would undoubtedly have laid bare the full depth of Soviet weakness and disunity. The immediate burden of sacrifice would have fallen upon one side; what was missing was a means of equalizing the cost throughout the whole course of the proposed arrangement. Moscow had no grounds for believing that the decision makers of the outside world viewed them or their ideology or their technique with such benevolence that any visible vulnerability would remain unexploited. Certainly the annihilation of mankind seemed remote and hypothetical when compared with the deprivations likely to follow at once the formation of a new international structure.

It was no necessary part of the analysis to assume that leading Soviet figures loved war (after the manner of Ghenghis Khan and other nomadic "shepherds of men"). We understood that it would be political suicide for individual leaders on either side to propose full unilateral disarmament by their own government, or even to champion a ceiling or a method of arms reduction that would be regarded by colleagues or constituencies as unfavorable to continuing independence.

Nor was it part of the analysis to assume that individuals are fully conscious of the values that influence their judgment and that the thrust of unconscious factors is toward voluntary union. So far at least as the upper levels of an active elite are concerned it is implausible to suggest that continuing uncertainty will generate unconscious factors making for trust in the benevolence and good faith of alien leaders. The evidence seems to support the contrary view that protracted insecurity renders it easy to perceive the "Other" as malevolent and devious. Hence the tendency is toward the perpetuation of seeming autonomy rather than in the direction of constructing a more inclusive system of public order.

We knew that the decision process of a body politic is to be understood as a complex and relatively stable network of communication and collaboration. A system acts to sustain rather than to revolutionize its own structure. This harmonizes with the fact that more acts must be repetitive than innovative if a system is stable. More specifically, structural stability is favored by the entrapment of each individual in a limited segment of the whole. The official or unofficial role of a participant determines what is available to his focus of attention, and with whom he may communicate or collaborate. The perspectives of a participant are the result of previous experience in the position, and in the sequence of positions through which he has passed. The playing of any role modifies predispositions by rewarding an act with value indulgences or by imposing value deprivations. As a strategy of maintaining and improving their net value position, individuals continually make and unmake coalitions of an explicit or tacit character. Enough information has long been available to show a qualified observer that the private coalitions upon which members of the Soviet or U. S. elite depend for personal advancement are coalitions whose effect is to sustain rather than to supersede a divided world. Obviously the coalitions entered into by top officers in the Red Army, Navy and Air Forces are not made with Americans; and *vice versa*. Nor do the corresponding coalitions of top diplomats, civil officials, or party officials cut across the intervening zone.

There are, political scientists know, typical situations in which active elite elements have expected to benefit by means of a more perfect union. Ruling families have intermarried. Today this institutional presupposition is missing; the top men of the USSR or the USA are not dynastic heads. It is a frail reed indeed to rely upon the hope that a Moscow-Hollywood fusion of infatuated youngsters or calculating oldsters will banish the perils of nuclear fission or fusion. Some historic unifications have been the outcome of duels between appointed champions in the manner of David and Goliath. This institutional predisposition is also missing. No one seriously expects to stake the issue of unity upon two doughty pilots armed with jets, or two teams of missile men lobbing away at one another in the South Seas. We also take note of the fact that thus far we have been unable to rely upon the appearance of an external group capable of being perceived as a common threat. The U.F.O., the unidentified flying objects, have not as yet been shown to be intelligence eyes of another planet against whom we may conceivably combine.

I have been indicating how the tools of the profession provided us with categories, propositions and cases adequate to the task of assessing the probable result of the appearance of unconventional weapons. These tools were, in fact, so used. I do not assert that all members of the profession refrained from adding to the lamentations that arose as this or that circle of humanity awoke to the poignancy of the fact that the planet is moving toward apparent doom. Limited catharsis has often been obtained by railing at the stupidity or malevolence of world elites for failing to bring the current nightmare to a peaceful end. Some among us found a measure of private satisfaction in the discovery of fresh evidence of the depravity of man and turned for consolation to the transempirical doctrines provided by one or another of the theological and metaphysical traditions of mankind. We need not deprecate these personal solutions so long as it is clear that they are not the distinctive roles for which our profession has sought to equip its members.

To assert that political scientists had tools that enabled us to assess a major development correctly is not to say that we are complacent about our part in the story of nuclear weapons. There is always a gap between fundamental theory and the data required to see how theoretical models explain or fail to explain specific configurations. As private scholars political scientists did not always have access to official information; and even when playing an official role a political scientist was not always shown every significant report in the possession of the government. Such limitations go beyond our responsibility as a profession. We must however assume responsibility for any limitation of theory or procedure that prevented us from making full use of every opportunity open to us.

I have been implying that it is possible to interpret our traditional body of theory as giving full recognition to the contextual character of politics. The classical literature made plain that specialized institutions of community-wide action are part of, and interact with, all institutions of the community, all personalities, all institutional and personal patterns in the surrounding world, and with the physical and biological environment. Modern logical technique has made it more apparent than it was formerly that the intellectual task before us is not the discovery of a small number of new fundamental categories with which to designate the context of interaction. Rather, it is apparent that all comprehensive systems are formally equivalent (hence interchangeable) at corresponding levels of abstraction (and regardless of possible differences in the number of key terms employed at each level). The inference is that within a rich intellectual tradition the most significant task is to construct a continuing institutional activity by which central theory is related continuously to events as they unfold. The fundamental categories are retained as constant features of a frame of reference elaborated and employed to delineate the contours of observational fields. The relevant context is the world political process as a whole.

The limited degree of success achieved by the profession in perfecting or in encouraging the body politic to perfect such an institutional process had adverse consequences for our role in regard to nuclear weapons. Long before atomic weapons were introduced we were well aware of the importance of scientific knowledge for the technology of fighting. But we did not correctly anticipate the approximate timing of the impact of nuclear physics upon military technology. Although we were equipped to assess the political consequences of sudden and stupendous increases of fighting effectiveness we did not foresee that such an emergent was imminent. Since technical developments were not explicitly anticipated we did not clarify in advance the main policy alternatives open to decision makers in this country or elsewhere. We did not create a literature or a body of oral analysis that seriously anticipated these issues. As political scientists we should have anticipated fully both the bomb and the significant problems of policy that came with it.

I do not want to create the impression that all would have been well if we had been better political scientists, and that we must bear upon our puny shoulders the burden of culpability for the situation of the world today. We are not so grandiose as to magnify our role or our responsibility beyond all proportion. Yet I cannot refrain from acknowledging, as I look back, that we left the minds of our decision makers flagrantly unprepared to meet the crisis precipitated by the bomb. I have no desire to hold a kangaroo court on President Truman's momentous decision or upon his principal advisers; or to give credence to the insinuation that "results" had become necessary in the face of Congressional restiveness about the cost of research and development. In the light of hindsight (that should have been foresight) I want to underline the probability that the new weapon was introduced in a manner that contributed unnecessarily to world insecurity. Perhaps the critics are right who say that the bomb should have been demonstrated on an uninhabited island before the live drops were made on Hiroshima and Nagasaki. More important is the question of how formal and effective control might have been extended beyond the decision makers of a single power. At least some members of the winning coalition might wisely have been brought into a system that operated through a common agency of inspection and direction.

Plainly there were not enough political scientists trained in physics, or sufficiently aware of the implication of impending scientific developments, to do much forward thinking and planning. This points to a failure of professional recruitment and training, and calls in question the then-prevailing conception of the political scientist's role. As a profession we are concerned with aggregate processes. It is not our job to supply the working politician with what he knows already, namely a bag of electoral and other manipulative tricks. Our distinctive perspective is not that of a trickster although we must be familiar with the trickster's outlook and his repertory if we are to assess the causes and consequences of his way of doing business for the decision process as a whole in any context. Nor is our role limited to reiterating and celebrating the ideal aspirations of the body politic, and exhibiting how value goals can be derived from fundamental postulates and principles. It is not exhausted by reporting historical sequences to be found in the rise, diffusion and restriction of myth and technique; or even by the formalization and verification of descriptive models of a scientific character. Part of our role, as the venerable metaphor has it, is scanning the horizon of the unfolding future with a view to defining in advance the probable import of what is foreseeable for the navigators of the Ship of State. It is our responsibility to flagellate our minds toward creativity, toward bringing into the stream of emerging events conceptions of future strategy that, if adopted, will increase the probability that ideal aspirations will be more approximately realized.

An implication for our future relation to science and armament is that we need to develop more political scientists who have the competence to infer the weapon implications of science and technology. It then becomes possible to anticipate the implications for collective policy.

Even a moderate degree of cross-disciplinary training or continuing contact should have enabled us to prepare for the advent of nuclear fission (and fusion). The *Review of Modern Physics* carried an article by Louis Turner of Princeton University in January 1940 in which 133 papers were appraised. They began with Fermi's original report of 1934 and came down to the Hahn-Strassman-Meitner researches which made explicit the import of Fermi's original experiment. In passing it may be noted that the contributions of a dozen nations were catalogued in

Turner's review. Not more than half a dozen of the 133 papers were by American authors. Perhaps American political scientists may be partially absolved for lack of foresight under these circumstances. But the over-all record of the profession is not thereby improved, since I do not find that colleagues in other countries were any more in touch than we were. Incidentally, it is worth recording that a standard college textbook in physics included a chapter in which the implications of current research were clearly spelled out. Ernest Pollard of Yale University referred in 1940 to the possibility of nuclear reactors that might generate electrical power or detonate as immensely destructive bombs; or that might produce radioactive substances for research and industrial processes or for a new and frightful kind of chemical warfare. I note further that at the time of the Fermi-Dunning experiment at the Columbia University cyclotron in early 1939 some science writers (especially of the New York *Times*) were quite definite about what was at stake.

Today in assessing the years ahead we need solid bases of inference about the degree to which the cost of producing unconventional weapons can be cut. Is it probable that the elites of intermediate powers will soon have at their disposal instruments capable of doing enough damage to outside powers to exert a strong deterrent effect? If so, the destiny of intermediate powers will be less grim than it has appeared to be in the recent past. If the drift toward bipolarity is reduced, there will be less hypocrisy or desperation among the elites of intermediate powers in clanging the cymbals of national loyalty in public while they readjust private family, business and political affairs in the light of the contingency that one or the other pole will dominate the globe.

It is important to estimate the likelihood that the instruments of defense can regain ground they have lost in recent times. In what period of time (if at all) is it probable that manned or unmanned flying objects can be harmlessly destroyed before they are on target? Is there any prospect that new knowledge may be used in a few years to seal off great areas of the globe behind impenetrable "energy" shells? This would open the not altogether uninviting possibility that disagreeable sectors of the globe may be sealed over and left to their own devices much as small boys put dishpans over snake pits or gopher holes.

In many ways the most disturbing result of the laggard position of political scientists in comprehending science and technology is that we have displayed no intellectual initiative in furnishing guidance to those who are in command of modern knowledge and its instrumentalities. Alert businessmen have long been on the lookout for promising applications in the marketplace. The professional military man is now accustomed to take the initiative. The question for us as political scientists is whether we have given enough serious attention to the task of reducing the human cost of whatever violence we cannot dispense with.

As an exercise in this line of thought I invite you to use your imagination to ask what an instrument of coercion would look like that incapacitates without killing, mutilating or in any way imposing permanent incapacity. You and I will probably come up with the same answer: a gas or a drug or a beam that when applied will induce sleep or a similar state of suspension. We spent several billion dollars on A and H bombs; and it is commonly said, with some plausibility, that scientists and engineers give you what you pay for. Our suggestion (and I repeat an old proposal) is that we go down the alphabet to the P bomb, the "paralysis bomb." The technical difficulties in the way of paralyzing a city or a region are very great, given current means of delivering a concentrated gas. Possibly the instrument can be a "P beam," a paralyzing beam of sound or of some other kind capable of accomplishing the purpose.

Without being in the least committed to the specific devices referred to, I nevertheless assert that in the future we need not remain as passive as we have been in approaching the problem of harmonizing considerations of humanity with the use of whatever coercion cannot be avoided.

So far as ultra-weapons are concerned it is apparent that the polar powers have reached an impasse. If they keep on they will have the capability of destroying one another several times over. Once would seem to be enough. (Diverting resources to blasting a grave assumes that it is not a common one.) The polar powers have a common affirmative interest in preventing the rise of an outlying gangster or maniac who might take advantage of the declining cost of nuclear weapons to hold up or gravely damage them both. It may be that workable policy proposals will emerge from concentrated study. For instance, in return for universal inspection of new installations the polar powers might be willing to contribute facilities and scientists to UN laboratories situated at intermediate points and devoted to research and development of new and fundamental scientific ideas. By providing for the possible exploitation of the results under collective auspices it may be possible to expedite the development of the UN into a genuine "third factor" that concurrently expresses an inclusive interest. Senator Anderson of the Joint Committee on Atomic Energy has already declared in favor of any policy that holds promise of joint activities that "obsolesce" old weapons around which vested and sentimental interests are crystallized.)

Since we are aware of the unforeseeable timing of the many factors that may affect a resort to arms it is evident that rational policies on behalf of peaceful cooperation do not rely upon a single avenue of approach. Wise strategy appeals to as many potential pockets of motivation as possible by making continual use of tactical ingenuity in applying every instrument of policy (diplomatic, military, economic, ideological).

It is generally believed that peaceful cooperation can be most readily encouraged in the field of economic growth. And there are grounds for predicting that developments that impend in the technology of production will rival the leaps that have recently occurred in weapon technology. This brings me to the consideration of our relationship as political scientists to these potentialities. Although the devices that contribute to production may also be employed for destructive purposes, my present concern is with the affirmative uses of science.

II. POLITICAL SCIENCE AND PRODUCTION

Impending is control of weather and climate. As our knowledge of the upper atmosphere increases it will be obvious that the seeding of local cloud formations is a relatively trivial precursor of hemispheric global control. Impending is the solution of the problem of obtaining pure water at low cost from the sea for irrigation purposes. Taken in conjunction with newly available energy sources it is not too early to anticipate the reclamation of the wastelands of the earth—the deserts, the polar ice caps, the tropical rain forests, the mountains (levelled to productive plateaus). As J. G. Harrar has told us, the total solar energy that reaches the earth every 48 hours is approximately equal to all the known reserves of coal, petroleum and wood. Clearly the conversion of relatively minute amounts to usable form would meet the energy needs of future generations. Already enough progress has been made to indicate that in the immediate future many local power needs can be supplied more economically by solar energy than by nuclear installations.

As political scientists we are conscious of the implications if great resource changes are introduced into a divided world. Imagine that the arid areas inside the Soviet zone are populated with the density of the fertile districts. Suppose further that the non-Soviet world does away with the arid lands of the United States, Mexico and South America, the Sahara, and the Middle East. If these regions become as populous as the more habitable parts of the countries where they are located the population of the non-Soviet world will be increased relatively more than the Soviet area.

Think next of the tropical forests. If the tropical rain forests of Central and Northern South America, of Mid-Africa, of India and of South-eastern Asia are made fit for human life to the same degree as the more temperate regions near them the relative population of the non-Soviet world will appreciably increase.

If mountainous areas are transformed into plateaus, and the plateaus are populated to the density of neighboring areas, the population of the non-Soviet world will also sustain a relative rise.

We know that the political consequences of changes in population and energy production depend upon the impact of these developments upon the "threat value" or the "asset value" of the members of the world community to one another. We expect that the flow of capital and know-how required to modernize production tends to conform the facts of economic growth to the configurations that predominate in the arena of world politics. One alternative of policy is to mitigate or modify this tendency to pour the concrete of capital investment into the mould of a current power alignment. To what extent can this result be achieved by instituting multilateral control of great programs of reclamation in selected districts? Can the Sahara, for instance, be jointly developed? Since the ruling circles of a split world pursue different objectives in terms of social structure and ideology it is only feasible to think of even restricted programs of multilateral cooperation within the frame of an agreement in which are prescribed the permissible proportions between governmentalized and non-governmentalized operation to be preserved at successive stages of the project. Further, it will be essential to determine whether the program is intended to consolidate an existing national unity or to lay the foundation for a new nation (one drawn, for example, from widely varying ethnic sources; or from a single principal source of people and culture).

The factor of geographical dispersion has an important bearing upon our expectations. The sources of solar and atomic energy are more capable of being widely distributed than the sources exploited by a technology of fossil fuels like petroleum and coal. It is axiomatic that a decentralized pattern of access to energy provides a favorable resource base for a decentralized outlook, and that the perspectives comprising such an outlook sustain a decentralized network of policy formation and execution. If a reversal is to occur in the trend toward bipolarizing the world, and a pattern resembling the Great Power System of the last century is to revive, two conditions at least must be fulfilled: a network of strong, coordinate centers of energy production; and cheaper costs of producing the newer weapons.

I have been talking of the resources found in the wastelands or neglected opportunities on the surface of the continental blocs. We must take the fact into account that new resources are in prospect whether we look beneath or above the land surface of the earth. To begin with the seas: we shall learn to mine the waters for minerals and to farm the oceans for foodstuffs on a scale hitherto unthinkable. In regard to resources above the surface: we are close to the first experimental expeditions to the moon; and, presently the planets. In this setting the traditional questions that center around the control of air space take on new significance.

As specialists in public law it is not difficult for us to anticipate the form in which conflicting claims to these new resources are likely to be phrased. In connection with the seas those who push particular claims to the exclusive exploitation of a given region will talk in terms of "the territorial sea," "contiguous zones," "jurisdiction" and the "continental shelf." Nation states whose officials push particular claims to share in exploiting the resources of an area will invoke the "freedom of the seas" and other internationalizing concepts. The probing of the upper atmosphere, satellite launching, space platforms and the like will pose the problem of how to adjust claims to exclusive control of "air space" against claims to share control. As expeditions to the moon or the planets become more imminent the question of "who owns what" or "who controls what" will bring into the debate the authoritative language traditionally employed in connection with the acquisition of territory ("exploration," "occupation," "conquest" and other concepts emphasizing priority in time and effectiveness of control).

As clarifiers of the goals and alternatives implicit in a decision process and as advisers of the participants we have an opportunity to reduce the amount of unnecessary friction by establishing a frame of reference in advance of the facts. When factual details appear they will of course exhibit some novel elements; common goals and principles will not. The members of the world community have a long history of accommodating "exclusive" claims and "sharing" claims with one another (as new resources provide new base values for the participants in the world arena).

It is, of course, essential that in taking advantage of this opportunity we deal with the entire context of value goals and principles as they relate to potential facts. I have referred to sets of doctrines that in all probability will be invoked when claims are made. The chief function of these formulations is to guide the attention of decision makers to the context in which pertinent activities occur. Formulas assist in recognizing and evaluating the consequences for international public order of accepting the exclusive or the sharing claim in particular cases or categories of cases.

When we examine past trends in world history it is not difficult to recognize that shifts have occurred in the relative emphasis laid upon exclusive or sharing claims. Grotius was speaking for the Netherlands and for other challengers of the claims of Spain, Portugal and England to monopolize great stretches of the seas. Sweeping readjustments were made in doctrine and in its applications relating to the seas. At first they were mainly in the direction of consolidating an international order in which sharing claims were widely accepted ("freedom of the seas"). In recent decades the trend has been the other way. As my colleague Myres S. McDougal has shown in some detail, claims to the exclusive enjoyment of resources have been accepted as "reasonable" in the light of facts that have appeared in the course of applying science and technology. A recent tabulation shows that no more than thirteen states accept the ancient three-mile rule for the territorial sea. Forty-five states repudiate it in varying degree, claiming wider limits. Contiguous zones of many kinds have been accepted for the administration of customs, the security of neutral states against belligerent activities, fishing conservation, appropriation of the resources of the sea-bed and of the continental shelf.

When we think configuratively about the problems raised in reference to the new resources it is clear that instead of relying on blanket principles (like "freedom of the seas" or "freedom of the air") the most fruitful policy alternatives are likely to emerge when we anticipate the appearance of characteristic factual contexts, and consider how the values chiefly at stake in them can be maximized. Hence we would not expect to apply the same prescription (1) to the sharing of air space for weather observation (where equipment is used that is expressly designed for the purpose and perhaps registered, and when the information obtained is made public) and (2) to the sharing of air space for projects of weather or climate control that may be deleterious to local values.

The contextual (or, synonymously, the configurative) approach is a challenge to imagine the full range of possible means of anticipating and resolving difficulties. On the most uncertain matters it is appropriate to call attention to the need of exploring the possibilities of agreement in advance of conflict. The inference is that no time should be lost, for instance, in putting into the hands of the UN the facilities for research, development and operation of satellites, "space platforms" and travel beyond the limits of the earth's atmospheric and gravitational fields. Doubtless the USA and the USSR will continue to compete with independent programs. Since the polar powers have a stake in moderating the conflict in which they are engaged in the hope of eventual harmony through agreement, not catastrophe, a practical method would appear to be to strengthen the "third factor," especially when both powers are also included within it.

The rapid introduction of new resources under present conditions calls for some degree of community and regional planning; and planning poses thorny questions about the structure and ideology of society. To an increasing extent questions of this kind need to be answered directly rather than by default. It must be conceded that American political scientists are not especially well equipped to participate in the planning function on the scale required. Although we are accustomed to corroborate the classical authorities and the Founding Fathers in praise of the middle classes as contributory to popular institutions of government, we have not as a rule dealt with these traditional doctrines in significant ways. For instance, we have not explored the principles of proportion that are most likely to consolidate or to sustain at various stages of industrial growth the perspectives and operational technique of popular government. Shall we, for example, rely upon a 30-40-50 rule to guide public policy in regard to the permissible degree of market control permitted to private interests? (For example: When one interest has 30% control of output, shall it be subject to special regulations designed to nullify the side-effects of power that go along with economic control? When one interest rises to 40% shall we put governmentally appointed trustees on the Board of Directors? At 50% shall government trustees predominate?)

Whatever the workable rules of proportion may be in representative contexts it is evident that we need to guide our studies of trend correlation and of comparative cases in order to improve the available bases of inference in such matters.

The same approach—the search for rules of proportion—applies to every institutional and personality pattern in a body politic. What are the optimum proportions of community resources to devote to elementary, intermediate, advanced and ultra-advanced education? To research and development in science and technology? To positive and negative sanctions for correctional and other purposes?

One way to jar "cakes of custom" out of the mind is to draft specifications for the first Mayflower expedition to establish continuing occupation outside the earth. (Possibly it could be "Noah's Jet"?) What proportion of men, women and children of which culture or combination of earth cultures shall we select? What ideological traditions, secular and sacred? What class backgrounds (elite, mid-elite, mass)? What individual and group interests? What personality structures?

By asking questions of this kind we are in a position to assess our present stock of knowledge concerning the interdependence of institutions specialized to power, and all other institutions in the social process of any community, together with the forms of personality involved. These, of course, are the recurring issues of political science and historical interpretation as well as policy.

III. POLITICAL SCIENCE AND EVOLUTION

I have been referring to a few implications of science and technology for weapons and production, and sketching some political ramifications. As political scientists we are perhaps even less well prepared to anticipate developments in genetics, experimental embryology and related disciplines. Taken together these fields signify that, as Julian Huxley has often put it, man is on the threshold of taking evolution into his own hands. By influencing the genes that constitute the key units in man's biological inheritance we affect the entire potential of future generations.

Important as recent innovations are in radioactivity I do not want to give more than passing notice to the dangers that they embody. The only feasible means of coping with these factors is by policies that avert war and preparation for war, and install proper precautions in the handling of high energy radiation for other purposes.

Quite recently the dangers that arise from radioactivity have been authoritatively brought to public notice: all high energy radiation that reaches the gonads stimulates gene mutations; more than 99 per cent of all mutations are dangerous; genes can only be eliminated by the death of the gene carrier or by his incapacity to reproduce. Nearly two years ago H. J. Müller told us that the bomb tests since the war had already exposed the inhabitants of the earth to radioactivity comparable with that of the inhabitants of Hiroshima and Nagasaki after the original explosions. He estimated that about 80,000 harmful mutations are involved and that "it will mean, in the end, several times this number of hampered lives."

It has been pointed out that perhaps the most satisfactory index of genetic damage is the sum of tangible defects existing among living individuals. We are speaking of such stigmata as "mental defects, epilepsy, congenital malformations, neuromuscular defects, hematological and endocrine defects, defects in vision or hearing, cutaneous and skeletal defects, or defects in the gastrointestinal or genitourinary tracts." We are informed that about 2 per cent of the live births in the United States have defects that are of "simple genetic origin and appear prior to sexual maturity." If mankind were subjected to a "double dosing" of radiation the present level of genetic defects would rise, and would eventually be doubled.

Regulatory measures are obviously needed against wars and weapon tests; and they are essential to the disposition of nuclear waste from industrial plants. (It has been remarked that a nuclear power plant is to be viewed as a large scale production of both highly poisonous gas and explosives under a single roof.)

The principal questions to which I desire to call attention pose issues of a relatively new and different order. Some of these questions have already come up in controversies over artificial insemination. They have embarrassed the champions of the orthodox prescriptions that prevail in several fields (theology, ethics, jurisprudence). Shall we call a child legitimate whose biological father is not identical with the sociological father? Even with the consent of the latter? With spermatozoa from a known or unknown source? (A possible international question is whether a nation state like the United States can claim the child as a citizen if the spermatozoa employed originated with an American mail order house and was sent by air mail for use abroad.)

Poignant as these issues are in specific cases they do not confront us with the consequences for public order that are to be anticipated if the progress of biology separates insemination and child bearing from genital contact. The assumption is often made that the continuation of sexual rectitude and even civic order depends upon charging every genital contact with the blessings and perils of procreation. The impending improvement of oral contraceptives, joined with other recent advances, are factors that already suggest the wisdom of other norms and sanctions of public order.

Other developments are threatening current ratios of the influence and power of the sexes. Given the millions and millions of spermatozoa produced by one male and the technique of canning by refrigeration, any very large number of males becomes relatively redundant for purposes of procreation. Must the male rest his future upon other values such as the strictly aesthetic appeal of the male contour? Before the female of the species becomes too complacent in this context it may be worth recalling the significance of some current experiments for the removal of the primordial female function from the body and into other receptacles. (Women, too, may have to rely upon their charm, a role for which their experience has provided extensive preparation.)

Apparently we are closer than most of us like to think to the production of species that occupy an intermediate position between man and the lower animals (or even plants). It is sometimes said, even in august quarters, that "one has not yet succeeded in making a species from another species." Theodosius Dobzhansky notes, however, that "the feat of obtaining a new species was accomplished more than a quarter of a century ago." In recent decades a fair number of new species have been brought into being. It is also true that some species that exist in nature have been recreated experimentally. A garrison police regime fully cognizant of science and technology can, in all probability, eventually aspire to biologize the class and caste system by selective breeding and training. Such beings can, in effect, be sown and harvested for specialized garrison police services or for other chosen operations.

Great strides have been taken in brain design. Experimental models of robots have been built who solve problems of a rather complex order in a given environment. Some of these machines look after themselves to a degree, obtaining and using the raw materials required for energy and repairs. Already it is claimed that the function of reproducing its kind, and of interacting with others, can be in-built.

The question then rises: Given our concern for human dignity when do we wisely extend all or part of the Universal Declaration of Human Rights to these forms? When do we accept the humanoids—the species intermediate between lower species and man, and which may resemble us in physique as well as in the possession of an approximately equivalent central nervous and cortical system—as at least partial participants in the body politic? And at what point do we accept the incorporation of relatively self-perpetuating and mutually influencing "super-machines" or "ex-robots" as beings entitled to the policies expressed in the Universal Declaration?

It is obvious that we are not too well equipped by cultural tradition to cope with these problems. A trait of our civilization is the intense sentimentalization of superficial differences in the visible format of the groupings to be found even within the human species. Recall the theologians, ethicists and jurists who have devoted themselves to the elaboration of symbols to show that the white race alone is genuinely human and hence solely entitled to the dignity of freedom. Recall, too, the counter-assertions, nourished in the soil of humiliation, that have arisen among ethnic groups that seek to overcome their contempt for themselves by dragging down the pretensions of the white imperialist.

Let us recognize that the traditions of certain non-Western civilizations are in some ways better adapted to the problem than the Graeco-Roman and Judeo-Christian perspectives. They possess a relatively broad basis for identifying the primary ego of the individual with a self that includes more than strictly human species in the congregation of living forms. A world view that includes the possibility of reincarnation in lower animal shapes, for example, may prepare its devotees to empathize more readily with other than strictly human species and varieties. Even they, however, may have their troubles with a mobile power plant in nearly human form.

The most disturbing question, perhaps, arises when we reflect upon the possibility that super-gifted men, or even new species possessing superior talent, will emerge as a result of research and development by geneticists, embryologists or machine makers. In principle, it is not too difficult to imagine a superior form. For instance, our sensory equipment does not enable us to take note of dangerous radiation levels in the environment. We have no inborn chattering of a Geiger counter.

I spoke before of taking the intellectual initiative for the use of science and technology for the fuller realization of our value goals. It is plain that if we bring certain kinds of living forms into the world we may be introducing a biological elite capable of treating us in the manner in which imperial powers have so often treated the weak. A question is whether the cultivation of superior qualities ought to be limited to intellectual capability. The answer, I feel confident you will agree, is in the negative. We need to be sufficiently vigilant to prevent the turning loose on the world of a hyper-intelligent species driven by an instinctual system especially inclined toward predation. The blood-stained story of our own species is only too familiar (the stories about succulent missionaries whose bodies were more readily incorporated than their messages are not wholly without foundation). Can we improve the prospects of developing a form of intelligent life copied not after our own image, but after the image of our nobler aspirations?

It is not to be overlooked that the problem of human capability can become acute if in the years ahead we escape from our present habitat on the earth, or are visited by other forms of intelligent life. There are, after all, untold millions of environments resembling our solar system, and it would be more remarkable to find that but one planet is inhabited by a complex living form than to encounter parallel developments. It would of course be embarrassing, at least, to discover that we are the savages or that we are put together on a markedly inferior biological plan.

IV. OUR FUTURE PROGRAM

The fact is that many of the problems to which I have been referring will be upon us long before we can make great changes in the ideological outlook or the socio-political patterns of life in this country or elsewhere. The same point applies to ourselves in our role as individuals and as members of the political science profession. Considering our present predispositions how can we improve the likelihood of contributing to the decision process at every level, from the neighborhood to the world as a whole?

It is abundantly clear that the impact of science and technology does not occur in a social vacuum, but in a context of human identifications, demands and expectations. I make the modest proposal that it is appropriate for political scientists, in company with other scientists and scholars dealing with human affairs, to improve our procedures of continuous deliberation upon the potential impacts of science and technology upon human affairs. No doubt the American Political Science Association and other professional societies constitute an appropriate network for the purpose. We can sustain continuing conferences devoted to the examination of emerging developments. As fellow professionals we have special responsibility for giving thought to the aggregate effects of any specific innovation.

Our first professional contribution, it appears, is to project a comprehensive image of the future for the purpose of indicating how our overriding goal values are likely to be affected if current policies continue.

A closely related contribution consists in clarifying the fundamental goal values of the body politic. We are accustomed to confront political ideologies with new factual contingencies and to suggest appropriate specific interpretations. We also confront political doctrines with rival doctrines, and with comprehensive theological and metaphysical systems. I have called attention to the point that the basic value systems of European civilization, in particular, are likely to be exposed to sweeping challenge as biology and engineering narrow the obvious differences between man and neighboring species, and between man and centrally operating machines. The crisis will be peculiarly sharp if we create or discover forms of life superior to man in intellect or instinctual predispositions. Our traditions have not been life-centered, but man-centered. We possess various paranoid-like traditions of being "chosen." Clearly a difficult task of modifying these egocentric perspectives lies ahead.

The third task is historical and scientific. It is historical in the sense that by mobilizing knowledge about the past we are enabled to recognize the appearance of new patterns and the diffusion or restriction of the old. It is scientific in the sense that we summarize the past in order to confirm (or disconfirm) propositions about the interplay of predisposition and environment. If we are to serve the aims of historic recognition and of scientific analysis, one of our professional responsibilities is to expedite the development of more perfect institutions specialized to continual self-observation on a global scale. Self-observation requires guidance by a system of theoretical models of the political process in which a continuing gradation is maintained between the most inclusive model and submodels adjusted to more limited contexts in time and space. Continual self-observation renders it necessary at each step through time to reevaluate the appropriateness of the operational indices for the variables and concepts employed at the most recent step. In this way all the concepts that figure in systematic, descriptive political science can be kept chronically pertinent to the ordering of political events as the future unfolds.

The fourth task is inventive and evaluative. It consists in originating policy alternatives by means of which goal values can be maximized. In estimating the likely occurrence of an event (or event category), it is essential to take into account the historical trends and the scientifically ascertained predispositions in the world arena or any pertinent part thereof.

The relationship of American political science to these tasks is in many ways unique. The typical department is a microcosm of the macrocosm of university faculties of the social sciences and humanities, and the school of law. It is no secret that a syndicate of philosophers, historians, behavioral scientists and public lawyers is capable of producing some degree of tension among themselves, especially when budgets are at stake. This has led to the suggestion that every component skill should be sent back where it came from—to the departments of philosophy, history, sociology and psychology, for example, and to the law school. In this way political science could be given back to the Indians. The catch is that we are not agreed who the Indians may be.

The present situation does make it possible for political scientists to take the lead in integrating rather than dividing our intellectual community. Compared with an entire university, which has become a noncommunicating aggregate of experts, each department of political science can be a true center of integration where normative and descriptive frames of reference are simultaneously and continuously applied to the consideration of the policy issues confronting the body politic as a whole over the near, middle and distant ranges of time.

The profession is advantageously situated therefore to take the lead in a configurative approach to the decision process in society. Where it plays this part, political science is the policy science, *par excellence*. If the implications of science and technology are to be correctly appraised, it will be essential to recruit some trained personnel from such fields into political science, to improve the science-content of professional education, and to provide for continuing cooperation among the professions involved.

It is quite unnecessary for any one individual to emulate the universal ambitions of renaissance man. But if we are to take the lead in performing the configurative or matrix function it is quite essential for the profession as a whole to achieve the division of labor, the understanding and the insight capable of realizing as fully as possible the dream of relevant universality. Each of us can at least widen the boundaries of the self and open the way to identify with living forms that differ from traditional images. We can step toward the possible reconciliation of a growing mastery over Nature with the dignity of freedom for all that lives. In the congregation of living forms human life may come to play a yet more distinguished role in generations to come, a role that transcends even the vision of the commonwealth of man championed by the distinguished political scientist and statesman, the centennial of whose birth we take pride in according special commemoration this year.

NOTES AND QUESTIONS

1. How would you characterize Lasswell's style of inquiry in light of reading Singer and Rapoport? Do you share Lasswell's confidence in the capacity of trained observers to contribute information that policy-makers can and should take into account? Is there enough time available in the policy-forming process to assess the relevance of speculations about remote objectives to present acts?

2. How would you use Lasswell's approach to develop the case for limited world government? What kinds of things would you want to think about? See McDougal and Lasswell in **II-1B**; and see McDougal, **II-1C**.

3. Do you agree with Lasswell's questioning of the decision to use atomic weapons in World War II? How might the United States have acted at the time to generalize control over the possession and right to use nuclear weapons? Is it safer to have the effective and formal control over nuclear weapons in an international institution than in the hands of several leading national governments? Why? See Chapter 4 and Volume IV for a fuller consideration of these issues.

4. Do Clark and Sohn make adequate provision for adapting to an evolving future? How does specialized knowledge get into the policy-making process operative in a totally disarmed world? Are central institutions required? Must a value consensus underlie the appropriation of knowledge by government? How do we choose from among preferred futures?

The Shimoda Case: Challenge and Response 4

Prior chapters have appraised the capacity of the international system to maintain minimum world public order by avoiding a major war. In addition, the Clark-Sohn plan has been used as a model to study the control of violence in an alternative international system. And finally, the prospects for transition from one to the other have been assayed in a variety of institutional and substantive settings. For purposes of transition the central questions are: What is acceptable? How can we act to enlarge the domain of what is acceptable?

These transition questions lead to the reality of political inertia that makes it difficult even to envisage a system change that is introduced in a period of peace by a drastic alteration in the constitutional basis of world order. On the other hand, in the event of a catastrophe in the form of a nuclear war, one can much more easily envisage an acceptance of a new basis for world order such as the one projected by Clark and Sohn. In the nuclear age this dependence upon the processes of traumatic transition may prove fatal. There seems to exist a flaw in human imagination that requires mankind to undergo the experience of tragedy so as to take steps to avoid it. And so the action taken under the sway of the tragic experience always seeks to avoid the repetition of a *prior* tragedy.

Perhaps, a way to begin to confront the dilemma is to reexperience the prior tragedy in such a way that it creates the social and political momentum needed for a solution of the transition problem, so that we use the events in the past to create enough anxiety about the future to dissipate the resistance of all sorts to drastic change in the ordering of the world. The limits of reason are quickly reached. One must engage the conscience as well as the mind to make convincing the demonstration of feasibility that has occupied our attention in the prior chapters. It is for this reason that we publish an extract from the *Shimoda* case dealing with the use of atomic bombs by the United States against Hiroshima and Nagasaki in the closing days of World War II. For this case is rooted in the tragic circumstance of these victims of the bombings that has lingered on so long after the events. To set a context for the decision itself we include a short commentary by one of the editors: "The Claimants of Hiroshima" by Richard A. Falk, adapted with the permission of *The Nation* from an article which first appeared in the February 15, 1965 issue.

RICHARD A. FALK
The Claimants of Hiroshima

On December 7, 1963, the District Court of Tokyo handed down a decision involving claims against the state brought by injured surviviors of the atomic attacks on Hiroshima and Nagasaki. The opinion of the Japanese court in the case of *Shimoda and Others v. Japan* has been recently translated into English.

The *Shimoda* opinion is long and complex. Only its most relevant features can be outlined and some tentative interpretations suggested. Five residents of Hiroshima and Nagasaki sought compensation from the Japanese Government for damages sustained by the atomic blasts. Japan was the defendant because in the Peace Treaty ending World War II Japan waived the claims of its nationals against the United States, but the United States was the real defendant—that is, the state whose alleged wrongs gave rise to the damage. It is an irony of the proceedings that the role of the Japanese Government as defendant required it to argue in behalf of the legitimacy of atomic attacks on two of its own leading cities. One senses the reluctance of Japan to press "its side" of the case. In the complaint, which is printed with the opinion, the claimants set forth the facts of the attack, the legal basis for their recovery, and specify the damage that they have individually sustained. The defense does not dispute the facts of the attack or damage, but confines itself to arguing that international law did not prohibit the use of atomic bombs by a belligerent and that, in any event, the Japanese Government has no responsibility to compensate individual victims of atomic damage.

The court recites the agonizing facts, examines, with the help of three expert advisers, the status of atomic weapons and arrives at several important conclusions. First, that it is neither possible, nor necessary, to conclude expressly that international law forbids the use of atomic (or nuclear) weapons, although the reasoning of the opinion suggests that such weapons would almost always be illegal if used against cities. Second, that the attacks upon Hiroshima and Nagasaki caused such severe and indiscriminate suffering that they did violate the most basic legal principles governing the conduct of war. And third, that these claimants have no remedy, since international law does not yet allow individuals, in the absence of an express stipulation in a treaty, to pursue claims on their own behalf against a government, especially against their own government.

These conclusions have great interest for international lawyers because they constitute the sole attempt by a legal tribunal to assess the relevance of the laws of war to the realities of the nuclear age, including especially the legality of nuclear weapons if used against cities and civilian populations. The decision has an added interest as it was rendered by a domestic court in a leading Asian country on the basis of Western legal concepts and sources of authority. It is also an opinion in which a principal belligerent policy of the victor in a war is brought under legal scrutiny by a tribunal of the defeated state. It should be noted, however, that the court, and even the complainants, make every effort not to pass judgment on the United States or its President, but to examine only the acts complained of. Reading the opinion, one feels a far greater sense of impartiality than that which pervaded the Tokyo and Nuremberg War Crimes Trials, those being trials conducted by the victors sitting in judgment over the defeated.

The *Shimoda* opinion also grapples in an interesting way with the status of individual claims for relief in international law in the absence of treaty rights, and thereby touches on the widely discussed question of whether individuals, as well as states, should become subjects of an evolving international legal system. This is not just an issue fit for academic speculation. Most abuses of human rights are perpetrated by governments against their own nationals. It is a crucial matter whether the victims of legal abuse themselves have the status and can gain access to a forum within which to assert their claim, embarrass their government, and perhaps arouse a response by the organized international community.

It is probable that the Tokyo opinion will be received favorably by international lawyers throughout the world, admiration being expressed for its dispassionate approach, careful and exhaustive examination of all the legal questions presented, and its conservative conclusions. The court was careful to refrain from making extravagant claims about the relevance of international law to the conditions of atomic attack and to avoid "legislating" on the delicate matters before it. At the same time, it reached the clear and momentous conclusion that the attacks on Hiroshima and Nagasaki were illegal. The court acknowledged the delicacy of its role in characteristic Japanese manner by rendering the decision on December 7, the anniversary of Pearl Harbor, thereby linking the aggressive Japanese initiation of World War II with an appraisal of its brutal termination. This was a most graceful way to impart a sense of humility upon the whole proceedings and to express the moral ambiguity of the judge's role in a legal controversy drawn from the events of a major war. The District Court of Tokyo deserves commendation for its competence and tact in handling the case.

But it is not for its contribution to international law that the *Shimoda* case is most important. It is rather that the specific context of the claim, especially the vividness supplied by the details of the injuries, has produced a text for the study of the whole relationship between nuclear weapons and human destiny. For we are confronted here with the suffering and with an attempt to assess the acts causing it in light of the moral and legal traditions of mankind. The magnitude of the horror caused at Hiroshima and Nagasaki, though at a level far below the destructive potential of current bombs, deprives us of the numbing abstractions about national security, credible deterrents, and the like.

The *Shimoda* case supplements existing attempts to prohibit the use of nuclear weapons in international conflict. In 1960, the United Nations General Assembly passed a resolution supported by most of its membership, but not by the United States, declaring nuclear weapons illegal and proposing a conference to implement the declaration. Plans are going forward for such a conference. This may eventually induce the Great Powers to consider more sympathetically the movement to create a tradition of no-first use of nuclear weapons, or—what amounts to the same thing—the restriction of nuclear weapons to reprisal for prior nuclear attack.

In my judgment, a tradition of no-first use, if seriously supported by the official proclamation of principal governments, would considerably improve the prospects for avoiding nuclear war. One doubts, for instance, that the United States would have defied the moral and legal tradition against poison gas or lethal germs if it had developed chemical or bacteriological weapons of mass destruction comparable to atomic weapons. We refrained from using poison gas against the Japanese in World War II, despite its relevance to the successful conduct of island and jungle warfare. We refrained more because the weapon was illegitimate than because we feared retaliation. If nuclear weapons could be banned by common tradition, then our defense planning would have to be changed so that security interests could be satisfied without reliance upon them.

However, such a tradition will lack its true moral foundation until Hiroshima and Nagasaki are reconsidered and responsibility accepted for the wrongs done there. Movies and books like *Hiroshima, Mon Amour, Red Alert, Dr. Strangelove, Seven Days in May* and *Fail-Safe* have usefully aroused some sense of fear about nuclear weapons, about the precarious basis of our "security," as long as it is premised upon the capability to destroy an enemy with nuclear weapons. The Japanese case supplements these efforts by analyzing the only historical antecedent.

The uncut version of *La Dolce Vita* contains a scene in which Steiner explains the murder of his children and his contemplated suicide by a lengthy speech that includes an indictment of the United States for having dropped atomic bombs on Nagasaki and Hiroshima. In the export version of the film, the scene is spliced down to a sentence or two of dialogue, Steiner making only the vague assertion that he is unwilling to bring up his children in a world in which nuclear warfare is a possibility. Steiner's violence seems out of proportion, dramatically unconvincing, and quite implausible as the film now stands. The excision was explained to me as having been prompted by a desire to spare American feelings—and by the recognition that Americans are not commercially responsive to anything that impugns the essential uprightness of their national behavior.

Even if *La Dolce Vita* was not doctored for quite the reasons ascribed, the explanation is credible. Hiroshima and Nagasaki are not yet properly implanted in our imagination. There is a reluctance to consider the moral question, an impatience with it, and a widespread sense of its irrelevance. To the extent that the issue has been discussed, it has been in technical and strategic terms: whether the Japanese were ready to surrender anyway; whether lives were ultimately saved, and how many; whether a comparable result could have been achieved by a demonstration blast in an uninhabited region. These questions are virtually unanswerable; they do not assess the moral responsibility of the United States for having set a precedent in favor of using nuclear weapons to achieve normal belligerent objectives, and for causing so much indiscriminate grief that lingers on because of the peculiarly grotesque qualities of radioactive diseases. And what does this precedent signify for the future? Has Pandora's box been let open forever, or is a nation, contemplating the use of nuclear weapons in the future, more likely to refrain by thinking back to what happened at Hiroshima and Nagasaki?

It is difficult to comprehend what it means to have crossed the nuclear threshold. It is hardly mitigating to suggest that the attacks upon Hiroshima and Nagasaki were no worse than the saturation bombings of Dresden and Hamburg, or the fire raids on Tokyo. To begin with, these attacks were themselves awesome rather than routine examples of what war at that time was like. Furthermore, the terrifying impact of atomic devices is enhanced because so much destruction is concentrated in a single detonation. The towering mushroom cloud and the huge blast that obliterates everything within a certain radius are ineradicable aspects of the experience. The impact of atomic war upon the political imagination is suggested by the reaction to atomic bombings in Japan, where a widespread revulsion to war is formalized in a clause of the new constitution that permanently forbids Japanese participation in or preparation for war. Pacifist feelings remain strong, especially among the younger generations, and there is a great distaste for any security arrangement that involves relying upon nuclear weapons. Is it necessary to suffer the trauma of nuclear attack to question seriously the wisdom and legitimacy of relying upon nuclear weapons to uphold traditional sovereign interests?

The United States' refusal to question the status of nuclear weapons reflects much more than an unwillingness to face unpleasant features in our nation's past. Since the end of World War II, our leadership in world affairs has depended upon our ability and willingness to use nuclear weapons against our enemies should circumstances warrant. Especially in Europe, we have made clear that we require nuclear weapons to offset what is alleged to be Soviet conventional superiority. And throughout the world we have tried to intimidate our adversaries by making the conditions of nuclear response uncertain so that acts of provocation might seem more risky. In the years immediately following World War II, our military preeminence was allowed to rest principally upon our nuclear monopoly. More recently, it has rested upon our nuclear superiority, insofar as that exists. Therefore, to withdraw legitimacy from nuclear weapons might be seen as a species of unilateral disarmament. For the United States would be giving up a military advantage without getting anything in exchange.

Some of the military objections to making nuclear weapons illegal, or even to reducing the stockpiles of such weapons, have grown weaker in the last few years. First, Soviet ICBM's and submarines make the United States itself vulnerable to awesome destruction. Second, the prospect of widespread dissemination of nuclear weaponry has increased since France and China acquired a nuclear capability; this diminishes the security and strategic value of nuclear weapons for both the United States and Russia. Third, it seems increasingly possible to arrange the defense of Europe on the basis of conventional weapons, and there appears to be much less fear that the Soviet Union will resort to military aggression for expansionist ends. Fourth, it becomes more plausible, although still by no means likely, that satisfactory disarmament agreements can be negotiated. Fifth, the main arenas of international conflict are likely to be internal wars (Vietnam, Laos, Congo) where nuclear weapons have little or no application; that is, the outcome of the cold war is seen to depend much less on the relative capacity to deliver nuclear destruction than upon the ability to influence political developments in certain crucial states of Asia, Africa and Latin America. In short, there is less reason now than earlier to resist the suggestion that it would be proper and sensible to ban or withdraw legitimacy from these weapons.

But it is not easy to reverse the direction of technological progress. Nuclear weapons have been used; the technique for their manufacture is now known throughout the world. Peaceful uses of atomic energy and the exploration of outer space assure the survival, even in a totally disarmed world, of the know-how and industrial capability to achieve rapid nuclear rearmament. No political system of constraint has ever managed either to avoid war permanently, or to prevent the use of any weapon that a belligerent thought would give it a decisive advantage; no nation has been willing to lose a major war rather than refrain from using some novel or horrible weapon thought more destructive than the weapons of its opponent. Present prospects for eliminating the danger of nuclear war are thus bleak, but a beginning can be made if especially we, the citizenry of the country that initiated the nuclear age and exercised leadership over its development, view with belated alarm our role in creating this unprecedented hazard to the future of man.

The court reviewed the various prohibitions directed at weapons in the past, beginning in 1886 with the St. Petersburg Declaration that prohibited explosives of less than 400 grams (explosive bullets), and continuing up through the 20th century when various formal efforts have been made at international meetings to outlaw poisonous gases, and to circumscribe rights to engage in aerial bombardment and submarine warfare. A painstaking examination is conducted to reach the conclusion that atomic bombs cannot be said to be legal just because they were new weapons at the time of their use. The emphasis in the opinion is less upon the status of the weapons themselves than upon the specific occasions of their use. Especially, the opinion concentrates upon the inability of an atomic attack upon an inhabited city to discriminate between military and non-military targets in a metropolitan area: *"Therefore, the act of atomic bombing. . . should be regarded. . .as a blind aerial bombardment; and it must be said to be a hostile act contrary to international law of the day."*

The court then considered the counter argument, advanced by the Japanese Government, that the concept of total war eliminates the distinction, traditional in international law, between combatant and noncombatant, and between military and nonmilitary objectives. The opinion rejects this argument, pointing to the continuing immunity from attack of such objects as schools, churches, shrines, hospitals and private houses. It rejects also the related argument that Hiroshima and Nagasaki represented targets where military objectives were so concentrated that zone bombing could be justified. It notes simply that military objectives were not particularly concentrated in either city.

The court examined the claim that the atomic bombing of these two cities was "contrary to the principle of international law that the means which give unnecessary pain in war and inhumane means are prohibited." Here, the court recognized that the law of war is formed by weighing considerations of humanity against those of military effectiveness. But it goes on to examine the various prohibitions of weapons—and decides that however great the inhumane result of the use of a weapon may be, the use of the weapon is not prohibited by international law, if it has a great military efficiency." The court emphasizes the bombings, not the weapons, concludes that they violate the most fundamental of all principles in the history of the law of war: "The destructive power of the atomic bomb is tremendous; but it is doubtful whether atomic bombing really had an appropriate military effect at that time and whether it was necessary. It is a deeply sorrowful reality that the atomic bombing on both cities. . .took the lives of many civilians, and that among the survivors there are people whose lives are still imperiled owing to radiation, even today, eighteen years later. In this sense, *it is not too much to say that the pain brought by atomic bombs is severer than that from poison and poison gas, and we can say that the act of dropping such a cruel bomb is contrary to the fundamental principle of the laws of war that unnecessary pain must not be given."*

This expresses the full and direct charge against the United States: We used these cruel weapons for doubtful military purposes, in an unusually inhumane way that has permanently seared the imagination of men, and has left an unextinguished legacy of suffering among civilians selected arbitrarily as victims of terror practiced on a gigantic scale.

The full force of *Shimoda and Others v. Japan* can be felt only by reading the whole document. This distinguished opinion by the Tokyo District

Court deprives us of our last excuse for forgetting the past.

There are some special issues. It can surely be argued that a reconsideration of the past does not reduce the prospect of its repetition. However, such an argument is hollow when made by Americans, for we have insistently urged the Germans to bring their war criminals to justice, conceiving such an encounter as an apt occasion for a moral catharsis.

Also, the augmented horrors of war in the nuclear age should not be allowed to diminish the horror of pre-nuclear war. One of the more bedeviling ambiguities in this subject of nuclear war arises because the existence of nuclear weapons may have avoided World War III, or at least postponed it.

Finally, there is the matter of whether it makes any sense to contend that there exists a national responsibility for Hiroshima and Nagasaki. For can it not be pointed out that the decision to drop atomic bombs was made in secret by President Truman and a small number of close advisers? The citizenry cannot so easily separate itself from moral participation in the decisions of its government. For one thing, our entire social and political system elevates to authority those whose values accord with and are representative of the moral consensus prevailing in the nation. For another, national reactions to the atomic bombing of Japan have ranged from apathy to endorsement. Such a response certainly is closely equivalent to mass ratification. As Americans, then, we remain implicated, at least so long as we shun the experience of Nagasaki and Hiroshima as being without interest or importance.

TOKYO DISTRICT COURT, DECEMBER 7, 1963*

PUBLIC INTERNATIONAL LAW—ATOMIC BOMBING OF HIROSHIMA AND NAGASAKI WAS AN ILLEGAL ACT IN VIOLATION OF INTERNATIONAL LAW.

PUBLIC INTERNATIONAL LAW—CUSTOMARY INTERNATIONAL LAW AS WELL AS POSITIVE INTERNATIONAL LAW (TREATIES) IS PART OF THE MUNICIPAL LAW OF JAPAN, AND VIOLATION GIVES INDIVIDUAL CLAIM FOR REDRESS UNDER MUNICIPAL LAW.

TREATIES—WAIVER OF MUNICIPAL LAW CLAIMS OF ATOMIC BOMB VICTIMS UNDER ARTICLE 19 (a) OF THE TREATY OF PEACE WAS NOT AN ILLEGAL ACT OF STATE UNDER ARTICLE 1 OF THE STATE COMPENSATION LAW.

DESIGNATION OF CASE:

Decision of the Tokyo District Court, December 7, 1963, Case No. 2,914 (wa) of 1955 and Case No. 4,177 (wa) of 1957.

PLAINTIFFS:

R. Shimoda (Ryuichi Shimoda), No. 945 Nakahiro-Machi, Hiroshima, and four others, represented by T. Kato (Takahisa Kato), Y. Matsui (Yasuhiro Matsui), K. Morikawa (Kinju Morikawa), K. Mizuta (Kenichi Mizuta), S. Furuno (Shuzo Furuno), T. Suzuki (Toru Suzuki), H. Ashida (Hiroshi Ashida), M. Ono (Masao Ono), and S. Shinagawa (Sumio Shinagawa), attorneys-at-law.

DEFENDANT:

The State (Japanese Government), represented by O. Kaya (Okinori Kaya), Minister of Justice, and H. Usami (Hatsuo Usami) and N. Minami (Noboru Minami), attorneys-at-law.

JUDGMENT:

1. The claims of the plaintiffs are dismissed on the merits.
2. The costs of litigation shall be borne by the plaintiffs.

FACTS:

I. Claims of the plaintiffs.

The plaintiffs seek the following judgment and declaration of provisiona

---

* 355 Hanrei Jiho [Decisions Bulletin] 17. Footnotes are added by the translator.

execution:

1. The defendant State shall pay R. Shimoda (Ryuichi Shimoda), plaintiff, 300,000 yen and interest thereon at the rate of 5% per annum from May 24, 1955, until paid in full.

2. The defendant State shall pay M. Tada (Maki Tada), plaintiff, 200,000 yen and interest thereon at the rate of 5% per annum from May 24, 1955, until paid in full.

3. The defendant State shall pay S. Hamabe (Suji Hamabe), plaintiff, 200,000 yen and interest thereon at the rate of 5% per annum from May 24, 1955, until paid in full.

4. The defendant State shall pay B. Iwabuchi (Bunji Iwabuchi), plaintiff, 200,000 yen and interest thereon at the rate of 5% per annum from May 25, 1955, until paid in full.

5. The defendant State shall pay T. Kawashima (Tochiko Kawashima), plaintiff, 200,000 yen and interest thereon at rate of 5% per annum from May 25, 1955, until paid in full.

6. The costs of litigation shall be borne by the plaintiffs.

II. Claim of the defendant State.

The defendant State seeks the judgment to the same effect as in the text of Judgment above.

III. Cause of the plaintiffs' claims.

1. Atomic bombing and its effect.

(1) Around 8:15 a.m. on August 6, 1945, a B-29 bomber piloted by Colonel Tibbetts, U.S. Army Air Forces, dropped a bomb called a uranium bomb on the City of Hiroshima under the orders of U.S. President H. S. Truman. The uranium bomb exploded in the air. A furious bomb-shell blast with a streak of strong flash followed, and buildings in Hiroshima collapsed with crash. The city was blacked out by a cloud of dust caused by the blast, and was everywhere enveloped in raging flames. All mortals including pregnant women and babies at the breasts of their mothers who were within a radius of some four kilometers of the epicenter, were killed in an instant. Also, in other areas people were horribly wounded on their bodies, owing to the special power of injury of the explosion; or they were flooded with radial rays and suffered from atomic bomb injuries, although they were not scarred on their bodies. And there is still no end to consequential deaths even today, ten and several years after.

(2)   Around 11:02 a.m. on August 9, 1945, three days after the aeria
bombardment of Hiroshima, another B-29 bomber piloted by Major Sweeney
U.S. Army Air Forces, dropped a bomb called plutonium bomb on the City o
Nagasaki. The plutonium bomb exploded in the air into a fire-ball of some
70 meters in diameter. The next instant, the fire-ball expanded quickly, struck
the earth, and turned into white smoke while changing all things on the earth
into radioactive things. Consequently, also in Nagasaki, the same destruction
and extremely cruel casualty to innocent people occurred as in Hiroshima.

(3)   Neither the existence nor the name of the uranium bomb which was
dropped on Hiroshima, or of the plutonium bomb dropped on Nagasaki, were
known to mankind that day; but they were later called atomic bombs, and were
to put the people of the world into deep fear. The atomic bomb discharges energy
generated from the nuclear fission of the uranium atom and the plutonium
atom, and energy generated from the chain reaction of the nuclear fission in
the shape of light, heat, radial rays, pressure from bomb explosion, etc. The
bomb not only has a destructive power beyond the imagination of mankind
both in quantity and in quality, but also by thermo-radiant ray sets fire to
things not directly destroyed, and gives people burns by flash (different from
burns by flame). The bomb inevitably results in indiscriminate casualties
over some four kilometers in radius from the epicenter, destroys buildings by
bomb-shell blast, and further gives rise to atomic bomb injuries by radial rays
and causes people to die gradually.

(4)   Among the casualties of the atomic bombs dropped on Hiroshima and
Nagasaki, the number of killed and wounded is shown in Exhibit I below.*
Numbers, however, fail to describe the disastrous scene after the atomic bombing. People in rags of hanging skin wandered about and lamented aloud among
dead bodies. It was an extremely sad sight beyond the description of a burning
hell, and beyond all imagination of anything heretofore known in human history. Thus, the effect of injury of the atomic bomb is remarkably great in
comparison with the highly efficient bombs of the past, and besides the atomic
bomb gives excessively unnecessary pain. Moreover, it is inevitable that atomic
bombing results in indiscriminate bombardment. Therefore, use of the atomic
bomb is an extremely cruel means of injuring the enemy.

2.   International law aspects.

The dropping of the atomic bomb was a hostile act taken by the United
States, which was then in a state of war with Japan, and was an illegal act
of hostility contrary to the positive international law of that day (treaties and
customary laws).

(1) (a)   By the St. Petersburg Declaration (December 11, 1868), the
parties agreed upon the following matters: The crisis of war must be limited
as much as possible with the advance of civilization.   The one just objective
of war is to weaken the enemy's military force, and in order to accomplish
his objective, as many people as possible must be placed out of battle.   The
use of a weapon designed to increase the pain of people placed out of battle,
or to bring about their death, is beyond the limits of the above objective of
war and contrary to humanity.   Therefore, in case of war, the contracting
parties promise to renounce the freedom of use by land forces or sea forces
of explosives and combustive projectiles under 400 grammes.

(b)   The Hague Regulations respecting the Laws and Customs of War
on Land, 1899, which are a code pertaining to the general law of war on land,
mention in article 22 the use of poison or poisonous weapons, and the use of
such weapons, projectiles, and other materials causing unnecessary pain as
matters especially prohibited.   The same Regulations prohibit in article 25
attack and bombardment on undefended cities, and provide for the necessity
of previous notice in case of bombardment (article 26) and the limitation of
the objective of attack to military objectives (article 27).

(c)   The same conclusion is also drawn from the interpretation of the
Declaration (1907) prohibiting the use of special projectiles (dum-dum bullets
by popular name), which was adopted at the Second Hague Conference, and
the Protocol (1925) respecting the prohibition of poison gas, etc., which was
adopted in Geneva.

(d)   Article 22 of the Draft Rules of Air Warfare, 1923, prohibits aerial
bombardment for the purpose of terrorizing the civilian population, destroying
private property not of military character, or injuring non-combatants.   The
same Draft Rules provide in article 24 that aerial bombardment is legitimate
only when directed at a military objective (paragraphs 1 and 2); that the
bombardment of cities, towns, villages, dwellings, or buildings not in the immediate neighborhood of operations of land forces is prohibited (paragraph 3);
that in cases where bombardment cannot be made without the indiscriminate
bombardment of the civilian population, bombardment must be abstained (paragraph 3); that in the immediate neighborhood of the operations of land forces,
bombardment is legitimate only where the military concentration is sufficiently
important to justify such bombardment, having regard to the danger caused
to the civilian population (paragraph 4); and that a belligerent State is liable
to pay compensation for injuries to person and property caused by violation
of the provisions of this article (paragraph 5).   The Draft Rules of Air War-

fare are not positive law, but we can recognize the effect of their content as a logical international law or a customary international law. The Conventio: on the Prevention and Punishment of Genocide was adopted by the Unite Nations General Assembly in 1948. The contents of this convention, whic] was adopted after the atomic bombing in question, existed as a logical inter national law of mankind before the dropping of the atomic bomb; and the were nothing but what was later stipulated.

(e)   The above international laws respecting acts of hostility naturall: apply to atomic bombing as positive international law of that day. Althoug] the atomic bomb is a new weapon, and it is difficult contextually to apply th above international laws directly or mutatis mutandis to the atomic bomb, w should apply the proper clauses directly or mutatis mutandis to the atomi bomb true to the spirit of legislation of the whole text, including the clause concerned; and we should not take the view that each of the above internationa laws does not apply or has become invalid by reason of change of circumstance by the appearance of the atomic bomb. Even if the above positive internationa laws do not apply directly or mutatis mutandis, their spirit must be said t have the effect of natural law or logical international law.

(2)   (a)   It was previously stated that the tremendous power of destruc tion of the atomic bombs dropped on Hiroshima and Nagasaki resulted i indiscriminate casualties without distinguishing between combatant and non combatant within a radius of some four kilometers of the epicenter. Thi effect of the atomic bomb was a well-known fact among persons who had hand in the research and production of the atomic bomb in the United States, in cluding President Truman. Further, the Hiroshima and Nagasaki of that da were not centers of war potential of Japan; and they were neither importan military bases nor so-called defended places against occupation. Therefore, th acts of atomic bombing Hiroshima and Nagasaki were so-called indiscriminat bombardments. The acts were clearly contrary to the express provisions o articles 25, 26 and 27 of the Hague Regulations respecting the Laws an Customs of War on Land, and to articles 22 and 24 of the Draft Rules o: Air Warfare.

(b)   The severity and cruelty of the pain caused to the human body b the power of injury of the atomic bomb, is more tremendous than that o: poison or poisonous weapons which are prohibited by article 26 of the Hagu Regulations respecting the Laws and Customs of War on Land; and the ac of use of the atomic bomb is necessarily illegal from the interpretation of th Declaration prohibiting dum-dum bullets and the Protocol respecting the pro ibition of poison gas, etc.

(c) Japan of that day had no atomic bomb, of course. It is a matter of general anticipation that the defeat of Japan was inevitable, and the defeat was regarded as a matter of time. Therefore, the atomic bombs were not dropped for the purpose of crushing the war potential of Japan, but as a terrorizing measure intended to make officials and people of Japan lose their fighting spirit. Nor were they dropped as a measure of defense of the United States, or for retaliation. Such is clear from the fact that a committee on the social and political meaning of atomic power, which was composed of seven scientists including Professor James Frank as chairman, recommended against the atomic bombing of Japan and so informed the Secretary of the Army. At the same time, 64 scientists who participated in the research and production of the atomic bomb presented a petition to the President to the same effect of the report of the above committee. The report and the petition, however, were disregarded; and the atomic bomb was dropped without notice on Hiroshima and Nagasaki.

(3) The defendant State alleges that it is difficult to form an immediate conclusion on the question whether the atomic bombing was contrary to international law, and as a reason alleges that no positive international law existed on the use of the atomic bomb, and that the illegality of the atomic bomb cannot be deduced from the interpretation of treaties like the Hague Regulations respecting the Laws and Customs of War on Land. However, since logical interpretation is admitted as a general principle of interpretation of international law, the allegation of the defendant State is without reason. The Japanese Government presented a letter of protest as stated in Exhibit III*** below, to the Government of the United States through the Government of Switzerland on August 10, 1945. The defendant State says that its present view results from objective considerations apart from the standpoint of a belligerent, but does it follow that the Japanese Government of that day did not make a proper interpretation of international law? The plaintiffs rather deem it even an honor as Japanese people that the Japanese Government made a great protest of the century after grasping the gist of the international law concerned in such a short time. Further, the defendant State seems to have the view that any measure except those definitely prohibited can be used in war until the enemy surrenders. This view is, however, that of a Merchant of Death, or a Politician of Death, and it is highly regrettable.

3. Municipal law aspects.

An act of atomic bombing is contrary to international law, as stated above, and it is contrary to municipal law at the same time.

(1)   That all homicides are illegal acts, is a universal principle of mar
kind, which is adopted in the law of every country. However, where homicid
is committed as an act of hostility, only where it is regarded as a legal ac
of hostility in international law may it be justified and excused in municipa
law. It cannot be said that all acts to which international law applies ar
governed only by international law, and that the application of municipa
law to such acts is never allowed. Since the act of atomic bombing is contrar
to international law, and is not justified, it therefore constitutes an illegal ac
in municipal law.

(2)   In the present case, those who assume responsibility for the illega
act are the United States and President Truman, who ordered the dropping c
the atomic bomb, but in order to claim damages against them a suit must b
filed in the district court of the United States. The *lex causae* applied in thi
case is decided by the conflict of laws of the United States, but there is n
doubt that in the case of an illegal act, the *lex causae* is the law of the plac
of the illegal act and where that place lies over two countries, the law of th
place of the result of the illegal act applies. Therefore, the *lex causae* in th
present case is the law of Japan, the place of the result of the illegal act. Ac
cording to the Japanese law of that day, it is clear that the State assume
responsibility for illegal acts performed by a member of the state organ, an
that the member himself was not excused from liability.

(3)   The defendant State tries to exclude the act of atomic bombin
from the object of judicial review, by broaching the theory of Act of Stat
(acte de gouvernement). Indeed, such an act as proclamation of war may b
an Act of State, but there is no reason why an individual act of hostility :
an Act of State. The so-called theory of Act of State is that, in case of co
flict between the Act of State and fundamental human rights, judicial revie
does not intervene in the conflict; and this is clear from the historical develo
ment of the theory.

(4)   Further, the defendant State broaches the old-fashioned theory c
Immunity of the Crown in English law, but it is sufficiently clear in th
Declaration of Independence of the United States that the United States di
not adopt the theory. Even if there is room for applying the theory, the a
plication must be subject to reasonable restriction; and it goes without sayin
that such exemption theory cannot apply to the use of atomic bombs, whic
people agree can evaporate the earth and ruin mankind. This suit must sta
off with calm, exact, and serious recognition of the horrible power of destructio

f the atomic bomb.

4. Claims for damages to sufferers.

(1) As stated above, the acts of atomic bombing by the United States
vere contrary to international law; and with regard to such acts, not only the
defendant State but also the injured individuals may claim damages in international law, both as the subject of rights in international law. Article 19
(a) of the Treaty of Peace with Japan (hereinafter referred to as the Japanese Peace Treaty), which provides that: "Japan waives all claims of Japan
nd its nationals against the Allied Powers and their nationals arising out of
he war or out of actions taken because of the existence of a state of war,"
learly assumes the existence of Japanese individuals' claims against the Allied
Powers (against the United States in the present case).

(2) The defendant State alleges that the plaintiffs' claims are abstract
nd theoretical, and are not rights since they have no means of realization.
f the view of the defendant State is recognized, international law in time of
ar will be denied generally. The logical extension of the defendant State's
iew is that, even if a country uses a weapon which is strictly prohibited,
he country is excused from a charge of illegality in case of victory; that, even
 it observes international law, a defeated country cannot charge the other
ountry's illegality; and that therefore, a country may use a prohibited weapon
 order to win a war. The defendant State's theory that a right which cannot
e exercised is not a right, is nothing but dogmatism. The rights of the plain-
ffs are exercised by the Government of Japan; and it is enough if the gov-
rnment of their own country can exercise their rights, since a democratic
ountry exists for its people. We must say that the theory that the rights of
eople in international law must depend on whether or not the government
 their own country exercises their rights for them, is a poor theory.

(3) Further, the defendant State alleges that the plaintiffs' claims do
ot exist; that their claims in international law did not exist even before the
nclusion of the peace treaty; and that there is no example in history where
 claim for damages by the sufferers of the defeated country was realized.
ghts, however, are always abstract in substance; their existence is confirmed
 the application of a country's norm of law or norm of international law.
he realization of a right is influenced by various relations of power such as
ilitary power or economic power, but the existence of a right itself is not
fluenced by them.

5. Waiver of claims in accordance with the Japanese Peace Treaty.

(1) Article 19 (a) of the Japanese Peace Treaty provides that: "Japan

waives all claims of Japan and its nationals against the Allied Powers and their nationals arising out of the war or out of actions taken because of the existence of a state of war." Japan has waived the claims in municipal law as well as the claims in international law against the United States and President Truman. Consequently, the plaintiffs legally have completely lost the claims for damages against the United States and President Truman.

(2)   The defendant State alleges that it cannot waive the claims of its nationals since the State of Japan is different from the nationals of Japan in personality. Even if there is logical room for such a point of view, the plaintiff's claims for damages will not be permitted by article 19 (a) of the Japanese Peace Treaty, since a treaty has the full force of law in the United States. Further, for the above reason, if the plaintiffs file a suit in the United States, they cannot easily obtain the cooperation of lawyers or the support of public opinion of the United States. It is even extremely difficult to find cooperators in Japan. Therefore, the plaintiffs' instituting a suit is almost impossible actually, and we may safely say that the plaintiffs have lost their claims.

6.   Responsibility of the defendant State for the waiver of claims.

(1)   In every democratic country, the government has the obligation to respect the rights of the people to the maximum. The defendant State illegally concluded the Japanese Peace Treaty and waived the plaintiffs' claims for damages against the United States and President Truman in accordance with article 19 (a) of the Peace Treaty; and we may safely say that the conclusion of a treaty is an exercise of public power. Therefore, the defendant State assumed the responsibility to compensate the damage suffered, in accordance with article 1 of the State Compensation Law,[1] to the plaintiffs who lost their claims by the defendant's illegal act and suffered damage.

(2)   Also, in the negotiations for conclusion of the Peace Treaty, the claims for damages by the atomic bombing must have been evaluated high, and such claims should be understood to have been appropriated to part of Japanese compensation in restitution of the United States. Japan must have profited in other aspects of the Peace Treaty by waiving the claims. Even if there were no express diplomatic negotiations, the conscience of the United States

---

1 *Kokka Baisho Ho*, Law No. 125 of October 27, 1947. "Article 1. (1) If an official or servant of the state or a public body intentionally or negligently commits an unlawful act and injures another in the course of performing his duties, the state or the public body is liable to make compensation therefor. (2) In the case of the preceding paragraph, if there has been intent or gross negligence, the state or the public body may claim compensation from the official or servant involved."

nd the people of the world necessarily inserted the claims in the balance sheet f the Peace Treaty, and with this expectation the defendant State intentionally vaived the claims. Therefore, by waiving the plaintiffs' claims for damages gainst the United States and President Truman, the defendant State should e regarded as having appropriated private properties of the plaintiffs for ublic use; and the defendant State is obliged to pay just compensation to the laintiffs in accordance with article 29 of the Japanese Constitution.[2]

(3) Assuming that claims for damages do not directly arise in accordance vith the above provision of the Constitution, and that the plaintiffs have no pecial claims for damages by reason of legal measures on compensation, the laintiffs have claims for damages of the same content against the defendant. n spite of waiver of the plaintiffs' claims for damages without compensation y the conclusion of the Japanese Peace Treaty, the defendant State has not aken any measure of compensation and therefore infringes on the rights of he plaintiffs. Therefore, it goes without saying that since this constitutes an llegal act, the defendant State assumes responsibility for paying damages to he plaintiffs.

(4) The defendant State alleges that even if the claims were waived by rticle 19 of the Japanese Peace Treaty, the plaintiffs have no claims for lamages against the defendant State. As reasons, the defendant State mentions hat the plaintiffs' claims are not legal questions and are abstract questions, hat the claims were destined to be necessarily waived by the defeated country n conclusion of the Peace Treaty, that they do not qualify as a property right nder the Constitution, and that article 29 of the Constitution does not directly rovide for claims for compensation against the state but only provide that oncrete measures of compensation shall be made by laws and regulations on xpropriation. However, with regard to the existence of the claims, what the efendant State alleges is only the relations of various powers, and the existence f the claims themselves is not influenced by them. It is also wrong to say hat the claims for compensation do not arise unless concrete, legal measures re taken as to compensation. For, the purpose of inviolable property right an be attained by inseparably providing for use or expropriation and the neasure of compensation before the actual use or expropriation is made. In he case of article 19(a) of the Japanese Peace Treaty, there was no room for nacting the law on expropriation, since the property of Japanese nationals was

---

Nihon Koku Kempo, November 3, 1947. "Article 29. (1) The right to own or to hold property is inviolable. (2) Property rights shall be defined by law, in conformity with the public welfare. (3) Private property may be taken for public use upon just compensation therefor."

appropriated and expropriated as indemnification for damage to the United States simultaneously with the conclusion of the Peace Treaty. Thus, if the defendant State can deny compensation by reason of lack of a law pertaining to compensation, while it takes unilaterally people's private property for public use, that is no better than confiscation and is far from the respect of human rights which is a fundamental idea of the Japanese Constitution.

(5) Further, the defendant State alleges that the way of consolation of sufferers of the atomic bombing must be determined by taking into consideration the financial conditions of the State as well as the consolation to other general war victims, and that since the question whether a measure for consolation should be taken in legislation and in finance is not a legal question but a political question, the defendant State has no obligation for compensation or indemnification to the plaintiffs at the present time when such measures have not been taken in legislation. As stated above, however, the claim for damages in this case is based on the municipal laws of Japan and the United States, and on international law; and it is not a political question.

The plaintiffs desire that the Japanese Government take proper measures promptly in legislation and finance, but such measures should be taken after strict confirmation of the claims of the sufferers against the defendant State and that they are different from groundless relief. In view of the fact that the damage caused by the atomic bomb is the cruelest damage, as some people say treason to mankind, compensation or indemnification for damage should be placed in the first consideration; and that is not impossible in the present financial conditions of the defendant State.

7. Damage of the plaintiffs.

(1) The plaintiff, Ryuichi Shimoda was a healthy man, 47 years old when the atomic bomb was dropped on Hiroshima. He lived with his family at No. 945, Nakahiro-machi, Hiroshima, and ran a small factory. His eldest daughter, Reiko (16 years old then), his third son, Kiyoshi (12 years old then), his second daughter, Yuriko (10 years old then), his third daughter, Kazue (7 years old then) and his fourth daughter, Toshiko (4 years old then) were killed by the atomic bomb. The plaintiff, his wife, Hina (40 years old then) and his fourth son, Katsuji (2 years old then) were injured by bomb-shell blast, heat ray, and radial rays. The plaintiff now has keloid in the right upper arm which is functionally disordered, and he also has keloid over the abdominal region and the left back which suppurates in the mild season of every spring. Also, he has physical handicap in the kidney and liver, and he cannot find employment at the present time. His wife, Hina, is suffering from

a feeling of languor in the whole body, a feeling of adynamia, and headaches. There sometimes appear symptoms of potential atomic bomb injury to his fourth son, Katsuji. On account of this situation, the family has no income and they barely live by the help of a little money and a few things sent monthly by the plaintiff's elder sister in Honolulu, Hawaii, the United States.

(2) The plaintiff, Maki Tada, resided at No. 2-262, Minami-machi, Hiroshima, when the atomic bomb was dropped, and lived a healthy and happy life with her husband who was an employee of Hiroshima Dentetsu Kabushiki Kaisha (Hiroshima Electric Railway Inc.). She was injured on the face, shoulders, chest and feet, and keloid is left in them. She has pains in her body even at the present time, and cannot continue working at daily wages. As her husband left home, disliking her disfigured looks, and has been missing ever since, she lives a miserable life with the help of government livelihood assistance.

(3) The plaintiff, Suji Hamabe, 54 years old when the atomic bomb was dropped on Nagasaki, lived alone from about May, 1944 at No. 54, Shirogane Saru-machi, Shiba, Tokyo, and worked at the head office of Mitsubishi Jukogyo Kabushiki Kaisha (Mitsubishi Heavy Industry Inc.), separated from his family who lived at No. 1-14, Shiroyama-machi, Nagasaki. However, the result was most tragic in human life in that all his family, his wife, Hana (48 years old then), his second daughter, Taeko (22 years old then), his third daughter, Noriko (19 years old then), his fourth daughter, Ryoko (16 years old then) and his fifth daughter, Tsuneko (14 years old then), were all killed by the atomic bomb, and that he alone survived.

(4) The plaintiff, Bunji Iwabuchi, resided with his family at No. 145, Nobori-cho, Hiroshima, but he and his wife, Fujino, were running a manufacturing industry of oil from root of pine at Yuno-mura, Saba-gun, Yamaguchi Prefecture when the atomic bomb was dropped on Hiroshima. Consequently, his adopted daughter, Toyoko (24 years old then), her husband, Kazutaka (26 years old then), and their first son, Kuniaki (1 year old then) were killed by the atomic bomb. The plaintiff and his wife, Fujino, alone survived and live the rest of their hopeless life at their relative's house which is located at their address.

(5) The plaintiff, Tochiko Kawashima, was 14 years old when the atomic bomb was dropped on Hiroshima. She lived a healthy life with her parents, brothers, and sisters at 2-chome, Minami-machi, Hiroshima. She was injured in the face and the left arm owing to the collapse of her house by bomb-shell blast, and scars still remains. Her father, Ototsuchi (50 years old then), who

worked at the Public Food Corporation at Hatchobori, Hiroshima, and her mother, Kimiyo (40 years old then), who served at the neighborhood association were injured by bomb-shell blast, heat rays, and radial rays. After medical treatment in a hospital in vain, her mother died on July 8, 1946, and following his wife her father died on the 20th of November in the same year. The young bereaved family including the plaintiff, who lost their parents, sold all their clothes and other personal effects for food and became unable to make a living. Consequently, they are now living such a sad life that the sisters are forced to live separately with relatives, and the plaintiff's younger sister Choko, has been adopted into a relative's family.

8. Claims for damages.

(1) The plaintiff, Ryuichi Shimoda, here claims against the defendant State the payment of 300,000 yen and interest thereon at the rate of 5% per annum from May 24, 1955, the day following service of process in this suit, until paid in full, as solatium for the extremely sorrowful, mental pain suffered by the death of a son and four daughters resulting from the bombing, and for property damage and mental pain resulting from injuries to the plaintiff himself.

(2) The plaintiff, Maki Tada, claims the payment of 200,000 yen and interest as in the previous paragraph, as solatium for property damage and indescribable agony resulting from injury.

(3) The plaintiff, Suji Hamabe, claims the payment of 200,000 yen and interest as in the paragraph (1), as solatium for the extremely sorrowful, mental pain suffered by the death of his wife and four children from the bombing.

(4) The plaintiff, Bunji Iwabuchi, claims the payment of 200,000 yen and interest thereon at the rate of 5% per annum from May 25, 1955, the day following service of process in this suit, until paid in full, as solatium for the extremely sorrowful, mental pain suffered by the death of his family members from the bombing.

(5) The plaintiff, Tochiko Kawashima, claims the payment of 200,000 yen and interest as in the previous paragraph, as solatium for property damage and agony resulting from injury and mental pain resulting from the death of her parents.

IV. Defendant State's answer.

1. The atomic bombing and its effect.

The defendant State admits the fact, as the plaintiffs allege, that so-called

tomic bombs were dropped on Hiroshima and Nagasaki by bombers of the
.S. Army Air Forces, and that a large number of people were killled by the
xplosion of the atomic bombs. However, the number of the killed and wounded
xclusive of the military personnel was as shown in Exhibit II below,** accord-
1g to the investigation of May, 1948 made by the Economic Stabilization Board.

2. International law aspects.

It is difficult to conclude that atomic bombing is necessarily contrary to
iternational law.

(1) Atomic weapons as a means of injuring the enemy, by harnessing
nergy from nuclear fission, were invented in the latter half of World War II;
nd they were generally unknown to mankind until used at Hiroshima and
Tagasaki. Accordingly, since there was neither a treaty prohibiting or per-
nitting the use of atomic weapons to injure the enemy, nor an international
1stomary law pertaining to such new weapons at that time, we should say
1at positive international law respecting atomic weapons did not exist; and
1erefore the question of violation of positive international law cannot arise.
ince the Hague Regulations respecting the Laws and Customs of War on
.and, and other treaties as mentioned by the plaintiffs, do not originally make
1e atomic bomb their object, we cannot put an expansive construction on
1eir intent. Further, since neither the Draft Rules of Air Warfare nor the
reaty respecting Prevention and Punishment of Genocide, was concluded as
treaty at the time when the atomic bombs were dropped, we cannot recog-
ize such treaties as positive law and cannot make them the source of inter-
ational law.

(2) Therefore, the question whether atomic bombing is contrary to inter-
ational law should be decided in the light of legal principles of international
w in time of war. From the viewpoint of international law, war is originally
1e condition in which a country is allowed to exercise all means deemed neces-
iry to cause the enemy to surrender, in other words, to force the enemy to
cept the condition proposed by the adversary and to determine to sue for
2ace. The first consideration is to crush the military force of the enemy.
owever, to destroy the enemy's economic power as a means of continuing
1ttle, and to foster defeatism among the people of the enemy can also effec-
vely hasten the surrender of the enemy; and necessary means may be ex-
cised to attain these purposes. Since the Middle Ages, belligerents, in
.ternational law, have been permitted to choose the means of injuring the
1emy in order to attain the special purpose of war, subject to certain con-
tions imposed by international customary law and treaties adapted to the

times.

The atomic bombs dropped on Hiroshima and Nagasaki were exceeding enormous in destructive power, and the damage was heaviest in history. is truly a matter of deep regret that a large number of non-combatant Japanes people were killed and wounded as a consequence. However, with the atom bombing of Hiroshima and Nagasaki, as a direct result, Japan ceased furth resistance and accepted the Potsdam Declaration. Thus, the purpose of Jap nese unconditional surrender was attained as the Allied Powers intended; an World War II came to an end. Thus, the use of atomic bombs hastened th Japanese surrender, and resulted in the prevention of casualties of human li of both belligerents which would be caused by the continuance of war. Ta ing an objective view of these circumstances, no one can easily conclude wheth the atomic bombing of Hiroshima and Nagasaki was contrary to internation law. Also, since no international agreement prohibiting the use of nucle weapons had been concluded yet, we think that we cannot decide readily o the propriety of the use of an atomic bomb as a means of injuring the enem in time of war.

(3) The Japanese Government issued, on August 10, 1945, through th Government of Switzerland, an official note in which it strongly demanded th the Government of the United States stop the use of atomic weapons instantl The content of the official note is as alleged by the plaintiffs. Such note wa however, the assertion as a belligerent that the use of a new-type bomb contrary to principles of international law and to the fundamental principl of humanity, but taking an objective view, apart from the position of a be ligerent, we cannot necessarily draw the same conclusion today.

3. Municipal law aspects.

The act of atomic bombing may be covered by international law, but not covered by municipal law by nature.

(1) War is a means of settling disputes of interest between sovereig states, and a state conducts a war for the benefit of the state itself and th people. Therefore, the legality of individual acts which compose such a wa should be treated exclusively by international law, and responsibility for ac deemed illegal should be solved by agreement between the countries concerne A country does not assume responsibility of compensation for damage resul ing from illegal acts directly inflicted on the people of the other country, i accordance with municipal law.

(2) In the municipal law of the United States, it is understood as limit of judicial power that the court shall deny judicial review of the exerci

f important political power and entrust the matter to the judgment of the
xecutive branch. The use of the atomic bomb by Truman, President of the
nited States, was aimed at the military and political effect of the atomic bomb
s a means of winning the war, and this is excluded from a judgment of
legality by a court. This necessarily results from the theory called Act
f State.

(3) Assuming that the municipal law of the United States applies to the
ct of atomic bombing, there was at the time a legal principle of State Im-
unity in the United States, which resembles the principle of Legal Immunity
f the Crown in English law. If a public servant of the federal government
r of a state government commits a tort in the performance of official duties,
e victim may not claim damages against the federal government, the state
overnment, or the public servant.

(4) As alleged by the plaintiffs, it is not possible to establish a tort
nder Japanese law by applying the conflict of law rules of the United States.
iewed in the light of the conflict of laws, in principle a country denies the
pplication of a foreign law if the application is contrary to the interest of
e country. However, since the state and its public servants do not assume
esponsibility under the laws of the United States, the *lex fori*, in principle
e *lex fori* applies cumulatively to that extent.

4. The sufferers' claims for damages.

The plaintiffs' claims for damages against the United States must be
enied, since it is difficult to say that atomic bombing is contrary to international
w. Even if the premise of the plaintiffs is recognized, however, it does not
llow that the plaintiffs have claims for damages.

(1) It is the United States which must compensate the damage resulting
om the atomic bombing, but it is the State of Japan and not the individual
aintiffs who are qualified to claim damages against the United States. The
asons are that individuals cannot be the subject of rights in international law,
d that, although there are some cases where individuals are the subject of
ternational law as expounded by some doctrines, they are limited to the case
here there is a provision to that effect in a treaty or other international law,
where the right of access to the International Court of Justice is granted
e individual. Accordingly, at the present time, when there is not such a
ovision in general international law respecting war, and when no individual
granted the right of access to the International Court of Justice, there is
reason why the claims for damages as a right in international law arise
the plaintiffs. In case of such a violation of international law, the country

to which the sufferers belong exercises the claim for damages against the country which caused damage. The claim in this case is not exercised by the country on behalf of the individual sufferers, but exercised by the country itself as its own right. If the country receives compensation as the result of exercising the claims, the distribution of compensation to the sufferers, and the amount of distribution, are decided by the country independently by its own authority.

(2) Even if the claims for damages were acquired by the plaintiffs for some reason, the claims must be abstract ones which have no possibility of realization. Since a plaintiff's claim is in international law, it should be realized by diplomatic negotiations first, and if the negotiations fail, it should be realized by access to the International Court of Justice. We must say, however, that since an individual citizen has no authority for diplomatic negotiations or the right of access to the International Court of Justice, he has no means or possibility to realize the claim as a right. Therefore, even if he has such a right, it does not come to an actual issue until the other country recognizes the right in a peace treaty and a concrete agreement is made. It is rather a right originating in the peace treaty itself, and it is outside the question of law as long as a concrete agreement is not made. Furthermore, there is no example in history where a defeated country has claimed against a victor country, compensation for damage resulting from acts of violation of international law by the latter, and where the claim has been realized. It is long-standing international custom that, even the victor country only claims compensation of a certain amount of money, or of certain utilities and construction services in accordance with the peace treaty. Therefore, we must say that even if the claims as alleged by the plaintiffs existed, they were destined to be necessarily extinguished with the conclusion of the Peace Treaty.

5. Waiver of the claims in accordance with the Japanese Peace Treaty.

It does not follow that Japan waived its individual citizens' claims for damages against the United States and President Truman in accordance with the provisions of article 19(a) of the Japanese Peace Treaty.

(1) It is the right of a state to negotiate with foreign countries on the basis of its individual citizens' claims for damages in international law, and there is no doubt that a state can waive this right by agreement with foreign countries. However, since an individual citizen's right to claim damages directly against a foreign country independently without the medium of his home government is different from the right of the state, it is not directly influenced by whatever agreement the state concludes with foreign countries by

reaty.

(2)   Therefore, it should be understood that the "claims of Japanese nationals" provided for in article 19(a) of the Japanese Peace Treaty only means claims for damages by the State of Japan on the basis of the nationals' own claims, that is, the so-called right of diplomatic protection. Japan can agree with another country that it will take necessary legislative and executive measures to prohibit its nationals from exercising their claims against the Allied Powers and their nationals. However, since the extinction clauses of claims and the compensation clauses substituted for the former as provided for in the peace treaty with Italy and five other countries are not provided for in the Japanese Peace Treaty, we cannot say that even such individual citizens' claims were waived. Even if article 19(a) of the Japanese Peace Treaty can be interpreted to have the intent to include the above individual citizens' claims, it amounts to no more than a statement that Japan waived what could not be waived, and the citizens' own claims are not extinguished by the statement. Therefore, if the plaintiffs had claims, it does not follow that the plaintiffs had rights infringed, since the claims were not waived in accordance with the Japanese Peace Treaty.

6.   The defendant State's responsibility for the waiver of claims.

(1)   The defendant State has no obligation for assuming responsibility for damages in accordance with the State Compensation Law. Since plaintiffs' claims were not worthy of a right by nature, and were destined to be waived by the defeated country on the conclusion of the Peace Treaty, the conclusion of the Japanese Peace Treaty did not result in the infringement of rights. Also, even if the contents of the Peace Treaty are out of keeping with the system of municipal law, the treaty itself cannot be regarded illegal. If a defeated country cannot conclude a peace treaty, because the peace treaty would be contrary to the prohibition clause of the constitution of the defeated country, or because legal procedures in the consitition cannot be taken, a defeated country could never conclude peace and consequently it would be required to continue the war as long as the capacity of conduct of war remains. Therefore, with regard to a peace treaty, even if there is doubt as to constitutionality, it is considered that the courts and the other state organs must recognize it as an accomplished fact like a revolution; that the power of conclusion of a treaty in time of war is not restricted by the constitution, on the theory of emergency of the state; and that a peace treaty is supreme over various powers in the constitution in application, on the theory of superiority of international law over municipal law. In the Japanese Peace Treaty, the position of the

defeated country, Japan, is not different from the above. Since the Japanese Peace Treaty is an international agreement which Japan, who surrendered unconditionally by accepting the Potsdam Declaration, "desired by force," in order to recover its independence, we cannot hold the treaty illegal even if there are provisions affecting the people's rights guaranteed by the Japanese Constitution.

(2) Even if the plaintiffs had the claims as alleged, and the claims were waived in accordance with article 19(a) of the Japanese Peace Treaty, it does not follow that a claim for compensation by the Japanese Government arises in accordance with article 29 of the Constitution. Article 29 of the Constitution does not directly grant the people a concrete claim for compensation; and this does not become possible until a concrete provision is made by the law respecting the matter concerned, that the people have a concrete claim for compensation against the State. In other words, the Constitution only orders that, when the State uses or expropriates private properties for public interest, the State should provide concretely the measure of compensation therefor; and it does not follow that the Constitution directly grants the people a concrete claim. Therefore, if the law provides that the State can use or expropriate private properties without preparing a measure of compensation, there are some cases where the law is made null and void as unconstitutional, but the people whose property was used or expropriated may not claim compensation against the State directly in accordance with the provisions of the Constitution. Also in this case, we do not think that the plaintiffs are entitled to claim compensation directly in accordance with the Treaty or the Constitution.

(3) The defendant State is unstinting in its deep sympathy with those who felt the explosion of the atomic bombs in the late war, which mankind had never before experienced. However, the way of consolation for these people must be balanced with the consolation for other general war victims, and by taking into due consideration the actual circumstances of finance of the State, etc. Whether measures should be taken in legislature and in finance is not a legal question, but a political question. This is the same as where the State receives indemnity from another country by exercising the right of diplomatic protection, and where the State can decide independently by its authority whether it will distribute the indemnity to the sufferers and also the method of distribution. Although the matter can thus be a question of domestic policy or of legislation, it does not follow that sufferers necessarily acquire claims for compensation. Therefore, at the present time while such measures have not been taken up by the legislature, the defendant State has no obligation to compensate or indemnify the plaintiffs; and the plaintiffs cannot immediately

regard the lack of such measures as an illegal act in civil law.

7. Damage of the plaintiffs.

The circumstances of casualties of the plaintiffs and the damage suffered thereby, are unknown to us.

Evidence. (Omitted by the decision.)

REASONS:

1. Atomic bombing and its effect.

(1) There is no dispute between the parties about the following facts. Around 8:15 a.m. on August 6, 1945, a B-29 bomber piloted by Colonel Tibbetts, U.S. Army Air Forces, dropped a uranium bomb on Hiroshima under the orders of U.S. President H.S. Truman, and around 11:02 a.m. on the 9th of the same month, a B-29 bomber piloted by Major Sweeney, U.S. Army Air Forces, dropped a plutonium bomb on Nagasaki under the orders of U.S. President Truman. These bombs (hereinafter referred to as "atomic bombs") exploded in the air. A furious bomb-shell blast with a flash, and both in Hiroshima and in Nagasaki almost all buildings in the cities collapsed. Simultaneously, fire broke out everywhere; and all people who were within a radius of some four kilometers of the epicenter were killled in an instant without distinction of age or sex. A large number of people elsewhere were burned on the skin by the flash, and others, bathed with the radiant rays, suffered from so-called atomic bomb injury. The number of killed and wounded, to say the least, amounted to more than 70,000 and 50,000 respectively, in Hiroshima, and to more than 20,000 and 40,000 respectively, in Nagasaki.

(2) Then, what is the explosion of an atomic bomb? This question is made clear theoretically without any room for doubt, and there are many results of experiment, which are collectd into materials by scientists for everyone's use. We will state the principle in brief as follows, by virtue of the "Effect of Nuclear Weapon" by Samuel Glaston (published by the U.S. Atomic Energy Commission). (Handbook of *Genshiryoku, Bakudan-hen,* in Japanese translation.)

When a free neutron enters into a atomic nucleus of uranium No. 235 or plutonium No. 239, the atomic nucleus is divided in two, and at that moment a large quantity of energy is discharged. Simultaniously, discharged by the reaction of that nuclear fission, more than two neutrons enter into the next atomic nucleus of uranium No. 235 or plutonium No. 239 and cause the reaction of nuclear fission. The neutrons discharged by this second nuclear

fission cause the next reaction similarly, and if there is a large quantity o
neutrons the reaction of nuclear fission is caused one after another like a
chain. In the process, part of the neutrons discharged disperse off, or par
are lost by the reaction of atomic nucleus which is not nuclear fission. How
ever, since the loss can be diminished relatively by increasing the quantit;
of uranium No. 235 or plutonium No. 239, or by reflecting neutrons with
reflector placed around, the reaction of nuclear fission is caused one after an
other like a chain by increasing the quantity of uranium No. 235 or plutonium
No. 239 to over the critical quantity; the energy is accumulated and the ex
plosion is caused finally. The time before the explosion is caused is very
short, and the energy discharged is tremendous. If a pound of uranium No
235 or plutonium No. 239 go into full neuclear fission, energy equivalent to the
explosion of a 9,000-ton TNT bomb is produced in less than one second. The
bombs dropped on Hiroshima and Nagasaki discharge energy equivalent in
quantity to 20,000 tons of TNT bombs, but at the present time far stronger
weapons which have the energy of megaton class, appear.

(3) Next, we will state in brief the effect caused by the explosion of
atomic bombs by virtue of the above-mentioned book.

The first effect comes from the bomb-shell blast. When an atomic bomb
explodes in the air, a fire ball composed of gas of very high temperature and
very high pressure arises at once and goes up engulfing the surrounding air.
From the fire ball, a wave of air (wave from bombardment) of high temperature
and high pressure is pushed up at once, and spreads in all directions quickly.
When the wave reaches the earth, it destroys buildings and other structures
as if an earthquake or typhoon occurred. The range of the effect is very wide.
In Nagasaki, houses within 1.4 miles from the epicenter collapsed, those
within 1.6 miles suffered rather heavy damage, and even those at the point
of 1.7 miles had their roofs and walls damaged.

The second effect comes from the heat rays. When a fire ball is made
by the explosion of an atomic bomb in the air, it begins to radiate heat rays
composed of heat of high temperature and light. The heat rays include
ultraviolate rays as well as visible rays and ultrared rays. The heat rays
reach the earth at the same speed as light, set fire to inflammable things on
the earth, burn the skin, and cause man's death according to the conditions.
In Hiroshima and Nagasaki, 20% to 30% of those killed are presumed killed
by burns; and in Nagasaki burns from the heat were recorded as far as
2.5 miles from the epicenter. While the effect of an ordinary high efficient
bomb (TNT bomb) is chiefly destruction by bomb-shell blast, the atomic bomb

ingularly possesses the effect of fire and burn by heat rays, together with destruction by bomb-shell blast.

The third and most peculiar effect comes from the first stage of nuclear radial rays and residual nuclear radioactivity. The radial rays which are radiated within one minute after the explosion of an atomic bomb are composed of neutron, gamma rays, alpha particles and beta particles; and they are called the first stage of nuclear radial rays. Among them, gamma rays and neutron have a flying leg of long range, and, when striking against the human body, they destroy or injure the cells and cause atomic disease (atomic bomb injury) by injury from radial rays. Atomic disease weakens the whole human body, and causes man's death several hours or weeks later; and if he fortunately saves his life a long term is required before his recovery. Also, the radiation of the first stage of nuclear radial rays causes leukaemia, cataract, and abortion of child, has various bad influences on various organs of the human body, and causes hereditarily bad influences.

The radial rays which are radiated chiefly from splinters of the bomb one minute after the explosion, are called the residual nuclear radial rays. These splinters spread wide in the air in the form of corpuscle, cause a radioactive rainfall by sticking to water drops, and flutter down to the earth in the form of the so-called ashes of death. The effect of radial rays on the human body is almost the same as that of the first stage of nuclear radial rays.

(4) Thus, one atomic bomb, even a small-scale bomb like the bombs dropped on Hiroshima and Nagasaki, discharges energy equivalent to a 20,-000-ton TNT bomb; and the power of destruction and effect of casualty by the bomb-shell blast are so remarkable that it cannot for a moment be compared with bombs of the past. Moreover, the power of destruction by the bomb-shell blast is only a part (some 50% of the energy) of the efficiency of atomic bomb; and the effect of incendiary and of casualty by heat rays (some 5% of the energy) has singularity which is not seen in a TNT bomb. We can see the strong power in that 20% to 30% of the deaths in Hiroshima and Nagasaki are presumed to result from burns. However, what strikes us with more terror is the radial rays or radioactivity caused by the atomic bomb; and we have already experienced the terror of atomic disease, leukaemia and various other injuries to the human body, which are caused by radial rays or radioactivity.

Thus, the atomic bomb is far stronger than weapons of the past in power of destruction and casualty. Besides, it has characteristics different from all kinds of weapons of the past in that it inflicts on the human body variou kinds of pain and bad influences. We must say that the atomic bomb is really cruel weapon.

2. International law aspects.

(1) There is no doubt that, whether or not an atomic bomb having such a character and effect is a weapon which is permitted in international law a a so-called nuclear weapon, is an important and very difficult question in inter national law. In this case, however, the point at issue is whether the acts o atomic bombing of Hiroshima and Nagasaki by the United States are regarded as illegal by positive international law at that time. Therefore, it is enough to consider this point only.

(2) As a premise for judging how the above acts of atomic bombing are treated by positive international law, we will begin by considering what inter national law has existed with regard to war, especially to hostile acts among modern countries since the latter half of 19th Century.

The following are the chronological enumeration of international laws con cerning this case:

1886. St. Petersburg Declaration respecting the prohibition of the ex plosives and incendiaries under 400 grammes.

1899. Convention respecting the Laws and Customs of War on Land (CON-VENTION CONCERNANT LES LOIS ET COUTUMES DE LA GUERRE SUR TERRE), concluded at the First Hague Peace Conference; and its annex Regulations respecting the Laws and Customs of War on Land (RÈGLEMENT CONCERNANT LES LOIS ET COUTUMES DE LA GUERRE SUR TERRE) (the so-called Regulations respecting War on Land).

1899. Declaration concerning expanding bullets (the so-called Declaration prohibiting dum-dum bullets).

1899. Declaration concerning projectiles launched from balloons in the air (the so-called Declaration prohibiting aerial bombardment).

1899. Declaration concerning projectiles diffusing asphyxiating or deleteri ous gases (the so-called Declaration prohibiting poison gases).

1907. Convention respecting the Laws and Customs of War on Land (CON VENTION CONCERNANT LES LOIS ET COUTUMES DE LA GUERRE SUR TERRE), which was concluded in the Second Hague Peace Conference (the revision of the Convention of the same name in the First Hague Peace Con ference).

1907. Declaration prohibiting aerial bombardment.

1922. Treaty of Five Countries concerning submarines and poisonous gases.

1923. Draft Rules concerning Air Warfare (Draft Rules of Air Warfare).

1925. Protocol prohibiting the use in war of asphyxiating, deleterious or other gases and bacteriological methods of warfare (Protocol respecting the prohibition of poison gases, etc.).

(3) In the above-mentioned laws and regulations, there is no direct provision with regard to the atomic bomb, a new weapon which appeared during World War II.

On the ground of this fact, the defendant State alleges that the question of violation of positive international law does not arise, since there was neither international customary law nor treaty law prohibiting the use of atomic bombs at that time, and the use is not prohibited clearly by positive international law.

Of course, it is right that the use of a new weapon is legal, as long as international law does not prohibit it. However, the prohibition in this case is understood to include not only the case where there is an express provision of direct prohibition but also the case where it is necessarily regarded that the use of a new weapon is prohibited, from the interpretation and analogical application of existing international laws and regulations (international customary laws and treaties). Further, we must understand that the prohibition includes also the case where, in the light of principles of international law which are the basis of the above-mentioned positive international laws and regulations, the use of a new weapon is admitted to be contrary to the principles. For there is no reason why the interpretation of international law must be limited to grammatical interpretation, any more than in the interpretation of municipal law. See Expert Opinions of K. Yasui (Kaoru Yasui), S. Tabata (Shigejiro Tabata), and Y. Takano (Yuichi Takano).)

(4) There is also an argument that a new weapon is not an object of regulation of international law at all, but such argument has not a sufficient ground as mentioned above. It is right and proper that any weapon contrary to the custom of civilized countries and to the principles of international law, should be prohibited even if there is no express provision in the laws and regulations. Only where there is no provision in the statutory [international] law, and as long as a new weapon is not contrary to the principles of international law, can the new weapon be used as a legal means of hostility.

Against this argument, some argue as follows. Although there are always many objections in every field against the invention and use of new weapons, they are soon regarded as advanced weapons, and the prohibition of the use of such weapons becomes altogether nonsensical. With the progress of civilization, a new weapon comes to be rather an efficient means of injuring the enemy.

This is as shown in history, and the atomic bomb is not an exception.

We cannot deny that in the past, although objections were made by variou interests against the appearance of a new weapon because international la was not yet developed, or a hostile feeling was strong against the people o the enemy or pagons, or the advance of general weapons was gradual, ne weapons nevertheless came to be regarded as legal with the later advancemen of civilization and the development of scientific techniques. This, however, i not always true. This will be clear from the recollection of the existence o the above-mentioned treaties prohibiting the use of dum-dum bullets and poison ous gases. Therefore, *we cannot regard a weapon as legal only because it i a new weapon, and it is still right that a new weapon must be exposed to th examination of positive international law.*

(5) Next, we will examine the international laws and regulations con cerned at that time, with regard to the act of atomic bombing.

First of all, there arises the question whether the act of atomic bombin is admitted by the laws and regulations respecting air raids, since the act i an aerial bombardment as a hostile act by military plane.

No general treaty respecting air raids has been concluded. However according to customary law recognized generally in international law with regar to a hostile act, a defended city and an undefended city are distinguished wit regard to bombardment by land forces, and a defended place and an undefende place are distinguished with regard to bombardment by naval forces. Agains the defended city and place, indiscriminate bombardment is permitted, while i the case of an undefended city and place, bombardment is permitted only agains combatant and military installations (military objectives) and bombardmen is not permitted against non-combatant and non-military installations (non military objectives). Any contrary bombardment is necessarily regarded as a illegal act of hostility. (See Expert Opinion of Shigejiro Tabata.) This prin ciple is clear from the following provisions: Article 25 of the Hague Regulation respecting War on Land provides that "the attack or bombardment, by an means whatever, of towns, villages, habitations, or buildings, which are no defended, is prohibited." "The Convention concerning bombardment by nava forces in time of war" (CONVENTION CONCERNANT LE BOMBARDMEN PAR DES FORCES NAVALES EN TEMPS DE GUERRE), adopted at th Hague Peace Conference of 1907, provides in article 1 that "the bombardmen of undefended ports, towns, villages, dwellings, or other buildings by nava forces is prohibited . . . ," and in article 2 that "among the above-mentione objects against which bombardment is prohibited are not included militar works, military or naval establishments, depots of arms or war material, work-shops or plants which could be utilized for the needs of a hostile fleet or army, and men-of-war in the harbor . . . ."

(6) With regard to air warfare, there are "Draft Rules of Air Warfare." Article 24 of the Draft Rules provides that: "(1) Aerial bombardment is legitimate only when directed at a military objective, that is to say, an object of which the destruction or injury would constitute a distinct military advantage to the belligerent. (2) Such bombardment is legitimate only when directed exclusively at the following objectives: military forces; military works; military establishments or depots; factories constituting important and well-known centers engaged in the manufacture of arms, ammunition, or distinctively military supplies; lines of communication or transportation used for military purposes. (3) The bombardment of cities, towns, villages, dwellings, or buildings not in the immediate neighborhood of the operations of land forces is prohibited. In cases where the objectives specified in paragraph (2) are so situated that they cannot be bombarded without the indiscriminate bombardment of the civilian population, the aircraft must abstain from bombardment. (4) In the immediate neighbourhood of the operations of land forces, the bombardment of cities, towns, villages, dwellings, or buildings is legitimate, provided there exists a reasonable presumption that the military concentration is sufficiently important to justify such bombardment, having regard to the danger thus caused to the civilian population . . . ." Further, article 22 provides for that "aerial bombardment for the purpose of terrorizing the civilian population, of destroying or damaging private property not of military character, or of injuring non-combatants, is prohibited." In other words, this Draft Rules of Air Warfare prohibit useless aerial bombardment and provide for the principle of military objective first of all. Then, together with that, the Draft Rules distinguish between places in the immediate neighborhood of the operations of land forces and other places, and provide that indiscriminate aerial bombardment against the former is permitted but that against the latter the aerial bombardment of military objectives only is permitted. In these provisions, stricter expressions are used than in the case of bombardment by land and naval forces, but what they mean is understood to be the same as the distinction between the defended city (place) and undefended city (place). The Draft Rules of Air Warfare cannot directly be called positive law, since they have not yet become effective as a treaty. However, international jurists regard the Draft Rules as authoritative with regard to air warfare. Some countries regard the substance of the Rules as a standard of action by armed forces,

and the fundamental provisions of the Draft Rules are consistently in conformity with international laws and regulations, and customs at that time. Therefore, we can safely say that the prohibition of indiscriminate aerial bombardment on an undefended city and the principle of military objective, which are provided for by the Draft Rules, are international customary law, also from the point that they are in common with the principle in land and sea warfare. Further, since the distinction of land, sea, and air warfare is made by the place and purpose of warfare, *we think that there is also sufficient reason for existence of the argument that, regarding the aerial bombardment of a city on land, the laws and regulations respecting land warfare analogically apply since the aerial bombardment is made on land.*

(7)   Then, what is the distinction between a defended city and an undefended city?   Generally speaking, a defended city is a city resisting any possible occupation attempt by land forces.   A city which is far distant from the battlefield, and is not in pressing danger of the enemy's occupation, even if there exist defensive installations or armed forces, cannot be said to be a defended city, since there is no military necessity of indiscriminate bombardment; and in this case the bombardment and aerial bombardment only against military objectives is admitted.   On the contrary, against a city resisting a possible occupation attempt by the enemy, indiscriminate bombardment is permitted out of military necessity, since an attack made upon the distinction between military objective and non-military objective has little military effect and cannot accomplish the expected purposes.   *Thus, we can say that it is a long-standing, generally recognized principle in international law respecting air raids, that indiscriminate aerial bombardment is not permitted on an undefended city and that only aerial bombardment on military objective is permitted.*   (Expert Opinions of Shigejiro Tabata and Yuichi Takano.)

Of course, it is naturally anticipated that the aerial bombardment of a military objective is attended with the destruction of non-military objectives or casualty of non-combatants; and this is not illegal if it is an inevitable result accompanying the aerial bombardment of a military objective. However, it necessarily follows that in an undefended city, an aerial bombardment directed at a non-military objective, and an aerial bombardment without distinction between military objectives and non-military objectives (the so-called blind aerial bombardment) is not permitted in the light of the above-mentioned principle.   (See Expert Opinion of Shigejiro Tabata.)

The power of injury and destruction of the atomic bomb is tremendous as already stated, and even such small-scale atomic bombs as those dropped on Hiroshima and Nagasaki discharge energy equivalent to a 20,000-ton TNT bomb in the past. If an atomic bomb of such power of destruction once explodes, it is clear that it brings almost the same result as complete destruction of a middle-size city, to say nothing of indiscrimination of military objective and non-military objective. *Therefore, the act of atomic bombing on an undefended city, setting aside that on a defended city, should be regarded in the same light as a blind aerial bombardment; and it must be said to be a hostile act contrary to international law of the day.*

(8) It is a well-known fact that Hiroshima and Nagasaki were not cities resisting a possible occupation attempt by land forces at that time. Further, it is clear as stated above that both cities did not come within the purview of the defended city, since they were not in the pressing danger of enemy's occupation, even if both cities were defended with anti-aircraft guns, etc. against air raids and had military installations. Also, it is clear that some 330,000 civilians in Hiroshima and some 270,000 civilians in Nagasaki maintained homes there, even though there were so-called military objectives such as armed forces, military installations, and munitions factories in both cities. Therefore, *since an aerial bombardment with an atomic bomb brings the same result as a blind aerial bombardment from the tremendous power of destruction, even if the aerial bombardment has only a military objective as the target of its attack, it is proper to understand that an aerial bombardment with an atomic bomb on both cities of Hiroshima and Nagasaki was an illegal act of hostility as the indiscriminate aerial bombardment on undefended cities.*

(9) Against the above conclusion, there is a counter-argument that the war of the day was the so-called total war, in which it was difficult to distinguish between combatant and non-combatant, and between military objective and non-military objective, and that the principle of military objective was not necessarily carried through during World War II.

The concept of military objective is prescribed in various expressions by the above-mentioned treaties, but the content is not always fixed and changes with time. It is difficult to deny that the scope is gradually spreading under the form of total war. For all the above reasons, however, we cannot say that the distinction between military objective and non-military objective has gone out of existence. For example, schools, churches, temples, shrines, hospitals and private houses cannot be military objectives, however total the war may be. If we understand the concept of total war to mean that all people who belong to a belligerent are more or less combatant, and all production means production injuring the enemy, there arises the necessity to destroy the whole people and all the property of the enemy; and it becomes nonsensical to distinguish between military objective and non-military objective. However, the advocacy of the concept of total war in recent times has the intent of pointing out the fact that the issue of a war is not decided only by armed forces and weapons, but that the other factors, that is to say, chiefly economic factors like source of energy, materials, productive capacity of industry, food, trade, etc., or human factors like population, man-power, etc., have a far-reaching control on the war method and war potential. The concept of total war is not advocated in such a vague meaning as stated above, and there was no actual example of such situation. *Accordingly, it is wrong to say that the distinction between military objective and non-military objective has gone out of existence because of total war.* (See Expert Opinions of Shigejiro Tabata and Yuichi Takano.)

(10)　During World War II, aerial bombardment was once made on the whole place where military objectives were concentrated, because it was impossible to confirm an individual military objective and attack it where munitions factories and military installations were concentrated in comparatively narrow places, and where defensive installations against air raids were very strong and solid; and there is an opinion regarding this as legal. Such aerial bombardment is called the aerial bombardment on an objective zone, and we cannot say that there is no room for regarding it as legal, even if it passes the bounds of the principle of military objective, since the proportion of the destruction of non-military objective is small in comparison with the large military interests and necessity. However, *the legal principle of the aerial bombardment on an objective zone cannot apply to the city of Hiroshima and the city of Nagasaki, since it is clear that both cities could not be said to be places where such military objectives concentrate.*

(11)　Besides, the atomic bombing on both cities of Hiroshima and Nagasaki is regarded as contrary to the principle of international law that the means which give unnecessary pain in war and inhumane means are prohibited as means of injuring the enemy. (See Expert Opinion of Shigejiro Tabata.)

In the argument of this point, it goes without saying that such an easy analogy that the atomic bomb is necessarily prohibited since it has characteristics different from former weapons in the inhumanity of its efficiency, is not admitted. For international law respecting war is not formed only by humane feelings, but it has as its basis both military necessity and efficiency and humane feelings, and is formed by weighing these two factors. With regard to this point, the doctrine mentions as its type the provision in the St.

Petersburg Declaration of 1886, which prohibits the use of projectiles under 400 grammes which are either explosive or charged with combustible or inflammable substances, and explains the reason as follows: These projectiles are so small that they have only such a power as to kill and wound one officer or man, but for that effect an ordinary bullet will do, and there is no need to use inhumane weapons which have no more profit. On the other hand, however great the inhumane result of the use of a weapon may be, the use of the weapon is not prohibited by international law, if it has a great military efficiency.

The issues in this sense are whether atomic bombing comes within the purview of "the employment of poison or poisonous weapons" prohibited by article 23(a) of the Hague Regulations respecting war on land, and of each forbidden provision of the "Declaration prohibiting each the use of projectiles the sole object of which is the diffusion of asphyxiating or deleterious gases" (DECLARATION CONCERNANT L'INTERDICTION DE L'EMPLOI DE PROJECTILES QUI ONT POUR BUT UNIQUE DE RÉPANDRE DES GAZ ASPHYXIANTS OR DÉLÉTÈRES) of 1899, and the "Protocol prohibiting the use in war of asphyxiating, poisonous and other gases, and bacteriological methods of warfare" of 1925. With regard to this point, there is not an established theory among international jurists in connection with the difference of poison, poison-gas, bacterium, etc. from atomic bombs. However, judging from the fact that the St. Petersburg Declaration declares that "... considering that the use of a weapon which increases uselessly the pain of people who are already placed out of battle and causes their death necessarily is beyond the scope of this purpose, and considering that the use of such a weapon is thus contrary to humanity . . ." and that article 23(e) of the Hague Regulations respecting War on Land prohibits "the employment of such arms, projectiles, and material as cause unnecessary injury," we can safely see that besides poison, poison-gas and bacterium the use of the means of injuring the enemy which causes at least the same or more injury is prohibited by international law. The destructive power of the atomic bomb is tremendous, but it is doubtful whether atomic bombing really had an appropriate military effect at that time and whether it was necessary. It is a deeply sorrowful reality that the atomic bombing on both cities of Hiroshima and Nagasaki took the lives of many civilians, and that among the survivors there are people whose lives are still imperilled owing to the radial rays, even today 18 years later. In this sense, *it is not too much to say that the pain brought by the atomic bombs is severer than that from poison and poison-gas, and we can say that the act of dropping such a cruel bomb is contrary to the fundamental principle of the laws of war that unnecessary pain must not be given.*

3. Municipal law aspects.

As stated above in detail, the act of atomic bombing was contrary to international law, but it is the next question whether it was contrary to the municipal laws of Japan and the United States of America at the same time.

(1) *Viewing Japanese law first of all, the prewar Imperial Constitution of Japan at the time when the atomic bombs were dropped, had no express provision with regard to the question what effect international law has in municipal law. However, it was understood that international customary law has its effect in muncipal law, and that treaties become effective as muncipal law by promulgation. Therefore, there is sufficient room for understanding that the act of atomic bombing is also contrary to municipal law, since it is contrary to international law.*

(2) *In the United States, it is clear that treaties have the effect as the supreme law of the land in accordance with article 6, paragraph 2 of the Constitution of the United States, and it is understood that international customary law is part of the law of the country. (See Expert Opinion of Shigejiro Tabata.) Such being the case, there seems to be a fair possibility that an act contrary to international law comes to be contrary to municipal law.*

(3) However, there is little meaning in the further abstract consideration of the question whether the acts of atomic bombing were contrary to the municipal laws of Japan and the United States. For the existence of the act contrary to municipal law, and the question whether the responsibility for the violation can be placed on some person and before what court the suit can be instituted in order to enforce the responsibility are different questions which must be considered separately. The question in this case is not concretely solved until these points are considered. This point will be commented on later together when the question of responsibility for acts contrary to international law is dealt with.

4. Claims for damages of the sufferers.

(1) *It is an established principle of international law that when a belligerent causes damage to the other belligerent by illegal acts of hostility in international law, the belligerent must compensate the other belligerent for the damage.*

Since it is a well-known fact that the atomic bombing of Hiroshima and Nagasaki was a regular act of hostility taken by an airplane of the U.S. Army

Air Forces, and that Japan suffered damage by the atomic bombing, it goes without saying that Japan has a claim for damages against the Unites States in international law. In these cases, however, the person who ordered that act does not assume responsibility as an individual. Accordingly, it is understood that compensation for damage cannot be claimed in international law against U.S. President Truman, who ordered the atomic bombing. It is a principle of international law that the State must directly assume responsibility for acts taken by a person as a state organ, and that the person who holds the position as a state organ does not assume responsibility as an individual.

(2)   Then, has the individual who suffered damage by the illegal act in international law a claim for damages in accordance with international law against the country which has caused the damage?

In the argument of this point, we must first of all consider the question whether an individual can be the subject of rights in international law. Traditional thinking limits the subject of rights in international law to the state, either because international law is the law which regulates the relations of the states, or because international law is formed on the basis of the common consent of the states. However, because international law has regulated chiefly the relations of the state hitherto, it does not necessarily follow that an individual does not become the subject of rights in international law; and the subject of forming international law is not always related to the subject of rights in international law. Further, there is a view that an individual cannot become the subject of rights because international law does not always have effect within a country. This view is, however, not proper, since it is possible in theory for international law to recognize the individual rights even when international law has no effect within a country. Thus, *even if we argue the essential qualities of international law, it does not draw out the conclusion that the subject of rights in international law is necessarily limited to a state.*

(3)   Then, on the contrary, can the individual always be the subject of rights in international law? The standing of the individual in international law does not come to question until international law (chiefly treaties) provides with regard to the rights and duties of the individual. In this case, as doctrine of international law, there are the following two opposing views: One is the view that if only rights and duties are stipulated in international law, the individual acquires certain rights and duties in international law by the existence of the stipulation alone. The other is the view that, unless there is a possibility that the individual can assert his rights and enforce his duties in his name in international law, it cannot be said that he acquires rights

and duties in international law. This opposition arises from a difference in understanding the subject of international law and in its turn the general nature of law. Generally speaking, the subject of a right in law is a person, who has the possibility of asserting his rights and of being bound by his duties in his own name. Accordingly, in order for a person to be a subject of a right in international law, there must be the possibility for him to assert his right and be bound by his duties in his name. Therefore, from this viewpoint, the latter of the above two views is right.

Next, we will examine the treaties recognizing the standing of the individual in international law in this meaning. As examples in which the individual's right of instituting suit is directly permitted, we can mention the economic clauses of the Treaty respecting the establishment of the International Prize Court, adopted at the Hague Peace Conference of 1907; the Treaty respecting the establishment of the Central American Court of Justice, concluded by five Central American countries in 1907; and the Versailles Treaty and the other peace treaties after World War I (Treaty of St. Germain-en-Laye, Treaty of Trianon, Treaty of Lausanne and Treaty of Neuilly-sur-Seine).

The Treaty respecting the establishment of the International Prize Court was not ratified and did not become a positive international law. Also, it provided for a special court which would have been an organ for appeal in case of dissatisfaction over the examination of the national prize courts. The Treaty respecting the establishment of the Central American Court of Justice was only effective for ten years in five Central American countries. Therefore, these two treaties are not adequate in the consideration of the present general questions.

On the other hand, the Versailles Treaty and other peace treaties provided for the establishment of mixed arbitral tribunals to deal with suits concerning property rights of the nationals of the countries involved in World War I. In the case of the Versailles Treaty, nationals of the Allied and Associated Powers were permitted to institute suits before mixed arbitral tribunals directly against the German Government for compensation for damage suffered by their properties, rights, and interests within German territory as a result of the application of extraordinary wartime steps or measures of transfer by the German Government. Moreover, it was stipulated that they could institute suits before mixed arbitral tribunals in their own names entirely independent of the intention of their home governments. Accordingly, in this case, we can say that individuals were the subject of rights in international law.

So, there is an argument that, by this example, individuals have generally been the subject of rights in international law; but this argument is not right. The reason is that, in the above case, the object of compensation was limited to damage to properties, rights, or interests within German territory resulting from the wartime application of extraordinary steps or measures of transfer by the German Government, and that the compensation did not cover all damages caused by the conduct of war by Germany. Another reason is that the above claim for damages was limited to nationals of the Allied and the Associated Powers, and nationals of the defeated countries did not have the right to bring action. Further, the mixed arbitral tribunals were *ad hoc* tribunals established individually by each victor country and Germany. The most important thing is that, they were all stipulated by and based on concrete treaties as stated above. Therefore, it is not enough to say on such ground that the rights of individuals in international law have been generally recognized, and that the procedure of asserting such rights in international law has been guaranteed. *It is still proper to understand that individuals are not the subject of rights in international law, unless it is concretely recognized by treaties as seen in the above example of mixed arbitral tribunals.*

(4) The plaintiffs allege that an individual has a claim in international law, since the right of the individual is exercised by the home government. However, if the purport is that the state exercise the right in international law in the citizen's name as his agent for his sake, there is no such example in international law and there is no reason in international law to recognize this.

Indeed, international law permits a state to demand from the other country reparations for damage caused to its nationals, in the name of the state for the sake of its nationals. This is called diplomatic protection, as is generally known. Diplomatic protection is, however, an act based on the state's own right of diplomatic protection, and the individual's claim itself is not asserted by this act. The claim for damages is asserted as the state's own claim. Whether the state exercises the right of diplomatic protection is decided by the state in its own judgment, and the state exercises the right in its name. It does not follow that the state acts on behalf of its nationals. Borchard and others call this phenomenon "immersion of the individual's claim into the state's claim." In this case, the state is not interfered with at all by the nationals in regard to how and what the state claims, and how it solves the question of the claim. With regard to the amount of compensation which the state claims, it does not always claim the compensation for the whole damage caused to the nationals. Further, the state can determine freely by its intention how the state distributes the compensation thus obtained. Therefore, in this case we must say that there is no room for regarding the individual as the subject of right in international law.

(5)   As understood from the above, there is no general way open to an individual who suffers damages from an illegal act of hostility in international law, to claim damages in international law. Accordingly, the possibility left to the individual comes to the question whether he can ask for redress before a domestic court of one or both belligerents.

Redress before a Japanese court, however, cannot be asked for. The sufferers must bring an action before a Japanese court against the other country as defendant, in this case, against the United States as defendant, but it is an established principle in international law that a country is not subject to the jurisdiction of the civil courts of other countries; and this principle is also recognized by Japan. (Daishinin (Court of Cassation), (Case No. (ku) 218 of 1928, Decision of December 28, 1928, 7 Minshu (Collection of Judicial Precedents Concerning Civil Affairs) 1128.)

(6)   Then, is redress before the court of the United States permitted?

With regard to this point, we must examine such questions in adjective law as whether the court of the United States has jurisdiction, and whether the plaintiffs in this case have the right to bring an action as foreigners, and also in substantive law. However, if we state the conclusion to the question is substantive law, the plaintiffs, in the law of the United States, cannot assert responsibility for the illegal act against the United States or President Truman.

In the law of the United States, the legal theory of so-called Sovereign Immunity has consistently applied since the 19th Century. This is the principle that the state does not assume responsibility of compensation for illegal acts committed by public servants in the performance of duty, like the principle in England that the "King can do no wrong." With regard to this legal theory of Sovereign Immunity, it is said that the theory is based on political measures imposed out of necessity, or it is explained that all the nationals improperly committed an illegal act, or that what the state does must be legal. Thus, the theory is rationalized by precedent and doctrine. The legal theory of Sovereign Immunity applies not only to the state but also to the highest executive organs of the state, including the presidency, and it is understood that the persons of these organs do not assume responsibility as individuals for their illegal acts comitted in the performance of their duties. As alleged by the plaintiffs, the English legal theory that the "King can do no wrong" was not adopted as such by the United States, and it is said that the reason why the theory of Sovereign Immunity which is almost the same as the English theory, has come to apply in the United States is not well known. There is, however, no room for denying that the theory of Sovereign Immunity generally applies in the United States. However great the atomic bomb may be in its distructive power as alleged by the plaintiffs, it cannot possibly be regarded that the atomic bomb has crushed off the theory of Sovereign Immunity.

After World War II, the United States has come to admit the responsibility of compensation by the state for illegal acts by enacting the Federal Tort Claims Act. The Act, however, has many exceptions; and it stipulates that the state does not assume responsibility when the administrative organs of the state perform discretionary duties, and that the state does not assume responsibility for hostile acts of land and sea forces. The Act also excludes claims arising in foreign countries. Accordingly, for the reasons stated above, *we can only say that the sufferers can not claim compensation for damages for torts by the United States or President Truman, in accordance with the law of the United States. It is a self-evident truth that this conclusion is the same whether a suit is instituted at the time of the atomic bombing or after the enactment of the Federal Tort Claims Act.*

(7) The above concerns the case where an individual exercises a claim in international law before the courts of Japan or the United States. The above argument will also apply in the case where an individual sues for damages before the courts of Japan or the United States for the reason that an illegal act is constituted under the law of Japan or the United States. Therefore, although there is no need to repeat it, the conclusion is that, with regard to a claim under municipal law, the individual cannot ask for redress before the courts of Japan or the United States.

5. Waiver of claims in accordance with the Japanese Peace Treaty.

(1) The greater part of the conclusion of this suit will be drawn from the above. However, all questions have not yet been examined. It requires further examination as to how the rights and duties arising out of the state of war between Japan and the United States are dealt with by the treaty between both countries, and how the individual's claim in international law is stipulated in the treaty.

(2) *Article 19(a) of the Peace Treaty between the Allied Powers and Japan ("the Japanese Peace Treaty"), concluded in San Francisco on September 8, 1958, effective April 28, 1952, provides that: "Japan waives all claims of*

*Japan and its nationals against the Allied Powers and their nationals arising
out of the war or out of actions taken because of the existence of a state of
war, and waives all claims arising from the presence, operations or actions of
forces or authorities of any of the Allied Powers in Japanese territory prior to
the coming into force of the present Treaty."*

It is clear that the "claims of Japan" which were waived by this provision
includes all claims which Japan had in accordance with treaties and inter
national customary laws. Accordingly, claims for compensation for damages
caused to Japan by illegal acts of hostility, for example, are necessarily
included.

(3)   Then, what will the waived "claims of Japan" indicate?

The defendant State alleges that the State of Japan cannot waive the
rights of its nationals, since the State of Japan and Japanese nationals are
different subjects of law; and accordingly what was waived was nothing
but the right of diplomatic protection of Japan.

This view is, however, not right. The right of diplomatic protection is
an inherent right of a state as already stated. Accordingly, it is included
in the "claims of Japan" in article 19(a). Further, while the "claims of
Japanese nationals," as a general expression, are understood to be substantive
rights, the right of diplomatic protection is understood to be an adjective
right, strictly speaking, even though there are many cases where the state
invokes the right of diplomatic protection, taking with its own nationals'
rights in the law of the other state against that state.

(4)   There is a view that a state cannot waive the claims of nationals
who are different subjects of law from the state. It is exactly as the above
if claims of nationals mean rights in international law. However, it must
be said that the state can waive its nationals' claims in municipal law. The
state has the sovereign right to create, change, and extinguish its nationals'
rights and duties in accordance with the regular procedures of municipal law;
and it is possible in legal theory for a state to promise to waive its nationals'
rights of the above nature against another state, setting aside the question
whether the promise is right or wrong. This is clear from the fact that
Japan recognizes in article 14(a)2(I) of the Japanese Peace Treaty that
the Allied Powers shall have the right to dispose of property of Japanese
nationals within the territory of the Allied Powers (so-called overseas assets).
And it will be easily understood that the object of waiver in this case is the
rights of nationals in municipal law.

(5)   *Such being the case, it will be natural to understand that the "claims*

of Japanese nationals" waived by article 19(a) are the claims of Japanese nationals in the municipal laws of Japan and of the Allied Powers, against the Allied Powers and their nationals. *The expert opinions of Kaoru Yasui, Shigejiro Tabata and Yuichi Takano unanimously conclude that the "claims of Japanese nationals" are the rights of Japanese nationals themselves. Further, the Japanese Government also regarded them as the rights of Japanese nationals.* This is clear from the fact that Kumao Nishimura (then Director of Treaties Bureau, Ministry of Foreign Affairs), government delegate in the ad hoc Committee on the Peace Treaty and the Security Treaty between Japan and the United States of America, House of Representatives, gave an explanation to the above effect in the article-by-article explanation of the Japanese Peace Treaty.

(6) The plaintiffs allege that an individual's claim in international law is included in the "claims of Japanese nationals."

However, as already stated, an individual's claim in international law is not recognized until it is provided for by a treaty and the right of bringing action and other procedural guarantees by which the individual can assert the claim have come into existence internationally. Such a procedural guarantee undoubtedly is not recognized by the Japanese Peace Treaty. Also, if we understand, as alleged by the plaintiffs, that the claims of Japanese nationals in international law are included in the Japanese Peace Treaty, we must conclude that claims for damages by Japanese nationals in international law are admitted for the first time by this treaty and that simultaneously the claims are waived by the same treaty. It is, however, unnatural to understand that such a special technique was used in the treaty; and there was no necessity to use such a technique. There is no example where individual claims for damages were recognized in customary international law at any time prior to the Japanese Peace Treaty. Accordingly, *it does not follow that the Japanese Peace Treaty admitted Japanese nationals' claims for damages in international law and accordingly made them the object of a waiver.* What were waived in article 19(a) of the Japanese Peace Treaty were Japanese nationals' claims under the municipal laws of Japan and of the Allied Powers.

6. Defendant's responsibility for waiver of claims.

(1) The plaintiffs allege that the defendant State lost the plaintiffs' claims for damages in international law and municipal law against the United States and President Truman by waiving them. *It is, however, as stated above, that claims in international law were not the object of waiver in the above-mentioned provisions; and it is as already explained that there is no admitting the ex-*

istence of even the claims in municipal law which were made the object of waiver. Such being the case, it follows that the plaintiffs had no rights to lose, and accordingly there is no reason for asserting the defendant's legal responsibility therefore.

(2) Everyone has a whole-hearted compassion for those who suffered damages by the dropping of the atomic bombs, which possess the largest-scale and strongest destructive power in human history. It is a common desire of mankind to totally abolish war, or at least to limit it to the minimum and confine damage to the minimum; and for that purpose we, mankind, are persevering in our efforts day and night.

However, if a war unfortunately occurs, it goes without saying that every country is required to minimize damage and to protect its nationals. In this light, the question of State redress on the basis of absolute liability will arise necessarily for war calamity. Actually, there is the "Law respecting Medical Treatment and the Like for Sufferers of the Atomic Bomb," which is related to this case; but it is clear that a law of this scale cannot possibly be sufficient for the relief or rescue of the suffers of the atomic bombs. The defendant State caused many nationals to die, injured them, and drove them to a precarious life by the war which it opened on its own authority and responsibility. Also, the seriousness of the damage cannot compare a moment with that of the general calamity. Needless to say the defendant state should take sufficient relief measures in this light.

That is, however, no longer the duty of the Court, but a duty which the Diet or legislature or the Cabinet or the executive must perform. Moreover it is by such a procedure that relief measures can be taken not only by the parties to this suit, but also by general sufferers of the atomic bombs; and there lies the *raison d'être* of the legislature and the administration. It cannot possibly be understood that the above is financially impossible in Japan, which has achieved a high degree of economic growth after the war. We cannot see this suit without regretting the political poverty.

7. Conclusion.

For the above reasons, the plaintiffs' claims in this suit are ruled improper, without considering the other issues; and we can only dismiss the plaintiffs' claims on the merits. Accordingly, applying articles 89 and 93 of the Code of Civil Procedure to the costs of litigation, we decide as in the text of the judgment above.

Civil Affairs Division No. 24, Tokyo District Court.

Presiding Judge T. Koseki (Toshimasa Koseki), Judge Y. Mibuchi (Yoıiko Mibuchi), Judge A. Takakuwa (Akira Takakuwa).

Exhibit I*

amaged District	Population prior to Damage	Casualties	
Hiroshima	413,889	Killed:	260,000
		Missing:	6,738
		Seriously wounded:	51,012
		Slightly wounded:	105,543
		Total:	423,293
Nagasaki	280,542	Killed:	73,884
		Wounded:	76,796
		Total:	150,680

Exhibit II**

amaged District	Population prior to Damage	Casualties	
Hiroshima	336,483 (1944)	Killed:	78,150
		Wounded:	51,408
Nagasaki	270,063 (1944)	Killed:	23,753
		Wounded:	41,847

Exhibit III***

A New-Type, Cruel Bomb Ignoring International Law; Imperial Govern-
ıent Protest to the Government of the United States.

With regard to the attack by a new-type bomb on the city of Hiroshima
.y a B-29 bomber on the 6th inst., the Imperial Government filed the following
rotest on the 10th inst., to the Government of the United States through the
ʃovernment of Switzerland, and gave instructions to the Japanese Minister
o Switzerland, Kase, to make the explanation of the same effect to the Inter-
ational Committee of Red Cross.

Protest against the Attack of a New-Type Bomb by American Airplane:

On the 6th of this month, an airplane of the United States dropped a new-
ype bomb on the urban district of the city of Hiroshima, and it killed and
.ounded a large number of the citizens and destroyed the bulk of the city.
ʰhe city of Hiroshima is an ordinary local city which is not provided with
ny military defensive preparations or establishments, and the whole city has

not a character of a military objective. In the statement on the aerial bombardment in this case, the United States President "Truman" asserts tha
they will destroy docks, factories and transport facilities. However, since th
bomb in this case, dropped by a parachute, explodes in the air and extend
the destructive effect to quite a wide sphere, it is clear to be quite impossibl
in technique to limit the effect of attack thereby to such specific objective
as mentioned above; and the above efficiency of the bomb in this case is alread
known to the United States. In the light of the actual state of damage, th
damaged district covers a wide area, and those who were in the district wer
all killed indiscriminately by bomb-shell blast and radiant heat without dis
tinction of combatant or non-combatant or of age or sex. The damaged spher
is general and immense, and judging from the individual state of injury, th
bomb in this case should be said to be the most cruel one that ever existed
It is a fundamental principle of international law in time of war that a
belligerent has not an unlimited right in chosing the means of injuring the
enemy, and should not use such weapons, projectiles, and other material as
cause unnecessary pain; and these are each expressly stipulated in the annex
of the Convention respecting the Laws and Customs of War on Land and
articles 22 and 23 (e) of the Regulations respecting the Laws and Customs of
War on Land. Since the beginning of the present World War, the Governmen
of the United States has declared repeatedly that the use of poison or othe
inhumane methods of warfare has been regarded as illegal by the public opinion in civilized countries, and that the United States would not use these
methods of warfare unless the other countries used these first. However, the
bomb in this case, which the United States used this time, exceeds by far the
indiscriminate and cruel character of efficiency, the poison and other weapons
the use of which has been prohibited hitherto because of such an efficiency
Disregarding a fundamental principle of international law and humanity, the
United States has already made indiscriminate aerial bombardments on cities of
the Empire in very wide areas, and it has already killed and injured a large
number of old people, children, and women, and collapsed or burned down
shrines, temples, schools, hospitals and ordinary private houses. Also, the United
States has used the new bomb in this case which has indiscriminate and cruel
character beyond comparison with all weapons and projectiles of the past. This
is a new offence against the civilization of mankind. The Imperial Government
impeaches the Government of the United States in its own name and the name
of all mankind and of civilization, and demands strongly that the Government
of the United States give up the use of such an inhumane weapon instantly.

NOTES AND QUESTIONS

1. Some sense of what World War III might be like can be derived from this extract from a statement on strategic objectives by United States Secretary of Defense Robert McNamara before the House Armed Service Committee on February 18, 1965:

NUCLEAR FORCES, U. S. AND SOVIET

The strategic objectives of our general nuclear war forces are:

1. To deter a deliberate nuclear attack upon the United States and its allies by maintaining a clear and convincing capability to inflict unacceptable damage on an attacker, even were the attacker to strike first;

2. In the event such a war should nevertheless occur, to limit damage to our populations and industrial capacities.

The first of these capabilities (required to deter potential aggressors) we call "assured destruction," i.e., the capability to destroy the aggressor as a viable society, even after a well-planned and executed surprise attack on our forces. The second capability we call "damage limitation," i.e., the capability to reduce the weight of the enemy attack by both offensive and defensive measures and to provide a degree of protection for the population against the effects of nuclear detonations.

The effectiveness of our strategic offensive forces in the damage limiting role would be critically dependent on the timing of an enemy attack on U. S. urban targets. Our missile forces would be most effective against the enemy bombers if the attack on our urban centers were withheld for an hour or more after an attack on U. S. military targets—an unlikely contingency. Our manned bomber forces would be effective in the damage-limiting role only if the enemy attack on our urban centers were witheld for several hours.

FATALITIES ESTIMATED

Based on the projected threat for the early nineteen-seventies and the most likely planning factors for that time period, our calculations show that even after absorbing a first strike, our already authorized strategic missile force, if it were directed against the aggressor's urban areas, could cause more than 100 million fatalities and destroy about 80 per cent of his industrial capacity. If our manned bombers were then to mount a follow-on attack against urban areas, fatalities would be increased by 10 to 15 million and industrial destruction by another per cent or two.

Although a deliberate nuclear attack upon the United States may seem a highly unlikely contingency in view of our unmistakable assured destruction capability, it must receive our urgent attention because of the enormous consequences it would have.

In this regard I should make two points clear. First, in order to preclude any possibility of miscalculation by others, I want to reiterate that although the U. S. would itself suffer severely in the event of a general nuclear war, we are fully committed to the defense of our allies. Second, we do not view damage limitation as a question of concern only to the U. S. Our offensive forces cover strategic enemy capabilities to inflict damage on our allies in Europe just as they cover enemy threats to the continental U. S.

In order to assess the potentials of various damage limiting programs we have examined a number of "balanced" defense postures at different budget levels. These postures are designed to defend against the assumed threat in the early nineteen-seventies.

To illustrate the critical nature of the timing of the attack, we used two limiting cases. First, we assumed that the enemy would initiate nuclear war with a simultaneous attack against our cities and military targets. Second, we assumed that the attack against our cities would be delayed long enough for us to retaliate against the aggressor's military targets with our own missiles. In both cases, we assumed that all new systems will perform essentially as estimated since our main purpose here was to gain an insight into the over-all problem of limiting damage.

(The results of Defense Secretary McNamara's analysis are summarized in the table below.)

"ESTIMATED EFFECT ON U. S. FATALITIES OF ADDITIONS TO THE APPROVED DAMAGE LIMITING PROGRAM"
(Based on 1970 population of 210 million)
(Millions of U. S. fatalities)

Additional Investment	Early urban attack	Delayed urban attack
$ 0 billion	149	122
$ 5 billion	120	90
$15 billion	96	59
$25 billion	78	41

The $5 billion of additional investment (of which about $2 billion would come from non-Federal sources) would provide a full fall-out shelter program for the entire population. The $15 billion level would add about $8.5 billion for a limited deployment of a low cost configuration of a missile defense system, plus about $1.5 billion for new manned bomber defenses. The $25 billion level would provide an additional $8.5 billion for antimissile defenses (for a total of about $17 billion) and another $1.5 billion for improved manned bomber defenses (for a total of $3 billion).

2. There has been an emerging trend in the General Assembly to declare that nuclear weapons are illegal instruments of warfare and to implement the declaration by convening a conference to draw up an international convention prohibiting the use of these weapons. A recent step in this trend was the passage in 1961 of Resolution 1653 (XVI) by a vote of 55-20-26, the United States voting against and the Soviet Union voting in favor. The text of this important resolution expressive of at least a moral consensus in the world community is reprinted in full:

Declaration on the Prohibition of the use of Nuclear and Thermo-Nuclear Weapons

The General Assembly,

Mindful of its responsibility under the Charter of the United Nations in the maintenance of international peace and security, as well as in the consideration of principles governing disarmament,

Gravely concerned that, while negotiations on disarmament have not so far achieved satisfactory results, the armaments race, particularly in the nuclear and thermo-nuclear fields, has reached a dangerous stage requiring all possible precautionary measures to protect humanity and civilization from the hazard of nuclear and thermo-nuclear catastrophe,

Recalling that the use of weapons of mass destruction, causing unnecessary human suffering, was in the past prohibited, as being contrary to the laws of humanity and to the principles of international law, by international declarations and binding agreements, such as the Declaration of St. Petersburg of 1868, the Declaration of the Brussels Conference of 1874, the Conventions of The Hague Peace Conference of 1899 and 1907, and the Geneva Protocol of 1925, to which the majority of nations are still parties,

Considering that the use of nuclear and thermo-nuclear weapons would bring about indiscriminate suffering and destruction to mankind and civilization to an even greater extent than the use of those weapons declared by the aforementioned international declarations and agreements to be contrary to the laws of humanity and a crime under international law,

Believing that the use of weapons of mass destruction, such as nuclear and thermo-nuclear weapons, is a direct negation of the high ideals and objectives which the United Nations has been established to achieve through the protection of succeeding generations from the scourge of war and through the preservation and promotion of their cultures,

1. Declares that:

(a) The use of nuclear and thermo-nuclear weapons is contrary to the spirit, letter and aims of the United Nations and, as such, a direct violation of the Charter of the United Nations;

(b) The use of nuclear and thermo-nuclear weapons would exceed even the scope of war and cause indiscriminate suffering and destruction to mankind and civilization and, as such, is contrary to the rules of international law and to the laws of humanity;

(c) The use of nuclear and thermo-nuclear weapons is a war directed not against an enemy or enemies alone but also against mankind in general, since the peoples of the world not involved in such a war will be subjected to all the evils generated by the use of such weapons;

(d) Any State using nuclear and thermo-nuclear weapons is to be considered as violating the Charter of the United Nations, as acting contrary to the laws of humanity and as committing a crime against mankind and civilization;

2. Requests the Secretary-General to consult the Governments of Member States to ascertain their views on the possibility of convening a special conference for signing a convention on the prohibition of the use of nuclear and thermo-nuclear weapons for war purposes and to report on the results of such consultation to the General Assembly at its seventeenth session.

3. The weight of General Assembly authority in support of outlawing the use of nuclear weapons should be related to the discussion of Robert Tucker's proposal for no first use of nuclear weapons. See **IV-3**. It should also be related to the discussions of the changing bases of international obligation as coming to include the norm-creating authority of a *relevant consensus* within the world community. This subject is considered more fully in **III-2** and **III-5A** in connection with the study of the law-creating effects of resolutions of the General Assembly.

4. At present, the official position of the United States on the issue of the legality of nuclear weapons is suggested in the various field manuals prepared for the guidance of military personnel. For example, Article 613 of the *Rules of Naval Warfare* reads as follows:

> There is at present no rule of international law expressly prohibiting states from the use of nuclear weapons in warfare. In the absence of express prohibition, the use of such weapons against enemy combatants and other military objectives is permitted.

Paragraph 35 of the U.S. Army *Rules of Land Warfare* read as follows:

> The use of explosive "atomic weapons," whether by air, sea or land forces, cannot as such be regarded as violative of international law in the absence of any customary rule of international law to the contrary.

Note that the Army formulation seems the more permissive as it does not confine the use of nuclear weapons to military objectives nor call attention to the distinction between combatants and non-combatants. On the basis of Article 613 would you conclude that the bombing of Hiroshima was an authorized use of nuclear weapons? The distinction between the status of these weapons as legal or not and the legal appraisal of their *use* is important to keep in mind.

5. International lawyers disagree about the legitimacy of nuclear weapons. There is no consensus one way or the other. The conclusions reached by the Tokyo District Court is certainly a datum that can be expected to exert some influence on the course of future legal controversy. Among the most important discussions to date are William V. O'Brien, "Legitimate Military Necessity in Nuclear War," *World*

Polity, vol. II, (1960) pp. 35–120; Georg Schwarzenberger, *The Legality of Nuclear Weapons* (Stevens & Sons, London, 1958); Myres S. McDougal and Florentino P. Feliciano, *Law and Minimum World Public Order; The Legal Regulation of International Coercion* (Yale University Press, 1961) pp. 77–8 and 659–668.

6. On the need to avoid nuclear war there is no dissent. Disagreement centers, among jurists and statesmen alike, upon what is permissible for a state to do to uphold its security interests, given the character of international society. There is also some controversy about the extent to which an indefinite threat to use nuclear weapons if provoked will influence the behavior of a potential aggressor.

7. Clark and Sohn authorize the United Nations Police Force to make use of nuclear weapons under certain circumstances. Their position is expressed in Article 4(6) of Annex II in *World Peace through World Law* (Harvard University Press, 1962) p. 330, the text of which is as follows:

> The United Nations Peace Force shall in no event employ nuclear weapons except when the General Assembly: (a) has declared that a nuclear weapon has actually been used either against a nation or against the United Nations itself or that there is a serious and imminent threat that a nuclear weapon will be so used; (b) has declared that nothing less than the use of a nuclear weapon or weapons by the Peace Force will suffice to prevent or suppress a serious breach of the peace or a violent and serious defiance of the authority of the United Nations; and (c) has authorized the United Nations Nuclear Energy Authority to transfer to the Peace Force one or more nuclear weapons. When the occasion for the use or possible use of a nuclear weapon or weapons by the Peace Force has ceased, or when the General Assembly so directs, any nuclear weapon or weapons so transferred to the Peace Force shall be forthwith returned to the Nuclear Energy Authority.

It is not entirely clear whether clauses (a) and (b) are cumulative or alternative conditions. Note that Clark and Sohn assume the potential legitimacy of nuclear weapons if used under the auspices of the United Nations. This suggests that even in their vision of a warless world Clark and Sohn believe that it is essential to preserve a nuclear capability and to set forth procedures for its invocation. Further consideration of these issues is postponed until **III-9**. For Clark and Sohn's rationale, see p. 319. Note the failure to specify the type of nuclear weapon retained for possible use by the Police Force.

Thomas C. Schelling, writing of the characteristics of a world police in a disarmed world, has this to say about its military requirements: "It will presumably need an 'invulnerable nuclear deterrent,' probably a more flexible and diversified deterrent than the major powers require now, with some redundancy as a safeguard against defection and sabotage." T. C. Schelling: "A World Force in Operation," in Lincoln P. Bloomfield, *International Military Forces* (Little, Brown, and Associates, Boston, 1964) p. 214. The entire essay by Schelling is included in **III-9C**. The implications of Schelling's remarks are that the prospect of nuclear war will remain active even in a disarmed world. It will never be possible for the world police force to assume that nuclear capability will not be retained. Therefore, a nuclear war between the world police force and a violator of the peace must remain a live possibility. Schelling estimates $25 billion as a realistic budget for an adequate world peace force, whereas Clark and Sohn advance a figure of $9 billion.

One of the most profound and comprehensive responses to the reality and prospect of nuclear warfare is the book by the celebrated German philosopher Karl Jaspers, *The Future of Mankind*, translated by E. B. Ashton, (University of Chicago Press, 1958). Jaspers is concerned with finding a way to think about the consequences of this radical new reality brought upon mankind by the development of nuclear weapons, and he carries forward the inquiry initiated by Singer, Rapoport, and Lasswell in the prior chapter about which modes of thought are most appropriate for the analysis of world order issues. There is, it would appear, some contrast between the philosophical style of response expressed by Jaspers and the more social scientific style of response of the authors presented in Chapter 3. Does Jaspers add anything? Does it help in assessing the basis for a system change in international society? Consider Jaspers' analysis and prescription also in light of the material on the causes of war in Chapter 2, especially the excerpt by Waltz on the three images, one of which is adopted by almost every theorist advancing a causal explanation of war.

KARL JASPERS

The New Fact

New weapons of destruction have always been called criminal, the first cannon as well as the recent unrestricted submarine warfare of World War I; yet habit soon made them unquestioned facts of life. The atom bomb of today is a fact novel in essence, for it leads mankind to the brink of self-destruction.

Experts say definitely that it is now possible for life on earth to be wiped out by human action. The scientists who brought the new fact into being have also publicized it. Neither they nor we laymen know how far atomic weapons manufacture has progressed, though each of us can apprehend that America and Russia, trailed by England, keep bending every effort to pile up more such bombs and to increase their destructiveness. The facts are shrouded in official secrecy. It is not publicly known whether — if all bombs in stock were dropped — the radioactive poisoning of the atmosphere would suffice to end life on this planet. One may be right in doubting that the day has come when all life on earth can be annihilated. But in ten years or less the day will come. This slight difference in time does not diminish the urgent need for reflection.

We may assume that the leaders of the two superpowers are informed — though nobody knows the extent to which secrets are guarded and compartmentalized, even among the leaders. Their plans are probably not clear to themselves. Not knowing what to do, they temporize, at the same time preparing for actions that seem inconceivable to all of them. The public is told nothing — except in such monstrous threats as Khrushchev's, which sound fantastic and contain no concrete data either. It is as if silence were imposed upon statesmen, not, as of old, by military secrecy alone, but by the very risk of speaking. There is a tendency abroad, fostered by governments, not to let matters alarm their people.

Alarm keeps growing, nonetheless, though perhaps in the wrong directions. There are protests against hydrogen bomb tests. There is concern about increased radioactivity everywhere. There is local opposition to the construction of atomic piles, lest they explode. Of course, the observation and publication of actually or potentially harmful phenomena is sensible and justified, but we must distinguish between three types of danger:

First, there are dangers inherent in the peaceful use of atomic energy, as well as in hydrogen bomb tests in peacetime. The dangers seem to be substantial; disease and mutations may result from the steady absorption of initially slight doses of radioactivity. But those are special problems and can be studied and met like other dangers. Though hundreds of thousands should succumb to the resulting injuries, the harm is limited, and constant efforts will probably limit it further.

Second, in case of war there are dangers of unprecedented destruction. The superbombs, whether delivered by plane or rocket, immediately exterminate all life in a large area. In a larger surrounding area the victims die slowly. In time, survivors in this vaguely circumscribed zone will note diseases and abnormalities in their offspring. Since this disaster will befall big cities and entire countries, there is now unanimous agreement that a new world war would destroy civilization. "I do not know what weapons will be used in the next war," Einstein said years ago, "but the one after that will be fought with bows and arrows."

The third danger, due to cumulative effects that may extend to lethal contamination of the whole atmosphere, is the destruction of mankind, of life itself.

All three dangers have this in common: we do not know to what extent they exist. But the concepts differ both in kind and in degree, progressing from local and special disasters to the end of civilization, and then to the end of mankind. Against the first, there are technological safeguards. From the second, remnants of humanity can be saved by protective measures, by straining the resources of technology to succeed, perhaps, in benefiting an infinitesimal fraction. Against the third, essentially new, danger there is no protection. What can be done in the face of it will be the theme of this book.

This third danger is intensified by dissembling. Attention is drawn from the genuinely new, unprecedented, overriding fact to other great but relatively superficial dangers. Overstatements of the present effect of the bomb tests, speculations about their possible effect — these are refutable; and when fears prove unfounded, a false calm results. There is at present no recognizable chance for a chain reaction to spread from its proper substance to matter at large, thus disintegrating the globe. The idea of one man pushing a button to explode the planet remains as illusory as ever. Another distraction is the fearful excitement about the perils of peaceful production and use of atomic energy. There are no "foolproof machines," nor can accidents be excluded, but credible reports tell us that a high safety rate can be achieved by the proper controls and that the dangerous atomic waste need not be feared either, since it can be buried and rendered harmless.

The refutation of these erroneous notions is deceptive. It tends to make the fact itself seem questionable, to shift an already real possibility into the realm of fantasy, to let our mood vacillate between misplaced exaggeration and a sense of calm where we should be profoundly alarmed.

We can rely on the natural scientists' judgment of facts. What they tell us is reality, not speculation. An intelligent person cannot read their statements without a sense of enormity; they have put the handwriting onto the wall for all to see. Until now an individual could take his own life, could kill or be killed in battle, and nations could be exterminated. Now, mankind as a whole can be wiped out by men. It has not merely become possible for this to happen; on purely rational reflection it is probable that it will happen.

This statement seems rash. We hesitate. We must examine it.

On the assumption that the scientists are right in their expert opinions — and we can scarcely doubt this — we mean to show here that this oppressive intellectual prognosis is indeed compelling, but also that it is not the last word. For probability is not certainty, and above all, we are dealing not only with recognizable, inexorable necessities of nature but with the future acts of men, with the potential of their freedom.

An effective awareness of the probability of total perdition is the only way by which the presently probable might become finally improbable, if not impossible. To this end we must make proper use of our factual knowledge. I may know something but insulate the knowledge, as it were: deny its validity, live as if it were not there. If knowledge is to bear fruit in us, we must think of it daily. Today the terrible threat of the hydrogen bomb seems not yet acute. It does not affect me bodily, here and now. I know of it, to be sure, when I am asked; but I think there is time. No, there is not much time. At most, it is a matter of decades, and perhaps the time is shorter. Perhaps the decisive moment is close at hand.

The atom bomb is today the greatest of all menaces to the future of mankind. In the past there have been imaginative notions of the world's end; its imminent expectation for their generation was the ethically and religiously effective error of John the Baptist, Jesus, and the first Christians. But now we face the real possibility of such an end. The possible reality which we must henceforth reckon with — and reckon with, at the increasing pace of developments, in the near future — is no longer a fictitious end of the world. It is no world's end at all, but the extinction of life on the surface of the planet.

A small thing, in this situation, yet a prerequisite of everything else, is to *think*: to look around us; to observe what is going on; to visualize the possibilities, the consequences of events and actions; to clarify the situation in the directions that emerge — until we feel the brutal new fact push our thinking to the very roots of human existence, where the question arises what man is and can be.

The basic human situation is to be in the world and not to know whence or whither. The possibility of total self-destruction makes us newly, differently conscious of this situation; it shows us a side of which no one has thought before. We must make sure of ourselves, in this new situation. True, our reason cannot plumb ultimate depths, but it can clarify what exists for us and what we want of it.

The atom bomb, as the problem of mankind's very existence, is equaled by only one other problem: the threat of totalitarian rule (not simply dictatorship, Marxism, or racial theory), with its terroristic structure that obliterates all liberty and human dignity. By one, we lose life; by the other, a life that is worth living. Both extreme possibilities bring us today to an awareness of what we want, how we would wish to live, what we must be prepared for.

The two problems seem fatefully linked. In practice, at least, they are inseparable. Neither one can be solved without the other, and the solution of both calls for forces in man to well up from such depths as to transform him in his moral, rational, political aspects — a transformation so extensive that it would become the turning point of history.

It is astonishing to find the obvious new fact not really acknowledged by people the world over, least of all in Russia and America. Thus the revolution in our way of thinking, which reflection upon the fact would seem to make inescapable, has not yet occurred. Our attention is distracted, drawn to side issues that are grave but not of absolute moment. Our vision is narrowed as we regard the fact in isolation, though it receives its full weight only in connection with the entirety of human existence, and with man's questions about himself. We tend to forget, preoccupied as we are with the momentary well-being of economic prosperity.

These distracting, narrowing, oblivious factors work involuntarily. They could be overcome only by total reflection and the ensuing change in, first, the individual. This inner change could spread through mankind like a wave — not just of alarm, not just of outrage at all agents of perdition, but of rational will. This will would lead to a re-examination of the whole of our humanity, of our lives, our motives. The eternal source could yield a new beginning of what we should be, to be worthy of life. It is only if consciousness of the new fact came to influence our lives that conventional politics, its interests and objectives, could be transformed into a new politics that might cope with the threat of extinction.

No book can bring this about. But if many tread parallel paths, the mere communication of thought can give notice and prepare the way.

To restate the present situation: we talk as if we knew and sound as if we did not want to know. What cannot but shock us in print is soon swamped by other sensations; what we may not doubt at the moment seems still too appalling to be given access to our hearts. We catch ourselves looking upon certainty as, after all, not quite certain. But then we are still ignorant of the fact. For knowledge, in this case, means conviction that we are dealing with the ultimate fact — with the point, so to speak, from which all that we are and can be would have to be put onto a different plane.

One is tempted to ask a question. If the first Christians believed in the end of the world, if they were sure of it even though they did not know, even though they were, in fact, mistaken — do we today, who know the fact, have to believe it as well, to accept its reality, and to make it a factor in our way of life?

We let it stand as if it did not concern us, since at this moment, here and now, it is not yet acute. As the sick man forgets his cancer, the healthy man his mortality, the bankrupt his plight — is this how we react to the atom bomb, covering up the horizon of our existence and muddling through, unthinkingly, a while longer?

We would prefer to know nothing of the atomic menace. We explain that neither politics nor planning is possible under the threat of total disaster; we want to live, not to die — but this catastrophe would finish everything, so there is no point in thinking of it. It seems to be one of these things which decency forbids mentioning, lest it make life unbearable. And yet, nothing but this very unbearableness can cause the event that might change it.

What a purposely blind state of life! Disregarding the possible controverts reason. Whoever is himself wants to know all there is to be known. And what poor politics! Today we find ourselves inescapably overshadowed by the cataclysm. Only the ostrich will, before thinking it through, treat a real possibility as if it would disappear if he ignored it.

Today the constant presence of the cataclysm as a possibility — indeed, a probability — offers a signal opportunity for reflection as such, and at the same time the one chance for the political rebirth that would avert the cataclysm. The stakes of the game should be part of everyone's life, as a call for reflection. There lies the horizon of reality in which we must stand. A refusal to know is already part of the disaster.

We hope that all men will know, and that this knowledge will be pervasive and consequential. For pervasive knowledge alone can prevent calamity. It not only enables individuals to act to a purpose; it enables man to change himself and his life, to recast his basic mold.

The threat of total extinction points to thoughts about the meaning of our existence. The atom bomb cannot be adequately comprehended as a special problem; man can prove equal to it only if his true self responds to the chance at hand. If he treats the matter as one among other difficulties, he will not master it.

It is the purpose of this book, therefore, to range to the best of my ability through all the fields in which the bomb poses questions. I want my words to convey a sense beyond their content, a sense of what truly counts. I want to bring my readers to a more conscious recognition of what they already know, to its re-examination, and, perhaps, to a view of it that may be clearer than mine.

Only by questioning in all directions can truth become manifest. I should like to approach the challenge of the bomb from every possible angle, each time in its own way, and to try out every road. I should like to give voice to all moods: the outraged, the aggressive, the hopeless, the despairing, the nonchalant, the trustful. I want to detach the arguments, insofar as they are objectively valid, from the moods. I should like to state the case for fundamentally different ways of thinking. As not all the questions and answers lie on the same level, they cannot be treated alike, as of the same kind; I want to test the ways of thinking on their own levels and to let each reveal its limits.

I am aiming at the whole of the politico-philosophical consciousness that can today become reality and truth. I know that if one man ventures to do so he will, at first, surely miss much and go wrong often; but the principle of thinking through the whole is vital. This is what mattered to me. One man's attempt to realize this aim is bound to fall short, but the important thing, to my mind, is to make the attempt, not just to state the aim in general terms. The idea of entirety must be at work in the background, whatever particulars are under investigation.

I hope that others traveling the same road will do better, without forgetting what this book touches upon. Such entire awareness, with its tensions, must become general if we are to reason with each other, to prepare our decisions with full clarity, and to reach them in the broadest scope.

Of all-encompassing importance is the distinction between two ways of thinking. *Intellectual thought* is the inventor and maker. Its precepts can be carried out and can multiply the making by infinite repetition. The result is a world in which a few minds devise the mechanics, creating, as it were, a second world in which the masses then assume the operative function. *Rational thought*, on the other hand, does not provide for the carrying-out of mass directives but requires each individual to do his own thinking, original thinking. Here, truth is not found by a machine reproducible at will, but by decision, resolve, and action whose self-willed performance, by each on his own, is what creates a common spirit.

What grows out of the free acts of countless men and comes upon us like an overwhelming tide of events is no mere tide of events. Every individual acts in it as a free agent. However powerless he may feel, no one is wholly powerless. We may quail before the course of history as before a relentlessly rising tidal wave, and we may be swept along. But we join in building dikes, and men have been able to stand fast. History differs from the tides of the sea. Those tides are mute. History speaks, and we answer. The very union of men is no mere natural phenomenon but an event animated by their freedom. However minute a quantity the individual may be among the factors that make history, he is a factor. He cannot attribute it all to a tide of events of which none is his doing.

The self-awareness of man is founded in the inner change that is incomprehensible, unreal even, to the intellect. If I base my awareness of existence on the mental attitude of the intellect, on its know-all and know-how, I sink into nothingness. Searching for myself along this road is futile; I shall have forgotten myself in mere intellectual thought. Reason brings me back to myself.

After the inner change, intellect and reason remain linked. Whatever is objectively, intellectually thinkable must be thought through to its limits, to be retained, conversely, in the realm of reason. The bounds of cognition are met and surpassed at the same time.

Everything along the way of presentation, taken by itself, will justify objections. Because it must first become clear by itself, it tempts us into a premature fixation on the question and answer of the moment; we get caught in discussions that made sense only along the way, from a limited point of view. It sounds final, so we allow ourselves to be trapped, so to speak, and lose ourselves in it.

In fact, however, nothing exists by itself. It is only after passing through all the perspectives with their emerging aspects that we can visualize the whole so as to serve our purpose. What we attain is not a system of the whole but an orderly discussion of the perspectives. Our aim is to make sure, within the scope of data and conceivabilities, of the ultimate motives from which our judgments and trends of action spring.

The parts of this book, therefore, complement one another. None seems to be dispensable. They can be understood only in the whole, and yet the whole itself is not visible. This corresponds to our human situation, which limits us to directions and ascertainments, and to an awareness of the foundations on which we live in history.

Not everything is solved, and the whole is never completed. If we beware of many premature, intellectually facile but unnecessary alternatives, we will the more decisively encounter the few alternatives that are true — because in our situation they are unbridgeable. They face us with the great historic decisions which in our temporal existence we cannot dodge. They seem inexorable, although we cannot sufficiently define them in rational form; if we could, the decisions would become mere arithmetical problems from a point of view outside the alternatives

— but we stand within the alternatives. We want to surmount them, and in truth we cannot see beyond them.

In complementary thinking, as well as in touching on our final alternatives, we can do no more than reach the space that seems to await us, limitless and beyond all perspective. There we find the resolution for what we do on our way of life — which is still not the way of all men. So, general suggestions must not be taken for ultimate truth, only for the medium in which — ever unsure of the whole — we know what we want here and now, in this situation, in the face of unsettled history.

The purpose of this book is not to take a "departmental" position — as, for example, from the viewpoint of philosophy as an academic discipline. I mean to address that part of man which is above departments. This intention is vulnerable, because it seems to involve bringing up anything and everything; but it is necessary because in no other way can we approach what matters. The problem is basic, and solving it takes all of man.

True, every task calls for a division of labor. We have special fields in science, organized departments in administration, a diversity of specialists in politics; we defer to the authority of expert knowledge, of professional standing, of official position, of membership in groups, nations, states. But all division presupposes the unity of the whole. Departments have a limited meaning. The whole which unites them also limits their realm of validity; it is their source and their guidepost. The whole, on the other hand, is common to all and belongs to no one or everyone — but only insofar as he realizes the whole, as he is a complete human being. Departmentalization ceases where all departments must be directed so that each can thrive. But the whole, or the source, or the final goal — these cannot in turn become matters for a department, or be departments themselves. It is from there, rather, that all the departments derive their meaning.

This same problem recurs in every sphere of our existence as thinking creatures. It encompasses the problem of intellect and reason, of specialized science and philosophy. Science is objectively compelling intellectual cognition; philosophy is rational self-enlightenment. Both are distinct and inseparable. Science becomes bottomless without philosophy; philosophy can take no step without the intellect, that is, without science.

A way of thinking that belongs to no department and does not surrender to any — this is a kind of philosophy we may expect of everyone.

It may be dormant, but in the true human being it can be raised to bright consciousness and critical assurance. "Philosophy is too high for me. . . . I'm no expert in philosophy. . . . I've never cared for philosophy. . . ." Such phrases serve to reject what everyone does unwittingly and, therefore, as a rule, poorly. This constant philosophy in all of us stamps our consciousness, determines our motivations, and is the bearer of all that we publicly take for granted.

It is the philosophers' fault — and in particular the fault of us professors of philosophy — if, instead of searching for the human language, we permit our thinking to limit itself and to degenerate into a department, into academic philosophy. We do not have mass incomprehension to complain about, but our own unseriousness and ineptitude.

This book is philosophical in intent. It makes no suggestions, performs no political act, offers no over-all solution. It belongs to no "department" and does not claim to be authorized by one. In the atom bomb question today, the typical procedure is for each expert in turn to state his case — physicist, biologist, military man, politician, theologian — and then to declare himself incompetent outside his special field. Yet all of them in so doing appeal to a listener or reader who is supposed to understand them all, to check their statements understandingly as best he can, to gain an over-all insight and to judge them, in his turn, on an over-all basis. Where is this complete man? He is every individual, including the lecturing specialists. We are too ready today to accede to such disclaimers as "I am not competent there" or "This is not my field." They may be true in regard to specialized knowledge and skills, but they become untrue if applied to concepts, decisions, and resolutions that concern the issue as a whole and thus the whole human being.

The limit of departmental thinking is the existence of issues that concern the whole and are up to everyone. This limit shows up in the question of the atom bomb. It is not a particular problem which experts might solve by special measures. It is today not one question among others; it is the one vital question: to be or not to be. Its shadow falls on whatever else we may do or inquire. Its solution lies at a depth of human existence which man achieves by no special knowledge, by no special activity, only by himself. Here he faces a task that he cannot meet with a "task force." It is vain to view the problem in isolation, as a particular threat that might be answered particularly and surmounted singly. The issue, rather, involves all of man and requires him to commit all his life to coping with it — in peacetime by his entire manner of living and in the crisis by courage and sacrifice. He has opportunities for which his intellect cannot plan, but which must be seized if he is to master the situation. Here, departmentalized thinking comes to a standstill. Truth, here, not only concerns everybody but must be grasped, created, realized by everybody from the depths of his existence. We are entering a zone where conventions fade, where departmental manners grow meaningless, where the foreground of respect for taboos, for silence, for mutual untouchability is breached.

Since we possess the power of total destruction, but not yet the power of controlling it with calculating certainty, everyone asks: What can be done? Where is the way out?

One wants an unequivocal, definitive answer. One wants concrete proposals: for actions, for institutions, for treaties, for gradual developments that would put everything right. One demands the impossible.

For a concrete moment, of course, stressing a particular idea or insisting upon a particular demand makes sense. These are political acts and can have meaning only in concrete situations, from the standpoint of the actor. They become true only insofar as all perspectives remain present in their own horizons.

These horizons can be shown. We can think and feel them through — we can, so to speak, experimentally place ourselves within them, thus realizing the inner condition from which proposals and actions spring at the concrete moment and can be examined. Thought sets the stage; clears up the premises; purveys the knowable data, the ground on which the way must be found. It is not easy to understand that, while our insight can develop only in a multiplicity of aspects and ways of thinking, the real action remains the plunge into the tide of history — and that is not deducible. It follows neither from general rules, like the solution of an arithmetical problem, nor from the manifest view of facts, of the state of the world.

In the nature of the case, therefore, a book like this should not be approached with false expectations. I do not show how to do things. I unveil no theory of what will happen. I take no definitive stand. I have no consoling final answer. I will indeed mention proposals, discuss projects for the future, assume occasional positions — but all this is by the way. I will try to survey our situation, but this, too, only in the possible perspectives. It will all remain in suspense. I will show that for thought alone there is no solution that might be worked out according to instructions.

Such thinking — which is granted to man without giving him the rest of a conclusion — takes stamina. It calls for endurance in the tensions of insolubility. It requires the candor of seeking fulfilment only from the ultimate source.

Yet in the end all suspense, all candor, all boundlessness of questioning is not skepticism but a will to make a resolute existence possible by thought. Existence itself is left free, left to its own responsibility which nothing can alleviate. Thinking helps to attain purity. Such thinking is the enthusiasm of reason.

A problem that has no lasting solution seems all the more formidable for being inescapable. It appears as soon as we see through the false intellectual premise that all problems are soluble — and that the insoluble ones are so because we ask the wrong questions. The intellect starts with the erroneous assumption that man can manage his affairs in the world; disappointed, it jumps to the erroneous conclusion that all is in vain and the world will surely perish.

Pronouncements by scientists, men of letters, philosophers, theologians, are all to the good insofar as they tell facts. If they go further, they are political in the narrow sense of the word, serving parties and states, whether or not they intend to — or else they would be prophetic proclamations, postulates by virtue of higher authority. One should hear them, read them, look at the speakers to see whether, in this sense, they merit credence. The present book wants to serve only for orientation, for clarification, and as a reminder. Action, not thought, will bring the solution of the mystery — the innumerable actions of innumerable people who have prepared themselves for this by thinking it through.

As for my thoughts about the consequences of the atom bomb, I have arranged them in three parts: first, general discussions that lead to dead ends; second, a review of the present world situation; third, a clarification of the human essence. In the first part, principles will be developed along the lines of the realities of our time, to show us that, while indispensable to our insight, they provide no solution but arrive at limits where they fail. The second part will show the concrete facts which no one in quest of reality can ignore. The third part will try, on the basis of the theoretical and concrete knowledge of the first two, to bring encompassing reason to the fore. Our new situation should revive our sense of what we are — our sense, as Kant put it, of what it means to be human.

The third part is the most extensive. It deals with the questions that came up most frequently, all but exclusively, in letters from my radio audience. It brings us to the philosophy that is not merely a matter of academic teaching but a reality in man as a truly human, as a rational creature.

In this tripartite arrangement, the end of the book should, from the beginning, play a part in our examination of particulars — and conversely, particular views should be kept in mind until the end. The basic ideas should keep recurring in variations. It will be seen from the outset that all politics depends on something above politics, but also that this suprapolitical element is not unequivocal. We may call it ethics, self-sacrifice, reason — yet each of these three is dependent upon the others, or at one with them. Distinction is only a way to make them communicable. It should help to make us aware of the mission of man; to lift our eyes beyond the world, to the source of our strength to fulfil our reality in the world.

KARL JASPERS

Initial Political Thinking About the New Fact

If a new world war comes, atom bombs are sure to fall. If an atomic holocaust is to be averted, no world war must break out. Every little war threatens to set off a world war. So there must be no more war.

Concretely, today the logic is as follows: Nuclear warfare is actually double suicide for the antagonists. They will not commit it, for their fear of the consequences will overcome their ill will.

But then the reasoning goes on: Because atomic war has become impossible, all war between the atomic superpowers has become impossible. Since at some stage of a world war for survival the nuclear threat would materialize, no great power will any longer risk starting a war. Since it would be a war of annihilation for all, it can no longer happen. Total peril engenders total deliverance. An extreme emergency compels forms of political existence which make not only the bomb but war itself impossible.

Yet this general idea does not dispel our worries. Fear alone is not enough to rely upon in the long run. Something must be done to assure permanence. As a result we are hearing two demands: first, the atom bomb must be abolished; second, world peace must be established not on fear alone, but on law.

The prevalent notion today is that we should stop testing atom bombs, forbid their manufacture, and destroy the ones on hand. This seems the simplest way. It could be done by agreement. A condition of the agreement would be mutual controls, which alone can guarantee observance.

This would be the act of salvation. But it would immediately do more than abolish the nuclear threat, for mutual controls would necessarily involve a transformation of political existence — a change from the status of nations facing each other like beasts in a state of nature to an international community founded on legal agreements guaranteed by common institutions. It would be the transition from a status of mere co-existence, unilaterally changeable to war at any moment by an act of violence, to a status of co-operation, with the freedom of all dependent upon their subordination to agreements jointly arrived at and put into effect by executive organs. It would be the beginning of world peace.

Such controls would, in the first place, entail a complete mutual privity, in itself a form of the mutual candor that would in turn produce the common spirit indispensable for peace. The resulting ubiquity of information would be the first act of making peace. The second result of controls would be the voluntary restriction of the sovereignty of all, by *de facto* recognition of the validity of treaties above sovereignty — treaties which, like all treaties, must rest not only on faith but on effective control agencies. The treaty powers would have to place such agencies above themselves. Only then would brute force no longer be free to tear up agreements.

The establishment of mutual controls would be the first and decisive step toward world peace. The rest of its realization would be incomparably easier. However, abolition of the atom bomb and establishment of an effective control agency do not seem possible as isolated, independent fruits of intelligent political planning, for several reasons.

First, any judgment of the reliability of controls presupposes the technical knowledge reached at the time. A conference of Russian, American, English, and, perhaps, other physicists — not politicians — would have to clarify the possible and necessary procedures for reliable controls. No such conference has done so at the time of this writing.

Second, no controls can function with absolute reliability in areas as vast as the American and Asian continents; even huge stores and factories can always be hidden underground. Even successful controls would be assured only in peacetime; all states in possession of the construction secrets could manufacture the bombs in case of war and use the peace to prepare their industrial plant for rapid manufacture. Finally, the difficulties of control would rise with the growing facility of atom bomb production and with the number of countries acquiring the bomb.

Third, the requisite scope of controls is apparent from the American Baruch Plan, dating from the time when Russia did not have the bomb as yet. All atomic energy on earth would have to be placed under an international authority which would not only control but own and administer all the uranium deposits on earth and all the industries producing and using atomic energy. Its officials were to be granted extraterritorial rights, like diplomatic envoys, and to be free to inspect and photograph anything they liked, anywhere in the world. In the directing councils of this authority there was to be majority rule without veto.

This plan — which America then offered to accept, while Russia hesitated — had one condition attached: it could only be carried out simultaneously with general disarmament. It was for this reason, too, that the existing bombs (then exclusively American) were to be destroyed only after the control machinery had started functioning.

We conclude: Controls are impossible without general disarmament. Not until world peace will be secured can they be adequate. The mere idea and attempt to establish controls cannot achieve their purpose.

There is no solution without eliminating war from the course of human events. War, which has existed as long as man, would have to cease. What used to be settled by war would have to find other ways of settlement; whatever courage and self-sacrifice or adventurous recklessness, wanton savagery, destructive hatred used to be released in war would have to find other outlets. Without world peace there is no preventing the extinction of mankind in an atomic holocaust.

In practice, however, controls are rejected today not only because no nation, not even the Western ones, will accept the premises of world peace. The decisive reason now is that controls and the totalitarian form of government are mutually exclusive. For totalitarianism to permit controls would be to abandon itself, to abdicate; for this form of government rests upon secrecy and state direction of all information. It can tolerate neither the free circulation of news nor the unlimited publication of ideas. To make known what the state itself does not make known counts as espionage or treason. Totalitarianism and its carriers, the leaders and the machine, must resist controls as long as they identify themselves with their form of government. Their minds must necessarily be set against controls as a matter of self-preservation: *principiis obsta*. And this attitude in turn must be disguised; they must talk as if, in principle, they were prepared to accept controls. They must constantly negotiate about them, but so as to strangle them at birth. They must invent controls that are ineffective and yet will serve to deceive those who are taken in by appearances.

In other words, the acceptance of controls presupposes a readiness for their infallible effect of assuring peace. By the very fact of their establishment, controls imply the solidarity they would create.

World peace will be achieved only by a new politics. Let us outline its principles, deducing them from its nature without asking now about the possibility of its realization — not dreaming up a fantasy of a utopian realm of immaculate spirits, but proceeding from the realities of human nature and freedom. This will gives us a yardstick to measure what we want and what already exists.

World peace rests on two premises: First, on *free will* — right and justice are to rule instead of force. Second, on *reality* — the human world is not and will never be one of right and perfect justice, but man can strive to make progress on the road to justice.

Nothing but the maintenance of this free pursuit of justice is definitive in existence. Everything is subject to revision: new realities appear; new questions are raised; tests are prepared in public discussion and carried out in legal forms that are revisable in their turn, but held inviolate for the duration of their validity. The one mortal foe of this freedom is a resort to violence.

As our condition can never be one of perfect justice, it can only be a condition of law that still includes some injustice — a condition of non-violence that still includes a minimum of force to maintain itself. The mortal enemy of this condition is indifference to wrong and to violence. Its survival depends on constant sensitivity to wrong and injustice, and on the energy to correct them.

On these two premises, the principles of this condition within and between states can be expressed as follows:

1. *To restrain violence, there must be binding commitments.*

a) All must be bound to recognize legality. Treaties must be acknowledged as legally in force as long as they are not altered by new negotiations.

b) All must be bound to renounce arbitrary action. Supremacy of law entails a renunciation of absolute sovereignty, as well as a renunciation of the veto power over decisions of any legally established authority.

c) There is always a remnant of force. It is an illusion that the right could be relied upon to prevail. As truth needs exponents, the right needs power — a power that is not inherent in it. War can be eliminated only if there is a supreme legal authority that can replace violence with law and arbitrate the gravest conflicts of opinion and interest. But this authority must dispose of effective means to enforce and maintain its decisions. A state cannot abolish the police, and states that bind themselves by treaty cannot abolish the force required to secure the treaties made under their guarantee. The creation of supranational authorities, which the nations would have to set up and to equip with unprecedented powers — the realization of the form in which the remaining force would, as a common force, be placed at the disposal of the legal authority — that is the great problem.

d) All must be bound to recognize the ballot, majority rule, and the determination of the popular will of the moment by free, secret elections. Let him who would act politically inform the people, use thought to persuade them, and reasons, points of view, and his own example to educate them. Truth must be able, in the long run, to win confirmation from the people. Only thus do men grow to partake in knowledge, to comprehend, and to resolve to make the change that is incumbent on mankind.

Those whom indignation at mass stupidity turns against free elections are forgetting that in the course of history — with some accidental exceptions — rulers have been no wiser, no more truthful, no better, no more responsible than a majority of the governed, and vice versa. They are forgetting also that, the greater the task, the more important is the education and co-operation of all.

We have no other means of inquiry than the ballot. To make it yield the best possible results is the responsibility of everyone, above all of those who seek power. Free secret elections are the only tangible means of political freedom as well as of peace — for only insofar as they follow the idea of democracy and recognize its commitments are the nations capable of peace.

2. *The establishment, maintenance, and development of binding commitments requires unrestricted communication.*

a) Freedom without violence is possible only if information is exchanged, if peoples mingle, and if discussion is public — and only when all this happens without restriction. The first act of peacemaking, therefore, is to permit the communication of news and the publicity of debate throughout the world, free from censorship and without risk for the individual. Real, world-wide, unlimited publicity is a premise of freedom and peace.

b) The principle of truthfulness demands that facts be admitted, that people put themselves in other people's shoes, that they see different interests, and voice their own true motives.

c) The community of peace exists only on the strength of a public communal spirit: a sensitive consciousness of right, which in most cases makes everyone co-responsible when any wrong is done. This alone will keep the wrong from attaining proportions that make violent rebellion irresistible and end the state of peace.

Ever since the time of the Seven Greek Sages, one rule has held for every citizen of a free state: The wrong that is done to another citizen is done to me. And what applies to the citizens of a state is true, in a peaceful world situation, among the citizens of all states. This world condition demands that we, through the community of nations, intervene to protect people anywhere who are deprived of their human rights. The internal tasks of each state are inseparable from its concern with the internal conduct of all other states — not, however, manifested by direct intervention, but by way of intervention on the part of supra-national authorities.

3. *To keep the unjust results of changing conditions from causing violence, the way for peaceful revision of all relationships must be left open.*

That men and nations have a claim to equal rights is a recognized principle, but this claim conflicts with the actual inequality of nations as well as men. Their native endowments — never finally determinable — differ as much as their strength, their talents, their visible accomplishments, their actions and the consequences of their actions, and their numbers. There can only be equality of opportunity within the external possibilities, no actual equality of all. If an external equality were established today, it would be changed by tomorrow into obvious inequality by the differences between men; in fact, their equalization beyond equality of opportunity would be the height of injustice. If there is to be peace, ineradicable inequalities must, as a matter of principle, be respected and allowed to grow non-violently into levels of rank.

But inequalities, and thus actual orders of rank, are constantly changing. Vested inequality is unjust. True, there is a historical continuity due to the actions and achievements of parents and ancestors; they have broken ground that remains fertile, bearing privileges of origin and inception — but only insofar as these credibly represent and prove themselves in the present. There are no definitive, permanently valid realities of rank by birth, descent, tradition, or property.

The principle of peace, therefore, is both to recognize inequalities and to be ready to revise the realities of rank on the basis of changes in fact — but only legally and after due reflection.

Likewise, political boundaries and treaties that have become unjust must be legally revisable. Subject peoples, or those evolving toward particularity, are to be freed on demand by a supranational authority.

It is easy to outline such principles of political peace, but thinking them out and proving them right does not make them real. Of course, it is still easier to smile at them and point to realities, to call them utopian and boast of one's own shrewd realism. Kant has given the answer to this attitude: "A constitution of the greatest possible human freedom, under laws which enable the freedom of each to endure together with that of all others, is at least a necessary idea. . . . Nothing can be more noxious and unworthy of a philosopher than the vulgar appeal to allegedly contrary experience — which, after all, would not exist if those measures had been taken in good time, in line with their ideas."

This is why those outlines are not utopian as long as they are understood in the ideal sense. They unfold the pattern of the idea whose realization remains an infinite task, and as such they are the standards for our critique and judgment of reality, and our guidelines for the efficacy of the idea within us.

In fact, to be sure, the principles of world peace are still rejected. Politics still runs in the same channels as ever, uses the same means and the same sophistry of argument. It is easy to show that the very opposite of the principles outlined above is in effect today — that within states they apply only partially and unreliably, while internationally they are either wholly ignored or slightly observed by only a few of the Western or Westernized nations. And they are not merely ignored in fact; as most men want peace, statesmen pronounce "principles of peace" — but theirs run diametrically counter to a truly peaceful world order.

What are the taboos? Absolute national sovereignty — hence, the demand for mutual non-interference and a veto right in common councils; equal rights for all to act arbitrarily; finally, peaceful coexistence of governmental and social systems based on concepts of law so utterly different as to be mutually exclusive, with mutual intercourse barred by iron curtains.

Let us examine these principles one by one.

Absolute sovereignty and non-interference are needed today to prevent the inevitable abuse of interference and to delay the outbreak of war; in a truly peaceful state of the world they would be unbearable. From a legal point of view, asking for absolute sovereignty and non-interference amounts to asking for the freedom, in a concrete situation, to decide alone and arbitrarily what is right — which means, in fact, the freedom to do wrong. It implies a readiness to break agreements and to make war if one has the power and if circumstances seem auspicious.

The holding of a veto on decision-making bodies thwarts any subordination of states to a rule of law.

Non-interference keeps the spirit of law from developing jointly in the mutual intercourse of nations. As every citizen should feel the wrong done to another as a wrong done to himself, every state should react to injustice suffered by citizens of another state as if its own had suffered it. Neither a nation nor an international community can long endure if its people remain indifferent to injustice practiced against people elsewhere. Governments ruling their subjects by terror constitute the antithesis of peace; they are a threat to world peace, being always ready to carry their violence from their own countries to the rest of mankind.

Equal rights thwart peace if they mean equal rights of arbitrary action, not just the same right to defend one's interests by legal means.

Failure to permit the free flow of news, to allow free public discussion, to tolerate the contest of parties in free elections — this bespeaks the determination of a power apparatus to retain the features it cannot risk showing in public. The need for concealment proves that wrong is being done. Concealment, stealth, and mendacity amount to potential violence. He who lacks power, or an opportune moment to use it, may for the time being resort to the fraud called "peaceful coexistence." By "peacefully" weakening his antagonist wherever possible, he will prepare for the final act of violence. Warding it off takes publicity. Not only the rulers but the peoples must talk to each other. Iron curtains mean violence and impairment of freedom.

The principles of absolute sovereignty, of veto powers, of equal rights for every state, including the right to maintain a reign of terror and refuse full public information — these principles are but a seemingly

moral smoke screen, behind which everyone does as he pleases to safeguard his power. Besides, they are a dam built in the public consciousness to delay the disaster, but a dam that may give way at any moment.
On the one hand, these principles leave room for the use of force; on the
other, they are available for the manipulation of a wavering public
opinion that is easily taken in by them, even at the very moment of
their violation.

Peace never comes from coexistence, only from co-operation. To gain
a breathing spell and at least to postpone war, one takes coexistence
into the bargain. In the present situation, even what is known to be
adverse to peace cannot be rejected — for to put the principles of peace
under law into practice unilaterally, without delay or limitations, would
be suicidal. The principles of world peace and the stated principles of
the present situation are poles apart. What then is to be done?

If we keep thinking politically, we should plan to make the peace-
promoting principles prevail, in time, over the ones now dominant.
Since humanity does not want to perish, nations would have to agree
to limit their sovereign power. What was done on a small scale when
governments were first instituted might be repeated with an international confederation. What scientific intelligence produced in the atom
bomb — the possibility of utter disaster — might be surmounted by the
same intelligence, by institutional techniques that would make treaties
effective.

If this effort succeeded, man would not need to change. By means of
intelligently conceived institutions, the will of all would restrain every
individual from further yielding to the basic human drives: the drive to
use force; the delight in violence and its risks; the urge to sacrifice oneself in violent action, to conquer or die; the love of high adventure as
a release from the tedium of our existence. Jointly imposed curbs would
now channel these drives into forms that would not menace the
community.

So far, however, this process fails to take place. What looks like it
turns out to be not progress but procrastination. Behind the veil of appearances, we rather find power positions being reinforced and preparations being made for extremity. True, the political arguments favoring an institutional improvement of the situation are plausible, and attempts along this way should never be abandoned. But they can never
suffice.

The way of politics itself needs another guidance. No man who has left a lasting mark in politics has ever acted from purely political motives. No politics fit for man has ever been self-sufficient. There are fortunate incidents in history, as in the English, Swiss, Dutch, and American struggles for freedom, when a truer ethos permeated the competence, the astuteness, the methods of politics — distinguished from great political achievements that are due to the superior skill of individuals and, as mere displays of skill, are ephemeral because they effect no political education.

Thus the continuation of political thinking brings us to the frontier where mere politics fails and a resolve is needed — the resolve of the human being in whom a change is wrought by extremity. There is, to be sure, an old, recurrent, and still widespread view that human nature is immutably the same we have always seen in practical politics, that wars are ineradicable, and so is the unscrupulous course of political action with its lies, betrayals, and trickery. This fact of nature should indeed not be forgotten, but neither should another fact: that one of the driving forces in politics is something above politics.

This is why purely political thinking, confined to political rules, is at a loss in extremities. Such thinking, supposedly realistic, is a smoke screen in which the human self is forgotten — just as the illusions of some other ways of thinking would have us forget the realities of human nature. Something above politics must guide political institutions, legislations, designs — if they are to endure. This is the font of the spirit that must pervade their reality in concrete situations, if they are to be trusted.

To us, the *suprapolitical* element is manifested in the ethical idea and in the valor of sacrifice. They can provide the conditions for the achievement of world peace — conditions impossible to create by treaties and institutions, but growing, rather, out of man's other side which the observer of tangible reality never perceives.

NOTES AND QUESTIONS

1. According to Jaspers what is the right kind of political thinking? Does the solution depend upon the transformation of man or the reconstitution of international society? Is Jaspers' response to "the new fact" compatible with the Clark-Sohn response? What are the principles that Jaspers posits as essential for the attainment of an enduring world peace? How does Jaspers propose to deal with the transition problem? What is the connection between the solution of the transition problem and what Jaspers calls "the *suprapolitical* element"?

2. Compare Jaspers' commendation for the right kind of thinking with Rapoport's comparison of strategic and systemic modes and with Singer's description of the several levels of analysis. What does philosophy have to contribute to the enterprise of war prevention? How does Jaspers answer this question? Would most Anglo-American philosophers agree with him? Do Clark and Sohn make sufficiently clear the philosophical bases of their proposals? Is a common conception of man and of human destiny a prerequisite of radical system change? Does Jaspers imply that it is?

We end as we began, with a problem and a plan, but we add to this a plea in the form of an essay by one of the editors. This essay, "The Study of War Prevention: Toward a Disciplined View" by Saul H. Mendlovitz, is adapted with the permission of the *Bulletin of the Atomic Scientists* from an article entitled "Teaching War Prevention" which first appeared in the February, 1964 issue. It seeks to state the case for war prevention as a serious field for academic study. Certainly, this is late to be making such an argument, but it is intended to orient your view of the future. When we ask "what can be done to prevent a major war?" one answer is to use our mental skills to the greatest advantage. We have already suggested that the mind is not sufficient by itself, that analysis must be animated by conscience if it is to transform our world-view. And let us be clear that nothing less is called for. Mendlovitz is asking us to devote a portion of our intellectual energy to the disciplined study of war prevention. It is this disciplined study that has helped with the solution of tormenting social problems in the past. The argument asks that we now consider war as a tormenting social problem susceptible to disciplined study. This set of readings seeks to be a preliminary demonstration of this potential for discipline.

SAUL H. MENDLOVITZ

The Study of War Prevention: Toward a Disciplined View

Should we ever be in a position to write a history of the successful world peace movement that is taking place in the second half of the twentieth century, there is little doubt that the academic community of the United States will emerge as a significant contributor. From the scientists' moment of stark comprehension that the bomb they helped assemble might actually be used, the concern and participation of academicians from all disciplines—as individuals, in groups, in official and unofficial capacities—have increased steadily, so that today the proportion of the academic community actively engaged in the peace movement probably exceeds that of any other vocational group. All this activity is misunderstood if it is seen only as the scholar acting as an ordinary citizen. For it represents the academic community carrying out one of its most important functions, that of expressing the conscience of the community in a manner that permits reasoned discussion, deepened understanding, and the invention of alternative courses of action.

Many situated in the academic community at once recognized that the new weapons of the nuclear age had radically altered the consequences of international violence in such a fashion that only the persistent and courageous mobilization of all the intellectual resources at the disposal of man would be able to contrive the means for transforming the existent war-prone system into a war prevention system without the experience of an intervening catastrophe. Members of the academic community have been moderately successful in awakening concern throughout the world with this range of problems.

To be sure, this concern has not always resulted in sensible behavior. Serious misunderstanding of Sino-Soviet intentions and capacities, research to bolster an already swollen defense establishment, and naive political action are familiar criticisms of the intellectual role of the academy. A further deficiency might, if corrected, affect the validity of these criticisms: the relatively small amount of time which scholars and educators give to the problems of world order and war prevention in their research and teaching.

There are some outstanding centers for peace research, but it is difficult to avoid the conclusion that the amount of peace research is minuscule, by any standard of reasonable comparison with the research going on in other subjects of human concern. J. David Singer has written that current peace research is being done by "the wrong people with the wrong questions," and is therefore of doubtful utility. In the classroom itself, peace education—or what is described as war prevention—is also conspicuously absent. In major universities, it is true, there may be one or two seminars that bear upon the subject, and in smaller schools an individual may on occasion offer a special course. But until very recently, it was rare to find a course on war prevention as an ordinary offering in social science departments, let alone in law and divinity school curricula.

In some ways this lack of attention is not surprising. It seems plausible to argue that with little research on the topic, it hardly makes sense to teach a course. Precisely what is it that ought to be taught? Should a course consider all patterns of group violence or should it confine itself to the specific dangers of nuclear war? Would the study of group violence lead to a better understanding of human behavior and social systems? Would this type of study produce beneficial theory? Isn't the very notion of war prevention so utopian that it would be irresponsible to impose it upon students? Even if these questions could be answered satisfactorily, there are those who would insist that standard international relations courses usually take up the problem of war prevention and that a separate course would introduce redundancy into the curriculum, being justified, if at all, only by its somewhat different emphasis. We are led to a single overwhelming issue: applying the same rigorous intellectual and academic standards that justify existing courses, is it possible to develop a course devoted to the study of war prevention? If the answer is yes, then—in view of the urgency and magnitude of the problem—the case for offering or even compelling college students to take such a course seems quite strong.

My own efforts to develop a course of war prevention may be considered to be part of the affirmative argument for taking seriously the academic claims of this subject. The impetus to create the course arose from the initiative of the publisher of these volumes, the World Law Fund. In the summer of 1961, the extension division of Rutgers University asked me to participate in an experimental program sponsored by the World Law Fund to encourage a serious reading of *World Peace through World Law* by Grenville Clark and Louis B. Sohn. The objective was to build a large-scale adult education program around this book. The Rutgers course was one of a number of pilot courses given in various universities. While not intimately acquainted with the book, I knew that it was generally characterized in academic circles as the most comprehensive and technically competent proposal for limited world government in being, but that it was nevertheless generally dismissed as unrealistic and somewhat utopian. However, as it offered the opportunity to deal directly with the problems of war prevention, I accepted the invitation to teach the course.

World Peace through World Law consists of a provision-by-provision comparison of the present United Nations Charter with a new Charter proposed by Clark and Sohn. The essence of the proposals is that an international system of law somewhat analogous to that found in domestic societies is needed if the international community is to achieve and maintain a stable peace. The Clark-Sohn revision of the Charter includes general and complete disarmament achieved and maintained by a strong structure of formal authority; development of an international police force to enforce disarmament and prevent international violence; establishment of mediation, conciliation, and compulsory court systems; creation of a reliable revenue base for United Nations operations which would also be used to support an ambitious world development program; and the grant of legislative authority to the General Assembly (with a considerably revised voting procedure based on weighted membership) to deal with war prevention.

Although these elements of a war prevention system are presented as a set of interrelated proposals, it is feasible and sensible to look at the merits of each element separately. In doing so, it becomes clear that the proposed model of world order is responsive to four troublesome dimensions of problem-solving in international society, and is especially sensitive to how solutions might be put into practice through the medium of an international organization. Many of the Clark-Sohn proposals seem to be designed to overcome the East-West political conflict, the North-South economic disparity, the reconciliation of population with other criteria for purposes of representation and voting within the authoritative decision-making structures; and the powers that would be given to the United Nations in relation to those retained by the states. This systematic attention to the major social and political problems of the world within the framework of a formal organization generated effectively the question of relevance to the creation and maintenance of a war prevention system. These questions raised the theoretical issues, as well as the practical ones, and were organized rather coherently around the Clark-Sohn model.

Three further considerations added to the attractiveness of this pedagogic scheme. First, the fact that the proposals were presented as a revision of the Charter of the United Nations encouraged an evaluation of the present role of formal international organization in controlling international violence. That this evaluation took place against the backdrop of a comprehensive model for world order made it natural to consider not only where we are and where we are going, but the transition question of how we are going to get there. An emphasis upon transition makes clear the necessity of constructing and using a relevant utopia as a model of a war prevention system. Even if the Clark-Sohn proposals should turn out to be impractical, the student is forced to consider what kind of stable war prevention system it is possible to attain; that is, the student must construct his own relevant utopia. To study the process of transition also provides a "realism" standard for the Clark-Sohn proposals.

Second, the Clark-Sohn scheme faces squarely a question about transition that the academic literature has tended to neglect: to what extent is it necessary and feasible to take a slow, step-by-step approach to world peace, as contrasted with taking a giant step by adopting all at once a set of interrelated proposals? Conventional wisdom on this issue is now firmly on the side of gradualism. The Clark-Sohn proposals can be read as a convincing argument for a more drastic approach to structural change in international society. On any single issue a particular nation might feel itself deprived of security, material goods, or political influence, but an integrated series of measures might provide a sufficient net gain for each nation so that it might be a more acceptable way of constructing a war prevention system than inching along in terms of universally acceptable action for all on each matter. This view of system change, introduced at the outset, with thorough discussion only after a fuller study of the scheme, could be a central focus of the course, but without precluding discussion of proposals and strategies that call for less comprehensive solutions. Finally, the elaborate detail of the Clark-Sohn proposals make it possible to test general principles of world order in terms of concrete behavior, sometimes even with a good deal of precision.

THE CONTRIBUTION OF LAW

Many competent scholars throughout the world have long considered law a dependent variable, the outcome of other social pressures, or, if you wish, epiphenomenal. Furthermore, international law, whatever its tradition of providing insight and rationalization for state behavior, certainly cannot be said to have had much impact upon state officials when it comes to their decisions about the use of organized violence in international relations. Since I wanted this course to be useful in law schools as well as in science departments, it was important to try to answer the question of what contribution, if any, law can make to the problem of war prevention. Since the question is complex and perhaps vulnerable to the criticism that it is not a sensible one, a few general remarks concerning the soundness of this "legal" perspective may be helpful.

Much of the discussion of the relationship of law to society depends, of course, on the particular definition of law posited; for our purposes it is sufficient to think of law as the empirical processes of legal institutions that an intelligent and moderately informed person would characterize as law. On this basis it is then reasonable to assert that within most modern states, law interacts with the significant social processes of the society, and that this is true whether law is viewed as a product of social forces or as an active agent within the social system. This constant interaction of law and social processes provides an initial rationale for the adoption of a legal perspective whenever a major social problem is being investigated, especially if one remains sensitive to the unsolved problems of causality in the interaction.

In all modern states, of course, legal institutions are used as principal means for the control and regulation of violence. Although the international legal system exhibits rather primitive formal structure at present, and regulates violence, to the extent that it does so, differently than does law in domestic societies, the legal perspective is nonetheless applicable to international problems. The literature and experience of international law provides a rich tradition bearing on the whole relationship of law to society in international life and on use of law to control international violence. And as supranational law develops within regional arrangements and world law structures begin to emerge, differences between systems of domestic law and the law of the international community will undoubtedly be chosen as focal points of study.

Turning from these theoretical considerations to the broad political problems of transition, and specifically to the design of a scheme of war prevention that might be acceptable to the peoples of the world, one should not minimize the fact that the experience of living under law is almost universal and that law can be appealed to in all societies as a rational method for achieving order and even justice in human affairs. To be sure, law has sometimes operated both oppressively and ineffectively, and there are good historical reasons for many people to be wary of legal solutions to human problems. These negative considerations are, however, not objections to law itself but to its substantive content or to a particular form of its application. Aside from a very few philosophical anarchists, most reasonable people— and this would include, for example, even revolutionaries and victims of oppression—envision a world in which law is properly used to control violence, resolve conflicts, redress harms, and promote social justice. In short, law as a method and goal for a world peace movement makes sense to the people of the world and to their governments.

It is on the basis of this reasoning that it seems possible to conclude that law does provide a realistic and logical point of departure for a serious study of war prevention.

Using *World Peace through World Law* as a model, the student is asked to evaluate whether the existing provisions of the United Nations Charter, the suggested Clark-Sohn revisions, or alternatives offered by other writers are necessary, feasible, and fair.

A vast literature of scholarly pretension (not to speak of official documents and speeches) on world affairs and war prevention does exist and in the absence of more and better research it seemed sensible to initiate study by evaluating the limitations and usefulness of what is available. Accordingly, a continuous theme throughout the course is the extent to which the proper issues are being discussed by various authors, whether there is suitable data present for an intelligent resolution of the issues, and whether it is possible to advance a more appropriate way of handling the issues. This methodological posture should, hopefully, lead to a clarification of what are the important and researchable problems in the war-peace area.

Certainly my work in teaching war prevention has convinced me that a course responsive to academic and intellectual standards can be put together, that it can be integrated into an existing curriculum in a rational way so as to satisfy pedagogic requirements, and that it will engage students in a meaningful fashion.

NOTES AND QUESTIONS

1. The Foreword to Kenneth S. Carlston's important book, *Law and Organization in World Society* (University of Illinois Press, 1962) p. vi, contains a passage relevant to the adoption of the legal perspective for the study of ordering and reconstituting international society:

> It is the lawyer's fate, no less than that of any man, to search continually for the truth. For if, in the words of Plato, law is "the leading string, golden and holy," which binds a society together, then the pattern of its golden skeins reveals the structure of the society itself. As it is the scientist's faith that there is an ultimate symmetry, order, and truth in nature, so it is the lawyer's faith that the body of law will express the full image of the society which it unites.

The Editors

RICHARD A. FALK. Albert G. Milbank Professor of International Law and Practice at Princeton University. Co-editor of *World Politics*. Author of *Law, Morality and War in the Contemporary World*, and *The Role of Domestic Courts in the International Legal Order*.

SAUL H. MENDLOVITZ. Professor of International Law at Rutgers University School of Law. Consultant to the World Law Fund, New York. Editor of *Legal and Political Problems of World Order*.

Notes on Authors

RICHARD J. BARNET. Co-director of the Institute for Policy Studies, Washington. Author of *Who Wants Disarmament?* and co-editor with Richard A. Falk of *Security in Disarmament*. Until 1963 he was Deputy Director of Political Research in the U.S. Arms Control and Disarmament Agency.

KENNETH E. BOULDING. Professor of Economics and co-director of the Center for Research in Conflict Resolution at the University of Michigan. Author of several books, including: *Conflict and Defense, The Economics of Peace, The Image*, and *Economic Analyses*.

ROBERTO DUCCI. Minister in Italian Ministry of Foreign Affairs. Former Counselor to the Italian Delegation of NATO. Chairman of the Drafting Committee of the Rome Treaties. Former Italian Ambassador to Finland.

HUGH GAITSKELL. Chancellor of the Exchequer, 1950–51. Leader of the Opposition in the British House of Commons from 1955 until his death in 1963.

ROBERT M. HUTCHINS. President of the Fund for the Republic. Formerly Dean of Yale Law School and Chancellor of the University of Chicago. Author of a number of books, including *Education for Freedom*, and *The University of Utopia*.

KARL JASPERS. German psychiatrist-philosopher. Winner of the German Peace Prize at the 1958 Frankfurt Book Fair for *The Future of Mankind*, and author of numerous books including *Reason and Existenz*.

POPE JOHN XXIII. Pope of the Roman Catholic Church from 1958 to June 3, 1963. Pope John is renowned for his championing of world peace, his initiative toward christian unity, and his efforts towards modernization and reform of the Roman Catholic Church. He convened Vatican II, the 21st Ecumenical Council, which he saw as a step toward the unity of all Christians.

HERMAN KAHN. Director, Hudson Institute, New York. Former Senior Staff Member, Physics Department, the RAND Corporation. Consultant to the Atomic Energy Commission and to the Office of Civil and Defense Mobilization. Author of *On Thermonuclear War*, and *Thinking About the Unthinkable*.

HAROLD D. LASSWELL. Edward J. Phelps Professor of International Law and Political Science at Yale University. Past President of the American Political Science Association. His books include *World Politics and Personal Insecurity*, and *National Security and Individual Freedom*.

WERNER LEVI. Professor of Political Science at the University of Hawaii. Author of *Fundamentals of World Organization, Free India in Asia*, and *Modern China's Foreign Policy*.

WALTER MILLIS. Staff Director of the Center for the Study of Democratic Institutions, Santa Barbara, California. His books include *Road to War, The Abolition of War* (with James Real), and *Arms and Men*.

H. L. NIEBURG. Associate Professor of Political Science at the University of Wisconsin. Author of *Nuclear Secrecy: A Study in Strategic Schizophrenia*.

ANATOL RAPOPORT. Professor of Mathematical Biology and Senior Research Mathematician at the Mental Health Research Institute of the University of Michigan. Author of *Science and the Goals of Man, Operational Philosophy, Flights, Games, and Debates*, and *Strategy and Conscience*.

J. DAVID SINGER. Professor of Political Science, University of Michigan. Member of the editorial board of the *Journal of Conflict Resolution*. Author of *Financing International Organization: The United Nations Budget Process*, and *Deterrence, Arms Control and Disarmament: Toward a Synthesis in National Security Policy*.

KENNETH N. WALTZ. Professor of Political Science at Swarthmore College. Author of *Man, the State and War*.

ALBERT J. WOHLSTETTER. Ford Research Professor, 1963–64, at the University of California at Berkeley. He has taught at various universities and written extensively on strategic topics. Former member of the Research Council, RAND Corporation.

QUINCY WRIGHT. Professor Emeritus of International Law, University of Chicago. Presently affiliated with the University of Virginia. Author of *The Study of International Relations, International Law and the United Nations,* and *A Study of War.*

RONALD J. YALEM. Associate Professor of International Relations at the University of Southern California. Author of *Regionalism and World Order.*

Permissions*

Kenneth E. Boulding. "The Prevention of World War III." Reprinted by permission of the author and publisher from *The Virginia Quarterly Review,* Vol. 38 (Winter, 1962) pp. 1–12.

Herman Kahn. "The Arms Race and Some of its Hazards." Reprinted by permission of the publisher from *Daedalus* (American Academy of Arts and Sciences, September, 1960) pp. 744–780, and based in part on *On Thermonuclear War* (Princeton University Press, 1960).

Richard J. Barnet. "Preparations for Progress." Reprinted by special permission of the publisher from *Who Wants Disarmament?* (Boston: Beacon Press, 1960) pp. 128–134. Copyright © 1960 by Richard J. Barnet.

Walter Millis. "Order and Change in a Warless World." Reprinted by permission of the publisher from the *Saturday Review,* (September 15, 1962) pp. 18–31. Also appeared in *A Warless World,* edited by Arthur Larson (NY: McGraw-Hill, 1962) pp. 40–50. Copyright © 1962, 1963 by the *Saturday Review.*

Robert M. Hutchins. "Constitutional Foundations for World Order." Reprinted by special permission of the Social Science Foundation, University of Denver, from *Foundation for World Order.* (Denver University Press, 1949) pp. 97–114.

*Permissions are listed to correspond to the sequence of the materials included in this volume.

J. David Singer. "The Level-of-Analysis Problem in International Rela-
tions." Reprinted by permission of the publisher from *The International
System,* edited by Klaus Knorr and Sidney Verba (Princeton University
Press, 1961) pp. 77–92.

Anatol Rapoport. "Systemic and Strategic Conflict." Reprinted by permission from *The Virginia Quarterly Review,* Vol. 40, No. 3 (Summer,
1964) pp. 337–368.

Harold D. Lasswell. "The Political Science of Science: An Inquiry into
the Possible Reconciliation of Mastery and Freedom." Reprinted with
permission from *The American Political Science Review,* Vol. 50, No. 4
(December, 1956) pp. 961–979.

Richard A. Falk. "The Claimants of Hiroshima." Reprinted with permission from *The Nation,* Vol. 200 (February 15, 1965) pp. 157–161.

"Shimoda and others versus Japan. Decision of the Tokyo District Court,
Dec. 7, 1963." Reprinted with permission from the Japan Branch of the
International Law Association, 355 Hanrei Jiho (Decisions Bulletin) 17.

Karl Jaspers. "The New Fact" and "Initial Political Thinking about the
New Fact." Reprinted by permission of the publisher from *The Future of
Mankind,* translated by E. B. Ashton (The University of Chicago Press,
1961) pp. 1–23.

Saul H. Mendlovitz. "The Study of War Prevention: Toward a Disciplined
View." Reprinted with permission from the *Bulletin of the Atomic Scientists* (Chicago: Educational Foundation for Nuclear Science, February,
1964) pp. 19–22.